University College of the Fraser Valley

COMMUNITIES OF THE AIR

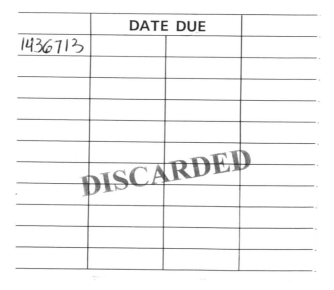

COMMUNITIES OF THE AIR

RADIO CENTURY, RADIO CULTURE

EDITED BY SUSAN MERRILL SQUIER

DUKE UNIVERSITY PRESS

DURHAM AND LONDON

2003

© 2003 Duke University Press

All rights reserved. Printed in the United

States of America on acid-free paper ∞ Designed by

Amy Ruth Buchanan. Typeset in Minion by Keystone

Typesetting, Inc. Library of Congress Cataloging-

in-Publication Data appear on the last printed

page of this book.

To the radio lovers:

JDS (The Shadow knows),

CCS *and* RDS (BBC World Service),

NCBS (KOTO) *and* VLS (KDNK)

To the Society for Literature and Science,

a good community in which to think about

communities of the air.

And to Gowen, Caitlin, *and* Toby,

for sharing the same frequency

for so many years.

CONTENTS

Radio Ideologies

ACKNOWLEDGMENTS

I would like to thank the members and audience of the radio panels at the 1998 Modern Language Association Convention, in San Francisco. The energy of our discussion convinced me this book should happen. Thanks, too, to my research assistants, Christina Jarvis, Julie Vedder, Elizabeth Mazzolini, and Megan Brown, who helped round up information on low-power radio, clip newspaper articles, communicate with the contributors, and check copy. Thanks to Sandy Steltz, of the Penn State University Rare Book Room, who kept her eyes peeled for anything relating to radio. And finally, a huge thank you to Reynolds Smith, whose enthusiasm for radio and engagement in this project made him the perfect editor.

Necessity spurred technological innovations that offered the public unprecedented access to its heroes. People accustomed to reading comparatively dry rehashes of events were now enthralled by vivid scenes rolling across the new Movietone newsreels. A public that had grown up with news illustrations and hazy photo layouts was now treated to breathtaking action shots facilitated by vastly improved photographic equipment. These images were now rapidly available thanks to wirephoto services, which had debuted in *Life* in the month that Pollard, Howard, and Smith formed their partnership.

But it was radio that had the greatest impact. In the 1920s the cost of a radio had been prohibitive—$120 or more—and all that bought was a box of unassembled parts. In unelectrified rural areas, radios ran on pricey, short-lived batteries. But with the 1930s came the advent of factory-built console, tabletop, and automobile radio sets, available for as little as $5. Thanks to President Roosevelt's Rural Electrification Administration, begun in 1936, electricity came to the quarter of the population that lived on farmlands. Rural families typically made the radio their second electric purchase, after the clothes iron. By 1935, when Seabiscuit began racing, two thirds of the nation's homes had radio. At the pinnacle of his career, that figure had jumped to 90 percent, plus eight million sets in cars. Enabling virtually all citizens to experience noteworthy events simultaneously and in entertaining form, radio created a vast common culture in America, arguably the first true mass culture the world had ever seen.

—LAURA HILLENBRAND, *Seabiscuit*

COMMUNITIES OF THE AIR:

INTRODUCING THE RADIO WORLD

Susan M. Squier

Radio . . . transforms the relation of everybody to everybody, regardless of programming.—Marshall McLuhan, *Essential McLuhan*

On December 31, 1999, *USA Today* ran a letters column in which readers
commented "on the most significant events of the past 1,000 years." One
letter, from a reader in Port Angeles, Washington, suggests the perspective
behind this collection of essays. The letter bears the headline "What Radio
Brought Us":

A big contribution for mankind during the millennium was the invention of
the radio—or the realization that one could transmit and receive radio electromagnetic energy through the air or vacuum of space.

    Think of the ramifications of the invention. It was followed by the invention
of TV, radio navigation, satellite navigation, police radar and so on. It has led to
instant communications around the world. And, yes, unfortunately TV and
radio have degenerated into vast cultural wastelands.

    When you think about how much we depend on this idea of transmitting
information electromagnetically—whether it be voice, pictures or data, it is
simply profound.[1]

While its assertion that radio has degenerated into a "vast cultural waste-
land" is certainly debatable, this celebration of radio's millennial importance grasps a crucial fact: radio is far more than just a new technology. By
putting people in touch with each other electromagnetically, radio creates a
set of overlapping communities of the air, including not only radio listeners but also those who study and theorize radio as a technological,
social, cultural, and historical phenomenon. The consumers of radio include (but are not limited to) the following: those who listen to talk radio;

supporters of National Public Radio; listeners to various alternative radio programs, from teen alternative music to political advocacy to arts programming; those who listen to country music, gospel, or Christian radio; those who need to listen to the radio for information, from the farm report to the weather report; people who are forced in an emergency to listen to CONELRAD; and workers in the Federal Emergency Management Agency (FEMA) who rely on radio in cases of national emergency, whether manmade or environmental.

We find a similar set of overlapping communities among those who write about radio or study its impact on culture and society, and this study deliberately addresses them, as well. Among those communities I would include those working on the impact of radio on modern culture; those interested in radio as a technoscience, linked to later technoscientific developments, preeminently the Internet; those working on radio's effects on political practice, dating from World War II and the powerful role played by radio in the Allied and Axis war efforts; those studying the role of radio in distance education, as in Australia; those studying how radio worked to consolidate nationhood (in the British Empire, as well as in newly emerging nations in the Caribbean); those considering how radio works to shape a national, racial, or sexual identity; those exploring the power of radio to promote cultural and artistic involvement; those interested in the ways that radio as a modern technology anticipates postmodern technologies such as computers and the World Wide Web (whether in its solicitation of multiple audiences, or in the pastiche of its programming, or in its dispersal across a global field). People interested in radio from a scholarly perspective include those working in theater (think of the radio theaters of the air so crucial in the 1930s and 1940s); in music (where radio can act to advance the growth of a new musical medium, as in the huge growth of rap and hip-hop); in literature (think of the "chapter-a-day" programs often aired by public radio stations); in cultural studies (where radio is understood as the leading edge of new cultural practices, as well as a vestige of what are now thought of as obsolete cultural positions and practices); in religious studies (examining the role of radio gospel and other religious radio programming); in women's studies (considering the development of gender segregation in radio programming, as well as in the staffing of radio stations); in history and media studies, where radio serves as the site of vivid historical documentation as well as the mark of a shifting mode of national communication. And I could go on.

Yet to make lists of "consumers" and "scholars" of radio is misleading, not only because it omits the crucial category of radio "producers" (from DJs to station owners and electricians to program hosts and producers) but because it obscures the valuable way radio *mixes up* those communities of the air. A more accurate representation of their overlapping relations would be to point out how DXers (those who tried to pick up distant radio signals), hams, and scholars who study how technologies affect social relations are all, for different reasons, interested in radio. Similarly, radio's music programming embodies these interwoven communities, offering a spectrum from fundamentalist Christian programs to the most self-consciously avant-garde, from residual/retro/niche to leading-edge cultural practices. Not surprising, then, that cultural studies scholars, so often fascinated by precisely that range of engagements, find radio programming a rich site of investigation. But that is only the most recent scholarly perspective to be drawn to radio.

Communities of the Air: Radio Century, Radio Culture began as several linked panels at the Modern Language Association Convention, sponsored by the Division of Literature and Science. The essays in this book reflect those origins, focusing on radio as cultural and material production, and incorporating the perspectives of literary and cultural studies, science studies, and feminist theory along with the more established field of radio history and the new field of radio studies. As I will map more extensively later, radio history has provided an internalist perspective on the development of radio as a technology, and of radio broadcasting. In contrast, radio studies has moved beyond an internalist perspective to a critical and interdisciplinary one.

From its inception in 1992, the *Journal of Radio Studies* addressed what one of its founders described as the "full sweep of radio history that started in the 1870s and extends to the present," considering radio as a developing science and technology as well as a set of institutional practices.[2] As the *JRS* continued to appear, the field of radio research shifted from a consideration of radio on its own technological and institutional terms to a new attention to the social context of radio, and then gradually to its symbolic, political, and theoretical implications. By 2000, the journal had established a research profile that moved beyond its primary dedication to scholarly investigations of "the practices of managers, programmers, researchers, ancillary industries, regulation, self-regulation, mergers and acquisitions, advertisers, marketers and promoters."[3] In addition to forewords by radio scholars and radio personalities, which were a regular feature of the journal, the *JRS Cumulative Index* listed essays on AM radio's future, Internet radio, talk radio, community and public radio, country music radio and international radio (especially Canadian and Scandinavian radio), archival research, studies of radio programming, contemporary research on subjects ranging from the economic implications of radio ownership arrangements to textual analyses of Garrison Keillor's *Prairie Home Companion,* radio history, and rhetorical studies of radio (both broadcast radio and radio dramas).[4] Gradually the categories concerning "interdisciplinary inquiries regarding radio's contemporary and historical subject matter" expanded, and the journal explicitly solicited an interchange between "broadcasters and academics," regularly featuring a forum in which members of both groups were asked to comment on questions concerning the challenges facing radio and make prognostications for its future.[5]

The important appearance in 1992 of the "Radio—Sound" issue of *Continuum: The Australian Journal of Media and Culture* nudged the analysis of radio from social science research to textual and cultural analysis. Toby Miller mapped the new stretch of the field in his superb "Editorial Introduction for Radio," arguing that radio studies had grafted to an interest in the everyday "as a category of contestation and valorization" a new understanding that radio functions as "transcoding device," that "the language of radio is a language that decodes and encodes other sign systems as part of the aural pictures painted by its promiscuous social tourism."[6] The journal grouped essays in three categories: "radio practice," "sound practice," and "questions of film culture."[7] The first two sections included articles on talkback radio, radio management, and various different forms of radio broadcasting (radical, feminist, public, and national radio), all under the rubric of an examination of the practices that characterized these different forms. The contributions to this issue examined radio as an assemblage of relations and practices, adhering to what one contributor called "a methodology which seeks to apprehend cultural phenomena within a discursive framework that refuses to give priority to text over context, production over reception, and deconstruction over interpretation (or, of course, the reverse)."[8] Their fresh perspectives on radio reflected an attention to "social negotiations, technological interconnexions and distributive structures which lend support to the development and extension of the artefact" over the production of "artefactual histories," "and to the investigation of intermedia connections, such as radio's links to gramophone recording, and to the telephone, and especially to film."[9]

For example, Tom O'Regan explores the reliance of talkback radio on the universal acceptance of the telephone and the widespread dissemination of radio as background noise in everyday professional and private settings; the growth of Top 40 radio programs and the shift from 78 rpm records to the new 33 and 45 rpm records that made possible "more plays over a shorter time," and thus a faster cycle of built-in obsolescence in popular music; and the "synergistic" relationship between radio and sound cinema, which was embraced sooner than it might have been in order to recapture the audience initially lost to radio.[10] Moving even farther afield from the exploration of intermedia connections, another essay in the "Radio—Sound" issue offered a deconstruction of a specific group of radio programs, *The Listening Room* programs on Paul Virilio, as part of a meta-commentary on the possibility of performing textual analysis on an aural medium. Rebecca Coyle conceptualized these radio programs as a "convocation" of Virilio's interest in accident and the producer Virginia Masden's strategy of bringing together transient voices and material from interviews to produce something "more like cinema and poetry than theatre."[11]

Coyle's essay in "Radio—Sound" exemplifies a focus on the theoretical implications of radio's treatment of sound that would be central to two crucial studies to emerge in the next half decade: Douglas Kahn and Gregory Whitehead's 1992 *Wireless Imagination: Sound, Radio, and the Avant-Garde,* and Adalaide Morris's 1997 collection *Sound States: Innovative Poetics and Acoustical Technologies.*[12] In both of these collections, the emphasis was on the intermedia technologies, and the contributions applied radio practices to other acoustic media. *Wireless Imagination* focused specifically on a period beginning with the avant-garde era and ending in the 1960s. It included essays exploring the role of radio and phonograph sound in the works of surrealist and avant-garde artists, as well as publishing excerpts from original works by Villiers de l'Isle-Adam, Alberto Savinio, Arseni Avraamov, F. T. Marinetti and Pino Masnata, and Antonin Artaud. Kahn's introduction reads almost as a manifesto for radio studies, for it claims the sonic as a cultural realm nearly unexplored: "While other historical fields may be busying themselves with things more detailed, the study of the relationship of sound and radio to the arts is open to a full range of investigations, including the most general."[13] The collection that follows illuminates the relations between modernism, the avant-garde, and postmodernism through an exploration of the experience of acoustic media, enacted in the form of vibration, inscription, and transmission (14).

Morris's collection also begins with the notion that twentieth-century thinkers have generally drawn their conceptual models from the visual media, claiming in contrast the intention of giving "the reader an earful."[14] Working to connect radio, tape transmissions, various sound-related performances, and theories of hearing, Morris's collection (like Miller's before it) approaches radio not as subject matter but as a set of (almost completely untheorized) practices. Yet where Kahn and Whitehead stop with the aural experiments of William S. Burroughs and other beats in the early 1960s, Morris pushes the relationship between radio and computer technologies, implicitly arguing that "the acoustical technologies that grew up with modernism also prepared the swerve toward the postmodern" (8).

Communities of the Air: Radio Century, Radio Culture also enacts a networked approach to radio, seeing it not only as a research area in its own right but as a set of practices that can illuminate questions in other fields, not only literary but also historical and sociocultural, from race relations and gender politics to the construction of regional and national identities. In addition to learning from writers, artists, and cultural studies scholars such as Morris, Kahn and Whitehead, and Miller who are exploring the avant-garde and performative aspects of radio, this volume is also greatly indebted to communications studies scholarship on radio, most notably that of Susan Douglas and Michele Hilmes. A prominent theme in such recent research is the double-valenced nature of the radio medium itself: its power to enforce the status quo (especially consumerism and stereotyping of race, gender, and ethnicity) and its capacity to provide a voice for resistance and critique.[15] Most recently, Michele Hilmes's *Hollywood and Broadcasting: From Radio to Cable* (1990) and *Radio Voices: American Broadcasting, 1922–1952* (1997) and Susan Douglas's *Inventing American Broadcasting, 1899–1922* (1987) and *Listening In: Radio and the American Imagination* (1999) have amplified our understanding of the social embeddedness of radio, emphasizing in particular the cognitive shift radio helped to produce, from the visual to the aural.[16] These valuable histories adopt distinctly different perspectives on the development and social effects of radio in the United States. Tracing the influence of the Hollywood studios on the development of radio broadcasting, Hilmes's *Hollywood and Broadcasting* explores the growth of the radio industry as a precarious balance of three interests: sponsor, network, and studio.[17] Sur-veying thirty years of radio, Hilmes emphasizes the medium's role as "a machine for the circulation of narratives that rehearse and justify the struc-tures of order underlying national identity." She explores how radio rein-forced the differences between us (of race, gender, and ethnicity) while consolidating what was held to be "truly American" (xvii). Hilmes ap-proaches radio as a place where social and cultural conflicts were worked out, and thus she finds in radio the traces of a continuing battle between the pluralist cultural consensus shaped by American commercial media and a range of diverse and conflicting popular alternatives.

In contrast, Susan Douglas stresses the subversive power of radio, even though she agrees that radio has played a powerful role in the creation of that new being, the "mass-mediated human." In *Listening In,* she explores radio's power to sustain emotional states, to spark the imagination, and to enable expression of stigmatized parts of the self.[18] Surveying the ways people listened to radio in the last hundred years, from DXers and jazz listeners of the 1920s and the radio comedy audiences of the 1930s to the broadcast news audiences of the 1940s, the sports and rock-and-roll au-diences of the 1950s and 1960s, and the FM and talk show listeners of the 1970s, 1980s, and 1990s, Douglas suggests that despite the frequently sub-versive uses of the medium, radio has moved gradually toward a conserva-tive, commercialized model: a listener tuning in mechanically to a mech-anized station. "The same device that worked so powerfully, through comedy and drama, sports and news, to forge a powerful sense of national identity in the 1930s is now working—along with cable TV, magazines, and niche advertising—to cultivate and encourage cultural segregation" (354). Douglas ends her book with a plea for a return to the core value of radio, a perspective she shares with Hilmes: "I think we want our imaginations back. I think we want—and need—to listen" (357). Hilmes and Douglas converge in their shared stress on radio's cultural power: to nourish our imaginations, to weave together a variety of different discourses into imag-ined communities, and to shift the dominant sense from visual to aural. As Douglas puts it, "You can't understand the importance of radio until you understand the importance of hearing" (7).

In their attention to the ways radio shaped imagined communities, including (re)defining the auditory contours of gender and race, these scholars have pioneered an approach to radio that considers it as an ensem-ble of social relations as well as a technology. Hilmes borrows from the work of British cultural studies scholar Stuart Hall to distinguish between the three "determinate moments" of the communicative act: the process of encoding, the form of the message, and the process of decoding.[19] We are familiar with the cultural studies analysis of the decoding process and of the message itself, but, as Hilmes points out, cultural studies also informs our understanding of the historical specificity of radio: the wireless possibilities that were actualized. That process of encoding includes the technological developments that shape radio—the battles over bandwidth, the invention of commercial advertisements, the successive development of new receivers and loudspeakers—just as much as the negotiations over the acceptable radio voice, or the target radio audience.

As the interdisciplinary approaches introduced by both Hilmes and Douglas demonstrate, radio deserves the attention of scholars in fields beyond media studies. This volume provides that wider perspective, drawing together essays by scholars in theater studies, history, English, science and technology studies, film studies, and women's studies, as well as radio writers, directors, and producers, and radio critics from the alternative press, to consider how radio has transformed the various social realms in which it has operated. The essays in this volume also exemplify the performative, practice-based orientation of cultural studies, in choosing to concentrate on different aspects of the radio experience: the encoding, the message, and the decoding. Finally, the collection also draws inspiration from Neil Strauss's brilliantly quirky *Radiotext(e)* (1993), which emphasizes radio's subversive, yeasty potential. Concentrating on the theoretical implications of radio as (social) text, and assuming that "radio is a box that needs to be opened," Strauss's volume animates the social processes, technological strategies, improvisations, and performance art pieces that participate in this "dangerous and mysterious" medium. Linking the "early sparks" of radio's possibilities to its "alternative histories," *Radiotext(e)* jumbles together the producers and consumers of radio, the medium's links to paranormal and extraterrestrial phenomena, and even the anarchic or totalitarian impulses of its cranks and control freaks.[20] "Radio knows no boundaries; its signal is as unavoidable as it is unstoppable," Strauss tells us, reminding us that our body itself "has a biological radio set, which can be triggered by a seizure of the temporal lobe" (9).

The essays included herein explore how radio has—both in its technological development and in its programming—put in place certain cultural and ideological practices that structure human relations. Marshall

McLuhan's term for this was a "grammar": as he explained, both television and radio are "immense extensions of ourselves which enable us to participate in one another's lives, much as a language does. But the modes of participation are already built into the technology; these new languages have their own grammars."[21] Although we tend to forget it in the glare of his media-pundit reputation, McLuhan was trained as an English professor, as this choice of terminology suggests. Thirty years after the peak of his influence, a rekindled interest in radio from a McLuhanesque perspective—as a grammar that can be manipulated and revised—has taken a prominent place in English studies.[22] English is itself a new discipline now, shaped by the converging forces of cultural studies, feminist theory, and science studies. All of these perspectives helped to shape the new cultural reading of radio this volume offers.

Although this volume reveals the marks of the communications studies scholars and cultural critics of radio that have preceded it, it takes a markedly different approach to its material. Linking the social, historical, and media studies orientations pioneered by Douglas and Hilmes to the theoretical and cultural studies orientations of Strauss's collection, the essays here consider how our era has been shaped as a "radio century," through the discourses we term, collectively, "radio culture." The essays included explore how radio—as both a century-long series of overlapping technological developments and a set of social practices and social relations—has shaped Anglo-American life in the twentieth century. They also explore the ways that radio constituted the Anglo-American "other," whether it be the West Indian poet, the North American woman, or the South African black. Finally, this book returns radio to its original position in the work of Marshall McLuhan, who, as the epigraph to this chapter reveals, appreciated the possibilities inherent in an aural, networked externalization of the human being. "Today men's nerves surround us; they have gone outside as electrical environment. The human nervous system itself can be reprogrammed biologically as readily as any radio network can alter its fare."[23]

In a reprise of some of McLuhan's major themes, the essays here consider radio's impact on our century and culture: its role in the important shift from a culture of the visual to a new culture of the aural; its consequent ability to elude or reframe gender, race, and class markers; its nearly paradigmatic status as an example of a technoscientific network linking human and nonhuman actors; its generic hybridity, incorporating music and the spoken word to the science of bandwidths and frequencies; its status as a thematic bridge between modernism and postmodernism, in its modern preoccupation with the biological perfectibility of the human being, and its proto-postmodern vision of the prosthetic extension of the self. Included are essays that address some of the "critically important genres of radio programming" omitted from Douglas's wide-ranging *Listening In,* including the modular science program, the radio drama, the children's broadcast, and the arts program (featuring poetry). Beginning with an assessment of the negotiations shaping the medium, its audience, and its place in the nation, the volume moves on to analyses of some of the various cultures, ideologies, and discourses that shaped, and were shaped by, this new technology.

Of course, given the interpenetration of radio into our biological and social worlds, these essays cannot pretend to offer the last word. Instead, they offer what might be called a first glimpse of how attention to the multiple significances and agencies of radio can give voice to the anxieties, hopes, fears, and wishes of a culture. Approaching radio as a powerful aural networking device that links and produces a range of different social relations and practices, from the elite to the popular, the dominant to the resistant, the canonical to the aesthetically transgressive, the essays are grouped in three parts, to explore the diverse cultures created by a century of radio. The first part looks at the development of radio as a technology, considering both the early initiatives that were foreclosed or preserved as certain possibilities of radio were exploited and others were ignored, the technical and aesthetic dimension of an individually programmed three-hour music program, and the implications of the more recent foray into low-power radio. The second part explores the role of radio to articulate and embody a range of marginal and alternative social worlds, whether of Caribbean nationalist poetry, black American consumer power, youth culture, or scientific literacy. Finally, the third part considers how radio shapes gendered identities on the national and individual levels, in the period from the early years of the century through the 1940s, to the 1990s.

A Century of Radio Culture

The field of radio studies incorporates a generally accepted time line of technological development beginning more than a century ago, when Guglielmo Marconi made his first trip to the United States, to broadcast the *America*'s Cup race on the new technology known as "wireless telegra-phy."[24] One year later, students and professors at the University of Wiscon-sin began to experiment with transmitting radio signals, and amateur radio was launched in the United States. This new technology led to con-flicts over government regulation of the spectrum, or as it was known at the beginning of the century, "the ether." Who should control this new collective resource? Those with claims on it ranged from radio amateurs and for-profit companies to the navy, eager to harness the potential for national defense that this new communications space represented.[25] Radio ushered in financial good fortune as increased public interest in wireless between 1906 and 1912 led to a boom in wireless company stocks prefigur-ing our late-1990s run on Internet stocks (195). However, radio was linked to disaster, as well. In April 1912, Marconi booked a steamship passage to the United States, canceling his trip only at the last minute. The ship he would have joined was the *Titanic*. It sank in the North Atlantic, its wireless distress signals nearly useless because nearby ships' wireless operators had turned off their sets for the night. Still, Marconi's invention did make possible the rescue of nearly nine hundred lives by the *Carpathia*, the only ship to receive the *Titanic*'s signals (228–31). The Radio Act of 1912 re-sponded to the tragedy of the *Titanic* by giving distress calls priority over all · other wireless transmissions, requiring all wireless operators to be licensed, and relegating amateurs to the shortwave part of the radio spectrum.[26] By 1915, the first experimental radio license had been granted, and by the 1920s, amateur ham radio operators were exploring the ether on their crystal sets, trying to "DX" the most distant radio station possible.

Beyond the United States, radio technology developed unevenly, in terms of its introduction into a country, the extent to which it was subject to state control, and the breadth and depth of its AM and FM offerings. While radio began as a state monopoly everywhere in the West except the United States, the reliance on radio to consolidate state power was most powerfully expressed during World War II.[27] Then, the Nazi party used radio broadcasts ranging from Hitler's speeches to the light entertainment of the *Wunschkonzert* to "bind together the *Volksgemeinschaft*, the commu-nity of the *Volk* or people as they called it, into one big happy family."[28] As an essay in this volume reveals, from its earliest days, British radio, too, used the trope of a radio family to build political stability. Yet British radio took a different developmental path than its U.S. cousin. Rather than the U.S. pattern of allocating the ether to commercial radio stations and gov-

ernmental uses, with only a small patch left for amateurs and ham operators, the British pattern of "duopoly" limited radio to state-owned and
private stations, with just the occasional community or pirate radio station
appearing (most notably in the 1960s) to disrupt that pattern.[29]

During World War II, Nazi propaganda broadcasts were combated by
free radio broadcasts, but the notion of free radio really got its start in
Italy in the 1970s, and in France and Japan in the 1980s.[30] Indeed, it was
theorist Félix Guattari who introduced the concept of free radio to Japan,
in an interview with Tetsuo Kogawa in 1980 that was published in *Nippon
Dokusho Shinbun,* a radical periodical.[31] Japanese free radio stations took
advantage of a government loophole that exempted so-called low-power
stations from licensing requirements to create a range of free radio stations,
each no more than "a gathering place with a transmitting device" (95).
Although their programming differed, these radio stations shared a commitment to an interactive model of radio based on a notion of activating
and extending already existing community involvement, whether based on
geography, on resistance, or on a shared political identity.

Radio histories differ, but what remains the same is the way radio functions as more than just a technology or a method of communication, but as
a node of cultural exchange, a process through which human beings can
represent and negotiate our wishes and fears. Even in its early years, radio
made its mark on the cultural imagination. It figured prominently in two
new genres of popular writing: adventure tales for young boys, which spun
tales of young heroes like Tom Swift and the "radio boys" who solved
crimes using the wireless, and science fiction.[32] "The father of science
fiction," Hugo Gernsback, was a wireless zealot, whose New York shop, the
Electro-Importing Company, sold wireless equipment directly to the public.[33] Founder of the Wireless Association of America, which claimed ten
thousand members by 1910, Gernsback also launched America's first science fiction magazine, *Amazing Stories.*[34] As a sampling of its issues between 1934 and 1939 reveals, this periodical used radio to probe the future,
offering the following inventive scenarios: a device that uses radio waves to
bore into an object; the tale of some mechanical servants called "Metanicals" who use the radio to revolt against their human masters and to
communicate with the past; a radio that picks up threats from a satellite
beyond the moon; a radio phone; radio used as an analogy to explain a
"magic machine" that can see into the past; the tale of aliens who tune into
Earth radio and use it as a means of domination once they take over the

earth; a "super-powerful radio" that can be tuned in to any station in the world and impells its listener to obey its alien communications; the notion of using a brain as a radio, transmitting sonic waves from an adult scientist's brain to the brain of a newborn, thus enabling the instantaneous wireless transfer of scientific knowledge; a radio that is used to broadcast the warnings of an invisible vigilante, the "Utopian reformer"; the story of a huge structure built to pass beyond the Kennelly-Heaviside layer of atmosphere, and thus to pick up telepathic transmissions requesting help from an alien people who inspire human beings to build a spaceship to save them; the tale of what seems to be radio communication between a man and a woman but is eventually understood to be mental telepathy; and the tale of "Myles Cabot the Radio Man, greatest scientist of two worlds," a former radio engineer who has invented a method of wireless transmission of matter, has accidentally transmitted himself to Venus by radio waves, and comes back to save the president of the United States.[35] Taken together, these stories reveal that in the 1930s, science fiction used radio as a vehicle to explore human wishes and fears, both realistic and fantastic, including our hopes for more efficient science education, our anxiety about the increasing power of the machines on which we depend, our concern for the future of the human race, and our awareness of the gendered nature of human communication, as well as fantasies of the existence of alien beings, the possibility of correcting the past, and the possibility of dominating other beings (by radio waves or telepathy).

By the time of World War II, radio had been harnessed to the military effort, while shortwave radio broadcasters provided carefully neutral, but still dramatic, fare for their loyal civilian listeners. The fifties and sixties saw the growth of a tremendous youth radio market. With the FM explosion of the 1950s and 1960s, a new breed of listener, largely male and obsessed with "high fidelity," joined the radio audience, making radio a battleground between automated playlists of Top 40 hits, and the free-form programming of largely college FM stations. By the 1970s and 1980s, the growth of talk radio brought us such seemingly incompatible formats as National Public Radio and the Rush Limbaugh show, both of them—as Susan Douglas astutely remarks—vehicles for a new radio-based activism, as well as alternative models for male selfhood in a postwar era.[36] By the end of the twentieth century, it often seemed that these battles between amateurs and professionals, young and older people, consumer-oriented and "public service" programming, were long past. Radio seemed to be taken for granted, overshadowed by new technologies such as computers, digital television, and cell phones.

Yet the forecast for radio in the twenty-first century is both more turbulent, and more mixed, than that late-twentieth-century narrative of radio's gentle decline into obscurity. Consolidation of stations after the 1996 FCC ruling that permitted the ownership of multiple stations in the same market has been reshaping both commercial and public radio in ominous as well as promising ways.[37] In February 2000 the thriving Chicano radio scene in Southern California lost a major outlet when Minnesota Public Radio acquired the lease of the financially strapped station KPCC of Pasadena City College and transformed its music-based programming into a twenty-four-hour all-news station. After a run of sixteen years, KPCC's *The Sancho Show,* a well-loved eclectic, multigenerational program with a strong following in the Chicano community, was summarily canceled and replaced, in an act of striking insensitivity on the part of NPR, by *Prairie Home Companion.* This was the second such change in as many years: in 1998 another Chicano station, KRLA, changed its format when acquired by new owners.[38] To frightened Los Angeles listeners, it not only presaged a move toward ethnic and geographic homogenization of radio programming but raised fears that the culture such radio programs addressed was endangered as well. "If Sancho's distinctive regional voice, with its obvious community service message, could be stilled . . . perhaps the culture he spoke for was no longer so distinctive nor as much of a community as it had imagined" (31).

In contrast, in the Northeast, demographic changes, coupled with the increasing cost of major-market radio stations, have led to an increase in ethnic programming on suburban stations. A recent report in the *New York Times* found that in the New York suburban region, ethnic programming was proliferating on "AM and FM stations; subcarrier stations that share a frequency with a major station but require a special radio or subscription; and pirate stations, which sneak in very local programming on empty frequencies."[39] These suburban radio stations increasingly broadcast quiz shows, music programs with call-in dedications, talk shows, soap operas, and news programs, in Polish, Russian, Chinese, Arabic, Spanish, Vietnamese, Korean, and several Indian languages, with more ethnic groups targeted every week. Profiting from the great increase in numbers of ethnic immigrants to the suburban rings around major metropolitan areas, these stations are able to reach their listeners without paying the inflated prices now attached to major-market radio stations. Moreover, they are also reaching listeners via the Internet. Bringing education, religious programming, entertainment, communication, and news to their listeners, and even providing family contacts to prisoners in the Union County (New Jersey) jail, these new radio stations reflect the increasing diversity of the Eastern suburbs just as urban radio stations, both Eastern and Western, are falling prey to disturbing economically driven homogenization.

Moreover, changes in radio technology are providing a variety of new programming models: Web-based radio, digital radio, low-power radio. Sometimes these can expand the communities that radio addresses. For example, even as *The Sancho Show* remained off the air in Pasadena, Web-based radio provided access to other Chicano radio stations, such as Radio Aztlan (KUCR-RM of UC Riverside) and Radio Bilingue of XHITT-FM in Tijuana, as well as Chicano stations in San Jose and Berkeley.[40] But in other cases, new technology simply provides an additional market for a commercial radio enterprise, as in the case of Channel 1031.com, a Web-only station. According to Charlie Rahilly, senior vice president for sales for the massive Clear Channel Communications: "We're trying to see if we can make this migration from over-the-air to over-the-Web work, if we can monetize it and produce positive operating results."[41] While their current link to PCs limits their entry into the crucial drive-time market, still the numbers of these Web-based stations are growing dramatically. Limited to only 56 in April 1996, by August 2000 there were almost 4,500 on-line radio stations, according to BRS Media.[42]

Essential to the Web-based format, digital radio has also made a major impact on conventional on-air radio. Although it caught on first in smaller, niche stations because of the technological demands its equipment places on DJs and engineers, the new digital radio format promises to dominate the industry within the decade, according to many experts in the field.[43] This new format has huge implications for the ways we produce, market, finance, consume, and even archive radio programs. "Virtually every aspect of a station's production and distribution—songs, commercials, listeners' calls, promotions, jingles—nearly everything you hear on the radio, can reside invisibly on computer hard drives and be packaged into shows by software" (E1). As with any other technological innovation, it produces challenges as well as opportunities. Although it offers DJs the possibility of greater control, permitting them to shape their show to screen out the repetition of specific song genres or of several songs by the same composer, or delete certain words or phrases from listeners' comments, digitized radio is also a far less forgiving technology. Radio engineers have to learn how to work around its limitations, a task that comes easily at the smaller, newer, younger stations but taxes the abilities of those who have been in the business for several decades or more. As Norm Avery of KABC radio in L.A. explains: "There's a learning curve to this digital equipment. With analog tape we know the failure rate and how to work around it. When you switch to digital, you're putting all your eggs in one basket. There's a big difference if your client's commercial doesn't play due to some digital glitch, and that client is a local merchant in a small town, than if that client is the Ford Motor Company and you're in LA" (E1). The massive scale of contemporary radio, as smaller stations have consolidated into huge regional stations, linked into national conglomerates with the blessing of the FCC, makes any misstep more costly. But along with the possibility of digitally produced mistakes comes the possibility of more ways of producing profit. With digital archives of programs, and listener call-ins, it is easier to produce celebrity station promotions, to track and confirm the airing of commercial spots, to distribute syndicated programs, and even to avoid weather-related disturbances to the radio signal (E8).

Yet if digital radio has made possible a move toward massive stations with linked programming, for a while it looked as if another much more low-tech innovation would enable an almost utopian return to community radio. In his 1972 yippie classic *Steal This Book,* Abbie Hoffman urged people to master the fundamentals of "low-power" or "guerrilla radio."[44] He explained that "under FCC Low Power Transmission Regulations, it is legal to broadcast on the AM band without even obtaining a license, if you transmit with 100 milliwatts of power or less on a free band space that doesn't interfere with a licensed station" (299). At the turn of the twenty-first century, FCC chairman William Kennard accomplished an ironic reprise of the seventies when he backed low-power FM radio. Kennard's proposed low-power initiative would have qualified more than a thousand noncommercial FM stations to broadcast at between 50 and 100 watts to a region within a radius of four to seven miles from their station, opening up new sectors of the airwaves to a mix of community groups and local programming. But a powerful coalition comprised of the National Association of Broadcasters and National Public Radio worked hard to gut the low-power movement, arguing that the low-power radio signal could disrupt existing stations (NAB) and could "interfere with radio reading services for the blind" (NPR).[45] In December 2000, Congress passed the Radio Broadcasting Preservation Act of 2000, sponsored by outgoing Republican senator Rod Grams of Minnesota, which transferred licensing authority on low-power radio from the FCC to Congress, ensuring that virtually no low-power radio stations could be licensed in metropolitan areas.[46] While opposition to low-power radio was customarily phrased in terms of bandwidth interference, the passage of the RBPA suggested otherwise to FCC chairman Kennard. As Frank Ahrens of the *Washington Post* reported, "The Grams bill also calls for the FCC to study the economic impact of the low-power stations on existing stations, which Kennard believes undercuts the NAB's argument that its opposition to low-power radio centers on potential interference. 'That is one of the more cynical aspects of the legislation,' Kennard said, 'It's all about protectionism.' "[47] In 2001, when Michael Powell (son of army chief of staff Colin Powell) swept into power with the Bush administration to become the replacement for FCC chairman Kennard, the liaison between corporate capitalism and radio seemed firm. Although there are no doubt many chapters still to come, with their own crises and reversals, thus far the low-power story demonstrates the same tension between centralized control and communicative pluralism, corporate capitalism and community service, that has characterized radio's technological development throughout its history.

Part I: Radio Technology across the Twentieth Century

The essays in this first part focus on the development of radio, sharing the premise that, in the process of constructing this new technology, certain aspects of its broad potential were foreclosed while others were enhanced, with important implications for women and minority groups. Steven Wurtzler argues that a "conceptual conservatism" characterized the emergence of radio, leading it to be modeled after already existing communications technologies, notably the telephone. Examining a 1923 struggle between a community access model of radio proposed briefly by AT&T, and the growing for-profit ideology that eventually prevailed, Wurtzler shows how the locus of control for radio moved from local to national, disenfranchising community radio while providing, in that brief moment, a model for community access television of the future. Examining the function of "community radio" in times of catastrophe, Bruce Campbell examines the role of ham radio lobbyists in shaping the uses of radio. He argues that a power struggle occurred between the private hobbyists who were the initial developers of radio technology and the government institutions that sought to harness that remarkable new power. The result, Campbell demonstrates, was a government co-optation and reconfiguration of radio itself, based on ham radio's role in catastrophe management, which marginalized women while enhancing the power of radio for a militarized state. Although the move to low-power radio initially seemed to promise many more community-based programs, Nina Huntemann examines the actual impact of such programming, to show that its "cluster mentality" and profit focus produces a "sameness and lost localism" in its stations.

Part II: Radio Cultures

The incidental effect of certain uses of radio on the gender, race, class, and ethnicity of its producers and consumers is the focus of the second group of essays. They examine the ways that radio technologies were used by or against different cultural formations, to constitute and voice identity and social position, to consolidate a marginalized or isolated cultural group, or to co-opt a resistant cultural role for mainstream purposes. The essays take a special look at several radio genres that, as Susan Douglas points out, are "critically important": arts programming focused on poetry, black radio, alternative music, and modular science programming.[48] Laurence Breiner explores the paradoxical role of the BBC Colonial Service radio in enabling the consolidation of an "imagined community" among West Indian poets and nationalists between World War II and 1958, the year of colonial independence, when the short-lived Federation of the West Indies came into being. Arguing that *Caribbean Voices,* the special West Indian poetry program of the BBC, both consolidated support for a political federation of noncontiguous colonies and forged a potent new poetic movement, Breiner demonstrates an interdisciplinary analysis that illuminates radio's complex cultural effects.

Focusing on the way the radio helped to create a "crowd mind" among African American radio listeners in the 1950s, Kathy Newman recovers the history of black radio listeners, to show how radio identified them as an explicit consumer group as early as the 1940s. This new "Negro market" not only gave black Americans an increased sense of consumer power but also schooled them in a tactic that contributed substantially to their political power: the use of the boycott, which became a prominent feature of the

Civil Rights movement of the 1960s. Lauren Goodlad offers a history of "alternative radio" culture since its inception in the late 1970s. She demonstrates how the resistant impulses of alternative music have been co-opted and repackaged by corporate culture into a less-challenging form that conspicuously reaffirms traditional gender boundaries.

Drawing on his work as a writer for the internationally syndicated program *A Moment of Science,* Donald Ulin demonstrates that the formal and institutional demands of this radio program can lead to an uncritical, self-congratulatory, internalist, and ideologically inflected representation of science. In contrast, Ulin argues, modular science programs that specifically target their information to regional audiences can escape the triumphant globalizing of nationally syndicated science spots in favor of the targeted delivery of local knowledge. In the last essay of this part, Martin Spinelli returns to the complex topic of poetry programming, this time on the NPR syndicated interview program, *Fresh Air.* In contrast to Breiner's appreciation for the aesthetically and politically consolidating effect of the BBC's *Caribbean Voices* program in the 1950s, Spinelli demonstrates the consumption-centered programming ethic of *Fresh Air.* Spinelli shares with Goodlad an appreciation of the way that such a consumption-centered focus can constrict listener choices under the guise of expanding them. However, "promo" spots for a poetry program can disrupt the smooth surface of public radio programming and draw listeners' attention to the formal properties of poetic language.

Part III: Radio Ideologies

Radio has been subjected to serious critique for its mass appeal, most powerfully expressed by Marshall McLuhan's analysis of its prominent role in fascist politics in the 1930s and 1940s. As McLuhan observed, both Hitler and his victims and critics "danced entranced to the tribal drum of radio that extended their central nervous system to create depth involvement for everybody."[49] Yet if radio can harness ideology, it can also resist it. This volume's final part examines radio's power to reinforce, or to resist, ideologies of gender, as well as race and nationality. Drawing together feminist film theory and McLuhan's concept of a radio as a "hot" medium, Adrienne Munich explores Queen Elizabeth II's recourse to radio broadcasting to consolidate and unify the empire she inherited, and to shape her image as a modern, global monarch within the discourse of family. Leah

Lowe examines how Gracie Allen's mock presidential campaign, launched in 1940 on the "Surprise Party" ticket, highlighted the power of radio to shape gender representations, as well as raising questions about the extent to which aural, rather than visual, media can escape gender role stereotypes. Like Queen Elizabeth's radio broadcast from South Africa, which as Munich demonstrates not only served, but also subverted, white patriarchy, Gracie's comic run for the presidency also embodied a feminine transgressive power. Mary Desjardins and Mark Williams consider the role of gendered direct address in *The Lonesome Gal,* an extremely successful radio program launched in the post–World War II era, demonstrating radio's power (here, as in Queen Elizabeth's radio broadcasts) to evoke a seductive maternal aural space while adapting itself to changing the gender role demands of the 1950s.

Conclusion: Radio's Postmodern Primal Scene

"Today men's nerves surround us; they have gone outside as electrical environment," Marshall McLuhan observed in 1964. My concluding essay explores radio as it was before the actualization of McLuhan's prescient vision of a convergence of the biological and the informatic. Comparing fictional representations and theorizations of radio in its early years, a short story from the late 1950s, and a contemporary science fiction novel and film (both of which extrapolate from radio's informatic potential), I trace how radio productively unsettles our narrative of the emergence of what has been called the posthuman body. That a technology as seemingly old-fashioned as the radio should also be as current as cyberspace has received little notice. Indeed, as Michele Hilmes points out, "[no] other medium has been more thoroughly forgotten, by the public, historians, and media scholars alike."[50] Even Sandy Stone pronounces not radio but "the telephone . . . the first electronic network prosthesis," despite a powerful passage in which she describes the first time she "fell in love with her own prostheses."[51]

The first time love struck was in 1950. I was hunkered down in the dark late at night, on my bed with the big iron bedstead on the second floor, listening absently to the crickets singing, and helping a friend scratch around on the surface of a galena crystal that was part of a primitive radio. We were looking for one of the hot spots, places where the crystal had active sites that worked like diodes and could detect radio waves. Nothing but silence for a long, long time, and then suddenly the earphones burst into life and there was a whole new universe raging in our heads—the ranting voice of Jean Shepherd, boiling into the atmosphere from the massive transmitter of WOR AM, 250 kilowatts strong and only a few miles away. At that distance we could have heard the signal in our tooth fillings if we'd had any, but the transmitter might well have been Rangoon, for all the fragrant breath of exotic worlds it suggested, I was hooked. Hooked on technology. I could take a couple of coils of wire and a hunk of galena and send a whole part of myself into the ether. An extension of my will, of my instrumentality—that's a prosthesis, all right. (394)

In this rich passage, Sandy Stone captures radio's primal scene. All the marks of summer nostalgia figure here: childhood experimentation after dark with the crickets singing, "hot spots" that open onto a whole new universe of experience, the "fragrant breath of exotic worlds." Stone's memory is saturated with technoeroticism, a serendipitous result of Stone's own transsexual subject position, which links the boy enthralled with his crystal radio set and the DXing ham radio amateur to the nostalgic and critical feminist theorist of the present. Stone's passage is strikingly parallel to Susan Douglas's memory of a similar early moment of radio listening:

Driving alone at night . . . or lying in bed tuned to a disembodied voice or music, evokes a spiritual, almost telepathic contact across space and time, a reassurance that we aren't alone in the void: we have kindred spirits. You engage with a phantom whose voice and presence you welcomed, needed. The feeling isn't some naive, bathetic sense of universal "brotherly love" (although under certain circumstances, and especially with various mind-altering substances, such an illusion is possible), but there is a sense of camaraderie and mutuality coming from the sky itself.[52]

In each passage, the ritual of bedtime radio listening invokes love, though Stone sexualizes while Douglas politicizes its nature. More than that, both passages capture the alien, otherworldly nature of radio: Douglas's allusion to "a spiritual, almost telepathic contact across space and time" recalls Sir Oliver Lodge's early tinkering with radio transmissions from the world beyond the grave, and Stone's allusion to the possibility of hearing the signal "in our tooth fillings" invokes the proto-postmodern genre of paranormal radio transmissions that John Keel has dubbed "biological radio."[53]

Hilmes and Douglas have emphasized the conflicts and tensions that define the development of radio, both as a technology and as a set of social processes (though even to phrase it that way distorts the networked unity that is radio as a technoscience). But the primal scenes of Douglas and Stone represent another aspect of radio: its function as a desiring mechanism that links the individual to the collectivity, the human to the machine, spaces geographically distant to each other. Sandy Stone sees the programmers who are designing computer-based games as having the power to structure "the major unacknowledged source of socialization and education in industrialized societies."[54] Yet even while admitting that her "choice of the term 'computer-based' is already becoming an anachronism, since the meanings of culturally defined objects such as television, telephone, cable, and computers, and the boundaries between them, are already in hot debate and considerable flux," Stone ignores the fact that radio served as a crucial precedent for this kind of socialization (406). Sensitized by Breiner's essay in this volume to the way that the development of radio was patterned on the telephone, we are not surprised when Stone acknowledges that her analysis came "from huddling under the covers with a galena crystal, listening to Stephen Hawking, doing phone sex, and incidentally paying attention to how none of these versions of me was unitary or complete" (404). That the primal scene in bed with the galena crystal led to her meditation on split subjectivity and multiple engagements with the body and voice, the ether and the meat, attests to radio's role in inaugurating the postmodern.

"Listening to radio was like being a child again, having stories read to you and being expected to have—and use—a vivid imagination." Susan Douglas observes in *Listening In*. Douglas is right to emphasize the pleasures of listening, particularly radio's role in kindling the imagination.[55] Yet that imagination was not entirely unconstrained. Like any other medium, radio's imaginative uses were shaped by its sociocultural context. The complex multiple meanings of radio are captured by Greg Howard in one issue of his comic strip *Sally Forth*. "Hilary asked me to explain a vulgar innuendo she heard on the radio today," Sally says to Ted, bemoaning the inability of "radio DJs" to "control themselves during the times they know parents are driving their kids to school." Ted empathizes with Sally's dig at popular radio, observing, "It seems . . . more and more DJs are abusing 'freedom of expression' in an attempt to boost their ratings." " 'Shock Radio,' " Ted quips, "a price we pay for living in an open society." Yet if Ted's response is resigned acceptance of the status quo. Sally's is more resistant and resourceful: "I guess I'll just delete the setting for that station." With that gesture, she subverts the patriotic orthodoxy of the new consumerism that reduces the "pursuit of happiness" to the "pursuit of market share."[56] Whether in service of high or popular culture, radio is still a site of contestation between corporate and consumer control, both of its transmission and of its reception.

The essays in this volume explore a number of the ways that radio was constructed by, and in its turn helped to shape, society and culture. We learn that radio's vulnerability to corporate control and its stress on emergency communications resulted in a set of class and gender exclusions that remain to be remedied. Yet if radio disenfranchised local, working-class community groups and women in its development, we also see that in arts programming and programming focused explicitly on African Americans, radio served to consolidate and strengthen the clout of a black audience, Afro-Caribbean in the first case, and African American in the second. Paradoxically, we also discover how the delineation and targeting of specific radio markets (audiences for alternative youth radio, popular science radio, and programming focused on poetry) can blunt their force, resulting in a co-optation of their alternative positioning in the service of a more centrist vision of each constituency. Finally, in the essays focusing on radio ideology and radio's primal scene, we learn how radio programming both inscribed and subverted stereotypes of gender, race, and nationality, as well as of the autonomous modern individual.

Fun in the Radio World

Susan Douglas has observed that radio listening is like being "a child again."[57] Perhaps that is why I am drawn, in conclusion, to E. Boyd Smith's 1923 children's book *Fun in the Radio World*. Its illustrations capture the magic and method of the new medium by focusing not on the technology but on its rejuvenating effect on listeners.[58] The genre of children's literature, like the encyclopedia, functions to consolidate already existing cultural practices. When read with a cultural studies lens, this playful children's picture book expresses many of the same cultural and ideological functions of radio that are anatomized by the essays in this volume. In its text as in its illustrations, *Fun in the Radio World* demonstrates the cultural

construction and functions of radio: as a developing technology, an auditory practice, a social network, a technology of race, gender, and perhaps
even species.

Smith's colored pen-and-ink drawings move from the familiar to the
exotic, in each case portraying various modes of *listening in* to the radio.
The illustrations feature farmyard animals with heads cocked in amaze-
ment at the sound of a musical broadcast; children at a swimming hole
reluctantly hearing the call to come home; Camp Fire girls and Boy Scouts
in rapt (if sex-segregated) groupings listening to radio programs; children
and adults capering to the radio on a hot summer day; sailors aboard ship
dancing the hornpipe to an unseen radio; African "savages" transfixed by a
radio broadcast played by white explorers; wild animals listening in puzzle-
ment to a radio concert; cowboys whooping it up on the ranch to the tune
of radio concerts; Indians on the warpath interrupting their dance to cock
their ears to the mysterious radio signal; Eskimos huddled in pleasure
beside a polar exploration vessel transmitting radio signals; and finally the
mysterious planet Saturn, where radio may someday reach.

Addressing its child readers, Smith's volume offers a lucid introduction
to the technology of radio: how it develops, how it is picked up by different
societies and cultures, how it constructs its users, what its potential is for
future development. Smith's narrative naturalizes radio technology, comparing its multidirectional signal to solar radiation: "When the big sending
stations, like Newark, send out their radio, it goes in every direction, just as
the sun sends out its light and heat, and anyone with a 'receiver' can pick it
up" (1). The book presents radio as relying on a global grammar (to bor-
row McLuhan's term) that transcends limitations of culture, even of species. Thus it can be appreciated by animals as well as people: "Music is a
pretty universal language, so perhaps they [barnyard animals] understood
it, though they must have been astonished to hear so much noise, with
nobody making it" (1, 3). And it presents the technologically conservative
response to radio, too, as naturalized, so that resistant human beings echo
the resistance of the barnyard fowl: "They [barnyard fowl] were like a good
many people and didn't like any change; 'standing pat' was good enough
for them. They wanted a quiet life and preferred to do their noise-making
themselves" (8).

Celebrating "fun in the radio world," Smith's children's book shows how
radio functions for recreation, showing people and even animals "listening
in" to baseball games, band concerts, and jazz concerts. More interesting

still, the book shows the ways radio can be used to instill discipline (anticipating similar uses of pagers and cell phones): "Willie has a mechanical bent and made a transmitter, so that he can send out radio messages for a short distance. . . . But, alas, his mother knows this and how to use it. So, in the best of the swimming he hears her call. . . . So radio is used in a practical way" (9, 11). It explains how radio can provide disaster relief and global positioning assistance: "The ship can even call up the stations on the shore, hundreds of miles away, and carry on conversations. So they no longer feel as though they were out of the world, and forgotten. If they get into trouble they can call for help. Or if they don't know just where they are, all they have to do is to ask the shore stations, and the right one will give them their position. To them the radio has already become a valuable thing" (27). It emphasizes that radio can create a sense of global community: "The traveler, the prospector, and mountain miner, and all people who live far off in remote places, no longer need feel lonely, for radio keeps them in touch with all the rest of the world" (43). Finally, in the scene of radio on an Indian reservation, Smith's story shows how radio can be used to enforce governmentality, nationalism, and generational differentiation:

Now, when they [the Indians] get worked up, and have too lively a dance which threatens trouble—all stripped, painted, and decked out with feathers—the Government agent, who is supposed to look after them, starts the radio going, to calm them.

Now this rival dance music, of some jazz band, attracts the young ones away from their old fighting music, and works for peace. In this way the agent finds his radio very useful—a lot better than soldiers.

Like most of us, they, too, soon become interested in the latest things. That, just now, is radio. So here is a good use for it, to civilize them, and make them good Americans. (43)

Like a basic civics lesson, *Fun in the Radio World* emphasizes how radio enforces some of the key American values: equality, uniformity, and personal choice. The effect is, paradoxically, simultaneously communal and individualistic, for although radio transmits impartially in all directions and treats us all alike, it also enables individuals to choose a station based on their own preferences, a central tenet of capitalist consumerism: "We are all alike in this, from one side of the country to the other, and radio treats us all alike; it just gives out the news and anyone can get it who listens in. And its program is so varied that there is something for every taste. And then, too, often several stations are broadcasting at about the same time, so that if you don't like one concert you can always tune up to another" (40). Radio serves not only the more benign aspects of human culture but also the more invidious ones, as well, such as gender stereotyping and racialization. The different ways that Camp Fire girls and Boy Scouts use radio, presented without any analysis in Smith's text and photos, embody that gender stereotyping. Camp Fire girls get "garden or cooking talks, something for every taste," and Boy Scouts get "good instructive advice" as well as "Brer Rabbit" stories (15). Boys with "mechanical instincts . . . want receivers of their own, at which they tinker and work until they can get in touch with very far-away stations. And some even make quite good homemade receivers" (19). Not only radio broadcasts but the technological history and hardware of radio are a male province, as Smith's text also illustrates: "Of course the boys want to know how it was invented—or they ought to. Well, they will find the beginning went away back to Benjamin Franklin, and others of his time; then Morse invented the telegraph, sending sound electrically through wire. The experiments of Hertz followed. Then Marconi succeeded in sending messages through the air by 'wireless.' Poulsen next developed the radio. And now in our own country men are steadily improving it" (19).

If the male sex is dominant in the history and present uses of radio, Smith's book suggests that it is a dominance especially enjoyed by white males. Perhaps the most egregiously stereotyped illustration in the volume is paired with text that explains how white explorers rely on radio to reinforce racial categories (figure 1). The illustration positions us with the white explorers, in pith helmets, who from their tent flap are tuning in a radio program while astonished savages in grass skirts and loincloths, spears in hands, the whites of their eyes shining, gaze open-mouthed at the technological miracle. White explorers necessarily rely on radio to instill dominance, the narrator straightforwardly explains: "Sometimes theirs is a dangerous life, and they have to deal with fierce savages. They, too, carry their receivers and can pick up the radio from home, this same radio which has crossed the ocean. They connect up and give the natives a concert. And these savage black men who might easily be very dangerous, are so astonished, and so impressed by the wonders of the white men that for the time they become quite safe to travel among" (28).

Smith's text explains that white explorers use radio almost as an aural drug, to create among the natives a kind of addiction and dependence that

FIGURE 1. "Savages" astonished by radio. E. Boyd Smith, *Fun in the Radio World* (New York: Frederick A. Stokes, 1923).

reduces their threat: "You can easily imagine the surprise of the natives; of course they think it is magic. No wonder, when they hear all this music, or talking, coming from nowhere. . . . When one concert ends the explorer tunes up for WBZ, or KYW—this means, of course, the big central broadcasting stations back in America—and gives them another. And so in time wins over the tribe, who will do anything for him now, to get more music" (31).

Yet if Smith (probably unintentionally) paints a picture of radio as a tool of racial dominance, readers enjoy glimpses of the ways that radio can open up a broader world to its listeners, thereby undercutting that same racial segregation. For example, omnipresent radio broadcasting brings jazz to those who might otherwise not listen to it: "And the radio, naturally, is here too, for now we find it everywhere, and plenty of receivers give us music. And the jazz sets the bathers capering around on the warm sand, the big and the little people. . . . We would miss it now. It is all about us, though we can't see it" (23).

By the end of Smith's children's story, we have discovered that the invisible technology of radio reaches so far, and is so liberatory, that it extends beyond the earth into outer space. The remarkable capacities of this new

FIGURE 2. Title page, E. Boyd Smith, *Fun in the Radio World.*

technology are so great, the text suggests, that it prompts a radical decentering from the human. The text thus combines the typically modernist perspective of expansionist nationalism with a proto-postmodern glimpse from another angle of vision. If polar explorers, broadcasting radio to the Eskimos, represent "the end of our world, the farthest we can go . . . no doubt radio keeps right on—off the world—right out into empty space. *And if it is strong enough perhaps it even reaches Mars, or ringed Saturn, or some of the other planets, so far, far away. We don't know whether any people live there or not. If they do, I wonder if they have receivers up there? Who knows?"* (47).

From the familiar barnyard and swimming hole to the rings of Saturn, the radio world promises fun to all. Yet this fun is experienced in different ways and from different positions, depending on one's species, class, race, sex, and age. The title page and splendid cover of the children's book make this point explicitly, if nonverbally. The title page, with the smiling face of a girl wearing headphones superimposed on a radio dial, suggests that if girls are included among the fun, their role will be not as transmitter but as radio receiver (figure 2). In contrast, on the cover, Father Time, his earphones on, listens in a relaxed pose to the transmissions of radio station TODAY, whose antenna is clasped by a naked infant New Year (gender not

FIGURE 3. Father Time listens to station TODAY, cover illustration, E. Boyd Smith, *Fun in the Radio World.*

specified, but traditionally male) (figure 3). The hourglass marks the medium's inherently temporal and aural character, and the owl raises the question of the moment: *Who can have fun in the radio world?* The essays that follow explore some of the cultural, technological, and political resonances of that question, taking as their point of departure McLuhan's observation that radio "transforms the relation of everybody to everybody, regardless of programming."

Notes

1 Don Kelm, *USA Today,* 31 December 1999, 29A.

2 Herbert M. Howard, "Foreword," *Journal of Radio Studies* 8, no. 1 (2001): v.

3 James E. Fletcher, "Foreword," *Journal of Radio Studies* 7, no. 1 (2000): v–vi.

4 *JRS Cumulative Index,* vols. 1–7, *Journal of Radio Studies* 7, no. 1 (2000): 249–54.

5 Frank Chorba, "Introduction," *Journal of Radio Studies* 8, no. 1 (2001): x.

6 Toby Miller, "An Editorial Introduction for Radio," *Continuum: The Australian Journal of Media and Culture* 6, no. 1 (1992), "Radio—Sound" issue. Available

from UMI's Proquest Direct, http://wwwmcc.murdoch.edu.au/ReadingRoom/6.1/Miller.html, 1–7, 2 (10 August 2001).

7 Title page, *Continuum: The Australian Journal of Media and Culture* 6, no. 1 (1992), "Radio—Sound" issue. Available from UMI's Proquest Direct, http://wwwmcc.murdoch.edu.au/ReadingRoom/6.1/Miller.html, 1–7, 2 (10 August 2001).

8 David Rose, " 'Just Warming 'Em Up': Radio Talkback and Its Renditions," *Continuum: The Australian Journal of Media and Culture* 6, no. 1 (1992): 1. Available from UMI's Proquest Direct, http://wwwmcc.murdoch.edu.au/ReadingRoom/6.1/Rose.html (10 August 2001).

9 Tom O'Regan, "Radio Daze: Some Historical and Technological Aspects of Radio," *Continuum: The Australian Journal of Media and Culture* 6, no. 1 (1992). Available from UMI's Proquest Direct, http://wwwmcc.murdoch.edu.au/ReadingRoom/6.1/O'Regan.html, 1–7, 1 (10 August 2001).

10 Ibid., 3, 5.

11 Rebecca Coyle, "Sound and Speed in Convocation: An Analysis of The Listening Room Programs on Paul Virilio," *Continuum: The Australian Journal of Media and Culture* 6, no. 1 (1992): 118–38.

12 Douglas Kahn and Gregory Whitehead, *Wireless Imagination: Sound, Radio, and the Avant-Garde* (Cambridge: MIT Press, 1992); Adalaide Morris, *Sound States: Innovative Poetics and Acoustical Technologies* (Chapel Hill: University of North Carolina Press, 1997).

13 Kahn and Whitehead, *Wireless Imagination*, 1.

14 Morris, *Sound States*, 2.

15 Peter Monaghan, "Exploring Radio's Sociocultural Legacy," *Chronicle of Higher Education*, 19 February 1999, A17–A19.

16 Michele Hilmes, *Hollywood and Broadcasting: From Radio to Cable* (Urbana and Chicago: University of Illinois Press, 1990), and *Radio Voices: American Broadcasting, 1922–1952* (Minneapolis: University of Minnesota Press, 1997); Susan Douglas, *Inventing American Broadcasting, 1899–1922* (Baltimore: Johns Hopkins University Press, 1987), and *Listening In: Radio and the American Imagination* (New York: Times Books, 1999).

17 Hilmes, *Hollywood and Broadcasting*, 3.

18 Douglas, *Listening In*, 5.

19 Hilmes, *Hollywood and Broadcasting*, 78.

20 Neil Strauss, *Radiotext(e)*, *Semiotext(e)* 6, no. 1 (1993).

21 Marshall McLuhan, "The Agenbite of Outwit," in *Media Research: Technology, Art, Communication*, ed. Michel A. Moos (The Netherlands: OPA, 1977), 123.

22 This is evidenced not only by this volume but in the many sessions focused on radio at the 1998 MLA convention.

23 Marshall McLuhan, "Notes on Burroughs," in *Media Research*, 86.

24 Henry Petroski, "Radio Days," *Civilization: The Magazine of the Library of Congress,* February–March 1997, 64.

25 Douglas, *Inventing American Broadcasting,* esp. chap. 6, "Popular Culture and Populist Technology: The Amateur Operators, 1906–1912," 187–215, and chap. 7, "The *Titanic* Disaster and the First Radio Regulation," 216–39.

26 Petroski, "Radio Days," 66; Douglas, *Inventing American Broadcasting,* 234. As Douglas observes, "The Radio Act of 1912 represents a watershed in wireless history, the point after which individual exploration of vast tracts of the ether would diminish and corporate management and exploitation, in close collaboration with the state, would increase. The American spectrum was partitioned: another frontier was partially closed. The 1912 law as a legislative artifact reveals American society's early struggle to come to terms with an invisible, enigmatic, communally held resource whose potential was still only partially appreciated" (236).

27 Mark Raboy, "Radio as an Emancipatory Cultural Practice," *Radiotext(e), Semiotext(e)* 6, no. 1 (1993).

28 David Bathrick, "Making a National Family with the Radio: The Nazi *Wunschkonzert,*" *Modernism/Modernity* 4, no. 1 (January 1997): 116.

29 Richard Barbrook, "A New Way of Talking: Community Radio in 1980s Britain," *Science as Culture* (London), pilot issue (1987): 81–129.

30 Tetsuo Kogawa, "Free Radio in Japan: The Mini FM Boom," *Radiotext(e), Semiotext(e)* 6, no. 1 (1993): 90.

31 Ibid., 91.

32 Allen Chapman, "The Radio Boys Trailing a Voice, or Solving a Wireless Mystery," *Radiotext(e), Semiotext(e)* 6, no. 1 (1993).

33 Douglas, *Inventing American Broadcasting,* 199–200. For a discussion of Gernsback's role in the growth of science fiction magazine publishing, see Andrew Ross, *Strange Weather: Culture, Science, and Technology in the Age of Limits* (London: Verso, 1991).

34 Douglas, *Inventing American Broadcasting,* 205.

35 Citations from *Amazing Stories* are as follows: Harl Vincent, "Cat's Eye," April 1934, 10–32; Francis Flagg, "The Metanicals," April 1934, 60–79; H. Haverstock Hill, "Terror Out of Space," part 3, April 1934, 80–108; L. B. Rosborough, "Hastings—1066," June 1934, 53–63; Walter Kateley, "Subjugating the Earth," June 1934, 64–100; Neil R. Jones, "Moon Pirates" (conclusion), October 1934, 53–83; P. Schuyler Miller, "The Pool of Life," June 1934, 12–52; Eando Binder, "Eighty-Five and Eighty-Seven," June 1934, 84–96; Edmond Hamilton, "Intelligence Undying," April 1936, 13–26; Isaac R. Nathanson, "A Modern Comedy of Science, April 1936, 27–55; Ralph Robin, "The Pygmies of Phobos," April 1936, 116–26; Robert Moore Williams, "The Man Who Ruled the World," June 1938, 10–29; Polton Cross, "The Master of the Golden City," June 1938, 44–71; John

Russell Fearn, "A Summons from Mars," June 1938, 82–106; and Ralph Milne Farley, "The Radio Man Returns," June 1939, 96–109. *The Radio Man,* also by Ralph Milne Farley [Roger Sherman Hoar, pseud.], appeared in 1948 (Los Angeles: Fantasy Publishing).

36 Douglas, *Listening In,* 26.

37 David W. Chen, "In Suburbs, Newcomers Are Welcomed As Ethnic Radio Grows," *New York Times,* 17 July 2001, A21.

38 Ariel Swartley, "Chicano Radio's Fading Signal," *New York Times,* 6 August 2000, sec. 2, p. 31.

39 Chen, "In Suburbs, Newcomers Are Welcomed," A21.

40 Swartley, "Chicano Radio's Fading Signal," 31.

41 Jordan Raphael, "Radio Station Leaves Earth and Enters Cyberspace," *New York Times,* 4 September 2000, C6.

42 Ibid.

43 Eric A. Taub, "New Format for Radio: All Digital," *New York Times,* 25 January 2001, E1, E8.

44 Abbie Hoffman, "Guerilla Radio," *Radiotext(e), Semiotext(e)* 6, no. 1 (1993): 299–301. Excerpted from *Steal This Book* (Contemporary Classics, 1972).

45 Brian Naylor, "Congress Votes to Limit the Development of Low-Power Radio," transcript, *All Things Considered,* National Public Radio, 19 December 2000.

46 Frank Ahrens, "Budget Bill Curbs Low-Power Radio; Stations Would Be Kept Out of Cities," *Washington Post,* 20 December 2000, E3.

47 Ibid.

48 Douglas, *Listening In,* 10.

49 Marshall McLuhan, *Understanding Media: The Extensions of Man* (New York: McGraw-Hill, 1965), 298.

50 Hilmes, *Radio Voices,* xiv.

51 Sandy Stone, "Split Subjects, Not Atoms, or How I Fell in Love with My Prosthesis," in *The Cyborg Handbook,* ed. Chris Hables Gray (New York: Routledge, 1995), 402.

52 Douglas, *Listening In,* 40.

53 John Keel, "Biological Radio," *Radiotext(e), Semiotext(e)* 6, no. 1 (1993): 344–45; Douglas, *Listening In,* 42–43.

54 Stone, "Split Subjects," 403.

55 Douglas, *Listening In,* 4.

56 Greg Howard, *Sally Forth, Centre Daily Times.*

57 Douglas, *Listening In,* 4.

58 E. Boyd Smith, *Fun in the Radio World* (New York: Frederick A. Stokes, 1923). Smith, born in St. John, New Brunswick, Canada, in 1860, was an artist, illustrator, and children's book author whose other works included *The Story of Pocahontas and Captain John Smith* (1906).

Works Cited

Ahrens, Frank. "Budget Bill Curbs Low-Power Radio: Stations Would Be Kept Out of Cities." *Washington Post*, 20 December 2000, E3.

Barbrook, Richard. "A New Way of Talking: Community Radio in 1980s Britain." *Science as Culture* no. 1 (1987): 81–129.

Bathrick, David. "Making a National Family with the Radio: The Nazi *Wunschkonzert*." *Modernism/Modernity* 4, no. 1 (January 1997): 114–27.

Binder, Eando. "Eighty-Five and Eighty-Seven." *Amazing Stories*, June 1934, 84–96.

Chapman, Allen. "The Radio Boys Trailing a Voice, or Solving a Wireless Mystery." *Radiotext(e)*, ed. Neil Strauss. *Semiotext(e)* 6, no. 1 (1993): 198–203.

Chen, David W. "In Suburbs, Newcomers Are Welcomed As Ethnic Radio Grows." *New York Times*, 17 July 2001, A21.

Chorba, Frank. "Introduction." *Journal of Radio Studies* 8, no. 1 (2001).

Cross, Polton. "The Master of Golden City." *Amazing Stories*, June 1938, 44–71.

Douglas, Susan. *Inventing American Broadcasting, 1899–1922*. Baltimore: Johns Hopkins University Press, 1987.

——. *Listening In: Radio and the American Imagination*. New York: Time Books, 1999.

Farley, Ralph Milne. *The Radio Man*. Los Angeles: Fantasy Publishing, 1948.

——. "The Radio Man Returns." *Amazing Stories*, June 1939, 96–109.

Fearn, John Russell. "A Summons from Mars." *Amazing Stories*, June 1938, 82–106.

Flagg, Francis. "The Metanicals." *Amazing Stories*, April 1934, 60–79.

Fletcher, James E. "Foreword." *Journal of Radio Studies* 7, no. 1 (2000): v–viii.

Hamilton, Edmond. "Intelligence Undying." *Amazing Stories*, April 1936, 13–26.

Hill, H. Haverstock. "Terror Out of Space." Part 3. *Amazing Stories*, April 1934, 80–108.

Hilmes, Michele. *Hollywood and Broadcasting: From Radio to Cable*. Urbana and Chicago: University of Illinois Press, 1990.

——. *Radio Voices: American Broadcasting, 1922–1952*. Minneapolis: University of Minnesota Press, 1997.

Hoffman, Abbie. "Guerilla Radio." *Radiotext(e)*, ed. Neil Strauss. *Semiotext(e)* 6, no. 1 (1993): 299–301. Excerpted from *Steal This Book* (Massachusetts: Contemporary Classics, 1972).

Howard, Herbert H. "Foreword." *Journal of Radio Studies* 8, no. 1 (2001): v–ix.

Jones, Neil R. "Moon Pirates" (conclusion). *Amazing Stories*, October 1934, 53–83.

JRS Cumulative Index, vols. 1–7. *Journal of Radio Studies* 7, no. 1 (2000): 249–54.

Kahn, Douglas, and Gregory Whitehead. *Wireless Imagination: Sound, Radio, and the Avant-Garde*. Cambridge: MIT Press, 1992.

Kateley, Walter. "Subjugating the Earth." *Amazing Stories*, June 1934, 64–100.

Keel, John. "Biological Radio." *Radiotext(e)*, ed. Neil Strauss. *Semiotext(e)* 6, no. 1 (1993): 344–45.

Kelm, Don. *USA Today,* 31 December 1999, 29A.

Kogawa, Tetsuo. "Free Radio in Japan: The Mini FM Boom." *Radiotext(e),* ed. Neil Strauss. *Semiotext(e)* 6, no. 1 (1993): 90–96.

McLuhan, Marshall. "The Agenbite of Outwit." In *Media Research: Technology, Art, Communication,* ed. Michael A. Moos. The Netherlands: OPA, 1977.

———. "A McLuhan Sourcebook." Assembled by William Kuhns. In *Essential McLuhan,* ed. Eric McLuhan and Frank Zingrone. Toronto: Basic Books, 1995.

———. "Notes on Burroughs." In *Media Research: Technology, Art Communication,* ed. Michael A. Moos. The Netherlands: OPA, 1977.

———. *Understanding Media: The Extensions of Man.* New York: McGraw-Hill, 1965.

Miller, P. Schuyler. "The Pool of Life." *Amazing Stories,* June 1934, 12–52.

Miller, Toby. "An Editorial Introduction for Radio." *Continuum: The Australian Journal of Media and Culture* 6, no. 1 (1992). Available at http://www.mcc.murdoch .edu.au/ReadingRoom.6.1/Miller.html.

Monaghan, Peter. "Exploring Radio's Sociocultural Legacy." *Chronicle of Higher Education,* 19 February 1999, A17–A19.

Morris, Adalaide. *Sound States: Innovative Poetics and Acoustical Technologies.* Chapel Hill: University of North Carolina Press, 1997.

Nathanson, Isaac R. "A Modern Comedy of Science." *Amazing Stories,* April 1936.

Naylor, Brian. "Congress Votes to Limit the Development of Low-Power Radio." Transcript, *All Things Considered* (National Public Radio), 19 December 2000.

O'Regan, Tom. "Radio Daze: Some Historical and Technological Aspects of Radio." *Continuum* 6, no. 1 (1992): Available at http://www.mcc.murdoch.edu.au/ ReadingRoom.6.1/O'Regan.html.

Petroski, Henry. "Radio Days." *Civilization: The Magazine of the Library of Congress,* February–March 1997, 64–73.

Raboy, Mark. "Radio as an Emancipatory Cultural Practice." *Radiotext(e),* ed. Neil Strauss. *Semiotext(e)* 6, no. 1 (1993): 129–34.

Raphael, Jordan. "Radio Station Leaves Earth and Enters Cyberspace." *New York Times,* 4 September 2000, C6.

Robin, Ralph. "The Pygmies of Phobos." *Amazing Stories,* April 1936, 116–26.

Rosborough, L. B. "Hastings–1066." *Amazing Stories,* June 1934, 53–63.

Rose, David. " 'Just Warming 'Em Up': Radio Talkback and Its Renditions." *Continuum* 6, no. 1 (1992): 1–10. Available at http://www.mcc.murdoch.edu.au/ ReadingRoom.6.1/Rose.html.

Ross, Andrew. *Strange Weather: Culture, Science, and Technology in the Age of Limits.* London: Verso, 1991.

Smith, E. Boyd. *Fun in the Radio World.* New York: Frederick A. Stokes, 1923.

Stone, Sandy. "Split Subjects, Not Atoms, or How I Fell in Love with My Prosthesis." In *The Cyborg Handbook,* ed. Chris Hables Gray. New York: Routledge, 1995.

Strauss, Neil, ed. *Radiotext(e). Semiotext(e)* 6, no. 1 (1993).

Swartley, Ariel. "Chicano Radio's Fading Signal." *New York Times,* 6 August 2000, sec. 2, pp. 1, 31.

Taub, Eric A. "New Format for Radio: All Digital." *New York Times,* 25 January 2001, E1.

Vincent, Harl. "Cat's Eye." *Amazing Stories,* April 1934, 10–32.

Williams, Robert Moore. "The Man Who Ruled the World." *Amazing Stories,* June 1938, 10–19.

RADIO TECHNOLOGY

ACROSS THE TWENTIETH CENTURY

AT&T INVENTS PUBLIC ACCESS

BROADCASTING IN 1923: A FORECLOSED

MODEL FOR AMERICAN RADIO

Steve Wurtzler

Recent work on the history of American mass media has productively reconsidered the emergence of various media technologies in the United States.[1] This latest generation of media histories has successfully challenged previous accounts that retrospectively imposed an evolutionary view of technological change whereby a combination of corporate and consumer behavior, governmental regulation, and successful research-and-development efforts led almost inexorably to today's media forms. Such teleological accounts, focusing almost exclusively on causal links between successful innovations, collapsed history with a particular vision of progress in which a given medium's social identity was more or less the logical outcome of the technology itself. Instead, these new histories of American media point us toward the nonlinear development of technological artifacts, the false starts. They often reveal the paths initially taken but then foreclosed, and the unsuccessful applications often elided or underemphasized by previous historical accounts.

Like all technologies, emerging media are characterized by a period of "interpretive flexibility"—a period during innovation in which a given technological artifact will initially have multiple potential identities and serve multiple potential social functions.[2] Emerging media are initially characterized by conflicting interpretations of what a technology is and what it might become. The phonograph, in its initial decades, for example, was alternately conceived as an aid to stenography and an instrument for public performance, but not as a home entertainment device. The development and deployment of any media form are the products of various attempts to precisely *define* a technology and its uses. Such development is always contested terrain, often won through the foreclosure of various alternative models of what a medium might become. The ultimate form of a media technology is thus never predetermined either by the technology itself or by a single powerful player in that struggle (such as a corporation exercising important patent rights or strategically investing in a specific use of a medium, a particular government regulatory framework, or a particular market-based model).[3]

The history of American broadcasting powerfully illustrates this process whereby plural potential identities are progressively foreclosed and a single, dominant model for a medium gains prominence. After the redefinition of wireless communication technology from point-to-point telephony applications to point-to-mass broadcasting applications there followed a series of struggles to determine what form such broadcasting would take. This period of interpretive flexibility for broadcasting was characterized by conflicting visions for both the deployment of radio and its potential roles in American life.[4] These struggles over the identity of radio offer from one perspective a utopian moment when the future of radio broadcasting could have been pushed in any number of directions. But before rewriting the history of American radio as a declension narrative—as a dramatic fall, as a tale of utopian potential betrayed—we might ask if it is really all that surprising that radio would eventually become an instrument of hegemonic discourse, an instrument mobilized at the service of corporate capitalism. In the United States, is it surprising that radio was disseminated according to the logic of capital? By posing this question in this way, it might appear that I am invoking "economics in the last instance" as the ultimate determinant of media development, that despite whatever countervailing voices, practices, and determinants are at work, in the last instance, a media system will conform to the prevailing array of economic relations. But a reconsideration of the advent of cable television, American radio in the 1920s, and late-1990s radio broadcasting illustrates that while capitalism is indeed victorious and apparently pervasive, it is not all-powerful as a determining factor in a technology's social identity. Within the history of any media technology there arise spaces in which countervailing practices can indeed gain a foothold. Once a particular identity for a media technology is foreclosed, once a model for that medium's role in American life is suppressed, that model is never entirely erased. Changing circumstances (further technological innovations, shifts in consumer behavior, market forces, etc.) can open up gaps in which that which was previously foreclosed can again return.

Public Access Television as an Alternative Model for American
Mass Media

Public access television is a case in point. Within a political economy of television dominated by professionally produced programming and large, interlocking corporate conglomerates there exists public access as an embattled alternative—a vision daily enacted of an entirely different social identity for television. The philosophy behind public access begins with the belief that ordinary citizens should be structurally enabled and indeed encouraged to function as *producers* as well as consumers of television programming. By providing citizens with access to, as well as training with, video technology and often a cable channel exclusively devoted to this use, public access efforts embody a geographically dispersed, locally originated, nonprofit model for media, the goal of which is to empower and give voice to citizens.

The origins of public access television in the United States illustrate that technological change, shifts in both regulatory frameworks and media-industry economic arrangements, and the organizing and lobbying efforts of activists can, and in fact do, create media models that function in direct opposition to a commercial status quo. Public access television resulted from the interaction of all these forces. The innovation and diffusion of cable as a television delivery system spawned a reconsideration of U.S. media regulatory policy. Largely because of the successful organizing efforts of access advocates and the lobbying efforts of groups such as the National League of Cities and the U.S. Conference of Mayors, the Federal Communications Commission (FCC) mandated that cable television providers include channel space and resources for locally produced public, educational, and government access. Although eventually struck down in 1979, these "must provide" provisions enabled local municipalities to require contractually that cable companies operating locally provide some form of public access. In exchange for the right to run cables through a community and for a virtual monopoly as a cable television provider in a given municipality, cable companies were required to provide channel space and, in some cases where local activists were particularly successful, facilities and financial resources underwriting access efforts. Local cable TV franchise agreements formally codified public access provisions in cities across the United States.[5]

In the case of public access television, a variety of determinants interacted to redefine the nature of television, albeit only in a highly marginalized and carefully contained manner. The continued, although almost perpetually imperiled, existence of public access television in a variety of forms attests to the fact that even once a medium such as television is successfully diffused and incorporated into U.S. society, the ultimate shape of that medium is never finally and forever determined. Public access television resulted, in part, from the technological possibilities offered by emerging cable television delivery systems and the consequent structural space created by that emergence, a space in which, due to new economic and regulatory arrangements, alternative visions of media could gain some momentary purchase. But the vision of an essentially egalitarian, dispersed, locally originated, nonprofit, and importantly *participatory* medium controlled and operated by members of a community did not originate among a committed group of 1970s-era American media activists. The model behind public access circulated during the initial period in which various forces struggled to shape the identity of American radio in the 1920s. A version of "public access" radio competed with other potential models for the deployment of broadcast technology during the initial struggles to shape the identity of American radio.

Radio in 1923

The interpretive flexibility of radio broadcasting in the 1920s is powerfully illustrated by some of the visions expressed by representatives of a single corporation, American Telephone and Telegraph (AT&T). In what follows I will focus on two events involving AT&T in February 1923 that illustrate radically different visions of radio's potential role in American life.

During a February 14, 1923, broadcast over AT&T-owned radio station WEAF, audiences heard described two competing (although not entirely incompatible) visions for the future of radio and other electrical sound technologies. The broadcast event was a meeting of the American Institute of Electrical Engineers (AIEE) held simultaneously in both New York and Chicago. Through the auspices of AT&T long distance, wired voice transmission, and public address installations in New York and Chicago, members of the AIEE heard the presentation of scientific papers and engaged in discussion of those papers despite the distance between the two convention sites. The broadcast event itself, albeit not of compelling interest to audiences broadly conceived, was of interest to many of those who in 1923 were involved in radio and thereby concerned with electrical developments.[6]

In an address to the AIEE, Frank Jewett, vice president of Western Electric (the wholly owned subsidiary of AT&T), celebrated sound technology's ability to transcend spatial limits and electrically unite dispersed members of a group, thereby reinforcing their group identity by eclipsing that space. "For the first time groups of men and women, separated by hundreds of miles, are gathered together in a common meeting under a single presiding officer to listen to papers presented in cities separated by half the span of a continent and to take part in the discussion of these papers with an ease characteristic of discussions in small and intimate gatherings."[7] According to Jewett, sound technology could (re)constitute community, an intimate gathering characterized by the (virtual) copresence (albeit electrically achieved) of all participants. Jewett's remarks emphasized technology's ability to foster a type of discourse characterized by rational discussion and exchange. In short, technology was here configured as an instrument that facilitated a utopian public sphere, although a public sphere applied not to the larger social body but to a scientific community.

Jewett also acknowledged in his remarks the implications of broadcasting the proceedings, as well. "At the same time unnumbered thousands in their homes are auditors of our deliberations through radio broadcasting."[8] The participatory public sphere of scientists had an audience as well, a "public" called into being through the auspices not of membership, or even of copresence (and not even the electrically augmented pseudopresence of reciprocal communication), but instead an audience constituted as overhearing the rational deliberation and debate. The scientific public sphere of the AIEE became an aural spectacle to be consumed by all of those absently overhearing, rather than participating in, the proceedings.

Later in the conference, chief engineer of Western Electric Edward B. Craft described yet another vision of radio. Craft noted to his New York City audience that the first mayor of New York in 1685 could easily have addressed his entire constituency of 1,100 without raising his voice. Craft continued by contrasting this earlier moment of direct unmediated address with the possibilities now available through electrical means. "The ideas on which this nation was founded were spread abroad largely by word-of-mouth. With the growth of the population, of the newspaper and of the mail service, the printed word gradually displaced the spoken word. The loud speaking telephone system will tend to reestablish oratory by making it worth while for the nation's leaders to sway the emotions of tremendous audiences."[9]

Although Craft invoked the model of a public addressed by its leaders, this vision was far from the public sphere of enlightenment ideology. Here, emotional sway replaced rational debate, and the model for political modes of address was not a dialogue but indeed precisely the one-way, theatrical performance that would be codified through the rise of radio networks, commercially sponsored broadcasting, equal time provisions, and other exclusionary methods of disciplining electrically augmented speech. Technological possibility was here foreshadowed as the perpetuating of power relations according to a preexisting status quo, all the while evoking an earlier utopian moment of copresence and unmediated address.

Taken together, the remarks of Jewett and Craft point toward many of the constitutive features of what American commercial radio would eventually become. The AIEE conference featured two-way reciprocal communication that fostered participation and technologically augmented the possibilities of the rational discourse of scientific exchange, arguably a model of greater inclusion. The broadcast obviously did not involve such reciprocal communication but instead involved one-way communication. Like membership in the AIEE, this entailed a necessary structural exclusion. In keeping with the celebratory rhetoric and the event's emphasis on, and attempted embodiment of, the utopian possibilities of technology, "participation" was rhetorically redefined as listening in on distant events.[10] Participation so defined elides the structural exclusion of one-way communication. While spatial absence was compensated for by broadcast, by dispersion into the ether, the "unnumbered thousands" of auditors in their homes mutely consumed the aural spectacle rather than genuinely participating in it. Jewett and Craft invoked two distinct modes of discourse, each of which is associated in their remarks with a particular technological configuration. The wired voice transmission and public address system employed by the AIEE facilitated the rational exchange of ideas, the discussion and deliberation among equals. The one-way broadcast, in Craft's words, facilitated the "emotional sway" of the powerful orchestrating consent from the governed.

All of which is not to say that a mode of communication or a technological application has endemic to it a particular mode of discourse and a specific configuration of power. Reciprocal communication is not inher-

ently egalitarian, nor does it in and of itself guarantee the rational deliberation of a public sphere, however defined. Still, we can trace in these remarks by AT&T officials some of the underwriting assumptions embodied
within the eventual U.S. commercial broadcasting system. Radio as a technology could be grafted onto and further solidify existing configurations of
power, maintaining existing structural exclusions while rhetorically celebrating an illusory enhanced participation in American political and cultural life carefully contained through the act of consumption. But neither
the ultimate form of American broadcasting nor the assumptions implicit
in Jewett's and Craft's remarks were necessarily inevitable in February 1923.

In the same month, an alternative model for the diffusion and use of
American radio arose within the combined corporate boundaries of AT&T.
This model combined a conception of radio as a one-way medium of
communication to an audience with a view of that audience as neither
national nor essentially anonymous but instead, like the members of the
AIEE, linked by shared identity, namely, geographic membership in a
community.

On February 26, 1923, AT&T held an internal conference attended by
representatives of associated Bell System companies to develop a strategy
for maintaining and consolidating their interest in radio. Although radio
as a medium in early 1923 had been more or less successfully defined as
predominantly a medium of broadcasting (as opposed to a two-way medium of wireless telephony), the ultimate shape through which the technology would be diffused was far from predetermined. Various corporate
interests (including Westinghouse, General Electric, the Radio Corporation of America, as well as AT&T) vied with entrepreneurial-minded inven-
tors and loosely aligned interest groups (including educators and the Amateur Radio Relay League) to develop an identity for the emerging media
form. At the 1923 conference, the representatives of the Bell System developed a coherent vision for radio's dissemination. That vision of radio's
future also contained implicit assumptions about the medium's role in
American cultural life. The Bell System's 1923 vision of radio bore a striking
resemblance to the later model of community-originated cable television
embodied in public access efforts some fifty years later.

AT&T proposed developing U.S. radio as a dispersed, largely decentralized array of noncompetitive local broadcast stations operating at transmission power levels designed to reach members within a specific community.[11] AT&T would construct, own, and operate a single broadcasting

station in virtually any town of consequence in the United States. Within this model, programming would be predominantly local in origination, with the community itself determining the content, standards, and nature of broadcast material. Programming policies and decisions were to be vested entirely in the hands of a local broadcasting association consisting of community leaders and the general public. When the local broadcast association wished it, AT&T would provide through a modified version of their long-distance telephone system interconnections between local stations for programming of abiding national or regional interest. Competition from private stations was to be minimized or foreclosed through the efforts of the local broadcasting associations to function inclusively, encouraging all in the community who were interested in radio to join in the shared, collective effort. Such a vision for American radio is a striking contrast to the eventual (predominantly) for-profit, advertising-supported, competitive oligopoly of powerful radio networks and their affiliates that would come to define American broadcasting well beyond the transition to television. By some standards, the AT&T proposal sounds almost utopian in nature; this model for radio reproduces and reinforces utopian notions of a locally defined public freely and collectively determining what is in their own community's best interest. That public is truly participatory, not simply the passive consumers of radio programming (an audience), but active participants both in shaping broadcast policy and in developing the resulting programming.

Whether or not AT&T genuinely intended for this system of radio to constitute a broadcasting version of an ever-illusory participatory public sphere (an issue I will address hereafter), such a model for radio would appear to have created the *structural* conditions within which a public access model of radio could have developed. One can imagine (or perhaps fantasize about) an alternative history of American broadcasting, a history that provided voice to those voices largely excluded from a for-profit medium that in the first instance (commercial programming) addressed its audience as consumers and in the second instance (community affairs, political commentary, political broadcasts) addressed its audience precisely as consumers of hegemonic discourse.

Beyond the structural conditions that could have created such a decentralized, community-controlled system of radio, some evidence from the period surrounding AT&T's proposal suggests what such a public access model of radio might have sounded like. In a community with a strong organized labor presence, working people might be addressed directly as a social class, perhaps by fellow working folks, precisely about labor issues. Such a mode of address was adopted a few years later by Chicago radio station wcfl before the pressures of competitive commercial broadcasting undermined the station's initial mission.[12] In a community with a strong ethnic population, programming might cultivate and address that identity rather than foster an ethos of assimilation. Broadcasting history includes examples of stations and programming that sought to address ethnicity as a shared cultural identity rather than either as merely a market segment or as a corporeal quality erased from attempts to address and thereby constitute a national consuming audience. Within such an alternative history of broadcasting, women might have played a far more active role both as listeners and as broadcasters. Susan Smulyan has tracked the extent to which the rise of commercial broadcasting hailed women as consumers and homemakers, thereby reinscribing them within patriarchal domination.[13] Widely circulated radio journals in 1923 and 1924 such as *Wireless Age,* however, offered countermodels for feminine—indeed, proto-feminist—uses of radio that incorporated women (as listeners *and* as broadcasters) into active roles within a political, rather than consumption-driven, public sphere. Although a journal such as *Wireless Age* did include articles on radio as a tool in engineering more efficient home economics, other models for women in radio prevailed before radio's full-scale commercialization.[14] Within at&t's proposed radio plan, when the corporation's desire to maintain profits by adding more stations to this broadcasting system combined with the increased diffusion of radio receivers to minority populations, a crucial point might have been reached when at&t would have constructed stations in predominantly African American communities such as Harlem or Chicago south of the Loop.

Such retrospective speculations about (or perhaps a longing for) a different radio history views technological innovation as potentially utopian in nature and perceives media developments as following a declension narrative in which radical or even reformist potential is progressively foreclosed through the almost inertial weight of capitalist investment and regulatory initiatives that structurally follow the logic of capital. But before reinvoking economics in the last instance as the ultimate arbiter of the social shaping of media technologies, it would be useful to examine at&t's rationale for this community-based model of radio. Despite its carefully managed rhetoric of "universal service" between 1910 and 1930, the Bell

System was not philanthropically proposing this approach to radio solely as a contribution to an actual or virtual communications democracy. In this historic instance at least, the interests of a large corporation briefly coincided with those who sought a noncommercial, decentralized system of U.S. broadcasting.

AT&T's 1923 plan for the diffusion of radio according to a locally controlled broadcasting model resulted from the interaction of multiple determinants that shaped the organization's perspective on radio. Foremost among these determinants was AT&T's desire to maximize profits by exercising its radio patent position and the "exclusive" rights granted to the organization by the radio patent pool agreement of 1919–1920 (an agreement that effectively split the field of radio among corporate participants Westinghouse, General Electric, AT&T, the United Fruit Company, and the newly formed Radio Corporation of America). AT&T maintained (a position later determined to be erroneous) that the patent pool granted them the exclusive rights to build, lease, sell, and license radio transmitters. In the short term (at least until those patents expired), AT&T could maximize profits by constructing and operating a large number of radio stations. A model for radio featuring a large number of stations operating at lower power levels, rather than fewer high-powered stations, financially appeared to be in the Bell System's best interest. Such a plan offered continuing long-term profits (although not as large) even after the expiration of basic patents. These ongoing profits could be secured through service contracts with local community broadcasting associations and through the introduction of improvements in transmission technology developed within the Bell System's established research initiatives. Such innovations in the "state of the art" could guarantee continued sources of profit through new patents as the old patents expired, thereby foreclosing potential competition from future organizations. AT&T's 1923 radio plan would also have successfully secured its role as the sole provider of interconnections between radio stations or for wired transmissions between remote events and broadcast transmitters. Radio, from this perspective, provided yet another potentially profitable use for an augmented version of the Bell System's existing long-distance facilities. This strategy was vigorously and ultimately successfully pursued by the Bell System, independently of its 1923 plan for the diffusion of radio.

Both the desire to maximize profits through the execution of their patent position and AT&T's desire to develop through radio a supplement to their income through the wired transmission of voices provided determinants shaping the 1923 radio proposal. But other forces shaped the plan, as well. A decentralized, local deployment of radio like that of the plan was consistent with ongoing public relations efforts within the Bell System that stressed the public service provided by this large, increasingly ubiquitous corporation. The proposed model for radio complemented both the Bell System's rhetoric of "universal service" and related attempts to carefully craft a benevolent public-service identity for the corporation to further forestall public antimonopoly sentiment and subsequent government regulatory intervention in corporate affairs.[15] Through local radio, the apparently otherwise ubiquitous AT&T could gain and nurture an additional local identity strategically linked to community leaders and a definition of radio broadcasting as a public service provided by the Bell System.

Elsewhere I have used the term "conceptual conservatism" to refer to the manner in which new communication technologies are often initially conceptualized in terms of, and their introduction modeled on, established communications forms (the telephone modeled on the telegraph, for example).[16] AT&T's plan for the proliferation of low-power, community-centered, local broadcasting facilities is an example of such conceptual conservatism. This plan for the diffusion of radio echoed the technological model through which the telephone had successfully been diffused. AT&T would be a communications *provider,* constructing, owning, and operating the instrumentality of communication while individual local consumers determined how best to use it. AT&T's 1923 plan for local radio thereby sought to apply the successful model for the diffusion of the telephone to a new and emerging media form. Such conceptual conservatism, in which a new technology is developed and deployed in light of existing established technologies, is quite common in the initial stages of emerging U.S. media forms.

Finally, AT&T's 1923 radio proposal should be understood in light of the organization's ongoing experience as an operator of a radio station, New York station WEAF. The company was on the verge of deciding that while ownership of a broadcasting facility provided certain long-range benefits (it could function as an augment to ongoing research-and-development efforts), the actual day-to-day operation of a radio station was neither consistent with its established corporate identity as a provider of communication facilities nor consistent with its existing areas of expertise.[17] AT&T attempted with mixed success to approach the operation of WEAF along the lines of existing telephone service—the company's role was to provide a broadcasting facility, the content of which was solely to be determined by whoever purchased the use of those facilities. The 1923 radio proposal thus abstracted to a national scale the experiences and approach of WEAF.

AT&T's desire to maximize the profits made possible by its patent position for broadcast transmission equipment, the proposal's consistency with the public presentation of the Bell System as a public service, and the conceptual conservatism that made logical a view that radio might best be deployed in a manner similar to the telephone all collaborated to underwrite the approach to radio outlined internally in 1923. Rther than any philanthropic, utopian, participatory vision of the technology, AT&T's plan for decentralized, noncommercial, publicly controlled radio arose out of a large corporation seeking to play by capitalism's rules. Nonetheless, despite its for-profit origins, this model for radio structurally enabled a drastically different approach to broadcasting than what eventually developed.

Although structurally enabled, a participatory version of radio faced substantial obstacles even within AT&T's plan. Despite its interpretation of the radio patent pool agreement, AT&T was not solely entitled to construct and to license broadcasting stations, and with an arbitration referee's decision in November 1924, the notion that AT&T could monopolize American radio through building and licensing transmitters came to an abrupt end. In fact, in a revised patent pool agreement of 1926, AT&T ceded the business of constructing radio stations to its competitors, withdrawing to instead focus its radio efforts on providing the wired transmission facilities connecting stations that were necessary for radio networks.

AT&T's own description of the February 1923 radio plan reveals traces of further obstacles to a truly participatory model of American radio. The anticipated constitution of local broadcasting associations was not free from commercial involvement and in fact would tend to reinforce hierarchical power in a given community. When outlining the plan, assistant vice president of AT&T A. H. Griswold noted "that in each locality an important group of people will get together and form a broadcasting association. In that group of people should be the type that the community looks to as being the leaders of the community. In it I would expect to see the chamber of commerce, the important newspapers, the department stores, especially the people interested in radio and the general public as well."[18] A community broadcasting association dominated by the chamber of commerce and large retail interests necessarily reproduces the manner in which power in a community was dispersed along lines of economic interests. Within the AT&T plan, the anticipated method of limiting competing stations posed a further potential obstacle to participatory community radio. Griswold continued, "Whatever monopoly feature there is in it will be created by the local group itself which will get everyone interested in radio into that local group and if any one desires to own his own private broadcasting station, they will say to him, 'Come in with the bunch, we represent this community in radio broadcasting.' "[19] When approaching or foreclosing potential competitors with the collaborative (not inherently *collective*) voice that maintains "*we* represent this community," local configurations of power determine who is included within, and importantly excluded from, that communal "we." The owner of a textile mill in a small southern town, to cite an obvious example, would clearly exert a powerful influence over how the communal "we" was in fact defined within that community. Precisely such concerns are today faced throughout the United States by public access television providers, and advocates of the access philosophy must fight intermittent struggles over how such a communal "we" will be defined. But contemporary public access, or for that matter the alternative vision of American radio proposed by AT&T, importantly provides a site for such struggles, whereas centralized for-profit media providers arguably allow only space for individual complaining or orchestrated interest-group pressure about the programming content that is directed at consumers.

Contemporary Radio Broadcasting

From some perspectives, the promise of citizen participation in broadcasting implicit in the 1923 AT&T radio plan and later embodied in public access television has today been fulfilled by so-called community radio stations. But shifts in the political economy of American broadcasting exacerbated by the 1996 Federal Communications Act have encroached on and undermined the community's involvement in "community" radio. Contemporary radio illustrates the ongoing struggle of citizens to participate in broadcasting, and it demonstrates as well that while a particular model for a mass-media technology may gain dominance, alternative approaches do, in fact, survive.

In a 1998 essay, Jon Bekken argues that a variety of forces have collaborated to powerfully reshape community radio efforts in the United States over the past fifteen or so years.[20] Bekken tracks the manner in which licensing and regulation, shifts in funding, and increased access to externally originated programming through satellite distribution systems have led to an increased professionalization of community radio broadcasting. With such professionalization has come an increase in bureaucratic station policies, an imposition of hierarchical management models, and an increased emphasis on programming as the exclusive domain of paid, professional staff. Widely publicized developments at San Francisco station KPFA and across the Pacifica network illustrate this process of professionalization and both the exclusionary programming policies and community outcry that ensue.[21] These developments have often in practice removed the community from community broadcasting, erecting institutional and policy barriers to citizen access to, and control over, what were once viewed as local media institutions. Whereas community radio had once arguably challenged, if not actually broken down, the barriers between broadcasters and listeners by structurally including regular citizens in both the production and management of local community radio, recent developments have established structural constraints to genuine community participation.

In the aftermath of the 1996 Federal Communications Act and both the subsequent consolidation of ownership of commercial radio in the United States and the ongoing management and programming changes to community radio stations, the prospect for citizens' access to the means of radio production seems increasingly eroded. Lately, however, political progressives, radicals, access advocates, and listeners seeking more variety in radio have directed their attention to another, apparently expanding alternative. Micropower radio broadcasting (elsewhere labeled "pirate radio") offers citizens a comparatively inexpensive method of introducing diverse voices and perspectives "into the ether."[22] Broadcasting well below the federally mandated minimum power requirements of 100 watts, micropower radio broadcasters present an alternative approach to radio that can be heard anywhere from a radius of a few blocks, a neighborhood or section of a large city, to an entire community. Because these operators broadcast clandestinely, or at least literally "beneath" the law, it is impossible to gauge precisely how many stations are broadcasting at any given time. Yet in the late 1990s, evidence indicated that micropower radio was a phenomenon more widespread, more substantial, than a few scofflaws amateurishly disrupting a commercial status quo. In August 1998, for example, the *New York Times* reported that in the previous year, an FCC "crackdown" on micropower radio caused some 250 unlicensed stations either to be shut down or to cease operation voluntarily.[23] In the same week, the FCC reported seizing the broadcasting equipment from fifteen such stations in Miami alone. Micropower broadcasters face greater penalities than the seizure of their broadcasting equipment. Subject to civil fines of up to $1,000, as well as criminal penalties extending to $100,000 and a year in prison, unlicensed broadcasters have successfully gained media attention and broader support—including listeners—in part because of their outlaw status. By some estimates virtually every major city has at least one micropower broadcasting station, and cities such as San Francisco can boast an estimated dozen of stations.

Micropower radio has been facilitated by technological developments, active advocates of the practice who often operate in open public defiance of the FCC, and a larger "do-it-yourself" culture that promotes active citizen participants in lieu of citizen-audiences. In the 1980s, the equipment necessary for a ten-watt micropower broadcasting station could weigh in excess of a thousand pounds and cost up to $10,000.[24] Today the necessary transmitting equipment can fit into a suitcase and be purchased (often from electrical wholesalers in Canada) for under $1,000 fully assembled or for a mere $200 in kit form. With experience and practice, a fully functional micropower radio broadcaster can assemble or break down her or his set in a couple of hours, rendering potentially more clandestine a station that continues to operate in defiance of FCC administrative warnings.

The current cost of purchasing a medium-sized station or even a small radio station has dramatically increased, in no small part owing to the economic developments in the aftermath of the Federal Communications Act of 1996, through which corporations were allowed to increase the number of radio stations they own nationally and within a given market. Micropower radio has created the possibility for broader participation in broadcasting. Micropower advocates such as Stephen Dunifer, founder in 1993 of micropower station Free Radio Berkeley, provide technical training and advice for would-be broadcasters.[25] Organizations like the Association of Micropower Broadcasters (AMPB), the Prometheus Radio Project, and the New York Free Media Alliance keep micropower broadcasters and their supporters abreast of technical and legal developments in this dispersed movement. The circulation of relevant legal briefs available from the National Lawyers Guild Committee on Democratic Communication, as well as simplified descriptions of the limitations on the FCC's authority ("When the FCC Knocks on Your Door"), all facilitate a growing, dispersed attempt to reclaim a space for direct citizen participation in radio.[26]

The growth of micropower broadcasting has been aided as well by a larger movement within American culture in which increasing numbers of citizens are redefining themselves as producers as well as consumers of media forms. The proliferation and increased cultural attention paid to, for example, zines and individuals' Web sites attest to at the most a shift in individual relationships to instruments of mass media and at the least a shift in consumption patterns (for example, a shift to consuming software for desktop publishing).[27]

Broadcasting at the lower end of the FM band or the upper end of the AM band, micropower radio stations offer programming every bit as diverse as their operators. Press accounts cite in the same paragraph micropower broadcasters as diverse as a fundamentalist church in Connecticut and New York City's "Steal This Radio," a station run collectively by a group of homeless and squatters, inspired, in name at least, by the late activist Abbie Hoffman. Some microbroadcasters are less closely identified with politicized programming, such as Portland, Maine's, "Basement Radio," which broadcast modern classic rock twenty-four hours a day, seven days a week in 1997 through a nine-watt transmitter that allowed the station to be heard clearly all over the city.[28]

Among the most celebrated microradio broadcasters are the legally embattled Free Radio Berkeley and Springfield, Illinois, community activist Mbanna Kantako, operator of Human Rights Radio. Dunifer openly sold suitcase-sized broadcasting equipment to would-be broadcasters even as he was engaged in a series of legal battles with the FCC, legal battles that continue today.[29] Kantako's broadcasting career is frequently cited as evidence of the political potential offered under the auspices of micropower radio. Since beginning to broadcast in 1987, Kantako's personal politics and programming policy underwent a series of changes as he became more aware that his broadcasts throughout the John Jay Homes public housing project in Springfield (and thereby reaching at one point an estimated 70 percent of the city's African American community) could become a tool for local political involvement and activism. After a series of 1989 broadcasts documenting police brutality that featured community members presenting personal testimony, Kantako was approached by the FCC and threatened with a $750 fine.[30] Kantako has kept broadcasting, and programming includes a mix of music and what Kantako describes as "like a Black Panther political education class on the radio."[31] The latter includes reading to listeners books such as Jeremy Rifkin's *The End of Work* and Jonathan Kozol's *Savage Inequality* and authors such as Ward Churchill, Bobby Seale, and Nat Turner.

Not surprisingly, micropower broadcasters invoke the ire and disdain of many commercial radio stations and organizations like the National Association of Broadcasters (NAB). Citing often illusory interference with their legal broadcast signals, as well as the apparent inequity in which legally licensed stations must conform to the costly and time-consuming engineering and record-keeping tasks mandated by the FCC while clandestine broadcasters clearly do not, organizations like the NAB disparage micropower broadcasters as a criminal scourge disrupting corporate radio's legally orchestrated colonization of the publicly owned broadcast spectrum. From most corporate broadcasters' perspectives, market competition should determine what type of programming is broadcast. From a broader public access perspective, however, structurally providing citizens with the means to communicate precisely serves, in the words of the Federal Radio Act of 1927, the greater "public interest, convenience and necessity."

Oddly enough, micropower broadcasters found a slightly sympathetic ear during the late 1990s in FCC chairman William E. Kennard. Expressing some concern with the aftermath of the 1996 Telecommunications Act, Kennard told the *New York Times*, "With consolidation, radio has become the province of multi-million-dollar corporations. The loss of small religious stations and local programming is very unfortunate."[32] On January 20, 2000, after almost two years of study and public comment, the FCC adopted rules creating a new low-power FM (LPFM) radio licensing procedure. Creating two new classes of stations at 10 watts and 100 watts of power (audible at approximately 1 to 2 and 3.5 miles respectively), the new licensing scheme went to some lengths to prevent interference with existing stations. Other provisions sought to guarantee that licensed LPFM stations would be noncommercial and, although only initially, locally owned. Current or former "pirate" broadcasters were excluded from the license application process. Congressional action in December 2000, largely the result of successful lobbying by the NAB and National Public Radio (NPR), further limited the number and location of possible stations under the FCC's new rules.[33]

Not all micropower broadcasters would take advantage of this "legalization" of their efforts, even if they were eligible. Kantako openly speaks against FCC sanctioning of micropower radio: "The question is, are there some things you just have the right to do? We think the right to communicate is a human right. So I'm not interested in the government authorizing us or giving us permission to do what we have a natural right to do."[34] In a more scholarly vein, Thomas Streeter notes that arguments invoking "access" to the broadcast spectrum presuppose that someone else already owns or controls that resource, leaving unquestioned the legitimacy of that ownership or control.[35] While the FCC moves through the process of licensing some low-power FM stations, other micropower broadcasters continue to operate throughout the United States in open defiance of the FCC and thereby implicitly question precisely the corporate control of the broadcast spectrum. While some advocates of media access speak in utopian terms of the possibilities offered for grassroots-originated media in both digital broadcasting and Internet radio, micropower broadcasters use the tools at hand to create alternative media today. It is particularly ironic that the struggle by micropower broadcasters to enact a model for American radio initially proposed by corporate giant AT&T would today often constitute a criminal offense.

In justifying the administrative crackdown on micropower radio in the 1990s, the FCC, its corporate supporters, and the NAB invoked the rhetorical specter of chaos, a dire prediction of overcrowded public airwaves and "legitimate" corporate broadcasting rendered inaudible by the cacophonous intrusions of unlicensed and unregulated airwave "pirates." The invocation of such chaos echoes throughout the history of U.S. broadcasting, for it was precisely the orchestrated articulation of such fears that underwrote the initial establishment within Herbert Hoover's Department of Commerce of regulatory and licensing powers over radio broadcasting in the 1920s. Subsequent regulatory efforts that effectively solidified and promulgated American broadcasting according to its current for-profit, oligopolistic status quo frequently invoked such fears of "noise," rhetorically promising to manage and to nurture a broadcast spectrum defined as a public resource. But for advocates of alternative, citizen-generated media forms, this apparent "chaos" promises more than cacophony. In a statement to the FCC in 1936, William Paley, chairman of CBS, noted, "Capital can adjust itself to orderly progress. It always does. But it retreats in the face of chaos."[36] While capital is certainly not yet in retreat in the face of low-power radio, micropower broadcasting provides a contemporary method for individual citizens to reclaim cheaply, albeit often extralegally, a free space within, adjacent to, or literally beneath corporate control of the mass media.

The history of emerging technologies such as radio in the 1920s and cable television delivery systems in the 1970s offers powerful lessons that the desire for community-controlled media and active citizen participation in both programming decisions and production are the product of hard-won struggles that must be intermittently waged. The rise of centralized, commercial, corporate-sponsored broadcasting in the 1920s and 1930s and its solidification into a hegemonic system (further augmented by "reforms" like the 1996 Telecommunications Act) exert a powerful inertia on the development of, and indeed our ability to conceptualize, existing and emerging media forms. Public access television showed us in the 1970s, and micropower radio illustrates today, that alternative models for media systems may be foreclosed, but they are never entirely eclipsed, and they can sometimes exist for decades in residual form, reemerging under different economic, regulatory, and technological conditions.

Notes

1 Some particularly important examples of this work include Susan J. Douglas, *Inventing American Broadcasting, 1899–1922* (Baltimore: Johns Hopkins University Press, 1987); Robert W. McChesney, *Telecommunications, Mass Media, and Democracy: The Battle for the Control of U.S. Broadcasting, 1928–1935* (New York: Oxford University Press, 1994); Susan Smulyan, *Selling Radio: The Commercialization of American Broadcasting, 1920–1934* (Washington, D.C.: Smithsonian Institution Press, 1994); Thomas Streeter, *Selling the Air: A Critique of the Policy of Commercial Broadcasting in the United States* (Chicago: University of Chicago Press, 1996); Michele Hilmes, *Radio Voices: American Broadcasting, 1922–1952* (Minneapolis: University of Minnesota Press, 1997); Brian Winston, *Misunderstanding Media* (Cambridge: Harvard University Press, 1986), *Technologies of Seeing: Photography, Cinematography, and Television* (London: British Film Institute, 1996), and *Media Technology and Society: A History from the Telegraph to the Internet* (New York: Routledge, 1998).

2 My theoretical model for considering histories of technological change owes much to work outside of media studies on the social construction of technologies. See T. J. Pinch and W. E. Bijker, "The Social Construction of Facts and Artifacts, or How the Sociology of Science and the Sociology of Technology Might Benefit Each Other," in *The Social Construction of Technological Systems: New Directions in the Sociology and History of Technology,* ed. W. E. Bijker, T. P.

Hughes, and T. J. Pinch (Cambridge: MIT Press, 1987), 17–50; and Wiebe E. Bijker, *Of Bicycles, Bakelites, and Bulbs: Toward a Theory of Sociotechnical Change* (Cambridge: MIT Press, 1995).

3 All these factors—patent rights, investment in a specific media application, regulatory efforts, market forces—can function as "closure mechanisms," that is, they can temporarily foreclose specific potential applications of a technology. But such forces do not in and of themselves determine a technology's ultimate identity of social use. On the concept of "closure mechanisms," see Pinch and Bijker, "The Social Construction of Facts."

4 Among recent accounts, these conflicting visions for radio are astutely traced by Douglas (for the period to 1922), Hilmes, and Smulyan. McChesney illustrates the extent to which a struggle over radio's social identity continued after the medium had been successfully introduced into American society.

5 For a more nuanced account of the origins of public access in the United States than I can provide in this context, see Streeter, *Selling the Air,* 174–81; Douglas Kellner, "Public Access Television: Alternative Views," *Radical Science* 16 (January 1985): 79–92; and Laura R. Linder, *Public Access Television: America's Electronic Soapbox* (Westport, Conn.: Praeger, 1999).

6 The fact that radio's audience had yet to be "broadly conceived" characterized, in part, the medium's interpretive flexibility in February 1923.

7 William Peck Banning, *Commercial Broadcasting Pioneer: The WEAF Experiment, 1922–1926* (Cambridge: Harvard University Press, 1946), 116.

8 Ibid., 116.

9 Ibid., 118.

10 Not coincidentally, the same argument was made surrounding potential radio broadcasts of Congress in the early and mid-1920s and, significantly, in the aftermath of the broadcast of the 1924 national conventions of the Democratic and Republican parties. Audiences were rhetorically constructed as participants in these events. See, for example, Ralph B. Howell and Nathaniel B. Dial, "Senators Howell and Dial on Broadcasting the Senate Proceedings," *Wireless Age* 12 (August 1924): 30–31, 79–80. Period rhetoric surrounding the broadcast of political conventions is illustrated in, for example, William A. Hurd, "How Broadcasting June Conventions Affects the November Elections," *Wireless Age* 12 (August 1924): 18–22, 57.

11 AT&T's 1923 radio plan is described in the Federal Communications Commission *Proposed Report Telephone Investigation* (Washington, D.C.: U.S. Government Printing Office, 1938), 455–58.

12 Nathan Godfried, *WCFL: Chicago's Voice of Labor, 1926–78* (Urbana: University of Illinois Press, 1997).

13 Susan Smulyan, "Radio Advertising to Women in Twenties America: 'A latchkey to every home,'" *Historical Journal of Film, Radio, and Television* 13 (1992): 299–314.

14 The view that radio could powerfully facilitate women's participation in the political realm is illustrated in Christine Frederick, "Women, Politics, and Radio," *Wireless Age* 12 (October 1924): 36–37, 76, 78. More common in the period, however, were articles constructing radio as a tool in developing more efficient home economics, such as Hortense Lee, "Cooking Eggs—via Radio," *Wireless Age* 11 (December 1923): 24–25.

15 Stuart Ewen, *PR! A Social History of Spin* (New York: Basic Books, 1996), 85–101, 192–96.

16 Steve James Wurtzler, "The Social Construction of Technological Change: American Mass Media and the Advent of Electrical Sound Technology," Ph.D. diss., University of Iowa, 2001.

17 At least this is the position taken in retrospective accounts of their operation of station WEAF. See Banning, *Commercial Broadcasting Pioneer.*

18 Federal Communications Commission, *Proposed Report Telephone Investigation,* 456.

19 Ibid.

20 Jon Bekken, "Community Radio at the Crossroads: Federal Policy and the Professionalization of a Grassroots Medium," in *Seizing the Airwaves: A Free Radio Handbook,* ed. Ron Sakolsky and Stephen Dunifer (San Francisco: AK Press, 1998), 29–46. Also see Nina Huntemann, "Corporate Interference: The Commercialization and Concentration of Radio Post the 1996 Telecommunications Act," *Journal of Communication Inquiry* 23, no. 4 (1999): 390–407.

21 For an account of the events at KPFA, see Matthew Lasar, *Pacifica Radio: The Rise of an Alternative Network,* rev. ed. (Philadelphia: Temple University Press, 2000), 231–52.

22 See Ron Sakolsky, "Anarchy on the Airwaves: A Brief History of the Micro-radio Movement in the U.S.A.," *Social Anarchism* 17 (1992): 11, for some reasons against using the label "pirate." I intentionally avoid the appellation "pirate broadcaster" because the label "pirate," in addition to invoking a swashbuckling lawbreaker ultimately functioning in the greater interest, implies theft, and micropower broadcasters cannot "steal" a resource—namely, the broadcast spectrum—that we all supposedly own. For accounts of the history of micropower broadcasting in the United States, see Greg Ruggiero, *Microradio and Democracy: (Low) Power to the People* (New York: Seven Stories, 1999); and Lawrence Soley, *Free Radio: Electronic Civil Disobedience* (Boulder: Westview, 1999).

23 Matt Richtel, "FCC Takes a Hard Look at 'Microradio' Stations," *New York Times,* 20 August 1998, sec. D, p. 7.

24 Al Diamon, "Pirate Radio," *Casco Bay Weekly,* 26 June 1997, 11.

25 Stephen Dunifer, "Micropower Broadcasting," in *Seizing the Airwaves: A Free Radio Handbook,* ed. Ron Sakolsky and Stephen Dunifer (San Francisco: AK Press, 1998), 185–205. Dunifer and others have extended the micropower movement beyond the United States to El Salvador, Chiapas, Haiti, and elsewhere.

Dunifer describes his efforts in the following way: "It's [program content] up to the communities involved. To me it's just providing the enabling technology" (Ron Sakolsky, "If You Can't Communicate, You Can't Organize, and If You Can't Organize, You Can't Fight Back: A Composite Interview with Stephen Dunifer," in *Seizing the Airwaves: A Free Radio Handbook,* ed. Ron Sakolsky and Stephen Dunifer (San Francisco: AK Press, 1998), 176, a view that sounds remarkably like that of Griswold of AT&T in 1923.

26 "When the FCC Knocks on Your Door," in *Seizing the Airwaves: A Free Radio Handbook,* ed. Ron Sakolsky and Stephen Dunifer (San Francisco: AK Press, 1998), 206–8.

27 For accounts of this "do-it-yourself" attitude applied to the media, see Gareth Branwyn, *Jamming the Media: A Citizen's Guide, Reclaiming the Tools of Communication* (San Francisco: Chronicle Books, 1997); and Don Hazen and Julie Winokur, eds., *We the Media: A Citizen's Guide to Fighting for Media Democracy* (New York: New Press, 1997), although both volumes perhaps also attest to the commodification of this "do-it-yourself" impulse.

28 Diamon, "Pirate Radio," 11.

29 Free Radio Berkeley and the Free Communications Coalition, "Reclaiming the Airwaves," May–June 1994, 5–6. Advertisements offering equipment for sale carried the caveat that the equipment was intended "for educational purposes only."

30 Sakolsky, "Anarchy on the Airwaves," 7.

31 Jerry Landy, " 'We're Part of the Restoration Process of the People': An Interview with Mbanna Kantako," in *Seizing the Airwaves: A Free Radio Handbook,* ed. Ron Sakolsky and Stephen Dunifer (San Francisco: AK Press, 1998), 94.

32 Richtel, "FCC Takes a Hard Look," 7.

33 Ron Sakolsky, "The LPFM Fiasco: Micropower Radio and the FCC's Low Power Trojan Horse." *LiP Magazine,* 17 January 2001 (on-line 11 June 2001). Available at http://www.lipmagazine.org/articles/featsakolsky_77_p.htm. Also see Federal Communications Commission, "Low Power FM Radio Service: Allegations and Facts" (on-line 11 June 2001). Available at http://www.fcc.gov/Bureaus/Mass _Media/Factsheets/lpfmfacto32900.html.

34 Landy, "We're Part of the Restoration," 97.

35 Streeter, *Selling the Air,* 195.

36 Ibid., 197.

Works Cited

Banning, William Peck. *Commercial Broadcasting Pioneer: The WEAF Experiment, 1922–1926.* Cambridge: Harvard University Press, 1946.

Bekken, Jon. "Community Radio at the Crossroads: Federal Policy and the Professionalization of a Grassroots Medium." In *Seizing the Airwaves: A Free Radio Handbook,* ed. Ron Sakolsky and Stephen Dunifer. San Francisco: AK Press, 1998.

Bijker, Wiebe E. *Of Bicycles, Bakelites, and Bulbs: Toward a Theory of Sociotechnical Change*. Cambridge: MIT Press, 1995.

Branwyn, Gareth. *Jamming the Media: A Citizen's Guide, Reclaiming the Tools of Communication*. San Francisco: Chronicle Books, 1997.

Diamon, Al. "Pirate Radio." *Casco Bay Weekly*, 26 June 1997, 11.

Douglas, Susan J. *Inventing American Broadcasting, 1899–1922*. Baltimore: Johns Hopkins University Press, 1987.

Dunifer, Stephen. "Micropower Broadcasting." In *Seizing the Airwaves: A Free Radio Handbook*, ed. Ron Sakolsky and Stephen Dunifer. San Francisco: AK Press, 1998.

Ewen, Stuart. *PR! A Social History of Spin*. New York: Basic Books, 1996.

Frederick, Christine. "Women Politics and Radio." *Wireless Age* 12 (October 1924): 36–37, 76, 78.

Free Radio Berkeley and the Free Communications Coalition. "Reclaiming the Airwaves," May–June 1994, 5–6.

Godfried, Nathan. *WCFL: Chicago's Voice of Labor, 1926–78*. Urbana: University of Illinois Press, 1997.

Hazen, Don, and Julie Winokur, eds. *We the Media: A Citizen's Guide to Fighting for Media Democracy*. New York: New Press, 1997.

Hilmes, Michele. *Radio Voices: American Broadcasting, 1922–1952*. Minneapolis: University of Minnesota Press, 1997.

Howell, Ralph B., and Nathaniel B. Dial. "Senators Howell and Dial on Broadcasting the Senate Proceedings." *Wireless Age* 12 (August 1924): 30–31, 79–80.

Huntemann, Nina. "Corporate Interference: The Commercialization and Concentration of Radio post the 1996 Telecommunications Act." *Journal of Communications Inquiry* 23, no. 4 (1999): 390–407.

Hurd, William A. "How Broadcasting June Conventions Affects the November Elections." *Wireless Age* 12 (August 1924): 18–22, 57.

Kellner, Douglas. "Public Access Television: Alternative Views." *Radical Science* 16 (January 1985): 79–92.

Landy, Jerry. "'We're Part of the Restoration Process of the People': An Interview with Mbanna Kantako." In *Seizing the Airwaves: A Free Radio Handbook*, ed. Ron Sakolsky and Stephen Dunifer. San Francisco: AK Press, 1998.

Lasar, Matthew. *Pacifica Radio: The Rise of an Alternative Network*. Rev. ed. Philadelphia: Temple University Press, 2000.

Lee, Hortense. "Cooking Eggs—via Radio." *Wireless Age* 11 (December 1923): 24–25.

Linder, Laura R. *Public Access Television: America's Electronic Soapbox*. Westport, Conn.: Praeger, 1999.

McChesney, Robert W. *Telecommunications, Mass Media, and Democracy: The Battle for the Control of U.S. Broadcasting, 1928–1935*. New York: Oxford University Press, 1994.

Pinch, T. J., and W. E. Bijker. "The Social Construction of Facts and Artifacts, or How the Sociology of Science and the Sociology of Technology Might Benefit Each

Other." In *The Social Construction of Technological Systems: New Directions in the Sociology and History of Technology,* ed. W. E. Bijker, T. P. Hughes, and T. J. Pinch. Cambridge: MIT Press, 1987.

Richtel, Matt. "FCC Takes a Hard Look at 'Microradio' Stations." *New York Times,* 20 August 1998, sec. D, p. 7.

Ruggiero, Greg. *Microradio and Democracy: (Low) Power to the People.* New York: Seven Stories, 1999.

Sakolsky, Ron. "Anarchy on the Airwaves: A Brief History of the Micro-radio Movement in the U.S.A." *Social Anarchism* 17 (1992).

——. "If You Can't Communicate, You Can't Organize, and If You Can't Organize, You Can't Fight Back: A Composite Interview with Stephen Dunifer." In *Seizing the Airwaves: A Free Radio Handbook,* ed. Ron Sakolsky and Stephen Dunifer. San Francisco: AK Press, 1998.

——. "The LPFM Fiasco: Micropower Radio and the FCC's Low Power Trojan Horse." *LiP Magazine,* 17 January 2001 (on-line 11 June 2001). Available at http://www.lipmagazine.org/articles/featsakolsky_77_p.htm.

Smulyan, Susan. "Radio Advertising to Women in Twenties America: 'A Latchkey to Every Home.'" *Historical Journal of Film, Radio, and Television* 13 (1992): 299–314.

——. *Selling Radio: The Commercialization of American Broadcasting, 1920–1934.* Washington, D.C.: Smithsonian Institution Press, 1994.

Soley, Lawrence. *Free Radio: Electronic Civil Disobedience.* Boulder: Westview, 1999.

Streeter, Thomas. *Selling the Air: A Critique of the Policy of Commercial Broadcasting in the United States.* Chicago: University of Chicago Press, 1996.

United States Federal Communications Commission. "Low Power FM Radio Service: Allegations and Facts." On-line 11 June 2001. Available at http://www.fcc.gov/Bureaus/Mass_Media/Factsheets/lpfmfact032900.html.

——. *Proposed Report Telephone Investigation.* Washington, D.C.: U.S. Government Printing Office, 1938.

"When the FCC Knocks on Your Door." In *Seizing the Airwaves: A Free Radio Handbook,* ed. Ron Sakolsky and Stephen Dunifer. San Francisco: AK Press, 1998.

Winston, Brian. *Media Technology and Society: A History from the Telegraph to the Internet.* New York: Routledge, 1998.

——. *Misunderstanding Media.* Cambridge: Harvard University Press, 1986.

——. *Technologies of Seeing: Photography, Cinematography, and Television.* London: British Film Institute, 1996.

Wurtzler, Steve James. "The Social Construction of Technological Change: American Mass Media and the Advent of Electrical Sound Technology." Ph.D. diss., University of Iowa, 2001.

COMPROMISING TECHNOLOGIES:

GOVERNMENT, THE RADIO HOBBY, AND

THE DISCOURSE OF CATASTROPHE IN

THE TWENTIETH CENTURY

Bruce Campbell

On March 29, 1998, tornadoes struck two small southern Minnesota farm communities, causing two fatalities and leaving hundreds homeless. With antennae down and phone lines cut, normal means of communication were impossible. But immediately after the storm ended, surviving amateur radio enthusiasts were on the air with the news of the disaster. Amateurs from around the state, acting according to previously made contingency plans, immediately stepped in with additional equipment and support. Together with local "hams," they helped restore public safety communications, provided voluntary communications for disaster relief agencies such as the Red Cross and Salvation Army, and transmitted urgent messages from survivors to loved ones to let them know what had happened. For roughly twenty-four hours, until the normal communications backbone could be restored, amateurs provided the only communications with the stricken areas.[1]

This is a true story, one of many selected at random, but there is more to it than meets the eye. It appeared in *QST,* the official publication of the American Radio Relay League (ARRL), the largest national organization of amateur radio enthusiasts. The publications and lore of the radio hobby are filled with similar accounts, and many of their activities are designed to prepare their members for emergency service. In fact, there is a "discourse of catastrophe" in amateur radio that is central to defining the identity of the hobby both inwardly and outwardly.[2] This discourse is one of the most powerful tools of the hobby in its fight to gain recognition and to protect its special privileges in society. While very effective as a tool, one of the unintended consequences of this discursive strategy has been to contribute to a marginalization of women.

Radio amateurs are in an unusual position within society. While closely regulated and supervised by the federal government, on the one hand, they are protected by both national and international laws, on the other hand.[3] They are routinely consulted by government on matters pertaining to their interests,[4] and they are often offered other forms of cooperation and privileges not available to other citizens.[5] In short, their role really needs to be seen as a kind of loose partnership with government that grants them a surprising degree of autonomy. One of the most valuable and important privileges secured to them by law is the reservation of significant portions of the radio spectrum for their exclusive or shared use.

Territory has always been an object of investment and speculation. In agricultural societies, land was one of the main sources of wealth and value. A technological society changes this age-old equation. Today one of the most valuable pieces of "real estate"—and one of the keenest objects of speculation—cannot be seen or felt by human beings. It is that part of the electromagnetic spectrum suitable for the transmission and reception of data: the radio spectrum.

National and international laws and treaties govern the use of the radio spectrum. One part is used for TV, another part is used for AM broadcast radio, still another for FM radio, and so on. From the beginning of government control of the airways, a part of the spectrum—indeed, a significant part—has been reserved for amateur radio hobbyists.[6] In effect, some of the most commercially valuable "property" belonging to the government (or to the people, depending on your point of view) is reserved for the exclusive use of hobbyists, surely a nearly unique situation.

Three reasons have served to justify this allocation of resources. To begin with, the hobbyists were among the first to "settle" the airwaves. They, alongside the entrepreneurs, helped to "invent" radio and develop uses for it, be they commercial or personal. Second, until the end of World War II (but gradually declining thereafter), the radio hobby was a significant source of radio training and a reservoir of trained radio operators. The allocation of this part of the spectrum was therefore originally a kind of admission by the government that it did not yet control the new technology and, as a result, signaled an agreement of partnership with private, independent enthusiasts: they would develop the technology and a body of trained operators, and in exchange the government would guarantee access to the airwaves.[7]

The development of technically more complex but simpler to operate radios, government-sponsored training of hundreds of thousands of radio operators during World War II and the Cold War, and similar efforts by the private sector and the university system for the uses of private enterprise have all broken the monopoly on mastery of the technology once held by amateurs. The weakening of the hobbyists' monopoly of knowledge has led to a growth in importance of the third justification as official representatives of the radio hobby battle to retain their use of the radio spectrum. This is the long and noble tradition of amateur radio enthusiasts voluntarily serving the public in emergencies.

There can be no question that amateur radio enthusiasts do serve the public with their skills and do provide important services, particularly during crises when the normal communications infrastructure is overstretched or damaged. The stories recounted in the publications of the radio world are neither invented nor particularly inflated. While most people are rarely conscious of the role hams play in public service, most remember recent events within the former Yugoslavia, where the only link to the outside world came in the form of amateur radio hobbyists broadcasting eyewitness accounts of civil war atrocities. A little thought might further bring up memories of hams helping with communications at fairs or parades, and there have been countless examples of the selfless public service in disasters such as the one that opened this chapter. Yet rightly or wrongly, few would accord amateur radio a major role in disaster preparedness and relief efforts.

Moreover, the genuine importance of amateurs as a strategic reservoir of people with special training and skills may also be fading. Modern communications equipment is more robust, cheaper, and simpler than ever before, allowing ever more routine and widespread use by personnel who do not need more than cursory training. What may have applied in an America where all telephones ran on wires strung from poles (and not sent by satellite) and radios were expensive, complicated, and cantankerous gadgets demanding considerable expertise and skill may not apply in a postmodern America, with its ubiquitous Internet and simple, sophisticated radios routinely assigned even to trash collectors and dog catchers.[8] Moreover, the radio spectrum that hams have for their exclusive or nearly exclusive use is increasingly valuable as users of the radio spectrum proliferate and new services for wireless telephone, data, and Internet services emerge.[9] As a result, amateur radio is under great pressure to give up or cede its pieces of the spectrum altogether, while other modes of communication, particularly the Internet and World Wide Web, are stealing away existing amateurs and potential future recruits into the hobby.[10] The response so far among hobbyists has been slow modification, and an ever greater emphasis on amateur radio's public service role,[11] leading to increased use of a discourse of catastrophe to define and legitimize the radio hobby.[12]

In a sense, amateur radio has always been under pressure to give up something. The existence of a private group that has been able to negotiate with the government and compel it to grant legal protection and a large measure of self-regulation and often arrogates to itself tasks properly the purview of government is something of an anomaly. From its inception, amateur radio has fought a running battle with government over its own independence.[13] The modern battle over spectrum is therefore nothing new. Throughout its entire existence, amateur radio has been forced to develop elaborate strategies to defend its very existence. Predictions about the future of amateur radio and its ability to retain its bits of the spectrum would be futile. The entire communications arena is in a period of extreme flux at the moment, with telecommunications, cable TV, and Internet access in a three-way competition for the radio spectrum. What is important here is that under mounting pressure, the discourse of catastrophe has never been more important to give cohesion and identity to the radio hobby.[14]

Amateur radio has deployed several versions of the discourse of catastrophe both to shape an identity for the hobby and to defend its hard-won privileges. They saturate the hobby press and together constitute one of the central, defining discourses of the hobby. The first kind of discourse of catastrophe involves preparedness. Articles routinely appear in the hobby press explaining how to prepare for emergency situations. One variety of this lies in technical preparedness: how to make battery packs, construct solar arrays, or build emergency or portable antennae.[15] Many nonemergency activities are given a new spin in this light. Other forms of public service, such as providing communications at parades or sporting events, for example, are extolled in part for their usefulness as a training ground for response to catastrophe.[16] Even normal home operating practices carried to an extreme, such as operation for extended periods of time without rest during contests, et cetera, may become training for emergency operations, though the link is often more implicit than explicit.[17] Similarly, the continued use of Morse code, a by now technically outmoded medium of communications, is sometimes justified for similar reasons.[18] Finally, the entire organized radio hobby takes part in an annual weekend-long exercise in disaster preparedness called "field day," when hams are encouraged to operate away from home and off the power grid.[19] This constant repetition of calls to preparedness has a practical element. The electricity does go out, and conventional communications do fail. Real catastrophes do happen. Yet the discourse of preparedness gives meaning and excitement to many otherwise rather mundane activities and, taken as a whole, helps give the radio hobby definition and an idealized purpose.

The second type of discourse of catastrophe is contained in stories about actual disasters where hams have helped. These are either firsthand accounts by participants or more objective (third-person) reports of recent incidents.[20] They are an ubiquitous fixture in the hobby press and rarely fail to make the point that this help justifies the radio hobby's special privileges.[21] Of course, the voluntary assistance of radio amateurs at public events and during disasters is not imaginary; they can and do provide extremely valuable assistance in often exemplary and selfless fashion. Such accounts of actual emergencies serve a practical function of teaching from experience, but this only really applies to the small group of amateurs who are organized for emergency activity. For the rest of the hobby, tales of real-life emergencies provide a kind of ideal identity of helpful competence, an example to all hobbyists and a source of real pride. They are also a store of moral capital, a common history of selfless service that reinforces the self-image of the hobby and can be tapped by all members to justify their activities and privileges.

The constant cultivation of identity within the hobby is quite important. After all, just what unites participants in amateur radio? An interest in radio technology and a desire to communicate with others through the "magic" of radio are certainly common denominators, and there is an undeniable camaraderie associated with the hobby. But radio is no longer seen as being at the cutting edge of technological modernity, so that the technical and experimental sides of radio no longer command the intense interest they did at the dawn of the century. Meanwhile other means of communication that do not demand strict testing and licensing standards, expensive equipment, or difficult technological knowledge have also siphoned off interest in radio, and many other hobbies provide a sense of camaraderie. The one area where radio as a hobby can command a unique purpose is in its public service tradition in general and in long-distance communications in emergencies in particular. This gives the discourse of catastrophe a special importance in a hobby that is flaking away at the edges and that some fear may be in decline.[22]

In recognition of this (and in an attempt to attract new members to the hobby), the FCC and the radio hobby have begun to evolve and search for ways of keeping amateur radio alive. One step was the creation in 1991 of an entry-level license class that did not require proficiency in Morse code.[23] Negotiations are currently under way on the national and international levels to further simplify the U.S. licensing structure and bring its requirements more in line with the current state of technology.

One would expect that technological and societal changes would open up the hobby to greater participation, including previously underrepresented groups. At the time the radio hobby began, just after the turn of the century, women were still restricted in their access to education, particularly technical education.[24] Many, though not all, of the first hobbyists were young men who had a technical or scientific education or the aspiration to obtain one,[25] and women's access to the hobby subcultures generated by advancing technological modernity was restricted, not least by the expectation that they would continue to be responsible for the bulk of all housework and child rearing. Thus it was merely a reflection of the times that women were absent or nearly so among the first generation of radio amateurs. Since then, the number of women interested and active in amateur radio has increased over time. In 1939 the first association of female amateur radio hobbyists was founded in the United States.[26] The number of women involved in amateur radio has grown over the century with the emancipation of women and the easier access to the hobby made possible by simpler, more sophisticated equipment and easier license standards for beginners. Yet women's proportion in what is still a male-dominated hobby has remained fairly small.[27]

Although there are good reasons for the historically small numbers of women in amateur radio, it is an unintended consequence of the discourse of catastrophe that the marginal role of women has been reinforced. Women do participate in the public service activities of amateur radio, even in the most dangerous of natural disasters,[28] but the gender stereotyping inherent in the discourse of catastrophe has tended to limit their ability to do so. For example, women, who usually have substantial child care and homemaking responsibilities, very often on top of a full- or part-time job, have difficulties finding the time for volunteer activities and training. This applies equally to nondisaster public service activities and training projects such as "field day." Thus a man who can leave home and children in the hands of a spouse in the midst of an emergency (or on any given Saturday afternoon) is much more likely to become involved in public service activities. This is not, of course, a consequence of the discourse of catastrophe per se, yet the failure of more women to take part in disaster relief activities such as overseeing a radio base station in the home is: helping in a disaster is unintentionally equated with being free of homebound responsibilities.[29] The extra burdens of homemaking and child rearing thus tend to leave women with less free time to participate in amateur disaster relief.[30] Even the need for Morse code proficiency for access to the higher license classes of amateur radio, a point of some pride for most amateurs, tends to restrict women. Its reputed difficulty is frightening to all beginners, but since it does require a certain time commitment to learn, women may be disproportionally disadvantaged and confined to the lowest license category.

A second perception common in the culture at large is the longstanding prejudice against women being in harm's way and the corresponding association of emergency workers with physical and mental toughness. This long-standing prejudice not only limits women's participation in amateur radio's disaster preparedness but has long limited women's access to professions perceived as dangerous such as fire fighting, emergency medicine, and soldiering.[31] Just as women active in nontraditional professions have shown themselves the equals of their male counterparts (not least because technology has reduced the importance of sheer physical strength in nearly every profession), so female amateur radio enthusiasts should eventually become represented in greater numbers. But this has not fully happened yet, and the discourse of catastrophe present in the hobby press continues to subtly cast the amateur radio disaster volunteer as male and having stereotypically male virtues. Accounts of successfully met disasters predominantly list male names and show photographs of male amateurs. Even where women were present, the articles still emphasize the male contribution.[32] This is still true despite an obvious attempt on the part of the ARRL to include women and portray amateur radio as a hobby open to, and appealing for, women.[33]

Thus the discourse of catastrophe gives identity to and helps unite a hobby that is otherwise united only by an interest in radio communications. It provides a powerful rationale for reserving valuable parts of the radio spectrum for amateur use, and not least, it encourages a true spirit of public service. But this same rhetorical strategy also tends to reinforce the already (for historical reasons) serious marginalization of women and other groups within the radio hobby. As the historical reasons for a lack of women in technological activities and nontraditional professions disappear, more and more women should discover an interest in amateur radio and all its related activities. But for this to happen, the radio hobby must either abandon its discourse of catastrophe, an unlikely and unwelcome scenario, or, more positively, find a way to make it more all-inclusive.

Notes

1   This story is condensed from a report entitled "Minnesota" in the "Happenings" column by Rick Lindquist, in *QST* 82, no. 6 (June 1998): 63. Similar accounts appear in nearly every issue of *QST* and similar publications for radio hobbyists, such as *CQ* and *73, Amateur Radio Today.*

2   "Catastrophe" has been proposed as one of the defining tropes of the twentieth century. See John Cawelti, "Pornography, Catastrophe, and Vengence: Shifting Narrative Structures in a Changing American Culture," in *The American Self: Myth, Ideology, and Popular Culture,* ed. Sam B. Girgus (Albuquerque: University of New Mexico Press, 1981), 182–92; and Ulrich Beck, *World Risk Society* (Cambridge: Blackwell, 1999). See also Kate Lacey, *Feminine Frequencies: Gender, German Radio, and the Public Sphere, 1923–1945* (Ann Arbor: University of Michigan Press, 1996), 4–6.

3   In the United States, amateur radio communications are regulated by the Federal Communications Commission under section 97 of its rules (47 C.F.R. §97). Internationally, amateur radio is regulated under §25 of the Radio Regulations of the International Telecommunications Union, which has the force of law by treaty for member countries. See also Larry van Horn, "Who Controls Government Frequencies?" *Monitoring Times* 17, no. 12 (December 1998): 72.

4   See, for example, "League Responds to Telecommunications Inquiry," *QST* 79, no. 6 (June 1990): 6.

5   Amateurs active in cooperation with emergency services benefit from special legal protection (according to Public Law 105–19) and are often given access to other resources such as training. A good example of issues relating to resources, training, and insurance protection may be found in Sonoma County Emergency Services, *Volunteer Handbook* (Sonoma, Calif.: Sonoma Op Area Auxiliary Communications Service, 1997–2001), available on-line at http://sonoma-county-acs.org/vol.htm. But privileges accorded to amateurs are also more blanket in nature. Aside from protected access to the airwaves, radio amateurs also have an

(albeit limited) ability to challenge local and state zoning restrictions in order to erect antennae. See Federal Communications Commission Rules Part 97 (Amateur Radio Service), Subpart A (General Provisions), §97.15. See also PRB-1, 101 FCC 2d 952 (1985) or Federal Communications Commission FCC 85-506 Memorandum Opinion and Order of 16 September 1985.

6 While parts of the radio spectrum are reserved for the exclusive use of hams, government can preempt this use in emergencies. Other parts of the spectrum are shared between hams and other users.

7 That this partnership was entered into reluctantly by the government is demonstrated by bills introduced into Congress in 1917 and 1918, in which the navy attempted to take complete control over national radio policy and exclude amateur radio completely. This move was defeated, and the navy soon turned instead to a policy of extensive cooperation with the radio hobby. Clinton B. DeSoto, *Two Hundred Meters and Down: The Story of Amateur Radio* (West Hartford, Conn.: American Radio Relay League, 1936), 52–54, 55–56; Susan Douglas, *Inventing American Broadcasting, 1899–1922* (Baltimore: Johns Hopkins University Press, 1987), chaps. 4 and 8. See also E. L. Battey, "Navy Day—1929," *QST* 14, no. 1 (January 1930): 18–20.

8 "Postmodern" is used here to characterize an advanced state of (technological) modernity in which the acceleration of the pace of life makes orientation difficult and meaning uncertain and superficial. This approaches the "postmodern condition" of Jean-François Lyotard but is not meant in any narrow theoretical sense. Jean-François Lyotard, *La condition postmoderne: Rapport sur le savoir* (Paris: Editions de Minuit, 1979).

9 There has been extensive discussion of the value of the radio spectrum in the financial press since the late 1990s. See "Battle of the Airwaves," *The Economist*, 29 July 2000, 57–58.

10 The Internet is also cutting into the allied hobby of shortwave listening (SWL) as international broadcasters begin moving to digital transmission and "rebroadcast" over the Web. See "Charting a Future for International Broadcasting," *Monitoring Times* 18, no. 12 (December 1999): 65, and 19, no. 1 (January 2000): 69. The same magazine now runs an occasional column on Internet radio.

11 A survey of *QST* between 1945 and February 2001 discloses a marked increase in emphasis on public service of all types since the end of World War II.

12 The association of radio with heroism, public service, and positive social benefits in general dates back to the origins of the technology. Susan Douglas, *Inventing American Broadcasting*, 25–27 and chap. 6.

13 Douglas, *Inventing American Broadcasting*, chaps. 6–8; and also no. 7 in this essay. Note that the situation in Germany was similar before 1945, save that the state was always able to maintain control over radio technology to the point of nearly excluding hobbyists from legal activity. See W. F. Körner, *Geschichte des Amateurfunks, 1909–1963* (Hamburg: FT Verlag Rojahn and Kraft, 1963).

14 Although the "discourse of catastrophe," as I term it, is the focus here, amateur radio also deploys other discourses, such as that of friendship and camaraderie, and that of the hobbyist-inventor. Both of these are powerful sources of identity and cohesion in their own right. See Douglas, *Inventing American Broadcasting,* 203–6, and *Listening In,* 332–44, 345–46.

15 For example, Cary Fishman and Bob Buus, "A Portable Antenna Support," *QST* 76, no. 5 (May 1992): 78–79.

16 See, for example, "Chicagoland Ham Mobilers Serve as Communications First-Liners," *QST* 34, no. 1 (January 1950): 26.

17 One example: Jim Miccolis, "Why I Like Field Day," *QST* 68, no. 5 (June 1994): 55.

18 L. Peter Carron Jr., *Morse Code: The Essential Language,* 2d ed. (Newington, Conn.: American Radio Relay League, 1991, 1996), 1.1–1.7.

19 See, for example, Dan Henderson and Billy Lunt, "1998 ARRL Field Day Results," *QST* 82, no. 12 (December 1998): 98–100; or Richard K. Arland, "QRP Field Day Survival Guide," *QST* 82, no. 6 (June 1998): 28–29.

20 See, for example, James D. Cain, "The Avianca Crash: Disaster and Discord," *QST* 89, no. 5 (May 1990): 14–17; or Rich Palm, "Hugo the Horrible: Accounts of Amateurs' Heroism in Danger's Path," *QST* 79, no. 2 (February 1990): 14–18.

21 *QST* contains a regular column devoted to public service, much of which is concerned with emergency activities or preparation. For example, a randomly chosen half year of *QST* (the first six months of vol. 59 [1975]) shows specific mention of hams helping in emergencies in all six issues.

22 See, for example, Frederick O. Maia, "Washington Readout," *CQ* 55, no. 3 (March 1999): 80–82; or Oscar Morales Jr., "A Ham Radio Growth Formula—from Cuba," *CQ VHF* 4, no. 3 (March 1999): 21. Another expression of the fear of a decline in amateur radio is a growing focus on ways of attracting young people to the hobby. See Jim Idelson, "A Journey to Sweepstakes: How Do We Attract More Young People to Amateur Radio? Could Contesting Provide the Answer?" *QST* 85, no. 2 (February 2001): 60–62.

23 "FCC Releases Codeless License Report and Order," *QST* 75, no. 2 (February 1991): 57–63; and David Sumner, "A Codeless Amateur License," *QST* 75, no. 2 (February 1991): 9.

24 Janet M. Hooks, *Women's Occupations through Seven Decades* (Washington: Zenger, 1978), table 9, p. 156. For a survey of the literature on women in scientific careers, see Carroll Wetzel Wilkinson, *Women Working in Nontraditional Fields: References and Resources, 1963–1988* (Boston: G. K. Hall, 1991).

25 De Soto, *Two Hundred Meters and Down,* 1–2, 24–27. Many of the first radio hobbyists became involved through university or school clubs. Susan Douglas, in *Listening In,* approaches the issue of women in radio from the opposite end and posits that radio had specific attraction for men in the first half of the century, having to do with changes and uncertainty in how masculinity was perceived and defined (12–13, 65–68).

26 This was the YLRL ("YL" is the Morse abbreviation for female, or "young lady," "OM," "old man," is the abbreviation for a male, particularly a male radio amateur). It still exists. See http://www.qsl.net/ylrl/for the Web page of the YLRL (as of August 2002). See also the obituary for Ethel M. Smith, the founder of the YLRL, "Two Who Made a Difference," *QST* 82, no. 8 (August 1998): 9.

27 Statistics on the number of female amateur radio operators are rare, and incomplete. Douglas states that 85 percent of current hams are male, but that women now account for nearly 40 percent of new license applications, suggesting that the number of women in amateur radio is rising (*Listening In,* 332). She is certainly correct, yet these figures are only approximations, given that neither the FCC nor the ARRL has accurate figures on the current number of licensed amateur radio operators who are women. It is clear that the ARRL is making an effort to include women in the running of the organization. As of January 2001, its vice president, two vice directors, and six out of the fifty section managers are women (e-mail communication from Steve Mansfield, ARRL legislative and public affairs manager, to the author, 17 January 2001). Nevertheless there is still a relative absence of women in amateur publications.

28 For example, see Rick Lindquist, "Bad Tornadoes Bring Out the Best in Hams," *QST* 82, no. 6 (June 1998): 63–65.

29 Or for that matter, a lack of any physical disabilities, even the most minor.

30 In many emergencies, radio amateurs on the scene of a disaster use relatively low-powered portable equipment to send messages to nearby hams at fixed stations using more powerful equipment, who send messages to their destination. U.S.-based hams also sometimes act as reception points for hams in disaster areas overseas and then pass the information on to aid organizations. A substantial portion of the communications contribution of hams in disasters therefore involves the passing on or relay of information and can be done by any skilled operator from a home station. See, for example, Rich Palm, "Hugo the Horrible: Accounts of Amateurs' Heroism in Danger's Path," *QST* 79, no. 2 (February 1990): 14–18. Women do participate in this and all other areas of emergency communications, but in small numbers.

31 The literature on this topic is voluminous. As a guide, see Wilkinson, *Women Working in Nontraditional Fields.* See also Paula J. Dubeck and Kathryn Borman, *Woman and Work, a Handbook* (New York: Garland, 1996); and Alice Kessler-Harris, *Out to Work: A History of Wage-Earning Women in the United States* (New York: Oxford University Press, 1982).

32 As just one example, see Paul W. Gerard, "Hams Put to the Test in Huge Oakland Fire," *QST* 76, no. 2 (February 1992): 23–29.

33 From at least the 1980s, pictures and mention of female amateurs have increased in *QST.* Perhaps the best example is the large number of women pictured in the most recent editions of *Now You're Talking!,* a book designed to provide a basic introduction to amateur radio and help future hams study for the two most basic

classes of amateur license. Larry D. Wolfgang and Joel P. Kleinman, eds., *Now You're Talking!* 3d ed. (Newington, Conn.: American Radio Relay League, 1997–1998). The book is also sold under license in Radio Shack stores.

Works Cited

Arland, Richard K. "QRP Field Day Survival Guide." *QST* 82, no. 6 (June 1998): 28–29.

Battey, E. L. "Navy Day—1929." *QST* 14, no. 1 (January 1930): 18–20.

"Battle of the Airwaves." *The Economics,* 29 July 2000, 57–58.

Beck, Ulrich. *World Risk Society.* Cambridge: Blackwell, 1999.

Cain, James D. "The Avianca Crash: Disaster and Discord." *QST* 89, no. 5 (May 1990): 14–17.

Carron, L. Peter, Jr. *Morse Code: The Essential Language.* 2d ed. Newington, Conn.: American Radio Relay League, 1991, 1996.

Cawelti, John. "Pornography, Catastrophe, and Vengeance: Shifting Narrative Structures in a Changing American Culture." In *The American Self: Myth, Ideology, and Popular Culture,* ed. Sam B. Girgus. Albuquerque: University of New Mexico Press, 1981.

"Charting a Future for International Broadcasting." *Monitoring Times* 18, no. 12 (December 1999): 65, and 19, no. 1 (January 2000): 69.

"Chicagoland Ham Mobilers Serve as Communications First-Liners." *QST* 34, no. 1 (January 1950): 26.

De Soto, Clinton B. *Two Hundred Meters and Down: The Story of Amateur Radio.* West Hartford, Conn.: American Radio Relay League, 1936.

Douglas, Susan. *Inventing American Broadcasting, 1899–1922.* Baltimore: Johns Hopkins University Press, 1987.

——. *Listening In: Radio and the American Imagination from Amos 'n' Andy to Wolfman Jack and Howard Stern.* New York: Random House, 1999.

Dubeck, Paula J., and Kathryn Borman. *Woman and Work, a Handbook.* New York: Garland, 1996.

"FCC Releases Codeless License Report and Order." *QST* 75, no. 2 (February 1991): 57–63.

Federal Communications Commission Rules Part 97 (Amateur Radio Service), Subpart A (General Provisions), §97.15.

Federal Communications Commission FCC 85-506, Memorandum Opinion and Order of 16 September 1985.

Fishman, Cary, and Bob Buus. "A Portable Antenna Support." *QST* 76, no. 5 (May 1992): 78–79.

Gerard, Paul W. "Hams Put to the Test in Huge Oakland Fire." *QST* 76, no. 2 (February 1992): 23–29.

Girgus, Sam B., ed. *The American Self: Myth, Ideology, and Popular Culture*. Albuquerque: University of New Mexico Press, 1981.

Henderson, Dan, and Billy Lunt. "1998 ARRL Field Day Results." *QST* 82, no. 12 (December 1998): 98–100.

Hooks, Janet M. *Women's Occupations through Seven Decades*. Washington: Zenger, 1978.

Idelson, Jim. "A Journey to Sweepstakes: How Do We Attract More Young People to Amateur Radio? Could Contesting Provide the Answer?" *QST* 85, no. 2 (February 2001): 60–62.

Kessler-Harris, Alice. *Out to Work: A History of Wage-Earning Women in the United States*. New York: Oxford University Press, 1982.

Körner, W. F. *Geschichte des Amateurfunks, 1909–1963*. Hamburg: FT Verlag Rojahn and Kraft, 1963.

Lacey, Kate. *Feminine Frequencies: Gender, German Radio, and the Public Sphere, 1923–1945*. Ann Arbor: University of Michigan Press, 1996.

"League Responds to Telecommunications Inquiry." *QST* 79, no. 6 (June 1990): 6.

Lindquist, Rick. "Bad Tornadoes Bring Out the Best in Hams." *QST* 82, no. 6 (June 1998): 63–65.

——. "Minnesota." *QST* 82, no. 6 (June 1998): 63.

Lyotard, Jean-François. *La condition postmoderne: Rapport sur le savoir*. Paris: Editions de Minuit, 1979.

Maia, Frederick O. "Washington Readout." *CQ* 55, no. 3 (March 1999): 80–82.

Miccolis, Jim. "Why I Like Field Day." *QST* 65, no. 5 (June 1994): 55.

Morales, Oscar Jr. "A Ham Radio Growth Formula—from Cuba." *CQ VHF* 4, no. 3 (March 1999): 21.

Palm, Rich. "Hugo the Horrible: Accounts of Amateurs' Heroism in Danger's Path." *QST* 79, no. 2 (February 1990): 14–18.

Sonoma County Emergency Services. *Volunteer Handbook*. Sonoma, Calif.: Sonoma Op Area Auxiliary Communications Service, 1997–2000. Available on-line at http: //www.cds1.net/acs/vol.htm.

Sumner, David. "A Codeless Amateur License." *QST* 75, no. 2 (February 1991): 9.

"Two Who Made a Difference." *QST* 82, no. 8 (August 1998): 9.

van Horn, Larry. "Who Controls Government Frequencies?" *Monitoring Times* 17, no. 12 (December 1998): 72.

Wilkinson, Carroll Wetzel. *Women Working in Nontraditional Fields: References and Resources, 1963–1988*. Boston: G. K. Hall, 1991.

Wolfgang, Larry D., and Joel P. Kleinman, eds. *Now You're Talking!* 3d ed. Newington, Conn.: American Radio Relay League, 1997–1998.

A PROMISE DIMINISHED:

THE POLITICS OF LOW-POWER RADIO

Nina Huntemann

On January 21, 2000, the Federal Communications Commission (FCC) voted to authorize a new class of broadcasting licenses: low-power radio service (LPFM). Low-power radio is defined by the FCC as radio broadcasting below 100 watts. Before the January vote, operating a station with less than 100 watts of power was illegal. Often referred to as "pirates," microradio broadcasters operating low-power radio without a license were subject to fines, seizure of broadcast equipment, and arrest.

Under the new FCC rules, low-power stations still require a license to broadcast, but a significant characteristic of these new licenses is the noncommercial requirement. Any individual or organization wishing to operate a LPFM station is prohibited from airing advertisements, although support from underwriting and program sponsorship is permitted. The noncommercial nature of LPFM is in stark contrast to the vast majority of radio stations in the United States, which are funded entirely by advertising revenue. In addition to the noncommercial requirement, LPFM licenses are available only to individuals or organizations who do not already own radio stations or any other media outlet (including cable systems, television stations, and newspapers), and at least for the first two years of licensing, LPFM operators must live within ten miles of their station.

The FCC's campaign to create LPFM and the specific requirements of low-power operators reflect an increasing concern for the concentration of radio ownership since the 1996 Telecommunications Act lifted national ownership caps. Particular effects of the change in ownership rules are format homogenization and the loss of radio's local focus as large-group owners controlled hundreds of stations across the country. Speaking to the National Association of Broadcasters (NAB) in October 1998, FCC chairman William Kennard advocated for LPFM as a means to remedy the trends of concentration:

As I have traveled around the country, I talk to many, many people who want to use the airwaves to speak to their communities. . . . There is a tremendous need for us to find ways to use the broadcast spectrum more efficiently so that we can bring more voices to the airwaves. . . . I believe that we have an obligation to explore ways to open the doors of opportunity to use the airwaves, particularly as consolidation closes those doors for new entrants.[1]

Consolidation Trends

On February 8, 1996, President Clinton signed into law the Telecommunications Act. The 106-page legislation enacted the most significant changes in media regulation since the 1934 Communications Act, which first established the FCC and the bulk of the law governing broadcasting. Regarding radio broadcasting, the act eliminated the restriction on the number of stations one owner could control nationally and relaxed local ownership restrictions, allowing control of up to eight stations in the largest radio markets. The ownership changes opened a floodgate of station mergers that has notably altered the landscape of commercial radio. According to former FCC commissioner Susan Ness, the consequences of the act "have changed irrecoverably the face of radio."[2]

According to the FCC, as of March 2000, the number of commercial radio owners decreased 22 percent in the four years since the act passed.[3] Of those that remain, the five largest radio group owners control over one hundred stations each. One entity, Clear Channel Communications, merged with AMFM Inc., increasing its holdings to over 1,000 stations— nearly a tenth of all commercial radio stations in the country.

Locally, many cities and towns have lost a third to nearly half of their radio owners over the four-year course of consolidation. For example, the Wilkes Barre/Scranton, Pennsylvania, market lost twelve owners, dropping from twenty-three in March 1996 to eleven in March 2000 for forty stations. In Springfield, Missouri, six owners left the market, leaving nine to operate twenty stations.[4]

A decrease in market owners means that local advertising revenue is concentrated into fewer hands. In the largest markets, cities such as New York, San Francisco, and Atlanta, 35 percent of market revenue is held by the top radio owner,[5] 24 percent by the second-largest owner, and 27 percent shared by the third and fourth owners.[6] In some of the smallest markets, towns such as Cheyenne, Wyoming, Jonesboro, Arkansas, and

Bangor, Maine, top owners control 50 percent of market revenue. And in nearly 60 percent of the nation's radio markets, one owner controls more than 40 percent of the total radio advertising revenue for that market.[7]

Losing Localism

In terms of communications technologies, radio is the most local of the mass media. Geographically bound by the physical properties of electromagnetic waves, radio has traditionally been defined by its broadcast range. Once available to community groups and grassroots organizations, garage bands and budding musicians, radio's localism has all but disappeared. This trend is a direct result of lifted ownership caps, which paved the way for group owners to consolidate operations by cutting staff and networking content.

The economies of scale enjoyed by large-group owners are best described in Clear Channel's 1999 annual report, which explains that profits are soaring as a result of consolidated ownership: "Create it once, use it often. That is the credo of the cluster."[8] The cluster refers to a geographic area where there exists a high concentration of radio stations owned by Clear Channel. Within a geographic cluster, Clear Channel solicits advertisers to place ads for a regional network of stations, instead of station by station.

But as the annual reports states, the "cluster mentality applies to format as well as geography."[9] As such, Clear Channel, through the subsidiary company Premiere Radio Network, creates programming for all its stations within a format. "Create it once, use it often" is accomplished by program packaging, where entire DJ shows, news, advertising, and station promotions are scripted, edited, and distributed to all the stations in the cluster format. It is quite possible, then, to turn on a Clear Channel rock station in El Paso, call a friend who is listening to a Clear Channel rock station in Houston, and both hear the same songs and DJ cut-ins. The local DJ is fast becoming a historical artifact as one DJ may serve a hundred format-specific stations across the country. As a result of cluster programming and market-researched playlists, local musicians are finding it even more difficult to cultivate fans via radio.

Syndicated programming also contributes to the sameness and lost localism of stations. Shows such as *The Rush Limbaugh Show, The Dr. Laura Program, The Rick Dees Weekly Top 40,* and *Heart to Heart with Naomi Judd* increasingly fill airtime, taking slots away from local call-in hosts. The claim that talk radio has democratized broadcasting by giving citizens a forum to voice concerns omits the fact that hundreds of thousands of listeners are vying for a few precious minutes on a syndicated program. Statistically, callers have a far greater chance getting on a local or even regional call-in show than the nationally syndicated *Michael Reagan Show.*

"Cluster contests" are particularly popular among radio group owners, as they allow stations to offer larger prizes financially supported by a multimillion-dollar radio company, not a single station. What listeners are not necessarily aware of is the wide reach of cluster contests. In some cases, when listeners call the toll-free line for a chance to win, they are competing with a nation of listeners, from Arizona to Maine, not just the audience of one station.

Even though music is the staple of commercial radio in the United States, only a handful of seconds per hour on most stations are devoted to news updates. As news is increasingly written and produced for regional and statewide stations, small towns have little hope of hearing about local events and concerns. The task of covering several counties' worth of news in a few short news breaks means that group-owned radio news departments are unable to adequately devote staff and airtime to local issues.

Profit Pressures

Due to the advantages of economies of scale, cluster programming, and staff consolidation, commercial radio has seen increasing profits during the years following ownership deregulation. Clear Channel reported its highest earnings ever in 2000, with net revenues of $5.3 billion, more than double the previous year.[10] Overall, radio properties have increased in value at an unprecedented rate, doubling pre–Telecommunications Act revenues. For example, adult-contemporary station KBLX, in the San Francisco market, posted revenues of $16.8 million for 1999, up from $7 million in 1993. In Philadelphia, soft rock station WBEB had an annual revenue of $7 million in 1993, which jumped to $24 million in 1999. Dallas–Fort Worth urban station KKDA tripled its value to $18 million in 1999, with its largest increase occurring between 1996 ($9.6 million) and 1997 ($13.3 million), a year after the act was passed.[11]

This profit has been essential to the financial survival of broadcasters in the face of massive mergers and acquisition debts incurred by many large-

radio-group owners. In response to debt-laden stations, radio group owners have aggressively sought to increase revenue streams. The tactics have
included increasing the cost of, and airtime devoted to, advertising. On
average, radio advertisements fill eighteen and as much as twenty minutes
per hour, up from six to eight minutes in the 1980s.[12]

Another controversial revenue-generating strategy is the reemergence of
a form of "payola" called pay-for-play. Payola, in its 1950s form, was the
practice of record labels paying DJs to air their artists. Rock radio's most
famous DJ, Alan Freed, was convicted in 1962 for accepting bribes in exchange for playing records. Shortly after Freed's conviction, the federal
government outlawed payola.

In its contemporary and legal form, pay-for-play, independent record
promoters act as brokers between record labels and radio stations. A promoter's job is to get the artists of the record label he or she represents
played on the air. For each airplay, the promoter is paid by the label and in
turn pays the station an average of $1,000 per play. A station in a medium-
sized market may gross $75,000 to $100,000 per year in pay-for-play deals.[13]
With consolidation, promoters can make deals with radio group owners to
place songs on format-specific playlists across the country. For example,
Chicago-based radio group Cumulus Media, which owns 210 stations, has a
$1 million dollar exclusive contract with Jeff McClusky Promotions.[14] Al-
though the result is the same as payola—paid placement—pay-for-play is
legal because money is exchanged between independent promoters and
radio station owners, not directly between record labels and disc jockeys.
Resting on this technicality, the FCC and other regulatory bodies are reluctant to investigate potential conflict-of-interest and anticompetitive-
practices concerns of musicians and small radio stations.

Critics argue that pay-for-play encourages stations to play only music
that will return direct cash benefits to the station, discouraging program
producers from adding artists not represented by a promoter. The effect is
that very little new music from unsigned or small, independent labels is
played on radio. Leo Ballinger, an advocate of low-power radio, argues that
the relationship between record labels and radio stations creates a funda-
mentally undemocratic medium, which "refuses to play much of the music
that is on the charts, let alone the wealth of sounds from the underground. . . . Commercial radio is corrupt, gladly taking money from record companies through third parties. Micropower [LPFM] radio must be
the voice of our music and our culture."[15]

(Low) Power to the People

These trends of a consolidated radio industry prompted the FCC to pro-
pose licensing rules for low-power radio stations in an effort to "foster
opportunities for new radio broadcast ownership and promote additional
diversity in radio voices and program services."[16] FCC chairman Kennard
began suggesting the idea of licensed low-power radio stations in 1998 as
the effects of broadcast deregulation crystallized. Bolstered by the enthusi-
astic response Kennard experienced when speaking about low-power radio
to community organizations, he placed the LPFM initiative on the FCC
agenda.[17]

On January 28, 1999, the FCC announced, as part of the rule-making
procedure, a period for public review during which all interested parties—
both opponents and proponents—could submit comments regarding the
commission's LPFM proposal. Interested in conducting extensive signal-
integrity studies, the NAB persuaded the FCC to extend the three-month
public comment period by six weeks. More than 3,500 comments were
collected, setting the highest record for public participation in an FCC rule-
making procedure.[18]

During the time of public comment, a political movement of microradio
broadcasters, free-speech advocates, radio enthusiasts, and commercial-free
media activists united resources to support the LPFM proposal. The groups
generated signal-integrity studies to counter the NAB's claim that new low-
power stations would cause frequency interference and solicited high-
profile backing from musicians (Amy Ray and Emily Sailers of the Indigo
Girls), lawyers (the American Civil Liberties Union), and consumer groups
(Consumers Union).

Although the FCC proposal was a flash point around which these various groups organized, the "free radio" movement had been challenging the
structure of broadcasting and the FCC's enforcement efforts against unlicensed microradio stations for years.[19] In the history of radio, thousands
of unlicensed stations have broadcast in the United States.[20] Microradio
broadcaster Stephen Dunifer, founder and operator of Free Radio Berkeley,
an unlicensed station in California, broadcast political commentary and
alternative music until the FCC shut him down and levied a $20,000 fine in
1998.

Dunifer's defense to a federal government injunction was to claim that
the FCC's refusal to grant him a broadcast license violated his First Amend-

ment rights. The corporate structure of radio and the procedures for licensing made it impossible for him to obtain a legal license to broadcast and thus restricted his right to free speech.[21] Furthermore, the FCC's mandate requires the commission to regulate in the "public convenience, interest, and necessity," issuing licenses to those who serve the community with their broadcasts. Dunifer claimed that the FCC was not fulfilling this mandate by issuing licenses to commercial radio stations that serve not the public interest but the interest of advertisers.[22]

Dunifer lost his case but gained national support that invigorated a movement to challenge the commercial and concentrated structure of radio. Dunifer continued to promote acts of civil disobedience by building inexpensive transmitters and teaching others how to establish microradio stations. The FCC enforcement arm continued to shut down microbroadcasters, even while Kennard was promoting the LPFM initiative.

The free-radio movement and LPFM proposal were met with fierce opposition from established commercial radio broadcasters. The NAB launched a public relations campaign and lobbied hard against Kennard's plan. In a 1998 press release, the NAB called microradio a "bad idea," claiming that the proposed FCC stations "would create small islands of usable coverage in an ocean of interference."[23] The NAB secured the support of U.S. representative Billy Tauzin (R-Louisiana), chair of the House Commerce Committee's communications subcommittee, which oversees communications policy. Part of Tauzin's strategy to derail LPFM was to question the FCC's ruling power and suggest that the Commission required policing: "[The FCC] is an agency out of control that demands congressional action to straighten it out."[24]

Recognizing that the fight for low-power radio was akin to a David-versus-Goliath struggle—small community and church groups against giant media corporations—the NAB convinced National Public Radio, a noncommercial public radio network, to take a stand on LPFM. Relying on NAB's signal-integrity studies, NPR also opposed LPFM on the grounds of frequency interference. Kevin Klose, president and CEO of NPR, stated that "the American public would not be well served by an FCC ruling that creates LPFM at the expense of the existing public radio services."[25]

Despite opposition, the FCC moved ahead with LPFM, revising the original proposal to create three new classes of stations (1,000, 100, and 10 watt) to opening licensing procedures for 100-watt and 10-watt stations only. Each station would have a maximum broadcast radius of one to three and one-half miles (seven miles in diameter, or less than forty square miles). The first window for filing applications opened in May 2000 for Alaska, California, the District of Columbia, Georgia, Indiana, Louisiana, Maine, Maryland, Oklahoma, Rhode Island, and Utah.

Having lost on the rule-making front, LPFM opponents, with the legislative support of Tauzin, lobbied for congressional action to stop the low-power stations from broadcasting. Drafted by Republican representative from Ohio Michael G. Oxley, the bill, known as the Radio Broadcasting Preservation Act of 2000, sought to curtail the FCC's LPFM initiative. The act required the FCC to hire an independent third party to conduct additional signal-integrity tests, prohibited the FCC from revising interference protection standards to expand eligibility for low-power radio without congressional approval, and reinstated the "third adjacent interference protection" rule.[26] In effect, the stations the FCC opened for licensing would be cut by 75 percent.[27]

Kennard's response to the act directly attacked the fear-mongering claims of interference and the political strong-arming of the NAB: "This attempt to kill low-power FM is not about ideology—it's about money. . . . The only group siding against the establishment of low-power FM is big radio, who in a textbook case of protectionism are trying to use the government to smother any potential competition."[28] The measure was attached to a House appropriations bill that President Clinton signed into law on December 21, 2000.

The Sky Is Falling

The arguments posed by the NAB and NPR against the FCC's LPFM initiative rested largely on the issue of signal interference. Both organizations asserted that the low-power signals originally proposed by the FCC could reduce the signal integrity of existing stations. By decreasing the adjacent interference protection requirement, broadcasters claimed that listeners would hear a degradation in signal quality, perhaps picking up nearby low-power stations on top of full-power stations.

Supporters of low-power radio questioned the motives behind the NAB and NPR opposition. Several technical studies showed little or no interference problems with current broadcasting technology. Furthermore, improved technologies were more efficient at maintaining signal quality, so the likelihood of inference from low-power radio stations using updated equipment was slim. Referring to the broadcasters' opposition as "sky is falling arguments," Kennard defended the technical engineering studies conducted by the FCC in a *Washington Post* column: "Our job is to act as guardian of the airwaves, not to degrade them. We have thoroughly tested this new service and are confident that there will not be any harmful interference."[29]

Revealing an apparent contradiction in the NAB's past relationship with the FCC regarding frequency allocation, Kennard wrote that established broadcasters had petitioned the FCC to allow "hundreds of full power stations to sit as close to each other on the dial as any new low-power FM station."[30] So why fear interference from significantly weaker signals? The free-radio movement argued that competition was the true meaning behind the NAB and NPR fight.

The principle behind LPFM is to create locally focused stations that serve the interest of communities within a noncommercial structure. Given the trends of consolidation—the loss of localism and rise in commercial messages—low-power radio may provide exactly what full-power stations have increasingly lost. There is some indication that changes in radio since deregulation, as well as the growth of Internet and satellite radio, have hurt the industry. Between 1989 and 1998, commercial radio experienced a 12 percent decline in listeners.[31] Even NPR-affiliated stations are turning away from local programming as the network has required stations to carry more NPR programming.[32]

In terms of audience, however, low-power radio is likely to capture only a very small portion of full-power radio station listeners. The broadcast range maximum is seven miles in diameter, not conducive to tuning in while driving, the time when most people listen to radio. Because low-power stations cannot carry commercials, full-power stations will have no new competition for advertising revenue with the added stations. In addition, the majority of low-power programming will offer highly specific content—church group sermons, community event calendars, local-issue talk shows, town government meetings, and eclectic musical programs. Due to the funding restraints of LPFM stations, most productions will be low quality, staffed by amateurs and volunteers. As a new entrant into the media landscape, a low-power radio station may be the equivalent threat to established stations as a local cable access channel is to HBO.

Although the potential for losing audiences is real, the lobbying effort and public relations campaign launched by LPFM opponents seemed lu-

dicrously disproportionate to the immediate effect that low-power stations would have on large-radio-group owners. However, as the free-radio
movement has proclaimed for years, what is at the heart of the low-power
radio struggle is a far greater challenge to established broadcasters than
competition. In announcing the LPFM initiative as a measure for giving
local communities a "voice," the FCC suggested what many media activists
have known: the current structure of the media does not adequately serve
the public interest. Furthermore, the near-monopoly ownership of media
outlets severely restricts basic principles of freedom of speech. To operate a
full-power radio station, a potential broadcaster must have access to hundreds of thousands of dollars for equipment and staff and program development. This financial barrier keeps corporate entities as the only feasible
owners of radio. As veteran microradio broadcaster Pete Tridish describes,
"American citizens have 17th century free speech rights. The right to hand
out a flyer on the street. Whereas corporations have 21st century rights. . . .
By dominating our communications system, they dominate our political
discourse."[33] The opportunities for a diversity of opinions have declined as
massive media corporations have conglomerated their operations into a
handful of entities. According to media critic Ben Bagdikian, ten corporations control the majority of the world's media.[34]

Radio and television broadcasters are particularly vulnerable to the
suggestion that their stations do not serve the public interest because, as
mandated by communications policy set forth decades ago, and reinforced
in the 1996 Telecommunications Act, the airwaves are a *public* resource.
Broadcasters merely "lease" space from the public, as allocated by the FCC.
If radio stations do not adequately meet public interest requirements, then
the long-standing assumption enjoyed by broadcasters that commercial
broadcasting is the best model for fulfilling public service obligations is
undermined. If successful, new models of broadcasting, like LPFM, may
upset a business logic that has enabled broadcasters to exploit deregulation
for economic gain.

Finally, low-power radio upsets the traditional relationship between
broadcaster and consumer. Because the new class of stations requires
owners to live in the community where they broadcast, and the voices on
the station are likely to be members of the community, the consumers
(audience) and producers of low-power radio are one and the same. Their
relationship with media access is democratized, involving far more participation than call-in shows and promotional contests. Your neighbor is

the weekly political columnist, your high school principal discusses the pros and cons of statewide testing, and your child is the after-school DJ.

What's Next

Even with the greatly reduced number of stations available owing to restrictions in the Radio Preservation Act, the FCC proceeded with the LPFM initiative. The first wave of applications brought in more than seven hundred interested parties, and the application windows for other states opened as scheduled.[35] The first licenses were granted on April 17, 2001.

In February 2001, the free-radio movement found an ally in the Senate, Senator John McCain (R-Arizona), whose political rhetoric reflected more populist positions during the 2000 presidential election, introduced a low-power radio bill to reverse the Radio Preservation Act slipped through Congress the year before. Perhaps recognizing the wide grassroots support for low-power radio, particularly from many conservative communities hoping to establish religious-oriented stations, McCain denounced the NAB and NPR effort to crush LPFM: "Last Congress, special interest forces opposed to low-power FM radio . . . mounted a successful behind-the-scenes campaign to kill low-power FM radio without a single debate on the Senate floor. This bill would reverse that language. . . . It's important that this bill be passed in the interest of would-be new broadcasters, existing broadcasters, but most of all, the listening public."[36] Specifically, the bill allows the FCC to license low-power stations without having to conduct additional technical studies, and it only restricts licenses to stations that actually interfere with existing stations. This allows the FCC to apply the second adjacent interference requirement, except in cases where interference is documented.

The fate of McCain's bill was unclear, as many changes occurred in Congress and the FCC during the first half of 2001. In late May, the Republican-controlled Senate shifted to the Democrats when Vermont senator Jim Jeffords switched his political affiliation from Republican to Independent. Overall, Democrats had been more supportive of the LPFM initiative and, with control of key senatorial committees now with the Democrats, were likely to give McCain's bill time on the Senate floor.

At the FCC, commissioner Michael Powell, Republican and son of Secretary of State Colin Powell, was appointed FCC chairman by President George W. Bush when Kennard stepped down. Although Powell voted for the LPFM proposal under Kennard, he had since questioned the FCC engineers' ability to conduct sound technical studies. When asked about his position on LPFM soon after his appointment, Powell replied, "I am still trying to figure it out."[37]

No matter the outcome of McCain's bill, a handful of low-power stations turned on their transmitters by the end of 2001. The free radio movement continues to defy FCC regulations by broadcasting unlicensed microradio. It is perhaps ironic that at the dawn of the twenty-first century and in the age of the Internet and digital media, the real information revolution may be launched by the oldest electronic mass medium—radio.

Notes

1 William E. Kennard, Federal Communications Commission chairman (speech given to the National Association of Broadcasters Radio Convention, Seattle, Wash., 16 October 1998).

2 Eric Boehlert, "One Big Happy Channel?" *Salon*, 28 June 2001. Available on-line at http://www.salon.com/tech/feature/2001/06/28/telecom_dereg/index.html.

3 Federal Communications Commission, Mass Media Bureau, Policy and Rules Division, *Review of the Radio Industry, 2000* (Washington, D.C., 2001), 3.

4 Ibid., appendix F.

5 Market revenue is calculated based on the total advertising dollars spent on radio in a given market. The percentage of market revenue refers to the portion of radio advertising dollars a station receives.

6 FCC, *Review of the Radio Industry, 2000*, 6.

7 Ibid.

8 Clear Channel Communications, Inc., *1999 Annual Report* (San Antonio, Tex., 1999).

9 Ibid.

10 Clear Channel Communications, Inc., *Clear Channel Reports Record Year-End and Fourth Quarter 2000 Results* (San Antonio, Tex., 2001).

11 Station revenue information obtained from the BIA Media Access Pro database, version 2.6, distributed by BIA Research Inc., Chantilly, Va.

12 James Duncan Jr. (speech given at the Paine Webber Media Conference, New York, December 1999).

13 Eric Boehlert, "Pay for Play." *Salon*, 14 March 2001. Available on-line at http://www.salon.com/ent/feature/2001/03/14/payola/index.html.

14 Chuck Philips, "Logs Link Payments with Radio Airplay," *Los Angeles Times*, 29 May 2001.

15 Leo Ballinger, "Broadcasting Confidential," in *Seizing the Airwaves: A Free Radio Handbook*, ed. R. Sakolsky and S. Dunifer (San Francisco: AK Press, 1998), 25–28.

16   Federal Communications Commission, Mass Media Bureau, *FCC Proposes Licensed Low Power FM Radio,* Rept. MM 99-1, Doc. MM-Docket 95-25, January 1999.

17   Kennard speech, 16 October 1998.

18   Pete Tridish, "The Prometheus Radio Project" (speech given at the University of Massachusetts–Amherst, 6 April 2001).

19   Neva Chonin, "A Pirate's Life," *San Francisco Chronicle,* 5 March 2000, 41.

20   Michael J. Aguilar, "Micro Radio: A Small Step in the Return to Localism, Diversity, and Competitiveness in Broadcasting," *Brooklyn Law Review,* winter 1999.

21   Stephen Dunifer, "Dunifer Responds to NAB & FCC," electronic mail, 5 October 1997. Available on-line at http://www.radio4all.org/news/dunifer-response.html.

22   Ibid.

23   National Association of Broadcasters, *NAB to FCC: Microradio Is a Bad Idea* (Washington, D.C., 1998).

24   "Top Legislator Blasts U.S. FCC Microradio Proposal" (Reuters News Service, 11 February 1999).

25   Alexander Cockburn and Jeffrey St. Clair, "Low Power Radio: Mayday! Mayday!" *Counterpunch,* 20 April 2000. Available on-line at http://www.counterpunch.org/microradio.html.

26   The adjacent interference protection rule buffer refers to the distribution of frequencies in a given geographic area. According to the current third adjacent interference protection requirements, if a station operates at 101.4, the next frequency available in that area is 101.7 or 100.1. The FCC's LPFM plan proposed decreasing that buffer to two.

27   Media Access Project, *Summary of the Anti-LPFM Legislation.* Available on-line at http://www.mediaaccess.org/programs/lpfm/rpa2000.html.

28   William E. Kennard, "The Voice of the People," *Washington Post,* 23 October 2000, A23.

29   Ibid.

30   Ibid.

31   Duncan speech.

32   "Hometown Radio," *Christian Science Monitor,* 17 April 2001, 10.

33   Tridish, "The Prometheus Radio Project."

34   Ben Bagdikian, *The Media Monopoly,* 5th ed. (Boston: Beacon Press, 1997).

35   Rachel Anderson, "Who's Got the Power: Challenges to Low-Power Radio," *Digital Beat Extra,* 18 July 2000. Available on-line at http://www.benton.org/News/Extra/pm071800.html.

36   John McCain, U.S. senator, *McCain Introduces Low Power Radio Bill* (Washington, D.C., 2001). Available on-line at http://www.senate.gov/~mccain/lpfm01.htm.

37   Christopher Stern, "New FCC Chairman Favors a Non-activist Approach," *Washington Post,* 7 February 2001, E1.

Works Cited

Aguilar, Michael J. "Micro Radio: A Small Step in the Return to Localism, Diversity, and Competitiveness in Broadcasting." *Brooklyn Law Review,* winter 1999.

Anderson, Rachel. "Who's Got the Power: Challenges to Low-Power Radio." *Digital Beat Extra,* 18 July 2000. Available on-line at http://www.benton.org/News/Extra/pm071800.html.

Bagdikian, Ben. *The Media Monopoly.* 5th ed. Boston: Beacon Press, 1997.

Ballinger, Leo. "Broadcasting Confidential." In *Seizing the Airwaves: A Free Radio Handbook,* ed. R. Sakolsky and S. Dunifer. San Francisco: AK Press, 1998.

BIA Media Access Pro. Chantilly, Va.: BIA Research Inc., version 2.6.

Boehlert, Eric. "One Big Happy Channel?" *Salon,* 28 June 2001. Available on-line at http://www.salon.com/tech/feature/2001/06/28/telecom_dereg/index.html.

——. "Pay for Play." *Salon,* 14 March 2001. Available on-line at http://www.salon.com/ent/feature/2001/03/14/payola/index.html.

Chonin, Neva. "A Pirate's Life." *San Francisco Chronicle,* 5 March 2000, 41.

Clear Channel Communications, Inc. *1999 Annual Report* (San Antonio, Tex., 1999).

——. *Clear Channel Reports Record Year-End and Fourth Quarter 2000 Results* (San Antonio, Tex., 2001).

Cockburn, Alexander, and Jeffrey St. Clair. "Low Power Radio: Mayday! Mayday!" *Counterpunch,* 20 April 2000. Available on-line at http://www.counterpunch.org/microradio.html.

Duncan, James, Jr. Speech given at the Paine Webber Media Conference, New York, N.Y., December 1999.

Dunifer, Stephen. "Dunifer Responds to NAB & FCC." Electronic mail, 5 October 1997. Available on-line at http://www.radio4all.org/news/dunifer-response.html.

Federal Communications Commission, Mass Media Bureau. *FCC Proposes Licensed Low Power FM Radio.* Washington, D.C., January 1999. Rept. MM 99-1, Doc. MM-Docket 95-25.

Federal Communications Commission, Mass Media Bureau, Policy and Rules Division. *Review of the Radio Industry, 2000.* Washington, D.C., 2001.

"Hometown Radio." *Christian Science Monitor,* 17 April 2001, 10.

Kennard, William E. Speech given at the National Association of Broadcasters Radio Convention, Seattle, Wash., 16 October 1998.

——. "The Voice of the People." *Washington Post,* 23 October 2000, A23.

McCain, John. *McCain Introduces Low Power Radio Bill.* Washington, D.C., 2001. Available on-line at http://www.senate.gov/~mccain/lpfm01.htm.

Media Access Project. *Summary of the Anti-LPFM Legislation.* Available on-line at http://www.mediaaccess.org/programs/lpfm/rpa2000.html.

National Association of Broadcasters. *NAB to FCC: Microradio Is a Bad Idea.* Washington, D.C., 1998.

Philips, Chuck. "Logs Link Payments with Radio Airplay." *Los Angeles Times*, 29 May 2001.

Stern, Christopher. "New FCC Chairman Favors a Non-activist Approach." *Washington Post*, 7 February 2001, E1.

"Top Legislator Blasts U.S. FCC Microradio Proposal." Reuters News Service, 11 February 1999.

Tridish, Pete. "The Prometheus Radio Project." Speech given at the University of Massachusetts–Amherst, 6 April 2001.

RADIO CULTURES

CARIBBEAN VOICES ON THE AIR:

RADIO, POETRY, AND NATIONALISM

IN THE ANGLOPHONE CARIBBEAN

Laurence A. Breiner

In June 1950, Eric Roach, a poet from the small Caribbean island of Tobago, published a poem entitled "Beyond" in which he addresses a poet envisioned as soaring like a bird over the landscape:

Pass over mountains;
Your cadenzas cascading, echoing, re-echoing,
Shall strain dark cataracted eyes
From cabbage beds, from damp potato ground;
They blinking in sun shall remember their youth

. . .

O, from your eyrie wash them with song
Like sunlight flooding, pouring through doors,
Through last slow closing shutters of the soul.
Wake them to pain, to laughter and to loveliness again.[1]

The rhetoric is high, and at first glance this is a predictably colonized text, originating from a point somewhere between Shelley and Swinburne. But it is curious that in Roach's work, this image of the bird/bard seems to come out of nowhere, suddenly prominent in the poems published in 1950 (after "Beyond" in June, "Transition" and "Frigate Bird Passing" in December). What inspires it? The opening of "Letter to Lamming in England" (1952) offers another instance of this imagery. Roach is here writing to— and about—a specific poet, the Barbadian George Lamming, who had recently emigrated, "jumped for England,"

. . . where, beyond my gaze,
I hear only your seasonal voice,

A lonely seagull's, crying on Atlantic.
My brother's is an echo's voice.[2]

In context, these lines indicate that the poem is inspired by the experience of listening to Lamming's voice broadcast across the Atlantic via BBC radio's *Caribbean Voices* program.[3] That program and its cultural impact will be the subject of this essay, but I want to begin by considering its impact on the individual poet who most fully recognized the potential of the medium. Roach's poem to Lamming does not emphasize the premise of the broadcast voice, but it is unmistakable, and it reveals for the first time the true source for this image of the disembodied voice of the soaring bird whose song inspires the people on the ground. Chronology supports this interpretation. "Beyond" and those other poems of 1950 must have been written almost immediately after Roach heard his own poetry broadcast on the BBC for the first time (in August 1949). From the start, then, Roach's rather Shelleyan metaphor of the soarer describes not a romantic fancy but an electronic reality, a technology that can transcend placedness without abandoning it. This technology makes it possible for a poet to be both everywhere and somewhere, to speak from the smallest island to the world at large, with the uncannily domestic intimacy characteristic of radio—a voice right here among us, and yet not.

The most important context for Roach's insight is the West Indian Federation, whose political manifestation was destined to fail shortly after its institution in 1958. During the 1940s and particularly after the war, the dispersed territories of the Anglophone Caribbean came to regard themselves as both a political and a cultural entity. The coincidence of cultural and political federation had long been an ideal of West Indies visionaries such as C. L. R. James (and before him W. Adolphe Roberts), who took note of the topographical analogy between the American archipelago of the Caribbean and the Mediterranean archipelago of the Greek islands and on that basis projected a cultural analogy. They saw great creative potential, akin to that of ancient Greece, in the region's dialectic of proximity and isolation. Many were dubious about the viability of political and especially of economic federation, but belief in the value of cultivating cultural affinities between the islands was much more widespread. As early as 1934, an editorial in the *West Indian Review,* in the course of arguing that there could be "no kind of uniformity of *political* outlook" in the Caribbean, nonetheless stated categorically that "there is a Federation of the mind, and of the spirit" in the region.[4]

Roach was an avid federationist, and there is a political dimension to the image of the poet that radio makes possible (and Shelley, too, managed to promote these same seemingly refractory conceptions of the poet, as transcendental soarer and as "unacknowledged legislator"). Soaring out of the village via the airwaves makes it possible for the poet to be heard in all the villages and to that extent gives him a politically meaningful power to gather all the islands while remaining on his own. Broadcast poetry is at once vividly embodied and literally disembodied—coming out of a box, coming out of the air. Between World War II and the imposition of immigration restrictions in 1962, migration to Britain presented a tempting alternative for writers struggling against the confinement of island society, and meditation on that paradox of embodiment seems to have influenced the decisions of several poets. Roach, for one, never migrated. There is good evidence that the experience of hearing his work read on the BBC was a factor in that decision. His perception of the potential of this technology went a long way toward resolving his doubts about any poet's raison d'être in a small colonial society, by suggesting that it was possible to stay at home while being effectually present elsewhere—throughout the region and even in the metropolitan center. Several of his poems present evidence that Roach's advocacy of federation was bound up with his faith in radio, a faith that through this technology he could genuinely speak from his own island to a much wider audience. Roach was not simply searching for his audience; he was trying to realize an identity for himself as a poet not for Tobago alone but for the West Indies, that mysterious transnational entity. The possibility of becoming a voice on the airwaves must have appeared to offer a powerful reconciliation, a way for the poet, at least, to be both squarely *here* and at the same time everywhere.

"Invented only in 1895, radio made it possible to . . . summon into being an aural representation of the imagined community where the printed page scarcely penetrated. Its role . . . generally in mid-twentieth-century nationalisms, has been much underestimated and understudied." So writes Benedict Anderson in *Imagined Communities,* where he touches on the importance of radio for the cultivation of nationalism in many colonial settings.[5] The convergence of radio and nationalism evokes some stereotypical images: on the one hand the romance of pirated frequencies and insurgents seizing the transmitter, on the other hand the new central government's control of broadcasting to promote both nationalist ideology and standardized language. Those are the grossly generalized "postcolonial" models. In specific cases, however, like that of Roach, the relation between radio and nationalism can be much more subtle. This essay considers such a case: the complex role played during the nationalist period by the *Caribbean Voices* program of the BBC Colonial Service, which was broadcast from England to the British West Indies between World War II and 1958, the year the colonies were consolidated as the independent (but short-lived) Federation of the West Indies.

The BBC *Caribbean Voices* program evolved at the end of World War II out of *Calling the West Indies,* a program produced primarily for West Indian servicemen during the war by the Jamaican poet and journalist Una Marson. Marson transformed the program into a literary magazine, and when she returned to Jamaica after the war, production of the program was taken over by Henry Swanzy. Thereafter known as *Caribbean Voices,* the program was discontinued in 1958 in conjunction with the transfer of political power from London to the West Indian Federation. Under the direction of Henry Swanzy, followed by V. S. Naipaul (after Swanzy's departure to Ghana in 1954), and finally Edgar Mittelholzer, who was at the time (1956) the most successful West Indian novelist, the program broadcast to the Caribbean readings of fiction, poetry, and even drama by West Indians.

A British program managed by West Indians resident in England and produced with the support of West Indians at home, *Caribbean Voices* did indeed create a number of communities, both in the Caribbean and in England. In England, the program drew on the resources of the growing community of migrants from the Caribbean. More and more West Indian writers (or aspiring writers) were resident in London after 1950, and this enriched the program, providing texts and a variety of island voices to read them over the air. Many who would go on to become important West Indian writers were taken on at the BBC as "freelances," and the famous "freelances' room" opposite Broadcasting House in Portland Place functioned as a cross between a literary club and a writers' workshop.[6] Hailing from Jamaica, Barbados, Trinidad, and Guyana, these writers—like other Caribbean migrants—were undergoing a progressive "West Indianification." Thrown together in London and indiscriminately regarded as "Jamaicans" by the British public, the migrants were increasingly inclined to identify themselves not with a specific island but with the "West Indies," even before that term had any actual political referent. Indeed, the development of a new regional consciousness among West Indians in London was crucial to the future of the Anglophone Caribbean.

John Figueroa reminds us that the program had more than one audience even in London: "The production of this programme offered to West Indians in London an opportunity to meet English and African writers and to discuss West Indian literature in particular and writing and art in general. Henry Swanzy, for instance, and myself held regular open-house meetings in connection with the programme."[7] Thus the program contributed to nascent "Commonwealth consciousness" as well.

The community in London was real. At home in the West Indies, *Caribbean Voices* created what must be called an *imaginary* community. It brought together literary texts from throughout the region and made them available to West Indian writers, but for the most part the writers themselves remained scattered across the islands of the Caribbean Basin, where there was no social (or even geographic) space in which they could actually be together. Thus when Lamming writes that the program "enabled writers in one island to keep in touch with the latest *work* of writers in another island," he is acknowledging that they could keep in touch with one another's work, but not with one another.[8]

Geoffrey Holder envisioned a profound but equally fanciful community in his review of the *Caribbean Voices* broadcast of Walcott's *Henri Christophe*—one of the program's most ambitious projects. The review praises the play, but Holder is most excited about the kind of audience that the occasion seemed to suggest might be within reach for West Indian writers:

I was listening at a wayside loudspeaker when the rain began to drizzle and three or four people took shelter. Two men, barefooted, were talking when Christophe momentarily flared up; then his voice grew quieter. . . . The two men stopped talking and even when the rain had ceased, they remained listening to the end of the play. At that late stage they could not have followed the events; they were held by the poetry, striking in its vividness and beauty and spoken with sympathy and sincerity. I thought of the Elizabethans.[9]

The BBC did not in fact induce a taste for blank verse among the peasantry. It did, however, cultivate small but serious localized audiences in the Caribbean, for whom the weekly broadcasts were a convivial and inspiring social ritual. Lamming has written about the significance of the program in Trinidad, where he lived before his emigration to England. At the time, writers had no local outlet for serious writing: "In an island where local radio is an incestuous concubinage between commerce and the official administration, these writers would look forward to that Sunday evening at half-past seven."[10] Lamming goes on to give a vivid and nostalgic account of the ritual that grew up around the broadcasts in Port of Spain, describing how he, with fellow poets Cecil Herbert and Clifford Sealey, would listen to the broadcast on a borrowed radio and then go down to what is now Independence Square for rum and "a carnival of disputatious argument." His perspective on such occasions is revealing: "The West Indian writer had no reputation to lose, and he had no audience sufficiently interested to recognise that he was acquiring one. Literature was, like cricket, his native sport."[11]

The successful interaction and cross-fertilization among these dispersed communities that the *Caribbean Voices* program facilitated was instrumental in consolidating support among West Indian intellectuals for a political federation of the noncontiguous colonies—the most ambitious of the program's imagined communities. Federation may have been the official British vision for the region's future, but it began as the vision of leading West Indian intellectuals, thoughtfully formulated in response to the problematic nature of Caribbean space.

If *Caribbean Voices* was important for the maturing cultural politics of the West Indies, it also played a crucial role in the emergence of Anglophone Caribbean literature, especially poetry. The emphasis on poetry is predictable enough: after drama, lyric poetry is undoubtedly the literary genre most congenial to radio, and drama was broadcast only rarely, because of time constraints and the expense of production. And *Caribbean Voices* certainly encouraged the development of poetry. Something on the order of three hundred poems were broadcast during the life of the program. Was the role of the BBC also formative; that is, did it encourage development *along particular lines?* The answer seems to be no. The extent to which the content of these British broadcasts reflected Caribbean tastes and expectations can be deduced from the editorial process and from the playlist of the program.[12]

It is particularly significant that during the era of *Caribbean Voices,* West Indians at home heard their work read aloud by West Indians in London (including the likes of Lamming, Kamau Brathwaite, and V. S. Naipaul). This necessarily drew attention to differences between West Indian dialects and thereby trained the ears of the audience while it presented writers with productive questions about their expressive options. It also established an association between poetry and live voices that has had enormous consequences for West Indian writers in the decades since 1970, a period dominated by an emphasis on performance poetry and the privileging of elements regarded as "oral."

The very existence of the program thus implied not only the respectability of writing by West Indians but the respectability of their spoken language, as well. It was a great piece of luck for the development of West Indian poetry that the cachet of metropolitan approval came first of all not in the form of publication by a British anthology or magazine (venues that, consciously or not, would have tended to encourage more exotic subject matter and less exotic language) but in the form of a radio program that made poets think about how their work would *sound* to a diverse West Indian audience listening *at home*. *Caribbean Voices* was much more hospitable in those formative days than any metropolitan publisher to the accurate representation of West Indian speech, and an entire generation's experience of listening to the program must be regarded as an important impetus behind the regional interest in orality and performance poetry after Independence.[13]

The individual writers had the visceral gratification of hearing their own work in public. That the work was usually heard in someone else's voice offers an apt emblem of the ineluctability of colonialism, particularly given the irony that imitative writers of the previous generation had been condemned for *writing* in a voice that was not their own. But we should be careful not to read the experience too narrowly. Even regarded within the colonial context, the transaction facilitated by *Caribbean Voices* is complex: the writer may feel pressure to write "British," but he may also feel pressure to write "exotic." The editor probably intends to select for "West Indianness," making a conscious effort not to be seduced by the merely exotic, yet he probably also has an unconscious predisposition for work with a recognizable relationship to the tradition. The text, on which all these conflicting judgments have been exercised, will be read by a West Indian who may not be all that familiar with reading to a microphone, and who will be performing in a BBC studio at the heart of Empire, presumably without an audience. His adjustment to that situation, which might standardize and even stilt his speech, must be further modulated in response to his awareness that he will be heard in the Caribbean by auditors who will be very sensitive to ways in which either the reader or the text may depart from their own sense of their normal language. Yet it is unpredictable—was even more so in the 1950s—whether any perceived deviation would be regarded negatively as a denial of roots, or positively as the achievement of a "better" accent.

The *Caribbean Voices* program was always self-conscious about balancing its real service to Caribbean culture (especially in default of any other medium) and its metropolitan filtration of the material. The initial collection and selection of material was made in Jamaica by Cedric Lindo, but no matter how many West Indians were involved as writers, readers, and editors, the specter of metropolitan evaluation was strong.[14] The BBC was being criticized even at the time of the broadcasts for condescension; in fact, Swanzy acknowledged complaints that the commentators were patronizing, and he went on to speak candidly of the program's value as temporary, pending the development of a *regional* outlet for West Indian writing.[15] At another point, Swanzy interrupts one of his own observations on the air to apologize for annoying the poets by talking about influences he perceives in their work.[16] In retrospect, however, the record of broadcasts is a record of editorial openness with relatively few critical blind spots. Indeed, Lamming writes: "The programme was intended to 'encourage' local talent; and it was a most salutary change when, under Henry Swanzy's direction, I'm sure, [Roy] Fuller and Calder Marshall became astringent." Sharper criticism meant sharper responses, and "tearing Fuller and Calder Marshall to pieces" was essential to the postbroadcast ritual in Port of Spain, as Lamming describes it.[17] Out of that imagined critical dialogue came sharper writing.

In the first year, poets were represented evenhandedly, at the rate of one or two poems each, with no showcasing of particular talents. The editors made an obvious effort at generational, and to a lesser extent geographic, representation. As was to be expected, there was a strong Jamaican contingent; quite apart from the effects of Lindo's editorial role, Jamaican work had the most visible public profile and most highly developed literary infrastructure. During that year there were nine Jamaicans of several generations. Even the two oldest, from the generation born in the 1880s, represented very different schools of poetic practice: Constance Hollar from the middle-class and old-fashioned Jamaican Poetry League, and Claude McKay, the constable who had emigrated to America and established himself as a modernist poet in the Harlem Renaissance. Younger poets such as H. D. Carberry and K. E. Ingram, then in their twenties, represented yet another "school." They were associated with the socialist and nationalist politics of the Peoples National Party, headed by Norman Manley, and with the literary magazine *Focus,* edited by his wife Edna. Besides the Jamaicans there was Frank Collymore from Barbados, and from Trinidad, interestingly enough, not any of the *Beacon* magazine group, which had dominated the local scene since the 1930s, but what might be called the established mavericks, A. M. Clarke and Harold Telemaque. Within a year or two, the broadcast included poets from British Guiana (now Guyana) and British Honduras (now Belize).

If there was concern to be representative of the various Caribbean territories, it is much less likely that anyone involved in the editorial process was paying attention to race and ethnicity as a variable to be taken into account, and quite unlikely that there was any sensitivity to gender. A few poems by women were broadcast in the early years, including work of Hollar, Marson, Daisy Myrie, and Louise Bennett. Indeed, the inclusion of Bennett was most impressive, not because she was female but because her poems, written in Jamaican dialect and intended for public performance, were generally dismissed as popular "entertainment." Apart from this prescient editorial decision by *Caribbean Voices,* critical recognition of Bennett as a serious poet did not come until the mid-1960s.[18] At the Commonwealth Arts Festival in London in 1965, she was still placed on the program among the folk singers, not the poets.[19] Bennett's "Bans O' Killing," broadcast in 1948, is apparently the first West Indian poem to use a form of expression that was still considered "dialect" as the vehicle for explicit claims about the dignity of Caribbean language. In this text a piece of "popular" Jamaican discourse voices a full consciousness of its historical antecedents in the slow emergence of English as a respectable literary language:

Dat dem start fe try tun language,
From de fourteen century,
Five hundred years gawn an dem got
More dialect dan we!

Arguing against those who would suppress nonstandard English in the Caribbean, Bennett points out that such a campaign would have to begin in Britain:

Yuh wi haffe kill de Lancashire
De Yorkshire, de Cockney
De broad Scotch an de Irish brogue
Before yuh start kill me!

Yuh wi haffe get de Oxford book
Of English verse, an tear
Out Chaucer, Burns, Lady Grizelle
An plenty o' Shakespeare![20]

With the reading of a set of ten poems by Harold Telemaque in 1947, the program began the practice of occasionally featuring a single author in relative depth. The event coincided with the publication of *Burnt Bush,* a volume in which thirty-five of Telemaque's poems appeared along with twenty-six by A. M. Clarke. Telemaque was a frequent and highly regarded contributor to the program through 1953, the year of his second volume *(Scarlet).*[21] On the other hand, *Caribbean Voices* appears to have broadcast only a single poem by Clarke. This might seem a convenient test case for the limits of BBC taste, but in fact the judgment is not at all idiosyncratic. Clarke's work is almost completely absent from later West Indian anthologies—even from Reinhard Sander's collection of Trinidadian literature during Clarke's heyday, the 1930s.[22]

In 1948 the program continued to feature individual writers, with a showcase of Lamming (nine poems) and later of Collymore (six poems). In 1949 Derek Walcott also appeared for the first time, with six poems. Walcott was a precocious nineteen years old at the time. His book *25 Poems* had appeared in a private printing the previous year; there was a second edition in 1949. The grouping is oddly assorted and uneven, but there are two major poems, "As John to Patmos" and "A City's Death by Fire," and the first of them is a claim-staking manifesto. Walcott in this early poem swears to remain at home and not only to be the poet of his place but also to be the poet for the people of that place.

Walcott was not the only poet who sensed that *Caribbean Voices* was the appropriate forum for such declarations. Fully ten years after he began publishing, Eric Roach's work enjoyed its first exposure outside Trinidad and Tobago in August 1949, when a set of five poems were broadcast together. The first poem, "Invocation," is an initiatory prayer for Roach's vocation, calling on the Muse to transform his verse.[23] Three of the other four—"March Trades," "Shallow Underground," and "The Old Man"—

introduce themes and tropes fundamental to the entire corpus of Roach's work. Although we cannot be certain whether the poet himself was primarily responsible for the specific selection for broadcast, we do know that none of these particular poems had been published anywhere before, and it is apparent that they constitute a very self-consciously designed debut.

Roach's work continued to appear frequently throughout the early 1950s, and he was by this time offering some of the most provocative material heard on the broadcast. "Haitian Trilogy" (1953), with its passages in Haitian creole, is among the earliest instances in all of West Indian poetry where local dialect is used without comic intent. The title of another poem, "Caribbean Coronation Verse," might lead us to expect the sort of bland occasional poem that justifies the existence of poets laureate. Roach, however, exploits the occasion to address the newly crowned Elizabeth directly, lobbying for a federation of the West Indies in surprisingly provocative terms:

. . . now my nigger voice from the slave islands
Proclaims her majesty in Shakespeare's tongue
To queen a commonwealth of flowering freedoms.[24]

These are individually among the most politically engaged poems by any author to be heard on the program, and taken along with the rest of Roach's broadcast poems, they provide a very plausible basis for his early reputation as the "blackest" of West Indian poets, and one of the angriest before independence.

It is noteworthy in this connection that the two most visibly political poets of that era are all but absent from the *Caribbean Voices* program. Both George Campbell in Jamaica and Martin Carter in Guyana were intimately associated with political movements in their respective countries, but it seems unlikely that the program's editors would have been skittish about such associations. Campbell was arguably the most famous poet in Jamaica in the years just after World War II, and he was certainly known to Cedric Lindo. His epoch-making book *First Poems* was reviewed on the program in 1946, but apart from a broadcast of his best-known poem "Holy" in 1948, his work was not heard again until the final programs of 1958, by which time he had emigrated to New York and apparently stopped writing. It was likewise only in that atmosphere of dismantling the colonial service in the face of federation that a single poem of Carter's—"University of Hunger"—was broadcast in 1958. This is puzzling; if there was a political objection to

Carter's work, there were many less trenchant poems from which to choose. This particular poem was written during Carter's imprisonment on political grounds in 1953 and appeared in the first of his books to be published outside Guyana, entitled (as if it were a clandestine dispatch) *Poems of Resistance from British Guiana*.[25] The neglect of these two poets is curious, but no obvious motive is apparent. Roach's poetic style was richer than Campbell's and more accessible than Carter's, but the work of both poets would have played very effectively on the radio.

It was in 1953 that the work of Edward Kamau Brathwaite was included for the first time (he was twenty-three years old and a student at Cambridge), with a debut of five poems. These poems, mostly under ten lines in length, are related in tone and style, but unlike most of Brathwaite's early work, they do not constitute a real sequence. Some are very accomplished, with hints of future technique rather than of future themes, but Brathwaite chose none of these poems for inclusion in *Other Exiles*, the volume that collects his early work. From the time that Edgar Mittelholzer took over the program in 1956, Brathwaite came to dominate the program both as a reader and as an author.[26] The poet's work at this point is still very well behaved, reflecting his travels in Europe and West Africa, and very much under the influence of T. S. Eliot. Brathwaite's broadcast poems, unlike those of Walcott and Roach, aspire to no grand statement about the poet's objectives or sense of self; that comes only with the publication of *Rights of Passage* in 1967.

Poetry by about a half-dozen women was broadcast during the life of the program, but no poem by a woman appeared after 1953—that is, just before Naipaul took over direction of the program. Naipaul, however, does not seem to have been the problem. After the prominence of women in the Jamaican Poetry League a generation earlier, poetry by women became almost invisible throughout the Anglophone Caribbean during the nationalist era of the 1950s and 1960s; women were writing throughout the period, but only about 1980 did women become important again as *publishing* poets. In the specific case of *Caribbean Voices*, the disappearance of women was a small part of a perceived disappearance of good poetry. When Naipaul looked back over the program's achievements in the final broadcast of 1958, he put forward the opinion that by 1954 (when he started), poetry seemed to be in general decline, judging from the preponderance of amateur and third-rate work submitted.[27] In any case, during the late 1950s, considerably less poetry was being broadcast on *Caribbean Voices* than formerly.

Caribbean Voices was terminated in 1958 as part of the general dismantling of British colonial apparatus. The move was certainly well-intentioned, but it came at a most inopportune time in many respects—*Caribbean Voices* was succeeded by no comparable regional radio programming. Thereafter radio in the West Indies played only a local role for each individual island, a role consistent with the atmosphere of micronationalism that marked the first two decades of independence. Brathwaite had early urged the value of the University of the West Indies, with its campuses in Jamaica, Trinidad, and Barbados, as a "West Indian" cultural space—perhaps implicitly sensing that it would have to take over the transnational functions of BBC cultural programming.[28] In any event, conferences, symposia, and even routine university business have provided frequent occasions for writers to assemble productively.[29]

To some extent, new technological developments compensated for the absence of regional radio. Largely under the influence of Brathwaite, West Indian poets in the 1970s explored the use of alternative media—especially audio- and videocassettes—for disseminating their work outside the narrow path of print. These technologies enhanced exciting innovations in contemporary poetry. At the same time, however, they are most compatible with a specific sector of poetic production, encompassing some forms of reggae and calypso, dub poetry (by writers such as Linton Kwesi Johnson, Mutabaruka, Jean Breeze), some recorded performance poetry (by Louise Bennett, Paul Keens-Douglas, Bruce St. John), and a few more traditional poets who happen to produce cassettes (especially Lorna Goodison). There are other limitations as well. Recorded poetry is mobile, portable, and cosmopolitan, yes, but those advantages are somewhat offset by recognition that such recordings are commodities privately held by migratory individuals, isolated even by their headsets. In comparison with the camaraderie of groups of writers gathered around borrowed radios, the "community" of owners of some particular compact disc or cassette is tenuous at best. In the Anglophone Caribbean, it was radio, and specifically *Caribbean Voices,* that provided the occasion for imagining a community, and the imagining went a considerable way toward realizing that community.

Caribbean scholars dream that new technologies will eventually bring us full circle, so that the surviving recordings of the *Caribbean Voices* program can be accessible again on CDs or a Web site. Thus far, however, it has not even been possible to collect for old-fashioned publication all the poetry that was heard on the broadcasts. What we do have is the gist of the BBC legacy, consolidated in an anthology within a decade after the termination of the program. Although it draws on a variety of sources, John Figueroa's anthology *Caribbean Voices* (vol. 1, 1966; vol. 2, 1970) relies heavily on material in the BBC scripts, and Figueroa explains that he chose his title in recognition of "the role played by the programme *Caribbean Voices* in encouraging West Indian writers at a time when it was, with the remarkable exception of [the Barbadian magazine] *Bim*, the sole regular opportunity for publishing West Indian verse."[30] Apart from its own historical importance, this anthology stands as a testament to the creativity that resulted from the benign West Indian "colonization" of a weekly segment of BBC programming.

Notes

1 E. M. Roach, *The Flowering Rock: Collected Poems, 1938–1974* (Leeds: Peepal Tree, 1992), 70.

2 Ibid., 81.

3 Roach presumably heard this very poem read back to him over the radio by Lamming himself (according to the BBC transcript of the broadcast, 13 April 1952). This would have given special resonance to the line "my brother's is an echo's voice." His brother poet is not only an alter ego but an actual echo; Roach's words come back to him, but in the accents of a different island.

4 Esther Chapman, "A Federation of Ideas," *West Indian Review* 1, no. 2 (October 1934): 11; italics mine.

5 Benedict Anderson, *Imagined Communities*, rev. ed. (London: Verso, 1991), 54.

6 V. S. Naipaul, *Finding the Center* (New York: Vintage, 1986), 3–4, 12.

7 John Figueroa, "Dreams and Visions: A Critical Introduction," in *Caribbean Voices: An Anthology of West Indian Poetry*, vol. 2 (London: Evans Brothers, 1970), 3.

8 George Lamming, *The Pleasures of Exile* (London: Allison and Busby, 1984), 65–66; italics mine.

9 Geoffrey A. Holder, review of *Henri Christophe*, by Derek Walcott, *Bim* 14 (June 1951): 142.

10 Lamming, *The Pleasures of Exile*, 65.

11 Ibid., 66.

12 Photocopied transcripts of the *Caribbean Voices* programs are preserved in the

libraries of the University of the West Indies; surviving audio recordings are preserved at the British National Sound Archive.

13 On this development see particularly Brathwaite's *History of the Voice* (London: New Beacon, 1984) and its extensive bibliographies.

14 For the context of Lindo's role see Anne Walmsley, *The Caribbean Artists Movement: 1966–1972* (London: New Beacon, 1992), 6.

15 BBC transcript (21 August 1949), 4.

16 BBC transcript (20 August 1950), 5.

17 Lamming, *The Pleasures of Exile,* 66.

18 Mervyn Morris's essay "On Reading Louise Bennett, Seriously," *Jamaica Journal* 1, no. 1 (December 1967); and Rex Nettleford's introduction to *Jamaica Labrish,* by Louise Bennett (Kingston: Sangster, 1966).

19 Walmsley, *The Caribbean Artists Movement,* 60.

20 Louise Bennett, *Jamaica Labrish* (Kingston: Sangster, 1966), 218–19.

21 Telemaque's is a story of frustrated promise in its own right; the termination of *Caribbean Voices* seems to have been a blow to him as it was to Roach. See Telemaque's comments and tone in a late interview with Anson Gonzalez, and his hope for a collection of his work even then, in Anson Gonzalez, *Trinidad and Tobago Literature: On Air* (Trinidad: National Cultural Council, 1974), 33–40.

22 Reinhard Sander, ed., *From Trinidad: An Anthology of Early West Indian Writing* (London: Hodder and Stoughton, 1978).

23 Roach, *The Flowering Rock,* 52.

24 Ibid., 100.

25 Martin Carter, *Poems of Resistance from British Guiana* (London: Lawrence and Wishart, 1954).

26 Brathwaite was represented by nine poems in 1955, eleven poems in a single program in 1956, and another nine in 1957.

27 BBC transcript (31 August 1958).

28 Edward Kamau Brathwaite, "The Role of the University in a Developing Society," in *Iouanaloa: Recent Writing from St. Lucia* (Castries: University of the West Indies, Department of Extra-mural Studies, 1963), 13–18.

29 The University's Radio Education Unit continues to play an important role in recording and archiving cultural events of all sorts: lectures, plays, performances, readings, panel discussions. Usually, however, such material enjoys little public exposure.

30 John Figueroa, introduction to *Caribbean Voices: An Anthology of West Indian Poetry,* vol. 1 (London: Evans Brothers, 1966), xiv.

Works Cited

Anderson, Benedict. *Imagined Communities.* Rev. ed. London: Verso, 1991.

Bennett, Louise. *Jamaica Labrish.* Kingston: Sangster, 1966.

Brathwaite, Edward Kamau. "The Role of the University in a Developing Society." In *Iouanaloa: Recent Writing from St. Lucia.* Castries: University of the West Indies, Department of Extra-mural Studies, 1963.

——. *History of the Voice.* London: New Beacon, 1984.

Caribbean Voices. Photocopied transcripts of the BBC radio program. Preserved at the libraries of the University of the West Indies at Mona, Jamaica, and St. Augustine, Trinidad and Tobago.

Carter, Martin. *Poems of Resistance from British Guiana.* London: Lawrence and Wishart, 1954.

Chapman, Esther. "A Federation of Ideas." *West Indian Review* 1, no. 2 (October 1934): 11.

Figueroa, John, ed. *Caribbean Voices: An Anthology of West Indian Poetry.* Vol. 1. London: Evans Brothers, 1966.

——. *Caribbean Voices: An Anthlogy of West Indian Poetry.* Vol. 2. London: Evans Brothers, 1970.

Gonzalez, Anson. *Trinidad and Tobago Literature: On Air.* Trinidad: National Cultural Council, 1974.

Holder, Geoffrey A. Review of *Henri Christophe,* by Derek Walcott. *Bim* 14 (June 1951): 141–42.

Lamming, George. *The Pleasures of Exile.* London: Allison and Busby, 1984.

Morris, Mervyn. "On Reading Louise Bennett, Seriously." *Jamaica Journal* 1, no. 1 (December 1967): 69–74.

Naipaul, V. S. *Finding the Center.* New York: Vintage, 1986.

Roach, E. M. *The Flowering Rock: Collected Poems, 1938–1974.* Leeds: Peepal Tree, 1992.

Sander, Reinhard, ed. *From Trinidad: An Anthology of Early West Indian Writing.* London: Hodder and Stoughton, 1978.

Walmsley, Anne. *The Caribbean Artists Movement: 1966–1972.* London: New Beacon, 1992.

THE FORGOTTEN FIFTEEN MILLION:

BLACK RADIO, RADICALISM, AND THE

CONSTRUCTION OF THE "NEGRO MARKET"

Kathy M. Newman

In 1949 *Sponsor* magazine used the following headline to grab the attention of national advertisers who had long ignored African American consumers—the "forgotten" fifteen million.

The forgotten 15,000,000: Ten billion a year Negro market is largely ignored by national advertisers. When a segment of the over-all American population that is larger than the population of the entire Dominion of Canada is overlooked and under-developed by U.S. national advertisers and their agencies, something would seem to be wrong. In the case of America's 15,000,000 Negroes, something very definitely is.[1]

With this article, *Sponsor* offered a new solution to an old problem in American advertising: the problem of racism versus the bottom line. To help advertisers overcome their racism toward the African American consumer, *Sponsor* used the success stories of radio stations that were already targeting the "Negro market." With testimonials from black radio stations all over the country, *Sponsor* argued that black radio could make black audiences into loyal listeners and loyal consumers.

Much of the evidence in *Sponsor*'s early features on the Negro market rested on the huge advertising success of one radio station in particular—WDIA, Memphis—the first radio station in the country to target all of its programming to African Americans. In its pioneer feature on the "forgotten 15,000,000," *Sponsor* reproduced one of WDIA's promotional brochures. With a picture of one of the black gospel groups promoted by the station, the brochure claimed that WDIA was "Out Front Down South" and was "the top choice with more than ½ MILLION NEGROES." By 1957, less than ten years later, there were over six hundred radio stations targeting 30 to 100 percent of their programming to African Americans in cities all over the country, and national advertisers were beginning to take black consumers more seriously—at least the ones they could reach via the airwaves.

Although these black consumers have been forgotten since the 1940s, we have much to gain by remembering them in the 1990s. First of all, their story challenges the idea that postwar consumer culture was marked by the standardization of the consumer. Advertisers who targeted the Negro market sought to construct an explicitly "Negro" consumer. Through radio, marketers sought a lower-income/working-class audience, for whom television was not yet a primary form of mass entertainment. This fact forces us to reconsider an accepted wisdom about the 1950s: the notion that advertisers were only interested in a homogeneous, white, middle-class market. Secondly, the story of the forgotten fifteen million challenges the accepted wisdom that African Americans were completely excluded from national advertising markets until the 1960s and 1970s. Their story shows us, instead, that African Americans were targeted by national advertising, through radio, starting in the 1940s.

These arguments draw from the pioneering social and cultural history of Robin Kelley, Robert Weems, and Lizabeth Cohen. They argue that there is a dialectic between consumer identity and political identity in the history of African American social movements. Robert Weems, in his pathbreaking *Desegregating the Dollar*, argues that after businesses recruited African American consumers in the 1930s and 1940s, African Americans used their economic power for political gain in the Civil Rights boycotts of the 1950s and 1960s. Focusing more on culture than politics, Robin Kelley shows that African American workers who participated in boycotts in the postwar era were conscious of their power as consumers, especially in their patronage of mass transit and downtown businesses: "Unlike in the workplace, where workers entered as disempowered producers dependent on wages for survival and beholden, ostensibly at least, to their superiors, working people entered public transportation as consumers—and with a sense of consumer entitlement."[2] In a similar vein, Lizabeth Cohen, writing about African American labor activism in Chicago in the 1920s and 1930s, argues that "participation in mainstream commercial life made blacks feel more independent and influential as a race."[3]

This argument—that participation in mainstream commercial life might have positive consequences for marginalized groups—is rarely made in progressive scholarship. A more emblematic response to consumer culture can be found in Manning Marable's account of marketing to African Americans in the twentieth century. Marable argues that "the impact of corporate America's massive exploitation of the Black consumer market has created a profoundly negative effect within Black culture and consciousness." He cites examples of companies that have used manipulative tactics to sell alcohol and tobacco to black consumers, such as Schieffelin's sponsoring of an advertisement for scotch with the testimony of Jesse Owens, and the Kool cigarettes sponsorship of the Kool Jazz Festivals. In these cases, Marable objects both to the nature of the products, alcohol and tobacco, and to the tactics used to sell them: black athletes and jazz music.[4]

But by focusing only on scotch and tobacco, and overlooking other products, and other advertising venues, such as radio, Marable misses the fact that corporate sponsorship of black culture has offered African Americans access to mainstream consumer culture and new outlets for black culture. Black radio pushed Schaefer beer, Philip Morris cigarettes, Nadinola skin lighteners, and Royal Crown hair products, but it also pushed Cadillacs, Quaker Oats, and GE appliances. Black radio provided news about the Ethiopian ambassador's visit to the United States and news about *Brown v. Board of Education*. Black radio offered rhythm and blues, gospel music, and homemaker shows. Black radio advocated higher education, recreation, and community service. Black radio supported voting rights, good health, and the "right to buy." Black radio, though it was a part of corporate America's exploitation of the black consumer, had some positive effects within black culture and black consciousness.

The Forgotten Fifteen Million

In 1947 an FCC report suggested that "a small segment of the listening audience carefully selected as a minority group, may, if it is loyally attached to the station, give it a unique fascination for advertisers." In 1947 television threatened to replace radio as the medium through which national advertisers could reach the broadest audience, and thus radio was looking for new and "narrower" markets. WDIA's success with programming for the Memphis black community—and *Sponsor*'s reporting of it—helped to ensure that African Americans would be the one of the first audiences to be "carefully selected as a minority group" by independent radio stations throughout the country.[5] Although the postwar period is generally thought of as a period of mass standardization of products and consumers, the history of the Negro market shows that marketing in the postwar era was a diverse, heterogeneous, and complex process. The diversity of advertising-sponsored media allowed marketers to use a medium like television to reach what they called the "class" market while using radio and magazines to reach a "mass" audience, a "working-class" audience, and a variety of minority audiences.

As a result, the sociology of marketing for difference became an industry unto itself, with a specialized professional discourse that was published in textbooks and advertising trade magazines. *Sponsor* magazine and its annual feature on black radio, for example, were the innovations of a World War II veteran named Norman Glenn, who began monthly publication of the magazine in 1946. He decided to start his own trade magazine after working in the advertising department of *Broadcasting* magazine. He noticed that *Broadcasting* was geared toward only one-half of the economic equation of the broadcast industry—stations and managers—rather than the needs of the product sponsor. And it was the sponsor, Glenn realized, that paid for radio. So why not devote a trade magazine to the sponsor's point of view? The magazine became a hit: *Sponsor* was the primary journal for broadcast advertisers—on radio and television—for much of its twenty-year life span.

In the fall of 1949 *Sponsor* hailed the potential of the "forgotten fifteen million" African American consumers and singled out black radio as one of the best ways to tap their $10 billion-per-year income. The magazine estimated that there were radios in the homes of between 68 and 84 percent of southern African Americans, arguing that in spite of the many factors that separated blacks and whites, there was no such thing as "segregated ears."[6] Three years later *Sponsor* expanded its coverage into a nineteen-page feature on the growing black radio industry. Using the 1950 U.S. Census, *Sponsor* showed that between 1940 and 1950, the number of African Americans living in urban centers increased by 46 percent, that the black median income rose by 192 percent (compared to 146 percent for whites), and that 91.5 percent of African Americans in the civilian labor force were employed. In a comparison of urban black consumer markets by size, the Memphis market ranked ninth, with African Americans making up nearly 50 percent of the city's total population.[7]

When *Time* magazine discovered the Negro market in 1954, the magazine seemed determined to show that cultivating the Negro market could lead to great social and economic change. In a story that featured the screening of an advertising film made by the Johnson Publishing Co., titled *The Secret of Selling the Negro, Time* reported that the economic rise of the African American "helped break down many segregation barriers."[8] *Time's* Freudian slip—the film was originally titled *The Secret of Selling the Negro Market*—is one of the many curious features of this article. But equally important is the fact that the article appeared in July 1954, just two months after the Supreme Court decision on *Brown v. the Board of Education.* Citing figures from Johnson's film and *Sponsor* magazine, *Time* made the connection between civil rights and the right to consume, concluding that the emergence of the Negro market was a good thing for the economy and for race relations: "Most retailers feel that even in Southern stores discrimination will disappear gradually, wiped out by the legal pressure against segregation and the economic rise of the South. Eventually, the Negro market will merge into and become indistinguishable from the overall market."[9] Therefore, at the same time that the Negro market was conceived of as a separate (and not necessarily equal) sphere, *Sponsor, Time,* and academics such as Joseph Johnson offered it as one route to integration. Between the courts and the democratic power of the dollar, they imagined, discrimination would disappear.

Even the *Pittsburgh Courier* reported that "many civic leaders below the Mason Dixon line are of the opinion that [Negro radio] will do more for lowering Jim Crow barriers than flowery oratory."[10] Black radio and its promise of the black consumer continued to draw praise throughout the mid-fifties: in 1956 Alex Haley coauthored a feature on black radio for *Harper's* with Albert Aberbanel, using much of the material provided by the previous five years of *Sponsor's* "Annual Negro Section":

"Negro radio" as it is popularly called, seems to have sprung up almost spontaneously, over night, all over the country. The surprising thing is that no one thought of it before, that for years talented Negroes knocked at closed doors, trying to get jobs in radio. . . . Almost all Negroes share a common desire for race progress, and the station and sponsors who make a special effort to attract them are showing an increased respect for Negroes as a people. Any discriminated-against minority group is also quick to take personal pride in the achievements of any of its members, so radio programs featuring Negroes offer excellent opportunities for listener identification. And finally, in segregated areas, such programs indirectly tell their listeners where they can go to shop without fear of being embarrassed.[11]

The irony here is palpable. Aberbanel and Haley described African Americans as a "discriminated-against minority" and as no more than "embarrassed" when they encountered discrimination in the marketplace. But understatement aside, these authors were not wrong in their basic premise: that the "Negro market" was founded on the double edge of segregation and race consciousness—especially in the South.

In 1957, a year when controversies over segregation and race consciousness drew the National Guard to Little Rock, Arkansas, *Time* returned to the subject of the Negro market—this time to report the successful sale of WDIA for $1 million. *Time* justified the "thumping price" with the argument that the Negro market was crucial to the national market: "The Negro market can make—or break—the sales programs of even the biggest advertisers. These 17.3 million customers are growing in power and influence . . . faster than the U.S. average. Though Negro stations were unheard-of ten years ago, they prosper today in every sizable city in the South and in big cities up North."[12] But perhaps because of controversies around school desegregation, this article made no mention of the integrationist potential of black buying power. Rather, the tone of the article focused on racial and class difference, on the "cotton pickers" who took portable radios to the field to hear "Theo ('Bless My Bones') Wade" and musical shows like *Tan Town Coffee Club, Wheelin' on Beale,* and *Hallelujah Jubilee.*

This emergence of the Negro market in the 1950s—and the importance of radio—challenges the conventional wisdom that marketers in the 1950s were interested only in finding (and producing) a standard white middle-class consumer. The rise of the Negro market shows that postwar marketing strategies were divided by media and by demographics, and that advertisers actively sought black consumers for national brands and products directed at the Negro market. Moreover, hair straighteners and skin lighteners were not the only products that sponsored black radio stations. A close look at the first black radio station, WDIA, will challenge the conventional wisdom that African Americans were largely excluded from exposure to national advertising until the 1960s. The history of marketing at WDIA shows that African Americans were encouraged to join in mainstream consumer behavior: to buy cars, washing machines, and new homes—to chew Wrigley's gum, eat Wonder Bread, listen to Philco radios, and drink Seven-Up.[13]

Ask Mr. Sponsor: WDIA *and the Production of the Negro Market*

In the 1940s and 1950s, black consumers were recruited through an expanding nexus of black newspapers and periodicals, such as *Ebony* magazine. But radio was the most prevalent form of nationally sponsored mass culture in African American homes in the 1950s and early 1960s: more African Americans owned radios than owned televisions, subscribed to newspapers, or subscribed to magazines. Radio was so prevalent in black homes, in fact, that *Ebony* magazine bought time on black radio stations to increase its circulation. In the mid-1950s it was estimated that on average, 94 percent of all black homes had at least one radio set. Regionally this was broken down into two statistics: radio penetration was equal to 98 percent in the North, and over 80 percent in the South. And thus more African Americans were exposed to national advertising on the radio than through any other black medium in the 1950s.[14]

Because of prejudice against black consumers, advertisers interested in targeting the Negro market had only a handful of academic studies and trade magazines like *Sponsor* for market research on black consumers. Racism was one factor; lack of telephones in black homes was another. The national rating companies, such as "Hooper" (which dominated the ratings market in the 1930s and 1940s), relied on the "telephone coincidental method" to obtain program ratings. With this system, researchers called radio listeners and asked them what program they were listening to at the time of the telephone call. In the 1940s fewer than 50 percent of Americans owned telephones, and the percentage of African Americans who owned telephones was much lower than the national average—especially in the South.

Thus radio station managers turned to *Sponsor* magazine's annual "Negro Radio" issue. *Sponsor* was the primary resource for advertisers interested in the Negro market, and WDIA was *Sponsor*'s most featured station. Thus the success of WDIA helped station managers around the country make the switch to black radio. And as the new black stations had success stories to share, their testimonials appeared in *Sponsor* magazine: black radio expanded at a rate of about one hundred new stations per year from 1949 to 1958. In the beginning, however, most of *Sponsor*'s advice on the Negro market was provided by Bert Ferguson, the white entrepreneur who was general manager and part owner of WDIA.

In 1948 Ferguson hired Nat D. Williams, a popular black high school teacher, to host the first show for black listeners in Memphis. Williams, who was also an entertainer and a nationally syndicated newspaper columnist in the Negro press, called his show *The Tan Town Jamboree*. To test the success of the show, Ferguson delivered pamphlets to the doorsteps of homes in black neighborhoods and asked listeners to write back with their comments on the new program. The response was overwhelming, and Ferguson began to expand WDIA's black programming. For the next eighteen months, he added black shows on an ad hoc basis until the station was completely converted from its previous format (though the news department, sales department, and general managers were staffed by whites until the 1960s). Williams helped to recruit a team of talented African American blues entertainers, comedians, teachers, and preachers to work as disc jockeys, and their shows ranged from gospel, blues, and rhythm and blues to sewing, agriculture, and homemaking.[15]

Early successes persuaded advertisers that WDIA was a good investment: General Home Service Co. was one of the first companies to sponsor the new programming: in the thirteen weeks that they sponsored fifteen-minute shows on WDIA, they sold 546 washers, "more than any other dealer had disposed of and almost as many as all the G.E. dealers in Memphis together had sold" in the same period.[16] In later years a station promotion in which listeners were asked to collect and send in Carnation Milk labels brought 168,364 labels into the station; when the Pure Oil company gave away free rabbit-foot key chains bearing potentially winning "serial numbers" with each fill-up, the company went through 50,000 key chains in thirteen weeks; in another case, a Memphis used-car dealer doubled the number of cars he sold per month after buying advertising on WDIA.[17] In 1954 station owners increased the WDIA signal from 250 to 50,000 watts, and by 1955 WDIA carried more national advertising than any other black station in the country.[18]

What made WDIA so successful? Why were African Americans in Memphis and the surrounding tri-state area willing to buy the products WDIA advertised? This is an important question; the fact that black incomes were rising after World War II did not guarantee that African American consumers were going to buy more, or buy more luxury goods. As Colin Campbell has argued, it is important to distinguish between the "presence in a population of a new *ability* to buy inessentials and a new *willingness* to do so."[19] WDIA successfully channeled the purchasing habits of African

Americans toward particular brands of essential food products, such as Lily White Flour, Southern Belle Sausage, and Carnation Canned Milk. And as for "inessentials," such as home appliances, remodeling services, travel, and automobiles, black radio stations advertised these products to a much larger audience than black periodicals such as *Ebony* magazine. And while black radio stations advertised many products that have been associated with the exploitation of black consumers, such as cigarettes, alcohol, skin lighteners and hair straighteners, black radio also advertised mainstream products associated with middle-class life in America.

It was this balance between segregation on the one hand and a growing race consciousness on the other that *Sponsor* used to explain the buying habits of Memphis African Americans. *Sponsor* taught advertisers how segregation shaped (and therefore helped to predict) black consumption patterns. *Sponsor* used charts to show that the median income for African Americans was about half the median income for whites in 1950, but pointed out that because of racial segregation in the real estate, restaurant, and recreational markets, African Americans spent less of their income on rent, vacations, and dining out: "Negroes still extend a lower-than-average patronage to many restaurants, night clubs, theaters, hotels, and vacation spots and generally spend less for out-of-home recreation than whites, since they can't always be sure they won't be embarrassed."[20] "Embarrassment" is a troubling euphemism for racism, but *Sponsor*'s point was clear enough: if discrimination discouraged African Americans from going out, broadcasters could capitalize on this by advertising products that African Americans would want to use while entertaining at home.

At the same time, *Sponsor* pointed out, African Americans spent a *higher* percentage of their income on staple food and household goods, thus "pay[ing] more and buy[ing] more of the things that are nationally advertised."[21] WDIA research found that African Americans were buying 80 percent of the rice, 70 percent of the canned milk, and 65 percent of the flour in Memphis grocery stores.[22] Other black radio stations reported advertising success with items like upholstery, tract homes, and packaged drug products, noting that blacks entertained more in their homes, could not move "just anywhere," and could not access the same quality of medical care as whites.[23] While black radio may have helped African Americans to imagine themselves as consumers of a lifestyle previously reserved for whites, it seems unlikely that an advertising appeal so integrated with the logic and consequences of segregation could result in the Negro market becoming indistinguishable from the overall market, as *Time* had prophesied in 1954.

On the other hand, as Robin Kelley has argued, segregation has often gone hand-in-hand with a positive sense of African American "congregation."[24] Kelley borrows this idea from the historian Earl Lewis, who explained that the difference between congregation and segregation was a difference in choice. Congregation, Lewis wrote, "symbolized an act of free will, whereas segregation represented the imposition of another's will."[25] Kelley uses this idea to suggest that we can learn something about collective action by examining the collective pleasures displayed in the consumption of transportation, music, and athletics: "Knowing what happens in these spaces of pleasure can help us understand the solidarity black people have shown at political mass meetings, illuminate the bonds of fellowship we find in churches and voluntary associations, and unveil the *conflicts* across class and gender lines that shape and constrain these collective struggles" (47). Kelley is not naively optimistic; he uses Lewis's words to warn us that "congregation in a Jim Crow environment produced more space than power." But in this space, he argues, African Americans could "gather their cultural bearings" and turn race prejudice into race pride (45).

The Negro market was founded on this dialectic between race prejudice and race pride, within the new "space" provided by black radio. *Sponsor* acknowledged segregation as the major reason for the existence of a separate Negro market, but it also recognized that a growing race pride in the accomplishments of African American artists and entertainers was one of segregation's unwitting effects: "The great mass of U.S. Negroes will continue as an identifiable group for a long, long time to come. As long as there is racial segregation or racial prejudice in this country, Negroes will continue to turn to their own news and entertainment media for everything from the interpretation of new legislation to the enjoyment of performing artists of their own race."[26] This quote suggests that if radio entrepreneurs and advertisers wanted to attract the Negro market to black radio, they needed to provide an African American "interpretation of new legislation" and feature black performers. It was not enough to know how much flour was purchased by black households in Memphis.

The most important factor in marketing to African Americans was the hiring of black disc jockeys. *Sponsor* argued that black listeners had more "confidence" in disc jockeys they could tell were black, and that racially specific listener identification had social, political, and commercial consequences: "Seldom can a Negro—particularly one who is getting more and more proud of his racial heritage as his status improves—find anything in the ordinary air show sponsored by a national advertiser with which he can identify himself. . . . Negro-appeal radio therefore is *the* radio in the increasingly race-conscious, race-proud world of millions of colored Americans."[27] Black disc jockeys were crucial to the sound of "race consciousness" on the radio. WDIA used its black staff for community outreach projects called the WDIA "goodwill" events. The WDIA staff volunteered its labor to host and perform in the station's first "Goodwill Revue" in 1949, and the funds raised were donated to a Christmas charity. In the same year, WDIA celebrated the radio debut of the "Teen Town Singers," a high school singing group. WDIA offered a $100 savings bond to local high school students for winning essays on the topic of "community life" and sponsored teen forums, an "I Speak for Democracy" contest, and an annual spelling bee.

The most famous of the WDIA disc jockeys, the blues singer B. B. King, remembers Bert Ferguson as a "fantastic person" who "believed in helping people." King called WDIA a "big learning center for people like myself." He remembers WDIA as a separate, safe space for the black staff members who worked there—an oasis, a place for black culture to flourish, and an interracial workplace in the segregated South:

At that time the South was segregated. But we had a feeling, us blacks did, when we got into the radio station, it was almost like being in a foreign country, and going to your embassy. When you get there, you know this is home. . . . So when we got into WDIA we felt like we meant something. We felt that we were citizens. We felt we were appreciated. And we didn't have to say, "Yes, sir" or "Yes, ma'am" or "No, sir," or "No, ma'am," unless we felt that it was honor that was due to someone, not simply because we were black and they were white. Everybody worked by that, and when you walked back on the streets it was again like leaving the embassy, in that foreign country, until it really changed, and WDIA did a lot to change it.[28]

B. B. King's memory of WDIA as a "home embassy" in a foreign country resonates with Earl Lewis's notion of the "congregation" that can come out of "segregation." WDIA was a product of segregation, but it provided jobs for black performers and offered black culture, music, news, and entertainment to the Memphis black community.

WDIA never promoted community without simultaneously offering a vision for "good citizenship" and "family values." The station news editor, Marie Wathen, and program director, Chris Spindel, developed many of the goodwill-instilling and audience-recruiting programs for the station in the early 1950s. Wathen initiated programs that counseled listeners on the "problems of marriage" and "family welfare." The 1952 license renewal application described the family welfare program as an "important educational service," designed to enjoin listeners "to live better, more productive, and happier lives."[29]

The station also campaigned against venereal disease and tuberculosis, offering free testing for both. Good citizenship also included voting: a record of public service announcements used for the month of July in 1952 includes spots for voter registration, the League of Women Voters, the Girl Scouts, the Elks Club, Civil Defense, AA, Farm Safety, three churches, a plug for the Red Sox (a Negro League baseball team), and the WDIA free movie program. This was another goodwill stunt aimed at the young: WDIA brought screens and speakers to neighborhoods where the kids were too poor to go to the movies in town, and the previews always included promotional films featuring the station's black disc jockey staff.[30]

By the mid-1950s, Ferguson and his staff had made WDIA into "not just a radio station but an advertising force."[31] Ferguson knew he was producing a loyal audience whose function was to consume the products advertised on the station. In 1957, after nearly ten years of experimenting with black radio, *Sponsor* agreed that the WDIA formula worked around the country, and that rhythm and blues, gospel music, black disc jockeys, community outreach, and goodwill projects were crucial to a black radio station's commercial success:

Many of these elements add up to a strong sense of loyalty, a need for identification with the Negro community even though there is a concurrent struggle for acceptance in the non-Negro community. The best of the Negro radio stations and newspapers encourage this search for identification—and they sell their advertisers' products better for doing this. They encourage fund raising for a new Negro hospital or help distribute Salk vaccine in Negro areas. They provide buses for handicapped Negro children or work to get better paving in Negro neighborhoods.[32]

Black disc jockeys, community involvement, and "goodwill" projects helped create a sense of black community identification, which in turn

increased the sales of products advertised on black stations. Racial "identification" was essential to commercialization.

WDIA provided the Memphis black community with a "home embassy"—a new space for entertainment, information, music, citizenship,
and "goodwill." WDIA also led to the increased participation of Memphis
African Americans in the mainstream commercial life of the region. By the
mid-1950s, the buying habits of the Memphis black community were noted
by white and African American business owners alike: "In the last decade . . . the trend in buying power among these people [African Ameri-
cans] has been sharply upward. This has been associated with the growing
industrial importance of this area, an increase in the wages of the Negro,
both in industry and in agriculture, and the general upward trend of
income throughout the U.S. This increased buying power has been keenly
felt by the retail establishment of Memphis."[33] Likewise, as the buying
power of African Americans increased, so did their sense of consumer
entitlement. WDIA symbolized the link between consumption and culture:
listeners knew that when they bought the products advertised on WDIA,
they helped to keep the station in business. Without their consumption,
WDIA would not have survived.

For WDIA and its black listeners, the relationship between commercialism and community was a dialectical one. WDIA did not "create" the black
community—the black community existed long before the radio station. Instead, WDIA used existing community leaders—teachers, preachers, homemakers, and talented entertainers—to sell advertising. WDIA even used the
idea of community—spelling bees, 4-H shows, neighborhood film screen-
ings, Little League baseball teams, schools for handicapped children, and
community fund-raisers—to sell advertising. But in the process WDIA gave
the black community access to the sounds of mainstream consumer culture,
new jobs in the field of mass media, exposure to national advertising, news
of interest to the black community, electronic mass culture created exclusively for a black audience, activities and social events that drew participants
from black listeners throughout the Memphis region, and information
about local products and retail outlets. WDIA used the black community for
profit, but the black community profited, too.

Moreover, the impact of WDIA went far beyond Memphis. Louis Cantor
argues in his book about WDIA that it "created the sound that changed
America" because WDIA became the model for black radio stations through-

out the country. WDIA proved that stations could make money selling products to black consumers, and as a result there was an explosion of black programs and stations over the course of the 1950s. In 1949 there was a handful of stations with programs for African Americans. In 1957 there were more than six hundred. In 1949 there were sixteen black disc jockeys. In 1957 there were more than one thousand. Black radio had become a commercial *and* a cultural force.

Black Radio Stations and the Color of Sound

Radio was the most prevalent form of nationally sponsored mass culture in African American homes in the postwar era. Black radio had an immediacy that helped create a new outlet for black community expression, but it was equally plagued by the ephemerality of radio sound. On the other hand, in spite of the ephemerality of radio sound, black radio had the power to unite, to unify, to bring together. Through stations like WDIA, radio helped to bind the African American community living in rural and urban neighborhoods in Memphis into a "regional family." Maurice "Hotrod" Hulbert, one of the most prominent disc jockeys at WDIA, remembers the first time he realized the power that black radio had to unite the black community:

I found out that the radio was a way to really help people. It had a power that I didn't know. There was a family that was burned out, burned out completely, [their house burned] completely to the ground. I asked for help [over the radio] and people began to bring in food, clothing, and I had my first automobile, that I owned, a little Chevrolet, and I was going to different places and picking up furniture, picking up food, picking up money, and it ended up that . . . people were bringing them furniture out there in trucks, bringing them money, clothes, and they had more than they had when the house burned down. That showed me something about radio. People responded.[34]

According to Hulbert, it was after seeing the response of the black community to the needs of the family whose house burned down that WDIA started the annual tradition of the "Goodwill Review." WDIA proved to product sponsors that it could sell goods, but it also brought the black community together in a new space: the space provided by the airwaves.

Radio had another advantage over television and the printed media: the American race problem was generally defined as a problem of color rather than sound.[35] Television was replacing radio as the new broadcast medium, and as radio researcher Henry Bullock pointed out, African Americans were not pictured as members of this new, broad, audience—in programming or in advertisements. It was easier for them to find themselves represented on the radio: "Negroes choose radio over television because of the greater opportunities for self-identification offered by the former medium. Radio gives greater freedom to the imagination, freeing the Negro from the 'left-out' feeling that a visual medium imposes."[36] African Americans were "left out" of mainstream media visual representations at the same time that the "black" sound, in music and in disc jockey style and voice, was being transmitted and imitated across the radio dial—even on stations that targeted a white audience. In essence, "black" voices could be used to sell over the airwaves where anyone might hear them, whereas black models were only seen within the enclosed pages of the Negro press.

On the other hand, even if the vast majority of African Americans owned and used radios, not all of them appreciated programs directed toward a black audience. As another radio researcher named William L. Smith argued, some black listeners found black radio itself to be a form of segregation, full of "detrimental racial stereotype[s]," lacking in quality and "too limited." Smith's study of black radio listeners in Columbus, Ohio, and Baton Rouge, Louisiana, found that even when 65 percent of the respondents in both areas listened to black radio, 60 percent of them preferred "general-appeal" programming.[37] As it turned out, finding the right sound, the right copy, and the right disc jockey for maximum black listener identification was hardly an exact science, especially since what it meant to sound authentically black was itself contested terrain.

This contest was most in evidence in the criticisms of black radio. A radio researcher named Henry Bullock found that middle- and upper-class African Americans in particular were resentful of black radio; in his research focus groups, they expressed their distaste for the medium.

"I for one," complained a participant, "would like to stand on the housetop and castigate every radio station in Houston that keys its market towards the Negro." Another participant confirmed this, saying, "I'd like to give them a piece of my mind." Showing the force of the alienation inherent in this type of radio programming, still another advised: "Do like I do. Don't buy the product."[38]

This participant thought that a boycott of the products advertised on black radio stations might discourage the "segregation" of the airwaves. But there is a trace of irony in this listener's disdain: black radio was one of the first national media to advertise a middle-class lifestyle for African Americans: luxury cars, suburban homes, remodeling services, and name-brand appliances.

The negative reaction of middle-class listeners was linked not only to the minstrel implications of the clowning black disc jockey—many of the early black disc jockeys got their entertainment training on the minstrel circuit— but also to black radio's southern roots. *Sponsor* revealed its knowledge of this problem in the following case study of inappropriate ad copy:

The WDAS, Philadelphia disk jockey didn't like the look of the copy. But he read it anyway. Within minutes, the Negro-appeal station's phones were ringing. Negro callers were furious. Station manager Bob Klein started checking in a hurry and soon discovered what had gone wrong. A large super market, anxious to stimulate weekend sales in its meat department, had sent over some last-minute copy which went something like this: "Say, folks . . . want some good ol' Southern eating? Well, just get a load of some of these weekend meat specials just waitin' for you to come in and buy 'em."

Sponsor explained that the ad was for the lowest-priced meat cuts, like "pig knuckles," "ham hocks," "chitlins" and "kidneys." One listener who lived in the "swank Lincoln Drive area of Germantown" complained to the station that she "wouldn't feed that kind of stuff to my poodle." Bob Klein, WDAS station manager, understood that "good ol' Southern eating was exactly the kind of thing Negroes don't look back to with any fond remembrance."[39]

Sponsor understood that there were other things that middle-class African Americans didn't want to be reminded of: the South was one; menial labor was another. *Sponsor* warned its readers about the mixed popularity of black actors in domestic positions: "Many Negro performers get a mixed reception from Negroes themselves—particularly those who appear in menial or subservient positions to white people. Negro tastes vary, just as whites' do; some stars are popular with one group of their own race, yet unpopular with another."[40] Phrases like "taste" and "class item" were frequently used in these articles to signal the class position of the listeners; these code words allowed *Sponsor* to hint at the class divisions within the black community without broadcasting the fact that in spite of black radio's popularity, the new medium drew its harshest critics from the black elite.

Though most of the time *Sponsor* tried to present an upscale image of the black radio audience, denying that the medium attracted "dollar-down" customers, some of its features highlighted "low-income" products. One national brand representative explained why his company chose black radio for its medicinal chewing gums, Feen-a-mint and Chooz: "Products of this type have traditionally shown more strength in lower-income, semi-skilled, or unskilled occupational groups. Since this is in the main true of the Negro group, as it is also true of certain white groups regionally, we feel the Negro market is one which should be shown attention."[41] This kind of confession was rare for a *Sponsor* feature. The magazine published an annual issue on black radio to combat the advertising world's negative view of the Negro market as a lower-income market. But in this same issue, *Sponsor* quoted a report published by the BBDO advertising agency, which suggested that black radio had "a greater appeal to the masses of lower income."[42] In 1957, because of the new prominence of television in middle-class markets, radio had a "greater appeal to the masses of lower income" regardless of race. Radio was now a demographically specific medium, with programming for teens, religious groups, lower-income housewives, and "working-class" listeners—both on and off the job.

But the appeal of black radio to working-class listeners was not simply a matter of "taste." It was also a matter of material circumstances. Radios were cheaper than televisions, newspapers, and magazines and thus easier for lower-income listeners to afford. Black radio was also a vital resource in areas in which African American literacy rates were low. Moreover, radio was popular among working-class listeners because black employment patterns often constrained leisure time. According to Henry Bullock, "a far lesser proportion of Negroes have leisure time to be more responsive to eye-absorbing (as contrasted with ear-absorbing) channels of entertainment."[43] Radio programming offered news and entertainment in a form that could be enjoyed not only as an alternative to work but as an accompaniment to it.

Sponsor showed its audience how to maximize this advantage, explaining that if stations targeted African Americans who worked for white employers, advertisers could get two markets for the price of one. The following example came from WRMA in Montgomery, Alabama:

Advertisers are missing a large Negro audience with double purchasing power during the hours from 9:00 a.m. to 3:00 p.m. Negro maids (there are 15,000 in this area) tune to this station while they are working in white homes. Many of them do some of the small-item grocery buying for the white family, such as bread, milk, coffee, tea, sugar, etc. Negro maids are the ones who actually *use* floor wax, furniture polish, glass cleaner, laundry starch, detergents, and soaps. They use them in their homes, too. If the maid suggests one brand over another, the white housewife will usually comply.[44]

As another *Sponsor* article put it, by making a direct pitch to black domestics, an advertiser could "sell both whites and Negroes."[45] But in order to "sell" them both, the African American domestic worker had to perform a disturbing double labor: she waxed the floor on the one hand, and sold floor wax to her white employer on the other.

Other testimonials, like one from WHOD in Pittsburgh, explained why employers and advertisers alike might have seen radio in the workplace as a good thing: "Early morning time is unusually good in Negro Radio due to the high percentage of factory workers in the Pittsburgh area who start on an 8:00 am shift. These same workers tune in during the day at their place of employment. We have talked with many employers who *like* their employees to listen to our shows while they work. Fast rhythm music means fast work tempo."[46] In this situation, black radio served the needs of capital on both ends, providing music to drive a "fast work tempo" in the factory, and advertisements to sell goods to the African American workers.

On the other hand, some black radio stations were aware of the class and taste differences among their listeners, offering different kinds of programming to appeal to these different groups. The results of a study that KBWR, San Francisco, did of the 150,000 black residents in the Bay Area showed that the station's black programming attracted a high percentage of *all* the area's black residents: "Radio is the only medium that penetrates this vast audience in widely separated areas. A personal survey showed that 96% of the interviewees are acquainted with our Sepia Serenade programs. Some 63% prefer to listen in the morning, 91% in the afternoon, 48% in the evening, and 65% on Sunday."[47] These statistics suggest that KBWR achieved phenomenal cross-class appeal. KBWR's survey also raises the possibility that black stations attracted audiences that varied by class, time of day, gender, and region. A black station in Chattanooga was most successful with singers, orchestras, and popular music; in Hollywood, the black station relied primarily on rhythm and blues; in Nashville, the black station used gospel shows and food talk shows to attract women listeners in the midmorning, and rhythm and blues shows in the early morning and late afternoon to attract a male audience.[48]

Black radio did not please everyone. For some black listeners, especially in the middle classes, black radio was more about "segregation" than "congregation." But throughout the 1950s, black radio still contributed to African Americans' sense of consumer power in four ways: it integrated black working-class and lower-income consumers, especially, into the mainstream of American consumer culture; it provided a cross-class space (similar to black churches and black lodges) for the expression of racial pride and identification; it provoked some black listeners, especially those in the middle classes, to consider the consumer realm as a realm for protest; and it sparked national interest in the phenomenon of the "Negro market," which made boycotting for civil rights an increasingly effective tactic. Black listeners who resented black radio, such as those quoted earlier, were quick to suggest the boycott as a remedy for the forms of commercialization that they resented. On a grander scale, as the nation began to take black consumers more seriously, the boycott became a more effective tactic for political activism. Black radio made the "Negro market" into a national reality.

Conclusion

The relationship between the emergence of the Negro market and the high incidence of African American boycotting during the Civil Rights movement is unique in the history of advertising and activism. No minority group in the history of broadcasting has ever been as self-consciously recruited, or as actively discriminated against, as the African American audience commodity. Nor has any group in American history used the consumer boycott to the same extent—or with the same success—as African Americans did during the Civil Rights movement.

But the relationship is suggestive: before there could be a "revolt" of the Negro market there had to *be* a market, and no other medium directed to the black community had as much advertising from national advertisers as black radio in the 1950s. Radio advertisements—and community programming—assured African Americans that they had consumer power. When they used that consumer power to exert *political* pressure on southern businesses and northern lunch counters, the nation was shocked. So, perhaps, were some of the very advertisers that used stations like WDIA to "sell" the Negro market.

In the act of remembering this story, the story of the "forgotten fifteen million," we are forced to rethink a number of conventional wisdoms about advertising, African Americans, and activism in the 1950s. This story shows us that advertisers sought to recruit, and create, a heterogeneous population of consumers in the postwar era. This story shows us that African Americans were exposed to national advertising before the 1960s. And finally this story shows us that participation in the marketplace, for African Americans, had some positive consequences for black culture and black consciousness. After a decade of black radio, and a decade of black consumption of national products, consumer activism became a central tactic in a national struggle for African American civil rights. Boycotting would have been a less effective strategy—especially in terms of publicity— had black radio not created a national context for, and awareness of, a national Negro market.

Even Martin Luther King Jr., in a 1967 address to the black National Association of Radio Announcers (NARA), acknowledged the social, political, and cultural impact of black radio. While he stressed the role of the announcer in the black community, he also recognized black radio as a cultural "bridge" between blacks and whites: "I have come to appreciate the role which the radio announcer plays in the life of our people; for better or for worse, you are opinion makers in the community. . . . The masses of Americans who have been deprived of educational opportunity are almost totally dependent on radio as their means of relating to the society at large. . . . In a real sense, you have paved the way for social and political change by creating a powerful cultural bridge between black and white."[49] Black radio, with its white-teen spin-offs, did "create the sound that changed America." But before black radio crossed over, it offered the black community the sounds of national advertising and postwar consumption. It changed America by turning "segregation" into "congregation." It changed America by providing a "home embassy" in the segregated South and the urban North. It changed America by remembering the "forgotten fifteen million"—so that today we can do the same.

Notes

1   "The Forgotten 15,000,000," *Sponsor,* 10 October 1949, 24. *Sponsor* magazine was the first trade magazine to promote the Negro market in an annual feature.

2   Robin Kelley, *Race Rebels: Culture, Politics, and the Black Working Class* (New York: Free Press, 1994), 61. Like Kelley, Dana Frank argues that the political

tactics associated with consumer power, such as the boycott, were often linked to labor struggles, especially strikes. Dana Frank, *Purchasing Power: Consumer Organizing, Gender, and the Seattle Labor Movement, 1919–1929* (New York: Cambridge University Press, 1994). Robert Weems has written the only synthetic history of black consumer activism, *Desegregating the Dollar: African American Consumerism in the Twentieth Century* (New York: New York University Press, 1998). See also Andor Skotnes, " 'Buy Where You Can Work': Boycotting for Jobs in African-American Baltimore, 1933–1934," *Journal of Social History* (summer 1994): 735–61. For the best overview of black radio, see William Barlow, *Voice Over: The Making of Black Radio* (Philadelphia: Temple University Press, 1998). An excellent history of WDIA also exists: Louis Cantor, *Wheelin' on Beale: How WDIA-Memphis Became the Nation's First All-Black Radio Station and Created the Sound that Changed America* (New York: Pharos Books, 1992), 41–55.

3 Lizabeth Cohen, *Making a New Deal: Industrial Workers in Chicago, 1919–1939* (Cambridge: Cambridge University Press, 1990), 154. Lizabeth Cohen has been kind enough to share with me some materials from her book, *A Consumer's Republic: The Politics of Mass Consumption in Postwar America* (New York: Alfred A. Knopf, 2003).

4 Manning Marable, *How Capitalism Underdeveloped Black America: Problems in Race, Political Economy, and Society* (Boston: South End Press, 1983), 161–63. With this critique, Marable echoes the critique of David Caplovitz, who shows how lower-income communities have long been inundated by alcohol advertising, tobacco advertising, and sleazy credit schemes. David Caplovitz, *The Poor Pay More: Consumer Practices of Low-Income Families* (New York: Free Press, 1963).

5 Peter Fornatale and Joshua E. Mills, *Radio in the TV Age* (Woodstock, N.Y.: Overlook Press, 1980), 15.

6 "The Forgotten 15,000,000," 25.

7 "The Negro Market: $15,000,000,000 to Spend," *Sponsor*, 28 July 1952, 31; Joseph T. Johnson, *The Potential Negro Market* (New York: Pageant Press, 1952).

8 "The Negro Market: How to Tap $15 Billion in Sales," *Time*, 5 July 1954, 70.

9 Ibid.

10 Article from the *Pittsburgh Courier*, quoted in Cantor, *Wheelin' on Beale*, 170.

11 Albert Abarbanel and Alex Haley, "A New Audience for Radio," *Harper's*, February 1956, 57–59. See also J. Fred MacDonald, *Don't Touch That Dial! Radio Programming in American Life, 1920–1960* (Chicago: Nelson-Hall, 1979). The black press confirms this as well—in 1947, one year before WDIA began experimenting with black-appeal programming, *Opportunity* lamented the state of black acceptance into the industry: "Up to now little has happened in radio to ennoble the medium in the eyes of the Negro, and it must be conceded, if somewhat reluctantly, that despite hope and fervent prayer, not very much more

is likely to happen in the foreseeable future" ("On Stage . . . " *Opportunity,* July–September, 1947, 167).

12   "Biggest Negro Station," *Time,* 11 November 1957, 50.

13   "Negro Radio's Clients," *Sponsor,* 26 September 1959, 40–42.

14   "4th Annual Negro Section," *Sponsor,* 19 September 1955, 116. "*Ebony* magazine, for instance, runs a monthly saturation campaign in two dozen major Negro markets that begins some three days prior to publication and continues through the date it hits the stands" (133).

15   This summary is drawn from "Breaking the Color Barrier," chap. 3 of Cantor's *Wheelin' on Beale,* 41–55.

16   "Negro Results: Rich Yield for All Types of Clients," *Sponsor,* 28 July 1952, 38–39.

17   "The Carnation Story," WDIA promotional brochure, WDIA collection, Center for Southern Folklore; "Case Histories: Stations Report Sales and Audience Results," *Sponsor,* 28 September 1957, 41; "Negro Radio Results: Documented 'Case Histories' in Story Below Dramatize the Sales Power of Negro-Slanted Air Medium during 1955 Season," *Sponsor,* 19 September 1955, 141.

18   "Negro Radio: Over 600 Stations Strong Today—Negro-Slanted Shows Are Aired in 39 of 48 States, Cover 3.5 Million Negro Homes," *Sponsor,* 19 September 1955, 148.

19   Colin Campbell, *The Romantic Ethic and the Spirit of Modern Consumerism* (Oxford: Basil Blackwell, 1989), 18.

20   "The Negro Market: $15 Billion Annually—U.S. Negroes Buy Top-Quality, Brand-Name Goods of All Types. But You Must Know Where, When, and Why," *Sponsor,* 24 August 1953, 66.

21   "The Negro Market: $15 Billion Annually," 67.

22   Cantor, *Wheelin' on Beale,* 145.

23   "Negro Radio Results," *Sponsor,* 20 September 1954, 53, 155, 157.

24   Kelley, *Race Rebels,* 45. Frances Fox Piven and Richard A. Cloward refer to this phenomenon in similar terms, noting that the possibilities for black organizing by midcentury were enhanced by the cadre of black business and cultural leaders sustained by black patronage. They argue that this base was built up during the economic modernization of the South and also resulted from African American economic, political, and cultural "separation and concentration." Frances Fox Piven and Richard A. Cloward, *Poor People's Movements: Why They Succeed, How They Fail* (New York: Vintage Books, 1977), 204–5.

25   Kelley, *Race Rebels,* 45.

26   "The Negro Market: 15,000,000,000 to Spend," *Sponsor,* 28 July 1952, 30.

27   Joseph Wootton, "a Negro himself," and black-appeal station representative, quoted in "Negro Radio: Keystone of Community Life," *Sponsor,* 24 August 1953, 68.

28   B. B. King, taped interview, aired on WDUQ, Pittsburgh, 15 February 1998.

29 Exhibit "E," Additional Program Data, application for renewal of license, 1952, WDIA collection, Center for Southern Folklore.

30 Cantor, *Wheelin' on Beale*, 235.

31 "The Carnation Story," WDIA promotional brochure, WDIA collection, Center for Southern Folklore.

32 "The Negro Market: Why Buyers Are Looking Twice," *Sponsor*, 28 September 1957, 33.

33 Paul Hardman Sisco, "The Retail Function of Memphis" (Ph.D. diss., University of Chicago, 1954), 31.

34 Maurice Hulbert, interview, aired on WDUQ, Pittsburgh, 15 February 1998.

35 A potent example: the radio show "*Amos 'n' Andy*" boasted millions of black and white listeners in the 1930s and 1940s but suffered a backlash from black audiences and skittish advertisers when it crossed over to television. Although both the radio and the TV show had their fans and critics, the criticism leveled against the TV show was much stronger, and more effective, than the criticisms of the radio show that preceded it. Melvin Ely, *The Adventures of Amos 'n' Andy: A Social History of an American Phenomenon* (New York: Free Press, 1991).

36 Henry Allen Bullock, "Consumer Motivations in Black and White—II," *Harvard Business Review* 39, no. 4 (July–August 1961): 117. Throughout this study, he quotes from his book-length study of the Houston Negro Market, *Pathways to the Houston Negro Market* (Ann Arbor: Edwards Brothers, 1957).

37 William L. Smith, "A Comparison of the Attitudes of Negro Respondents in Columbus, Ohio, and Baton Rouge, Louisiana, toward Negro-Appeal Radio Programs Being Broadcast in Those Areas" (M.A. thesis, Ohio State University, 1957), 93–94.

38 Henry Allen Bullock, "Consumer Motivations in Black and White—I," *Harvard Business Review* 39, no. 3 (May–June 1961): 90.

39 "Tips on Selling via Negro Radio," *Sponsor*, 20 September 1954, 144.

40 "The Forgotten 15,000,000," 54.

41 Agency Analysis: Admen Tell Why and How They Buy Negro Radio," *Sponsor*, 28 September 1957, 39.

42 "The Negro Market: Why Buyers Are Looking Twice," 33.

43 Bullock, "Consumer Motivations in Black and White—II," 116.

44 Tips on Selling via Negro Radio," 148.

45 The Forgotten 15,000,000," 55.

46 "Tips on Selling via Negro Radio," 148.

47 "Tips on How to Get Most Out of Negro Radio," 78.

48 "Tips on Selling via Negro Radio," 148.

49 William Barlow, "Commercial and Noncommercial Radio," in *Split Image: African Americans in the Mass Media*, ed. William Barlow and Jannette L. Dates (Washington, D.C.: Howard University Press, 1990), 225.

Works Cited

Barlow, William. *Voice Over: The Making of Black Radio.* Philadelphia: Temple University Press, 1999.

Barlow, William, and Jannette L. Dates, eds. *Split Image: African Americans in the Mass Media.* Washington, D.C.: Howard University Press, 1990.

"Biggest Negro Station." *Time,* 11 November 1957, 50.

Bullock, Henry Allen. "Consumer Motivations in Black and White—I." *Harvard Business Review* 39, no. 3 (May–June 1961): 89–124.

——. "Consumer Motivations in Black and White—II." *Harvard Business Review* 39, no. 4 (July–August 1961): 112–33.

Campbell, Colin. *The Romantic Ethic and the Spirit of Modern Consumerism.* Oxford: Basil Blackwell, 1989.

Cantor, Louis. *Wheelin' on Beale: How WDIA-Memphis Became the Nation's First All-Black Radio Station and Created the Sound That Changed America.* New York: Pharos Books, 1992.

Caplovitz, David. *The Poor Pay More: Consumer Practices of Low-Income Families.* New York: Free Press, 1963.

Cohen, Lizabeth. *A Consumers' Republic: The Politics of Mass Consumption in Postwar America.* New York: Alfred A. Knopf, 2003.

——. *Making a New Deal: Industrial Workers in Chicago, 1919–1939.* Cambridge: Cambridge University Press, 1990.

Ely, Melvin. *The Adventures of Amos 'n' Andy: A Social History of an American Phenomenon.* New York: Free Press, 1991.

Fortnatale, Peter, and Joshua E. Mills. *Radio in the TV Age.* Woodstock, N.Y.: Overlook Press, 1980.

Frank, Dana. *Purchasing Power: Consumer Organizing, Gender, and the Seattle Labor Movement, 1919–1929.* New York: Cambridge University Press, 1994.

Kelley, Robin. *Race Rebels: Culture, Politics, and the Black Working Class.* New York: Free Press, 1994.

MacDonald, J. Fred. *Radio Programming in American Life, 1920–1960.* Chicago: Nelson-Hall, 1979.

Marable, Manning. *How Capitalism Underdeveloped Black America: Problems in Race, Political Economy, and Society.* Boston: South End Press, 1983.

"On Stage . . . " *Opportunity,* July–September 1947, 167.

Piven, Frances Fox, and Richard A. Cloward. *Poor People's Movements: Why They Succeed, How They Fail.* New York: Vintage Books, 1977.

Sisco, Paul Hardman. "The Retail Function of Memphis." Ph.D. diss., University of Chicago, 1954.

Skotnes, Andor. " 'Buy Where You Can Work': Boycotting for Jobs in African-American Baltimore, 1933–1934." *Journal of Social History* (summer 1994): 735–61.

Smith, William L. "A Comparison of the Attitudes of Negro Respondents in Columbus, Ohio, and Baton Rouge, Louisiana, toward Negro-Appeal Radio Programs Being Broadcast in those Areas." M.A. thesis, Ohio State University, 1957.

Sponsor Magazine, 1945–1968.

WDIA collection, Center for Southern Folklore, Memphis, Tennessee.

Weems, Robert E. *Desegregating the Dollar: African American Consumerism in the Twentieth Century.* New York: New York University Press, 1998.

PACKAGED ALTERNATIVES:

THE INCORPORATION AND GENDERING

OF "ALTERNATIVE" RADIO

Lauren M. E. Goodlad

A young couple talks at cross-purposes. She *wants desperately to share her feelings, communicate, and be validated by him.* He *wants to extoll the merits of a Canon photocopying machine. When he suggests a trip to the mall to snap up this hot commodity, she exults, "Shopping! You really* do *understand me . . . "*

A popular clothing outlet helps young men to interact successfully with their female peers. As a kid tries to chat up a girl he likes, his slacker's gaffes are corrected by a professional announcer's smooth talk. Rather than praise the girl's looks and invite her to watch mud wrestling, he should feign interest in poetry and ice dancing. With a final plug for the unspoken eloquence of cool male fashion, the spot concludes: "If you don't talk, she won't know how stupid you are."

Two teenage boys contrast the delights of dating girls and eating at Taco Bell. While girls are all too likely to demand conversation and commitment, they conclude a taco is a hungry guy's most obliging partner.

All of these advertisements were produced with young male consumers in mind. And all have been broadcast on KNDD 107.7, The End, Seattle's self-proclaimed leader in "new," which is to say "alternative," rock music—a classification presupposing a young, white, middle-class, and (increasingly) *male* audience.[1] It is not, I think, surprising to find these commercials—each of which tacitly appeals to rigid masculine norms—airing at a time when men compose only 40 percent of all U.S. students pursuing college degrees, and the liberal arts major, in particular, is perceived as a feminine domain.[2] Such commercials, in other words, not only bespeak an era of corporate-packaged youth culture but also suggest the reciprocities between marketing objectives and a turn-of-the-century society obsessed by sexual difference, dominated by an increasingly deterministic logic of hardwiring, hormones, Venusian women and Martian men.

In this essay, I attempt to situate this contemporary phenomenon in three overlapping historical contexts. The first is a material history of deregulation and the subsequent concentration of radio and other mass media within fewer and ever more powerful corporate hands. The second describes the corresponding efflorescence and "incorporation" of alternative music and the surrounding youth cultures. The third concerns my shifting personal relations to alternative radio as ardent fan and consumer, skeptical materialist critic, and, most recently, concerned feminist. Although my general purpose is to relate a condensed history of "alternative" radio and youth culture, from the late 1970s to the present day, my specific focus is on sex/gender. As an increasingly monopolistic entertainment industry seeks to segregate markets, I argue, a youth culture once known for its gender-blurring androgyny has conformed to, and now perpetuates, profitable patterns of sexual difference.

The Public Interest

It is instructive to recall that in the 1920s, one of the most conservative decades in U.S. history, Congress instituted the "public interest" doctrine, mandating that commercial broadcasters "emphasize" the "interests, needs, and convenience" of the people. Although repeatedly upheld after the introduction of television, this legislative doctrine was effectively undermined by the Reagan era's notion that market forces express, rather than compromise, the public's interest. Since 1981 both television and radio industries have been subject to increasing deregulation, and the public's ownership of the airwaves has been all but forgotten. Rules instituted over many decades to ensure that "broadcasters give back to their communities"—including those mandating public programming and limiting commercials—have been repealed or simply neglected.[3] The most important consequence of deregulation, however, has been to enable multiple ownership of radio, television, and cable stations, especially within the same broadcasting area. By effectively removing the limits placed on nationwide ownership, the Telecommunications Act of 1996 has completed the redefinition of the public and its interest from a model based on *citizenship* to one based on *consumption*.[4]

The rise of a media oligopoly, concentrating broadcasting and production within a few corporate hands, has further resulted in a drastic homogenization of content. In music radio, as newly acquired stations are expected to generate revenues in excess of their debts, emphasis on profitability translates into narrowly defined formats, hit-oriented playlists, slick DJs, and, of course, constant promotions and advertising. Although the total number of stations has grown, commercial radio has become increasingly formulaic. Programming in most major cities is identical, with, for example, "classic rock," Top 40, and "adult-oriented rock" stations playing the same songs to reach similar audiences. Because media conglomerates are, as Robert McChesney notes, "risk-averse," and wedded to "what has been commercially successful in the past," they shun diversity and experimentation in hopes of securing the large and demographically coherent audiences that advertisers pay to reach.[5] Listener complaints about repetition and lack of variety fall on deaf ears. Commercial DJs adhere to computer-generated playlists, taking few, if any, unpredictable requests.[6]

Mainstream Alternatives

Ironically, it was because of these effects that in the early 1980s, deregulation helped to codify "alternative" as a category designating the kind of music that commercial stations refused to play.[7] In the mid-1980s—when, as a recent college graduate, I worked in the "creative" department of a large corporation—alternative music culture helped me to define my own ostensible opposition to the mainstream. Although I did not immediately realize it, the postpunk, gothic, and industrial youth cultures with which I identified had already become the institutionalized products of a handful of entertainment conglomerates. At the same time, my local "alternative" radio station, New York's 92.7 WLIR was conforming to an ever more commercial format to attract new listeners and raise advertising revenues.[8]

It would be a mistake, however, to reduce alternative music culture entirely to the effect of deregulated radio. Readers of Dick Hebdige's classic account of the reappropriation of British punk in the late 1970s will be familiar with the manifold commodifying processes by which a youth culture's subversive meanings are first "diffused" (mass-produced) and consequently "defused" (politically neutralized).[9] Indeed, it is fair to say that the unanticipated profitability of punk subculture, in a market just beginning to exploit the global potential of MTV,[10] anticipated the entertainment industry's determination to cultivate and promote its own margins: to reappropriate "alternative" by establishing it in the paradoxical form of an institutionalized opposition to institutionalized culture. Hence, by the late 1980s and early 1990s, postpunk youth culture had developed the distinctly paradoxical and postmodern form of a mainstream avant-garde: a mass "alternative" for the self-consciously hip.[11]

In this commodified but ostensibly subcultural form, the postpunk music of this era, usually described as "new music" or "modern rock" by the radio stations that played it, provided stylistic and structural foundations for young middle-class identities. Marketed in the United States for white, usually college-bound or college-educated youth, the appeal of "alternative" was its deliberate challenge to the suburban norms that make such people demographically recognizable in the first place. Like most commercial alternative radio at this time, and in common with many noncommercial college stations, WLIR specialized in the latest new wave, gothic rock, and industrial dance music from the U.K. In the eyes of America's bored suburban teens and restless young professionals, Britain's mostly male, mostly working-class Thatcher-era bands, still riding hard on punk's leather coattails, were glamorously androgynous, exotically déclassé, and—if not precisely politically coherent—were, at any rate, rebellious, and in-your-face.

Of course, American youth might instead have sought alternatives in the contemporaneous hip-hop culture of urban African Americans. By and large, however, and despite some noteworthy crossovers, the postpunk preferred by white suburban youth remained aloof from inner-city music cultures. Through radio, clubs, magazines and fanzines, comic books, role-playing games, films, boutiques, and "postmodern MTV," white youths celebrated their dark sides in a U.K.-inspired, class- and gender-bending postpunk masquerade. In so doing, they tacitly declined to breach far more resistant boundaries of race.

Men Who Feel and Cry

As gothic rock, new wave, and punk-inflected alternative music entered the pop charts in the late 1980s and early 1990s, its distinctive trait was the cultivated display of androgynous masculinity: of men who feel and cry.

Male superstars of this era such as REM's Michael Stipe, the Cure's Robert Smith, U2's Bono, the Smiths' Morrissey, and eventually Nirvana's Kurt Cobain represented striking variations on the masculine heterosexual norm. These cult heroes of the suburban middle classes seemed to legitimate the oppositional edge of a mainstream "alternative." Their spectacular commercial successes entailed the popularization of nonheterosexist, antibinarizing notions of gender and sexuality, the trumpeting of progressive political causes, and the representation of male experience in a high-romantic and often decadent-aesthetic language of depth, pain, and failed transcendence.[12] Thus to the minds of many fans, the platinum albums, chart-topping hits, buzz-bin videos, and Grammy awards were not necessarily subcultural sellouts, but triumphs of the Other—an Other much like the gothic-artist-in-the-suburbs portrayed in Tim Burton's *Edward Scissorhands* (1990).

From a feminist point of view, this mainstream "alternative" represented a kind of antisexist sexism. For all its conspicuous androgyny, that is to say, postpunk music culture was unabashedly dominated by male musicians, prone to appropriating "femininity" as a male aesthetic credential rather than to empowering women. The gothic genres so integral to postpunk style obsessively rehearsed narratives of heterosexual masculinity in crisis. Through a familiar pattern in which traumatic loss (usually of a female beloved) finds expression in androgyny (as the lost female is replaced by a cathartic experience of "femininity"), normative male subjectivities were disrupted, refigured, and—to a certain extent—restored.[13] Despite obvious limitations, the effect of this androgynous male performance was to stress *likeness* between the sexes. Alternative's male icons ranged from introspective poets to veritable drama queens—always ready to cry, bleed, and shriek for the sake of articulating their passions. Such men might obsessively mourn the loss of a female beloved, or rail against the limitations of human understanding—but they could never be content to bond with a taco.

Indeed, this "homologizing" effect was evident in many distinctive features of the alternative music culture of this era.[14] For example, alternative music videos rarely featured the gratuitous display of female extras so common in more typically mainstream fare. Interviews with alternative musicians were unlikely to dwell on backstage sexual encounters with groupies. Commercial magazines and fanzines dedicated to the subject were produced with fans of both sexes in mind. The DJs at WLIR, glibly professional though they were, were interchangeably male and female, noteworthy for their in-depth knowledge of, and enthusiasm for, music, rather than for the cultivation of slick gendered personae.

Like most rock music fandoms, the alternative scene of the 1980s and early 1990s probably included more males than females. By and large, however, the experience was of a nongendered youth culture, equally accessible to both sexes and, just as important, tolerant toward nonheteronormative sexualities of many kinds. Indeed, defying normative expectations of gender and sexuality (and, to a lesser degree, of class) was precisely the point of the androgynous aesthetic—of being "alternative."

Mind the Gap

In the early 1990s, U.S. and U.K. alternative music cultures diverged for the first time in their respective histories. In the United States, bands such as Nirvana and Pearl Jam popularized grunge, a non-dance-oriented, angst-ridden variation on rock, with little relevance to the sped-up, hedonistic rave scene preferred by young post-Thatcherite Britons. Grunge fused a retrospective identification with the blues- and gospel-oriented rock of the early 1970s, with striking articulations of postpunk isolation, anger, and ennui.[15] By contrast, Britain's rave and techno were aggressively upbeat club- and dance-oriented music cultures—sites of a pointedly group-style escapism.

By the mid- and late 1990s, a variety of new transatlantic hybrids emerged.[16] At the same time, however, alternative music culture in the postgrunge era has become difficult to account for in primarily musical or stylistic terms. As the broadcasting and recording industries become increasingly monopolistic, industry profits depend more on the concerted constitution and cultivation of segregated markets. This underlying imperative deeply impresses the current musical product of today, with "alternative" proving no exception. When I interviewed her in 1998, Kim Monroe, a Seattle DJ, asserted that the late 1990s had produced the worst music she recalled in more than twenty years of listening to, and working in, radio. I agreed. But it is important to stress that the difference between alternative music before and after the 1990s is not reducible to the limitations of individual recording artists or particular trends.

New Order

Many factors contribute to the likelihood that, in the twenty-first century, alternative radio culture will be less "alternative" than ever. Artificially pumped up throughout the 1980s by the introduction of compact discs, today's highly consolidated music industry demands more profits and takes fewer risks. Starved of radio play, independent labels continue to founder or be acquired by entertainment giants such as AOL–Time Warner and Sony. The higher costs of promotion further militate against diversification and toward the hyping of a few chart-topping bands in each category.

Radio stations, meanwhile, attempt to maximize audience share by repeatedly playing the most popular singles in their category. Rather than compete by offering a wide range of music, commercial stations attempt to carve up the local market by creating class-, gender-, and age-specific demographics. In Seattle, for example, older fans of alternative music can listen to KMTT 100.3, The Mountain, a kinder, gentler alternative station, featuring more '80s hits, avoiding harder-edged new music, and airing lots of commercials for Volvos, Web TV, and life insurance. Younger fans, by contrast—and, in particular, younger *male* fans—are expected to prefer The End. The distinction reflects a common trend whereby alternative stations must decide whether to "stay young with their listening audience" or to age with them.[17]

Of course, were The Mountain and The End competitors, they might be loath to define themselves so narrowly and thus limit their potential listening audience. But The Mountain and The End are *not* competitors. Both stations are owned by Entercom, the fifth-largest radio broadcaster in the United States—a NYSE corporation owning forty-two radio stations nationwide, seven of which are in Seattle.[18] Unsurprisingly, stations owned and managed under the same corporate umbrella often find it more desirable to "share resources" than to compete: for example, choosing to broadcast certain artists, singles, and events on one station rather than on all stations, in order to more precisely define the audience of each.[19]

Although it is probable that as many as 40 percent of The End's listeners are female, the station considers its "core" audience to be men between ages eighteen and thirty-five. (In actuality, many listeners are much younger, but the self-proclaimed young-adult profile is more appealing to advertisers, and more suitable to the mature content of much of The End's broadcasting.) Although The End does not explicitly discourage female listeners, its deliberate male bias has become increasingly evident since 1996, when the station was purchased by Entercom.[20] By contrast, KBKS Kiss 106—another Seattle-based station, owned by CBS Radio—is expressly tailored to meet perceived feminine preferences.[21] Alternative music culture has thus become *gendered,* and the gender-blurring androgyny that dominated and arguably defined the category in its first decade is now passed over as an idiosyncrasy of the 1980s, or exploited as meaningless 1990s pastiche.

I Know What Boys Like

While classification by age has long been a factor in commercial radio (demonstrated by the long-standing popularity of "oldies" stations), sex/gender is a comparatively recent demographic emphasis. Here radio exemplifies a wider trend in which gender increasingly determines marketing strategies in publishing, television, movies, and various Internet-related media, and even on college campuses.[22] The fact is that for corporate broadcasters, demographic coherence is often more important than the actual number of listeners, making a sexually divided music culture an enhancement to profits. Unsurprisingly, what results is a vicious cycle of sorts: the more sexual difference is emphasized, the more segregation occurs, thus justifying even further amplification of gendered norms.

Rising to the challenge of the new "Martian" masculinity, The End cultivates a self-consciously hard, PC-bashing, if also somewhat juvenile, male persona. By contrast, Kiss 106—garnering the lion's share of supermarket, diet-pill, and shopping-mall advertising—features a more pop-oriented playlist, a pink Web site, and a larger number of female and soft-edged alternative artists. Kiss's approach to programming, blending pop with alternative, also represents a notable shift from classifying music by categories to classifying music according to perceived gender preferences. Crossovers—when, for example, an alternative band enters the pop charts and is consequently played on "hit" radio stations—have always been a factor.[23] Nevertheless when Kiss deliberately chooses to play popular artists such as Madonna and the Spice Girls alongside soft-edged alternative musicians, the logic is entirely different. Rather than allegiance to a music-specific style, Kiss's programming presupposes a feminine taste that privileges musical softness over any other factor. With a similar logic in mind, Kiss does not play Pearl Jam's hits—even though many are acoustic ballads—because the band's identification with grunge is, by now, perceived as a hard or masculine preference. Conversely, The End often avoids the softer alternative hits favored by Kiss and The Mountain.[24]

All of Seattle's commercial music radio stations—including The End, The Mountain, and Kiss—are dominated by male DJs. Kim Monroe is The End's only full-time female DJ, a singular status that she admits she enjoys. On the air she projects a tough, arguably "postfeminist" persona that is both distinct from, and harmonious with, the antics of some of her male colleagues.[25] The pattern of one or perhaps two full-time female DJs is, at least in Seattle, the apparent norm for commercial radio regardless of category. Rather than hire female DJs, stations express their degree of interest in female listeners largely through male DJs' personalities. Thus The Mountain's male DJs are neutral and professional; the ones on Kiss tend to be more chatty and gregarious; and The End's DJs distinguish themselves by digressing on subjects as varied as their favorite porn videos, their hangovers, and their experiments with Viagra.

Nice Guys Finish Last

One of the most telling indications of alternative radio's now rampant commercialism is its capitulation to "shock jock" programming, a genre pioneered by New York's Howard Stern. Here stations such as The End are responding to a national trend aimed at stanching the decline in targeted listeners by drawing in a young male audience by any means possible.[26] Across the FM dial, the dulcet tones of men behaving badly have become as familiar to Seattle mornings as the café latte. One notable example of the thirst for "shock" is the success of the L.A.-based Tom Leykis show, syndicated on seventy stations nationwide, including Seattle's KQBZ 100.7, The Buzz, yet another Entercom holding. When he first entered the Seattle market in 1999, Leykis's image was plastered all over the city's buses, accompanied by the telling phrase "Women hate nice guys." Leykis's show, the "stated 'public service'" of which is "to help men get their balls back,"[27] features a telephone format in which male callers vent their anger at women and inveigh against the alleged rule of political correctness. On one typical show, callers were invited to debunk the feminist myth of the "glass ceiling." Women don't become CEOs, the show concluded, because they are too lazy, too obsessed with child rearing, and too content with mooching off of men.

Significantly, this familiar brand of misogyny—damning women both if they do and if they do not conform to feminine stereotypes—has permeated alternative music culture. Recent radio hits have proclaimed that "nice guys finish last," have glamorized the lifestyle of the all-powerful pimp, and have staged monologues in which a hard-done-by guy rebels against his hyper-critical girlfriend, demanding, "What do I do right?"[28]

In another convergence between shock jock antics and alternative music radio, New York's 102.7 WNEW, once a legendary rock station that competed with WLIR for alternative listeners, has shifted to a talk-only format. As journalist Jesse Oxfeld notes, talk radio on the FM dial "is a relatively new development, created in recent years as increasingly formulaic music stations have foundered." WNEW's current hit is the Opie and Anthony show, New York's first-ranked program in the young male demographic. Where the Leykis show plays on pent-up male anger, Opie and Anthony specialize in "sophomoric sex humor." This approach is epitomized by the show's trademark "Whip 'em Out Wednesdays," during which female New Yorkers are encouraged to expose their breasts to male drivers sporting "W.O.W." bumper stickers. Like Leykis's harder-edged fare, such boys-will-be-boys antics invite young men to reclaim a state of nature putatively denied to them at home and in the workplace.[29] Men are encouraged to see themselves as forced to capitulate to female expectations in exchange for sex and companionship—and to rebel against those artificial constraints as often as possible. A similar dilemma is expressed in "She's Got the Look," a recent End hit by the postpunk band Guttermouth. Rehearsing a litany of gendered differences between himself and his girlfriend, the speaker promises, nevertheless, to change himself ("For you I'd do it . . . "), vowing to wash his car, secure employment, use foot deodorant, recycle his beer cans, and cancel his subscription to *Jugs* magazine. For Guttermouth as for the shock jocks, women thus ambivalently represent both indispensable sexual gratification and emasculating discipline.[30]

Situated within this context, it must be said that The End's talk-dominated morning show, introduced in 1997, and hosted by Andy Savage, represents a relatively tame variation on a growing national trend. Not unlike Opie and Anthony, the show features Howard Stern–like escapades, guest appearances by sex mavens and *Playboy* centerfolds, discussion of the day's trivia, telephone pranks, and listener call-ins. Interviews with, and live performances by, musicians also take place regularly. Savage, a self-professed admirer of David Letterman (rather than Stern), is rarely nasty and resentful in the manner of Leykis, usually less juvenile than Opie and Anthony, and displays nothing like the right-wing partisanship of Rush Limbaugh and his ilk. Carolyn Coffey, Savage's female cohost until 1998, was subordinate to Savage, but nevertheless a voice in her own right. She frequently disagreed with Savage and never lapsed into the trite supportive role to which so many female cohosts are relegated.[31] When, as they often did, Savage and Coffey gave advice to listeners who called in with personal problems, the advice was usually compassionate and sound, never crudely exploitative.

Some of the "shock" elements of the show do, however, warrant comment. One recurrent setup called "the roses" emulates the sensationalism of television shows like *Jerry Springer*.[32] I confess to having thoroughly enjoyed a bicycle race wherein contestants—stark naked except for the numbers pasted to their genitals, pedaled up Seattle's steep Capitol Hill to win concert tickets. When I interviewed Savage, he did not understand why I insisted on distinguishing between this display of athletic prowess—as well as male cheek—and a subsequent promotion in which a naked woman was driven down Seattle's busiest freeway in the back of a pickup truck. Several months before, I had written to the station suggesting that they air a debate over whether to play a recent single entitled "Smack My Bitch Up." The morning show aired the debate, and although there was no definite consensus among callers, the single is, to my knowledge, now played only after midnight.[33] In a sense, it is because so much of the show is far better than the Howard Stern prototype—so much of it genuinely and uninvidiously humorous and affable (if not remotely alternative)—that the lapses into misogyny are so disturbing.

An example occurred when on a day after Coffey had been let go, Savage and another male DJ conducted a telephone interview with the band Green Day. The host asked if it is true that "nice guys finish last," to which Green Day, known for their irreverent, bad-boy humor, replied, yes, and especially in love: James Brown did it to his woman with a crowbar, and he is the king of soul. All the guys laughed, and Green Day followed by asking if the kid whom they pulled onstage when they last played Seattle now "gets lots of chicks." Yes, replied Savage, "I think he gets laid a lot." Asked what they planned to give each other for Christmas, one band member described a giant dildo, and the other mentioned a butt plug. This presumably hilarious conversation was rebroadcast at various points during the day to promote the morning show's singular attractions.

The irony is that while Savage's show is often entertaining, most fans of "alternative" would prefer to hear *music* in the morning. The problem is partly that so many other stations have moved to shock-oriented formats that Seattle's DJs now vie for media attention as well as audience share.[34] Savage explains that his goal is to make people laugh, and not to offend anyone, but he seems genuinely to believe that frequent discussion of sex and antics involving female nudity are what it takes to get people's attention.[35] Yet while Savage's show appears to have won a satisfactory audience, The End has since truncated it.[36] During drive time (the popular listening hours between 9 and 10 A.M. and 5 and 6 P.M.), the station broadcasts "end-to-end music." Ironically, "end-to-end music" features a more diverse and less repetitive playlist, with more personalized input from the DJ and fewer commercial interruptions: precisely what alternative radio offered in the days before corporate profits were its self-evident priority.

Presumably, were the station to adopt an "end-to-end music" format all day long, it would have a happier core audience, but one that is more demographically diffuse, less disproportionately male, and possibly smaller. (They would also have far less time to air commercials and advertise the station's own promotions.) Describing the difference between the station's 1991 debut and the current avatar, one unhappy listener explains, "They have killed what the original End Team built by pounding the same songs into our heads over and over."[37] Because young men have been found to listen to radio for only a few minutes at a time, the logic is that only by playing the most popular songs as often as possible—including the most popular older songs—can the station successfully increase its target audience. Nevertheless it seems likely that by attempting to overcome the problem of fickle listeners, commercial radio has in fact exacerbated it. Alternative radio fans in the 1980s were typically extremely loyal to their radio station, since they closely identified it with their alternative way of life.[38] By revealing the underlying commercialism, and, especially, by reducing variety, stations such as The End have increased listeners' proclivity to "surf" from channel to channel. Hence another reason why emphasizing masculinity is so potentially desirable a feature. In the station's present-day form, Seattle's young males might no longer distinguish greatly between the alternative credentials of The End's music and that of competing formats—but they might, nevertheless, be persuaded to identify themselves with the station that brings topless women into the studio and promotes such stunts on its Web site.

We Can Be Heroes

Nevertheless it seems clear that there is only so much mileage to be had from a topless woman in a pickup truck. For obvious reasons, radio is not the ideal medium through which to exploit nudity: the description of Seattle drivers' responses to a topless woman during rush hour, delivered live by an intern named Snot, is not the kind of programming to generate long-term listener interest. The fact remains that the recording industry, and, to an extent, the music radio industry, have a considerable investment in making sure that youths of both sexes continue to find heroes in popstars: alternative or otherwise. Yet as the diversion to shock radio suggests, that investment has, to a certain extent, been damaged by commercialism.

Indeed, after years of declining sales, during which the recording industry lost out to video games and the Internet, some insiders began to opine that alternative music needed to recuperate the passion of its postpunk and grunge-era glory days.[39] Androgynous masculinity returned in the late 1990s in the form of Marilyn Manson, whose calculated homage to David Bowie is, perhaps, convincing for fans too young to remember the original Ziggy Stardust.[40] Although many catchy, inventive, and moving songs do get played on the radio, the commercial "alternatives" of today often take the form of trendy pastiche. This was especially true of 1997 and 1998, years in which End listeners harked to Oasis's incongruous blend of crass machismo and imitative Beatlemania, and witnessed the bizarre resurgence of swing.[41]

With some notable exceptions (e.g., Manson, Rage against the Machine, Radiohead),[42] fewer and fewer alternative bands are cultivating the enduring fandoms that once characterized a youth culture in which favored musicians were revered as prophets. I have no doubt that today's young fans are drawn to alternative music for the same reasons as their predecessors, and with many of the same effects. But in today's ultracompetitive and profit-driven market, the rhythm has changed. Record labels—determined to find and to milk the next big thing—seldom promote more than one or two singles off of individual albums. Popular singles are played incessantly while they are hot, and then disappear. Only a rare few join the hundred or so songs deemed sufficiently popular to constitute the station's regular catalog. What was once a pantheon of alternative heroes increasingly resembles a crowded field of fallen wonders, forgotten flashes in the pan.

What is clear, therefore, is a potential divide between the kind of "alternative" music culture that serves radio stations like The End, and the kind that serves the Napster-besieged recording industry.[43] Radio stations can thrive off of catchy, overplayed hits that attract a mass audience, using promotions and shock-jock antics to boost listener interest. Record companies, by contrast, rely on a more dedicated consumer, willing to spend as much as twenty dollars to buy a full-length compact disc (complete with the liner notes and other trimmings unavailable through free downloads). As young male consumers spend more time and money on everything from hit movies to computer games, soda pop, fast food, fashion, sports equipment, car stereos, and chat lines—all products that are advertised on The End—the share they devote to music diminishes. Moreover, even as they help to create a male consumer with numerous extramusical desires, stations such as The End are in a position to increase their own revenues by sponsoring and promoting special concert events.[44]

Since the late 1990s, one of the most notable trends in alternative radio has been the fusion of rap and hip-hop with rock and heavy metal. This marks a difference between the 1980s, when white alternative fans expressed little interest in a largely black hip-hop culture, and the 1990s, when white alternative musicians began consciously to model themselves on African American precedents. Along with the Beastie Boys, one of the most influential pioneers of rap-rock fusion is Rage against the Machine, a racially mixed L.A. band, who—significantly—represent an important exception to the apolitical commercialism of recent "alternatives."[45] It is ironic, therefore, to find the hard-rocking, aggressive rap sound that many fans identify with Rage's leftist politics appropriated by newer artists such as Kid Rock and Limp Bizkit. For these newcomers, black hip-hop and political militance provide desirable stylistic models for the crafting of commercial masculine personae. Hence Limp Bizkit's "Nookie," ranked number one by End listeners in 1999, translates a discernibly Rage-indebted sound into depoliticized anger at an unfaithful girlfriend.[46] In Kid Rock's seventh-ranked "Bawitdaba," the white speaker identifies himself with inner-city life, attributing the plight of his incarcerated "homies" and misunderstood "hoods" to everything from crooked police officers and hookers to the IRS. Unfortunately, this cross-race identification lapses into misogynistic fantasy in "Cowboy," another Kid Rock favorite, in which the speaker imagines himself as an L.A. pimp.[47] An even more over-the-top instance of fantasized, hip-hop-inspired omnipotence is Crazy Town's "Revolving Door," a 2001 hit in which the speaker boasts about his mansion, "the way that [he's] hung," and his consequent ability to keep an endless supply of women "in rotation."[48] Hence, as in hip-hop itself, commercialization has defused the political opposition voiced in Rage's groundbreaking fusion, or in African American pioneers such as Public Enemy. Moreover, as political radicalism is reduced to stylistic pastiche, male political passion is conflated with misogyny, sexism, and homophobia.[49]

As I write (in mid-2001), it is as yet too soon to determine the extent to which the current surge of rap-rock fusions is a passing fad. To be sure, rap-rock has already outlasted such minor ephemera as swing, and judging by its commercial success, it may well enjoy as long a run as grunge did. But even if it does, will this latest "alternative" provide the lasting heroes of grunge and its postpunk precursors? Glancing at the station's "Top End Songs of the Millennium," what stands out is how very few late 1990s hits— rap-rock or otherwise—made it into the top two hundred. Is it possible that those who voted were conscious of a qualitative difference between men who feel and cry, and the recent emphasis on posturing machismo? Is it evident, perhaps, that when music and music videos follow the cue of shock jocks, porn flicks, men's magazines, and late-night TV, the entire notion of "alternative" music collapses, reduced as it is to a kind of license for brazenness? If the answer to these questions is yes, can the recording industry survive in the postdigital age by peddling ever more explicit musical products, to an ever younger audience?

Given the uncertainty ahead, it is unsurprising to find the recording industry exploring strategies of many kinds. In lieu of advertising new releases and indirectly promoting radio play, labels might begin simply to buy blocks of airtime for the music they want to pitch to consumers. When this proposal was discussed on The End's morning show, both listeners and DJs were predictably skeptical. The DJs were loath to be stripped of what little autonomy over programming remains to them. Listeners, for their part, are already compelled to change channels frequently in order to hear music they like. It seems likely, however, that neither DJs nor listeners, but rather corporate executives, will decide whether to develop the idea further.

An Alternative to "Alternative"

There is, in fact, another option available to Seattle's alternative music enthusiasts. Indeed, the city is fortunate in supporting a bona fide (non-commercial) alternative radio station, 90.3 KCMU, licensed through the University of Washington, but funded directly by listeners through semiannual pledge drives.[50] Although KCMU easily raises the support it needs to cover its operating budget, the station remains vulnerable to outside interests eager to purchase it and turn it into yet another commercial enterprise. So far the University of Washington remains committed to public radio and uninterested in instituting the kind of management that would make the station more competitive with commercial counterparts.[51]

What is interesting about KCMU is how emphatically it contrasts with commercial radio stations, even the comparatively "alternative" commercial stations of the 1980s. KCMU not only airs no commercials (apart from mentioning community sponsors) but also conforms to no established commercial format. The morning show, hosted by John Richards, is among the most recognizable of its offerings, concentrating on recent alternative and indie rock (some of which is eventually played on commercial stations). But other shows are either devoted to specialty categories that would, on commercial radio, receive little or no airplay (indie rap and hip-hop, blues, world music, reggae, jazz), or they are so diverse and unpredictable as to suggest no particular category. Although, to be sure, it is possible to construct a KCMU listener profile—one that would doubtless demonstrate that listeners are, by and large, college-educated and middle-class—the management of the station has no interest in this endeavor. KCMU believes that it serves a comparatively wide age demographic, plays far more non-European and African American music than any other station claiming "alternative" status, and makes no assumptions about the tastes of male and female listeners.[52]

The Girl with the Thorn in Her Side

In 1994, when I first moved to Seattle, I immediately became a loyal End listener. On The End I discovered many of the same bands that were then being played regularly on WLIR, with, perhaps, some additional emphasis on grunge (an obvious Seattle favorite). Friends of mine were already devotees of KCMU, and I occasionally tuned into the station while in their company. I found it jarring when the programming shifted from experimental forms of alternative rock, to hip-hop, to country music or world music. I was not necessarily opposed to any of this music; I was fully capable of enjoying it on a case-by-case basis. But, to put it simply, KCMU was too alternative a station to suit my well-entrenched "alternative" predilections.

Although I did not fully realize it for quite some time, I had become identified with a commercial music culture that, however glib and formulaic, provided me with an idiom that I valued, both as a teacher, and for its own sake. By keeping up to date with "alternative," I believed I could track the passions and interests of my students; I could peer into their cultural unconscious while simultaneously enlivening my own. By functioning as a "mainstream avant-garde," alternative music culture could help me to identify with students considerably younger than myself, just as it had helped me, as a college student, to relate to male peers, and, as a young professional, to relate to like-minded individuals at the workplace. The best part of all is that I could do all this while taking part in a culture that seemed deliberately, even insistently, to blur artificial boundaries between the sexes.

That gender-transcending potential is, I believe, at least for the present, almost entirely gone. Although I still enjoy some of The End's programming, too often I feel as though I am poaching on the terrain of teenage boys.[53] Moreover, the more I listen to KCMU, the less tolerance I have for overplayed singles—much less for commercials, promotions, and the swagger of DJs. I also no longer wish, as I once did, that KCMU would commit itself exclusively to playing alternative rock music. In the absence of a viable youth-culture community, it seems unjustifiable to wish to exclude forms of music that are already all but inaudible from this rare public forum—this truer alternative. Indeed, perhaps through more concerted support of public radio, through a wider recognition of its value, it might be possible to form a community based on diversity and the public interest rather than on what—at least since World War II—has become the most typical "subcultural" foundation: the alienation of youth. That was undoubtedly the vision of those who nearly succeeded in enabling community organizations to broadcast on low-power radio stations, a plan killed by commercial broadcasters and National Public Radio in December 2000.[54]

Like so many of the new products it advertises and discusses—movies and television like *Orgazmo* and *The Men's Show*, the Hooters restaurant chain, *Maxim* or *Gear* magazine—The End and its ilk have helped to concretize a new masculine "nature," exemplified by the careless misogyny of DJs, and encapsulated in the tag line from a frequently played commercial: "If you don't talk, she won't know how stupid you are." Men, according to this formula, are simpleminded, instinct driven, goal oriented, competitive, and unemotional. But for their relentless sex drives, they would be content to play video games and turn up their tunes. Women, by contrast, are complex, inscrutable, sensorial, creative, unpredictable, demanding, and maddening. The irony is that women are everything that alternative's male musicians once were. Indeed, it is perhaps for that very reason that today's men are expected—even encouraged—to resent women so deeply.

To the seasoned ear, the recent successes of Korn and Marilyn Manson, both of whom have captured large male audiences by dramatizing male pain and frustration, may seem woefully imitative and insincere.[55] Yet whatever their limitations, the success of these bands testifies to the continuing relevance of the man who feels and cries. Indeed, even white rapper Eminem's disturbingly homophobic and misogynistic music represents, as Richard Kim has observed, male "pain and negativity" in a deliberately commercialized form. "Faggot," says Eminem, "doesn't necessary mean gay people," but "just . . . taking away your manhood," an experience he ties to his humiliating past as a "poor white trash" schoolboy.[56] Where 1980s predecessors had sought to heal such traumatic losses by an alternative exploration of the feminine, today's more rigid sexual norms have invited a new generation of male sufferers to *negate* the feminine in a kind of anesthetizing psychic disavowal. Hence Eminem's imagined violence against women and "faggots" is but the darker obverse of Kid Rock's omnipotent "Cowboy"—whose limitless mastery over women implies his invulnerability. What is certain, in any case, is that ostensibly passé forms of masculinity are inscribed everyday in the music of bands who are unlikely—at least for now—to be played on radio stations like The End.[57] For all of these reasons, it remains possible and even important to believe that the man content to bond with a taco, and the man behind the "Revolving Door," are still largely the wished-for projections of their corporate sponsors.

Epilogue

In March 2001, 90.3 KCMU became KEXP, reflecting a new "partnership" between the station, the University of Washington, and Experience Music

Project, a recently opened interactive music museum, described by the *Seattle Times* as Microsoft billionaire Paul Allen's "$240 million rock 'n' roll plaything."[58] When rumors first surfaced about the contemplated changes, fans of the station feared that the University had succumbed to commercial pressure in one of its most insidious forms.[59] But for the time being at least, the partnership has enhanced the profile of the station without any discernible changes to its programming or staff. KEXP, now located off-campus, has almost double the broadcast signal of its predecessor, and—even more significant—its CD-quality audio stream is at the vanguard of Web broadcasting technology.[60] Hence Seattle's community music radio station—still largely supported by local listeners—is now at the forefront of a new radio technology that "could make the AM/FM dial obsolete."[61]

If, as is expected, the Internet goes wireless, it will almost certainly transform radio as we know it. To be sure, a theoretically infinite wireless Internet will provide a means to bypassing corporate radio; but will it provide a means to realizing the community interest? In fact, some of the most innovative Internet broadcasting options offer a personalized playlist, a feature that not only removes "radio" from a local context but also dispenses with the tangible listening community that the current technology provides.[62] For the moment, however, commercial stations (many of which, like The End, also broadcast over the Web), still dominate despite the growing popular malaise—not least because listeners continue to tune in to traditional radio in their cars.

Since my first draft of this essay in 1999, several additional changes have taken place in Seattle radio. Kiss 106, Seattle's not so subtly "feminine" station, is now a memory; replaced in 2000 by a more hits-oriented adult contemporary format. Howard Stern has at long last entered the Seattle market, with the city's buses currently proclaiming his appearance on 99.9 KISW, Entercom's classic rock station. Andy Savage has a new and younger female cohost on The End's morning show. Although it is difficult to document such changes without inside knowledge, it appears to me that his show has begun to recognize the station's large adolescent listenership. To be sure, sex is still a recurring theme: cropping up in general discussion, through guests hawking sex-related products, or through gags such as inviting strangers to "make out" in the studio to win free concert tickets. Savage himself has recently married, prompting his younger and single cohosts to tease him about his newfound enthusiasm for "relationships."

What seems clear, in any case, is that events involving public nudity figure less, and interviews with bands figure more.

Last week, according to The End's Web site, Mark Hoppus, a member of Blink 182, called, allowing the DJs to discuss the "inside scoop on the new CD and the truth on farts and poop." Despite this unpromising start, I clicked on the file; the band in question records a catchy and often enjoyable variety of postpunk pop. The discussion focuses on the new video (which I have not seen). When the record label wanted to spend $750,000, the band resisted, preferring an unscripted approach, shot on the streets of L.A. with a handheld camera. In the end, the video *was* shot on the streets but still cost $500,000 to make. Hoppus verifies that the homeless person who is found in the video and taken to a strip club was a real homeless person—though what became of him afterward, Hoppus does not know. The old lady seen shaving her head was paid only $100 for her trouble and, Hoppus muses, may not have hair again for many years to come. I click off before the discussion turns to farts and poop.

It could be my imagination, but in the last few weeks I have sensed a certain sea change. Rap-rock acts from 1999 and 2000 such as Kid Rock, Limp Bizkit, and Eminem are no longer new, and more recent examples of the genre, such as Crazy Town's "Revolving Door," have slipped from the charts. In the meantime, newer End favorites are tending more toward postpunk and other rock fusions—familiar musical fare, in which young male angst is less frequently tied to misogyny. A commercial for a local car dealership is urging men not to be too "practical" when they choose a car; the right choice, they are told, requires "bonding" and "passion."

The End is currently playing two songs that, to my mind, represent the best in today's alternative music. The first is "Short Skirt, Long Jacket" by Cake, a band played frequently on KCMU before crossing over into the mainstream. What I like most is the song's witty ironization of male expectations of women as they are often voiced in song. The girl whom the speaker desires will cut through red tape with a machete, tour facilities, drive a Chrysler Le Baron, and have "a voice that is dark like tinted glass." She will wear a "short skirt" and a "loooooooooong jacket." In the last four days, driving to and from work for about twenty minutes during the most popular radio hours, I have managed to hear the song every day, and sometimes once each way. The second song is "Rexall," from the new solo album by Dave Navarro, a musician who started out in 1991 as the guitarist for Jane's Addiction, a dark-edged, hard-rocking California band. The song recalls me to grunge at its best—the last wave of "alternative" music to focus on the experience of men who feel and cry. It is a brooding tale of dying love that manages to convey the speaker's pain without misogyny: "There is no love left in your eyes, / There is love between your thighs."

When I heard the song on The End this afternoon, the DJ introduced Navarro as the man now having sex with MTV celebrity and *Maxim* cover girl Carmen Electra.

Notes

Early versions of this essay were presented at an MLA session on radio in December 1998, and at the Radiocracy conference in Cardiff in November 1999. My thanks to DJs Kim Monroe, Andy Savage, Carolyn Coffey, and John Richards. Sara Pourghasemi's independent study on radio culture catalyzed my interest in this area, Bryce Bernard's research assistance was most helpful, and Ken Nagelberg's expertise was invaluable. Thanks also to Mark Sammons and Kelly Davis, and to Susan Squier for her superb editorial comments.

1 Like most commercial stations of its kind, the current management of KNDD does not explicitly describe itself as an "alternative" radio station, preferring more neutral terms such as "new music." But End listeners frequently use the term to describe the music they hear on the station, and the station and its ilk are described as "alternative" within industry circles. The term "alternative" has become increasingly vexed, simultaneously signifying opposition to, and an established sector *within,* mainstream commercial music. In this essay, unless otherwise specified, I use the term to connote a paradoxical category that both is and claims not to be mainstream and commercial. Wherever appropriate I use quotation marks to emphasize attendant ironies and ambiguities.

2 On the declining enrollment of young men, see Tamar Lewin, "American Colleges Begin to Ask, Where Have All the Men Gone?" *New York Times,* 6 December 1998 (on-line).

3 Janine Jaquet, "Taking Back the People's Air," *The Nation* 266, no. 21 (8 June 1998): 13. See also Charles Fairchild, "Deterritorializing Radio Deregulation and the Continuing Triumph of the Corporatist Perspective in the USA," *Media, Culture, and Society* 21, no. 4 (1999): 549–61; and, for the most extensive account, Robert W. McChesney, *Rich Media, Poor Democracy: Communication Politics in Dubious Times* (New York: New Press, 2000), esp. chap. 1.

4 Fairchild, "Deterritorializing Radio," 552–53. On the concentration of media, see also Robert L. Hillard, *The Broadcast Century* (Boston: Focal Press, 1992), 226–80; Fairchild, 553–55; and McChesney, *Rich Media,* esp. 29–31, 85–87, and 163–64. As McChesney succinctly puts it in a recent article, the 1996 act "transformed

[radio] almost overnight . . . into a highly concentrated market in which a handful of firms own hundreds of stations and nearly every market is dominated by two or three firms maxed out with six to eight stations each" ("Kennard, the Public, and the FCC," *The Nation* 272, no. 19 [14 March 2001]: 19).

5 McChesney, *Rich Media,* 33.

6 My description of deregulation's effects on music radio is indebted to Sara Pourghasemi's unpublished essay "Radio Culture." A 1998 article in *The Stranger,* a free Seattle weekly, was devoted to readers' complaints about The End. One reader claimed to have received the following response when he called to complain about repetition: "I'm playing what the people want to hear, you stupid fuck! Nobody listens to the radio for more than ten minutes!" (Kathleen Wilson, "Stick a Fork in Them," *The Stranger Music Quarterly,* 15 October 1998, 3). I should add that many of the DJs I interviewed said that verbal abuse, particularly from young listeners, was one of the most difficult aspects of their jobs. Andy Savage, The End's morning DJ, has aired conversations with callers in which he explains (civilly) that the station is obligated to play what people are buying, for as long as they are buying it, in order to attract the largest listening audience. The explanation indicates how little the station conceals its commercial priorities and also how much it relies on its "alternative" image to distinguish itself from a "hits" station pure and simple.

7 In contrast to my more general use of the term, Nagelberg strictly defines "alternative" music and radio as noncommercial (usually either public or college-owned radio). In so doing, he demonstrates why it is so difficult to stabilize the definition; in particular, why it is both easy and desirable to appropriate "alternative" for decidedly commercial purposes. "Alternative radio," he explains, "program[s] music that is either too new, too complex, or too controversial to be played on commercial radio stations." Noncommercial radio is thus implicated in legitimating the lucrative "alternative" credentials of many highly successful commercial products. Corporate producers and broadcasters monitor the reception of bands signed to independent labels with an eye toward developing the latest in commercial "alternatives." Indeed, profitable indie labels (such as the Seattle-based Sub-Pop) are frequently purchased by huge entertainment conglomerates. Hence, in addition to promoting commercial "alternatives" to commercial music, the current climate features "independent" record labels that are both directly and indirectly dependent on corporate support. My thanks to Ken Nagelberg for permitting me to cite his unpublished conference paper "What Is the Frequency, Kenneth? A Case Study of the Mainstreaming of College Radio." See also Ken Nagelberg, "No Alternative: The Death of Alternative Radio in Baton Rouge," *Radio Resistors Bulletin* 9 (March 1995).

8 Characteristic of the effects of deregulation during this period, WLIR (broadcast from Long Island) was for a time WDRE but is now WLIR again. It was and remains a commercial (rather than public or college-owned) radio station.

9 Dick Hebdige, *Subculture: The Meaning of Style* (New York: Routledge, 1979), esp. 92–99.

10 Other important merchandising developments in the popular music industry in the 1980s and early 1990s included tie-ins with movies, Lollapalooza-style mega-tours, and, of course, the Internet.

11 I describe these notions at length in the introduction to *Goth Style*, a forthcoming coedited anthology. Some of my thoughts on the subject have been published in "Postmodern Gothic: The Lost Brides of Frankenstein and the 'Dark Taste of Fear,'" *Diegesis: Journal for the Association of Research in Popular Culture* 1 (fall 1997): 21–53.

12 On the representation of male experience, see my "Postmodern Gothic."

13 See my discussion of the gothic rock music of the Cure, the popular comic book novella *The Crow,* the film version of Anne Rice's *Interview with the Vampire,* and Poppy Z. Brite's popular novel *Lost Souls* in my "Postmodern Gothic."

14 On the modern (post-Enlightenment) shift from "homologous" to "incommensurable" constructions of sexual difference—a shift from understanding sexual difference as a difference in *degree* to understanding it as a difference in *kind*—see Thomas Laqueur, "Orgasm, Generation, and the Politics of Reproduction," in *The Making of the Modern Body,* ed. Catherine Gallagher and Thomas Laqueur (Berkeley: University of California Press, 1987), 1–41.

15 The failure of grunge to attract a sizable U.K. audience is discussed in Flavia, "Rebels without a Clue," *Cups* 87 (February 1998): 18–19.

16 Bands like Rage against the Machine (U.S.) and the Prodigy (U.K.), for example, fused hip-hop beats and raps with elements of the gothic, industrial, grunge, and techno long familiar to alternative fans.

17 Interviews with Kim Monroe, May–September 1998.

18 Entercom has almost doubled in size since my first draft of this paper in 1999: as of June 2001 they own ninety-five stations nationwide and boast of operating "multistation groups" in eighteen markets including twelve of the nation's top fifty markets, one of which is Seattle. Significantly, the company's Web site boasts that "radio enables advertisers to pinpoint their message to specific consumer groups with demographically specific radio stations that maximize their advertising investment." See www.entercom.com.

19 Interview with John Richards, February 1999.

20 Prior to Entercom, The End was owned by Viacom, owners of MTV. I am not suggesting that Entercom invented or even intentionally deployed a masculinizing strategy as such. It seems far more likely that having acquired The End while already operating The Mountain, Entercom encouraged the station to pursue its "core" audience (men under age thirty-five) in ways that minimized overlap with their "adult" radio station. That, in the postgrunge era, such men (often adolescents) would be expected to desire a "hard" masculine persona is not, of course, the result of any single corporate policy.

21 Like The End, Kiss does not make its gender preference explicit. According to its (pink-shaded) Web site, 62 percent of its listeners are female, and over 90 percent are between the ages of eighteen and forty-four. (Radio stations seem loath to admit that many of their listeners are under eighteen, although the Kiss Web site is happy to inform potential advertisers that a significant share of its listeners are the parents of young children.) On Kiss's format change in 2000, see the epilogue to this essay.

22 See Lewin, "American Colleges," for a report on how liberal arts colleges have begun to design different brochures for male and female students, emphasizing internships for the former and intimate classroom experience for the latter.

23 When, for example, "Lovesong," a catchy single off the Cure's otherwise brooding and lyrically disturbing album *Disintegration* (1989), peaked at number two, long-standing fans might have heard the song on "alternative" stations such as WLIR (then WDRE), or they might have heard it on Z100, a Top 40 station in the same listening area.

24 The latest releases from Alanis Morrissette—an artist heavily played on The End as recently as 1997—received very little KNDD airplay. Yet the Grammy-winning Morrissette was among the most heavily played "alternative" artists on the "feminine" Kiss 106. Again, it is not necessarily the case that The End consciously conspires against softer and female alternative artists. In addition to monitoring sales and nationwide airplay, the station introduces new music during specialty shows and tracks listener requests. Such active listeners—probably among the youngest of The End's audience—are the most likely to be influenced by the kinds of music the station has already committed to playing. Thus the "masculine" preference becomes a self-fulfilling prophecy. Moreover, the most frequently played singles in any given period are played on an almost hourly basis, for weeks and even months at a time, allowing for astonishingly little variety. This means that the great majority of new alternative singles, let alone new music, receive little or no airplay.

25 Monroe, for example, has commented on music videos featuring partial female nudity, protesting against the absence of "equal time" for men. Carolyn Coffey, the female cohost of The End's morning show until 1998, often voiced comparable opinions. It is perhaps fair to say that the station's deliberate anti-PC rebelliousness is, at best, offset by the predisposition to favor "equality" between the sexes. Unfortunately, while "equality" is sometimes invoked to criticize "PC" preferences—for example, the Lilith Fair tour's preference for female backup bands, which was criticized by The End's morning DJ—it is, to my knowledge, never invoked to question why so few female artists are played, or so few female DJs are employed. On the whole, however, I feel disposed to congratulate Monroe and Coffey for the spirit and integrity they display on the air. Their voices, however circumscribed, offer important exceptions to what would otherwise be an unmitigated boy's club.

26 According to one survey, listening among those age twenty-five and under de-
    clined by 10 percent between 1993 and 1999. Cited in Richard A. Martin, "Brave
    New Radio," *Seattle Weekly,* 12–18 August 1999 (on-line).

27 Mark Rahner, "Shock Jock Tom Leykis Strikes a Receptive Chord in Men—and
    Brings in Plenty of Static Too," *Seattle Times,* 13 August 2000 (on-line).

28 "Nice Guys Finish Last" is the title of a 1998 song by the postpunk band Green
    Day; Kid Rock's "Cowboy," one of the Top 20 End hits of 1999, narrates a fantasy
    of watching "lots a crotch," rocking "bitches," and finding "West Coast pussy" for
    one's friends back in Detroit: "[What Do I] Do Right" by Jimmie's Chicken
    Shack was ranked 105th by End listeners in 1999.

29 Jesse Oxfeld, "Not So Dumb Jocks," *Brill's Content* 4, no. 5 (June 2001): 100–103,
    137. According to a Manhattan radio consultant, the show is so popular with men
    because "every day society gets progressively more PC, so their opportunity to be
    a guy gets diminished" (102).

30 To do justice to Guttermouth—who, having recorded postpunk albums on inde-
    pendent labels since 1991, are making their first-ever foray into commercial
    radio—the song is not without some nuance. The lyrics imply that in addition to
    Venus/Mars sexual difference, the speaker is troubled by his girlfriend's per-
    sistent interest in "doing" his friends and fellow band members. On the other
    hand, female infidelity has become a common theme in alternative music,
    providing a handy justification for male anger. It is worth noting that while most
    alternative musicians are in their teens or twenties, the shock jocks tend to be
    considerably older. According to Oxfeld, Opie and Anthony are, respectively,
    thirty-six and thirty-nine years old; according to Rahner, Leykis is forty-four.
    Andy Savage, the host of The End's morning show, did not divulge his age during
    our interview or on his Web site: he looks to be about forty. Howard Stern has
    been around forever.

31 After several months during which The End's morning show DJs were all male, in
    2000, another female cohost joined its ranks: younger and slimmer than the
    departed Coffey, but, like the latter, a voice in her own right.

32 Listeners (usually women) who suspect that their partners are cheating on them
    are encouraged to call in. Savage then calls the suspected two-timer and tells him
    that his name has been drawn to receive a free bouquet of roses that he might
    send to his sweetheart. If he then provides the name of another woman, he finds
    that he is part of a radio hoax and that his aggrieved partner is on the line ready
    to have it out with him, all for the delectation of the Seattle listening area. When
    one male listener learned by these means that his live-in girlfriend had been
    straying, he was especially piqued that the "boob job" he had paid for was now
    being "worked" by another man. The girlfriend replied that he deserved it for
    destroying her self-esteem.

33 For more on this controversial single by the Prodigy, see Flavia, "Rebels without
    a Clue."

34 Typical of the kind of media attention that morning-show antics garner, in 1999 the *Seattle Weekly* (another free local paper) did a cover story on the subject. The article is accompanied by several photographs of Savage dreamily ogling an obviously nude (but discreetly posed) model. The cover of the *Weekly* features one such photograph alongside the words "SEX in the Morning." Not only Savage but several other local morning shows are described. See J. Kingston Pierce, "Radio Raunch," *Seattle Weekly,* 8 April 1999.

35 Interview with Andy Savage and Carolyn Coffey, September 1998. Again, I want to emphasize that most of the discussion of sex is nonexploitative and—while inappropriate for children—usually interesting.

36 According to Pierce, in 1999 Savage's show ranked number three with listeners between the ages of eighteen and thirty-four.

37 Cited by Wilson, "Stick a Fork in Them," 2.

38 John Richards interview.

39 This was the opinion of a record industry representative who appeared as a guest on The End's morning show but declined to be interviewed.

40 For an interesting article on Manson, see Chris Heath, "The Love Song of Marilyn Manson," *Rolling Stone,* 15 October 1998. In his earlier embodiment as "Antichrist Superstar," Manson was likened to heavy metal legend Alice Cooper rather than glam rocker Bowie. Manson's "Family Values" tour succeeded in rousing the ire of a number of respectable communities across the United States. One cannot help but admire Manson's genius for reinventing himself in ways using manifold cult predecessors to create an ever-transforming "alternative" pastiche. Most recently Manson has been promoting his December 2000 album, *Holy Wood,* through an art exhibition.

41 After two best-selling albums, Oasis's popularity has plummeted, and the swing fad is all but forgotten.

42 Radiohead, whose 1996 album *O.K. Computer* was a Grammy nominee and a commercial success, despite comparatively little radio support, is, of all of the most recent bands, the most comparable to the postpunk, pregrunge-era alternative scene. In fact, the band has been together since 1990. Singles off of Radiohead's two most recent albums, *Kid A* (2000) and *Amnesia* (2001), have enjoyed modest airplay on The End.

43 Of course, the same corporate entities sometimes have considerable holdings in both broadcasting and production. Napster is one of several Internet sites that allow users to "trade" downloads of digitized music.

44 Each year The End organizes and incessantly promotes at least two concert extravaganzas, featuring the year's hottest alternative artists: "Deck the Hall Ball," an indoor concert in December (tickets conveniently go on sale months before so that young listeners can purchase them prior to seasonal shopping), and "Endfest," an outdoor summer concert. The End has also sponsored and promoted "Board This," an early-spring outdoor event featuring snowboarding and

other popular sports as well as music. The obvious lucrativeness of promoting mass youth culture events while effectively advertising them free of charge on one's own radio station demonstrates The End's incentive to expand its adolescent audience, in addition to the adult male listeners that constitute its official "core."

45   Among many other political activities, the L.A.-based Rage, who have been building a following since the early 1990s, played a free concert to fans and demonstrators during the 2000 Democratic National Convention. The band's Web site, www.ratm.com, is devoted to various political causes. The Beastie Boys' variation on rap-rock fusion, dating back to the late 1980s, is marked by a more humorous, often tongue-in-cheek, and wholly apolitical tone.

46   The song features an enraged speaker railing against the unfaithful "girlie" who has "fucked" his "homies" and reduced him to a "chump." In the oft-repeated refrain, he protests that he "did it all for the nookie," so she can take "that cookie" and "stick it up [her]—yeah." In the popular video, this theme of wounded pride is undercut somewhat, since it features the lead vocalist being followed by a throng of adoring women. At the same time, the video attributes Rage-like political credentials to the band by having the police arrest the lead singer for performing an illegal concert. One Seattle mother told me how difficult it was when her eleven-year-old son, whose classmates were also Bizkit fans, insisted on buying the album (she eventually agreed that he could listen to it in his room, out of earshot of herself and her seven-year-old daughter). She was not clear whether her son had heard the song on The End, a Top 40 station, or perhaps both.

47   See note 28 on "Cowboy."

48   With hip-hop and Rage against the Machine doubtless in mind, Crazy Town's promoters portray the band as products of L.A.'s urban tensions; but one band member rather more honestly likens himself to "an X-rated Dennis the Menace." In the video for "Revolving Door," which was shot by a porn director, the band is surrounded by barely clad women. In contrast to these groupies, two skater girls express initial reluctance until, at the very end, they remove their sweatsuits to reveal that—in the words of one band member—"they're the two most bangin' girls there." See John Wiederhorn, "Crazy Town into the Skater Chicks in New Vid," *MTV News Online*, 7 June 2001. Crazy Town has been cited as one of several bands played on The End whose "explicit content music" is advertised during after-school programming. Eric Schumacher-Rasmussen, "Blink 182, Crazy Town, Too Explicit for Teens, Report Says," *MTV News Online*, 24 April 2001.

49   Homophobia is most notoriously at play in the music of the Grammy Award–winning Eminem, another white rapper and recent End favorite. It is worth noting, however, that the most controversial elements in Eminem's music are not especially evident in the radio hits. For a superb analysis of Eminem, see Richard Kim, "Eminem—Bad Rap?" *The Nation* 272, no. 9 (5 March 2001): 5–6.

50 On March 30, 2001, KCMU became KEXP, a development I describe in the epilogue to this essay.

51 For a detailed description of Louisiana State University's very different attitude toward the management of its college radio station, see Nagelberg, "What's the Frequency, Kenneth?" and Nagelberg, "No Alternative."

52 John Richards interview.

53 My experience is not atypical, nor is it limited to listeners of my age and sex. One twenty-eight-year-old man conveyed a typical opinion when he told me that he no longer "feels comfortable with the End," which strikes him as serving a kind of trendy, slackerlike male adolescent identity. However, my college-age students (female as well as male) often listen to The End, and I have also heard it playing at day care centers, cafés, and other places where young people work.

54 On the industry's intense lobbying efforts to kill the plan, and the subsequent curtailment of the Federal Communications Commission's authority to issue licenses, see Stephen Labaton, "Congress Severely Curtails Plan for Lower-Power Radio Stations," *New York Times*, 19 December 2000 (on-line).

55 Korn is particularly recognizable as a derivative of Nine Inch Nails, a pioneering industrial-gothic band that remains popular with young listeners.

56 Kim, "Eminem," 5.

57 A good example is Pedro the Lion, the recording artist name for David Bazan, a Seattle-based indie musician frequently played on KCMU. Bazan's minimalist music and intimate first-person lyrics are almost startlingly intense.

58 "EMP: The Experience Continues—Smoothly—with Big Names, Happy Fans," *Seattle Times*, 25 June 2000 (on-line).

59 See, for example, Bill Virgin, "Proposed Change for UW's KCMU Raises Concerns," *Seattle Post-Intelligencer*, 23 September 1999, D5; Eric Scigliano, "Station Break," *Seattle Weekly*, 23–29 September 1999 (on-line); and Eric Scigliano, "Radio Static," *Seattle Weekly*, 30 September–6 October 1999 (on-line).

60 See "KCMU Radio, University of Washington, and EMP Launch Innovative Partnership," the station's 30 March 2001 press release, available on-line at www.raptorial.com/zine/reviews/kexp_pr.htm.

61 Martin, "Brave New Radio."

62 A 1999 survey found that two-thirds of all teenagers were willing to pay a subscription fee to receive commercial-free programming, a statistic that bodes well for this kind of venture. For this citation and a description of various Web broadcasting formats, see Martin, "Brave New Radio."

Works Cited

"EMP: The Experience Continues—Smoothly—with Big Names, Happy Fans." *Seattle Times*, 25 June 2000 (on-line).

Entercom Official Web page. www.entercom.com.

Fairchild, Charles. "Deterritorializing Radio: Deregulation and the Continuing Triumph of the Corporatist Perspective in the USA." *Media, Culture, and Society* 21, no. 4 (1999): 549–61.

Flavia. "Rebels without a Clue." *Cups* 87 (February 1998): 18–19.

Goodlad, Lauren M. E. "Postmodern Gothic: The Lost Brides of Frankenstein and the 'Dark Taste of Fear.'" *Diegesis: Journal for the Association of Research in Popular Culture* 1 (fall 1997): 21–53.

———. Introduction to *Goth Style: Essays on Postpunk Culture*, ed. Lauren M. E. Goodlad and Michael Bibby. Durham: Duke University Press, forthcoming.

Heath, Chris. "The Love Song of Marilyn Manson." *Rolling Stone*, 15 October 1998, 36–43, 124.

Hebdige, Dick. *Subculture: The Meaning of Style*. New York: Routledge, 1979.

Hillard, Robert L. *The Broadcast Century*. Boston: Focal Press, 1992.

Jaquet, Janine. "Taking Back the People's Air." *The Nation* 266, no. 21 (8 June 1998): 13–16.

"KCMU Radio, University of Washington, and EMP Launch Innovative Partnership." 30 March 2001 Press Release. www.raptorial.com/zine/reviews/kexp_pr.htm.

Kim, Richard. "Eminem—Bad Rap?" *The Nation* 272, no. 9 (5 March 2001): 5–6.

KNDD 107.7 The End Web site. www.1077theend.com.

Labaton, Stephen. "Congress Severely Curtails Plan for Lower-Power Radio Stations." *New York Times*, 19 December 2000 (on-line).

Laqueur, Thomas. "Orgasm, Generation, and the Politics of Reproduction." In *The Making of the Modern Body*, ed. Catherine Gallager and Thomas Laqueur. Berkeley: University of California Press, 1987.

Lewin, Tamar. "American Colleges Begin to Ask, Where Have All the Men Gone?" *New York Times*, 6 December 1998 (on-line).

Martin, Richard A. "Brave New Radio." *Seattle Weekly*, 12–18 August 1999 (on-line).

McChesney, Robert W. "Kennard, the Public, and the FCC." *The Nation* 272, no. 19 (14 March 2001): 17–20.

———. *Rich Media, Poor Democracy: Communication Politics in Dubious Times*. New York: New Press, 2000.

Monroe, Kim. Interviews by author, May–September 1998.

Nagelberg, Kenneth. "No Alternative: The Death of Alternative Radio in Baton Rouge." Reprint of *Radio Resistors Bulletin* 9 (March 1995).

———. "What Is the Frequency, Kenneth? The Death of Alternative Radio in Baton Rouge." Manuscript.

Pierce, J. Kingston. "Radio Raunch." *Seattle Weekly*, 8 April 1999.

Pourghasemi, Sara. "Radio Culture." Manuscript.

Rage against the Machine Official Web site. www.ratm.com.

Rahner, Mark. "Shock Jock Tom Leykis Strikes a Receptive Chord in Men—and Brings in Plenty of Static Too." *Seattle Times*, 13 August 2000 (on-line).

Richards, John. Interview by author, February 1999.

Schumacher-Rasmussen, Eric. "Blink 182, Crazy Town, Too Explicit for Teens, Report Says," *MTV News Online,* 24 April 2001.

Scigliano, Eric. "Radio Static." *Seattle Weekly,* 30 September–6 October 1999 (on-line).

——. "Station Break." *Seattle Weekly,* 23–29 September 1999 (on-line).

Wiederhorn, John. "Crazy Town into the Skater Chicks in New Vid." *MTV News Online,* 7 June 2001.

Wilson, Kathleen. "Stick a Fork in Them." *The Stranger Music Quarterly,* 15 October 1998, 2–3.

SCIENCE LITERACIES:

THE MANDATE AND COMPLICITY OF

POPULAR SCIENCE ON THE RADIO

Donald Ulin

Scientific literacy . . . means the capacity to reason in quantitative terms. It means familiarity with a basic scientific vocabulary and with fundamental concepts about physical and biological processes. . . .

Without a basic understanding of science, how can we, as a people, make well-informed decisions on the technical issues that affect our society?—Paul Gray, "America's Ignorance of Science and Technology Poses a Threat to the Democratic Process Itself"

In the Middle Ages, people believed that the earth was flat for which they had at least the evidence of the senses: we believe it to be round, not because as many as one percent of us could give physical reasons for so quaint a belief, but because modern science has convinced us that nothing that is obvious is true, and that everything that is magical, improbable, extraordinary, gigantic, microscopic, heartless, or outrageous is scientific.—George Bernard Shaw, *Saint Joan*

The outcry for greater science literacy is hardly new. At least since the Soviet launch of the Sputnik program, polls have tracked what is usually taken to be a dismally inadequate public knowledge of science. Today, however, the demand for science literacy is driven by a different and more diffuse set of imperatives and contained in a different rhetoric. Most important for the purposes of this essay is the shift from a concern with recruiting and training scientists to a concern for a more broad-based "public understanding of science" or "scientific literacy."[1] The latter phrase echoes E. D. Hirsch's "cultural literacy," by which he means the body of knowledge necessary for one to function successfully in society. For Hirsch, promoting cultural literacy amounts to promoting democracy, not only because it confers the skills necessary for individual survival but because "literate culture is the most democratic culture in our land: it excludes nobody."[2] As my first epigraph indicates, promoters of scientific literacy typically make similar claims: the scientifically literate individual is both a better citizen, able to participate more effectively in the democratic process in a technological society, and a smarter consumer, less easily taken in by false advertising. Given its historic association in this country with the idea of democracy, radio would seem well situated to promote not only popular but populist scientific literacy.[3] Certainly there is no shortage of science radio programs bringing us daily doses of information to boost our scientific literacy. What is badly needed, however, is a more careful consideration than has generally been given to (1) the real aims of scientific literacy (particularly individual empowerment and a more effective participatory democracy), (2) the types of knowledge that would constitute the canon of scientific literacy, and (3) the tendency of the medium to filter, refract, or structure that canon. Without such consideration, efforts at improving "scientific literacy" are likely only to reproduce and reinforce the ideology of late-twentieth-century technological capitalism.

While much of what can be said on these grounds is relevant to any genre of popular science, I am especially interested here in the role of radio and, in particular, of the science "spot," or "sound bite," known in broadcasting as "modular programming." These prerecorded programs, such as *Earthnote, StarDate,* or *A Moment of Science,* are typically five minutes or less and are often distributed by a single institution to subscribing stations (most often National Public Radio affiliates) around the country. Some, like *StarDate,* focus on a single branch of science; others, like *A Moment of Science* or Bayer Corporation's *Everyday Science,* take science in general as their province. Most are relatively simple, relying on only a single narrator and some background music.[4] The format is ideal for the programming director struggling to make the most of an already crowded program. Furthermore, such a short program is relatively inexpensive to produce and can therefore be distributed at little or no cost to the individual stations. Perhaps for this reason, science modules are particularly attractive to smaller stations, often in rural areas. And yet many of the same science modules enjoy shortwave exposure around the world through the Armed Forces Radio network, which broadcasts more than twenty different modules on health, science, nature, and technology.

In the late 1980s and early 1990s, I produced several hundred scripts for

A Moment of Science. This two-minute general science radio program is produced by WFIU at Indiana University and distributed to sixty stations in the United States and to an even wider audience through the Armed Forces network and the English-language service of Deutsche Welle. The stated aims of "AMOS" are relatively simple, stressing entertainment and information in that order, but as I became more acutely aware of the power of the medium (radio) and the genre (the module) to shape the knowledge I was presenting, I found myself facing a somewhat different challenge. Was it possible, I wondered, for my two-minute radio programs to reflect the social, cultural, and economic investments of science? And, a more theoretical problem, what could this genre of popular science contribute to my own understanding of the social construction of science? In the decade or so during which the study of science and literature has been developing, it has addressed a wide variety of texts, both lowbrow and highbrow, from more narrowly and canonically literary genres such as lyric poetry, the novel, and so forth, to political treatises, advertising, travel narratives, and science fiction in both print and visual media. Yet in spite of a nationwide resurgence in the popularity of radio, remarkably little attention has been paid to this medium, and as far as I know, no one has yet addressed the impact of the science module on either popular attitudes toward, or the popular understanding of, science. This essay, then, represents a decade of reflection on a problem that I have come to view as crucial to our understanding of the public perception of science. The essay's mode is speculative and exploratory rather than exhortative, its intention being, first, to invite a more sophisticated and contextualized understanding of science literacy and, second, to situate science radio in relation to the expanded field of science literacy.

Teaching Literacy, Constructing Knowledge

Textbooks and advocates of scientific literacy typically stress the empirical nature of science—the idea that scientific knowledge, unlike other forms of knowledge, is verifiable by observation of the material world. The linchpin of this view of science is the "hypothetico-deductive model," according to which the scientist, inspired by some natural anomaly or curiosity, proposes a reasonable explanation (the hypothesis), which is then tested experimentally, either refuting or substantiating that hypothesis. Popular science books for children, like Salvatore Tocci's *Chemistry around You,* echo this simplified narrative as the basis for an equation between popular and populist science. Chemistry, Tocci assures us, "is not limited to people working in laboratories; you deal with chemical principles, concepts, and reactions whenever you cook, take aspirin tablets, or wash clothes. Your home is, in fact, a chemical laboratory, providing you with an opportunity to observe, record, explain, and discover the world of chemistry as it operates in your kitchen, bathroom, laundry room, garage, and backyard."[5] With open minds and some rudimentary training, we can all do science on a daily basis.

Tocci's aims are simpler than those of some promoters of scientific literacy, but they are typical in harnessing popular science to effective consumption. "Many of the projects in this book," he writes, "are designed to make you an educated consumer who will buy products not on the basis of advertising gimmicks or manufacturers' claims but on the knowledge gained from your experimental results. With the information in this book, you'll know how to determine which orange juice provides the most vitamin C, . . . which detergent is most effective in cleaning clothes."[6] In his *Dictionary of Scientific Literacy*, Richard Brennan points to our increasingly complex world, where "science, both basic and applied, has much to do with the nature of the work we do, how we travel and communicate," and so on. "Scientific literacy," he writes, "is the ticket for admission to such a world" and the means by which we "make informed decisions about public and personal matters involving science and technology."[7] Although more modest, the claims of science radio are often similar; Bayer Corporation, for example, produces the two-minute program *Everyday Science* as part of an initiative, it says, to "advance our company's values and beliefs, involve employees in their hometowns and help improve our communities."[8] Given the powerful role of science and technology in shaping our lives and our understanding of the world, a public understanding of those forces would seem a prerequisite in directing them toward appropriate, humane ends.

For at least a couple of decades, however, a growing number of media critics have questioned the claims made for scientific literacy. Is there a significant correlation between one's level of scientific sophistication and one's shopping habits? Is the behavior of the scientist in the supermarket or drugstore more rational than that of the nonscientist? Compared with nonscientists, do scientists smoke less, avoid saturated fats, or purchase less-toxic household cleaners? Leon Trachtman suggests that such is not the case, and he raises equally provocative questions about the relationship between scientific literacy and the democratic process. He notes, for example, that on the science-related issues that most concern voters (such as abortion, nuclear power, or the Endangered Species Act), "positions may be quite easily understood without very much scientific information. Someone whose convictions dictate opposition to abortion will not find his ability to make political judgments or take political action enhanced by a more profound understanding of the mechanism of conception."[9] In short, it seems unlikely that an individual's level of scientific knowledge would have any significant effect on choices regarding either public policy or personal matters.

Unlikely, that is, as long as we assume the value of that knowledge to be politically and ethically neutral. In fact, it is hardly neutral but is instead deeply influenced by the constraints of the media and possibly, though less obviously, by the interests of those most involved in the campaign for science literacy. Too often efforts at promoting science literacy are aimed principally at promoting the values of science and technology, while measurements of science literacy frequently confuse an understanding of science with an uncritical belief in its explanatory powers. Thus, under the constraints of the media and the oversight of vested interests, the construction of scientific knowledge—in other words, of a canon of science literacy—may actually disempower the nonscientist and thereby inhibit genuine public dialogue on science-related issues. Before turning to the media, however, it will be useful to look briefly at a couple of surveys designed to measure the public understanding of science.

Belying common claims for the verifiability of science, a Harris poll administered in 1994 to test the level of scientific literacy among American adults focused on information that was not only unverifiable by mere observation but contrary to what such observation would suggest. For example, as responses to the question "Which of these is the nearest living relative of the dinosaur *Tyrannosaurus Rex?*" respondents were offered the chicken, the crocodile, the lizard, and the elephant.[10] Not surprisingly, 30 percent guessed the lizard, while only 10 percent correctly identified the chicken. To "know" the correct answer would require one to have set aside the evidence of one's senses (which would suggest the lizard), and to accept a vision of science, suggested half-ironically by George Bernard Shaw in my second epigraph, as that which is "magical, improbable, extraordinary, gigantic, microscopic, heartless, or outrageous." Such neat "factoids" are fun because they are counterintuitive, and useful to social researchers because they represent a knowledge than can easily be tested. However, they also constitute a dangerously skewed representation of knowledge as a collection of universal truths divorced from any social or political considerations, unchallengeable by the nonscientist, and independent of any local variables.

In contrast to the Harris poll, a "Bioregional Quiz" published in 1981 in *CoEvolution Quarterly* focused exclusively on knowledge that might require observation in one's own environment, such as "What are the major plant associations in your region?" and "Trace your drinking water from the source to the tap."[11] Most of us in this age of transnational culture, information, and ideology are likely to fare even worse on the bioregional quiz than on the Harris poll, and I would guess that most people find the latter more exciting by virtue of its clarity and counterintuitiveness. However, if the aim of science literacy is to produce better consumers and citizens, we might consider whether an understanding of the botany and hydrogeology of one's own region would be more useful than the knowledge that chickens are descended from dinosaurs. In a global economy informed by global (or at least nonlocal) media, such local knowledge is necessarily devalued. Both questionnaires ask respondents to identify their homes, but the difference is telling: in the Harris poll, the answer is "the Milky Way." Far beyond the human scale and outside the realm of any practical concerns, this answer is valid and marketable (if you are producing a science radio program) anywhere in the world. Most of the questions on the "Bioregional Quiz" also ask respondents to identify their home, but the answers are local and require a knowledge less easily accommodated by a global medium: "home" here is not a galaxy but a watershed, an ecosystem, a climate. In any case, if one aim of scientific literacy is really to impress on people the verifiability of scientific knowledge and its immediate relevance to their everyday lives, we might do well to consider what kinds of knowledge we treat as representative of science—or to examine more critically the aims of "science literacy."

Not surprisingly, it is the factoids that are most easily accommodated by the strict requirements of modular science programming, making it an ideal medium to promote precisely the sort of scientific literacy suggested by the Harris poll. With its brevity (as little as thirty seconds), the modular program can hardly be expected to explain the principle behind nuclear fission, let alone explore the politics and economics of the energy industry.

Nor is a program destined for national or international distribution likely to explore the locally distinctive features of the estuary whose waters would be used for cooling a proposed nuclear power plant. Some programs like *A Moment of Science* are written months before they are broadcast or are written for repeated broadcasts, making timeliness as difficult to achieve as localness. The aim, then, is typically on the scale of the *90-Second Naturalist,* which aims to "amaze listeners with some of the most unbelievable facts and feats of nature." The result in this case is what one newspaper called "a cross between Trivial Pursuit and *National Geographic.*" Citing that description on its original Web site for the program, the Cincinnati Zoo (which is no longer associated with the program) was evidently ambivalent about the description: "While it is true that an adult female blue whale's tongue weighs as much as an elephant (10,000) pounds [*sic*], there is nothing trivial about nature."[12] Whatever their tendency to misrepresent either science or nature, such nifty factoids, easily packaged and marketed, have a strong appeal to the producers of modular science. What media critics would do well to consider is the extent to which a program's need to *impress* its listeners may shape the content and the message of the program itself.[13]

Of course there is no conspiracy to exclude local knowledge or to obscure the messy politics of science as it is really practiced. But the production of general knowledge at the expense of local and specific knowledge is more than the incidental outcome of big media; it is the lifeblood of an increasingly global economy, the precondition for NAFTA, GATT, and the exploitation of world markets and resources. It is this type of knowledge that allows multinational agricultural or pharmaceutical companies to maximize profits through economies of scale. The green revolution offers one example of the seductive power of such knowledge and its devastating consequences. Fired by the laudable dream of feeding the world's poor, scientists trained in the United States and Europe developed new high-yield crops for use in developing countries around the world. The initial results were good, but they required higher chemical inputs than indigenous strains, and many were unsuitable for sustained production in their new environments. In the end, millions of subsistence farmers were ruined by capital outlays for tractors, seed, pesticides, and so on; the fertility of the soil was depleted, and often the indigenous seed strains were lost, having been abandoned for several years. The science embodied in the green revolution, in the mainstream movement for science literacy, and in the factoids of popular science modules have at least this much in common: all three encourage us to value the universal over the local and the technical over the experiential. It is not surprising, then, that funding for many of these programs comes from the organizations responsible for producing and using the kind of knowledge that is valuable in a global economy, including Bayer Corporation (with it multi-billion-dollar agro-chemical division), NASA, the National Science Foundation, Bristol-Myers Squibb, and International Paper, to name just a few of the sponsors of science radio programs.[14]

Representing the Scientific Process—But Which Process?

Serious proponents of science literacy, however, point out that facts make up only one component of science literacy, the other being the scientific "process." In a study of science literacy, published in *Nature,* John R. Durant and his coauthors emphasized the need for both an "understanding of the process of scientific inquiry" and a "knowledge of the elementary findings of science."[15] Survey questions aimed at measuring the former tested respondents' ability to identify the components of the hypothetico-deductive method and to recognize that not "all of today's scientific theories will still be accepted in a hundred years" (13). Other questions from this portion of the survey required that respondents identify Einstein's theory of relativity and Darwin's theory of evolution as "well established explanation" rather than "a hunch or idea" or "a proven fact." By including in the definition of science literacy a recognition that science's most fundamental beliefs might be subject to question, Durant et al. take a more realistic view of science as something always liable to change. Such a measure of science literacy might also measure the public willingness to engage critically with scientific orthodoxy.

Ironically, however, if this portion of their survey rewarded a recognition of the inevitable uncertainty of science, the portion designed to test the respondent's "knowledge of the elementary findings of science" reduced science to the binary certainty of true-false propositions: "the oxygen we breathe comes from plants," "diamonds are made of carbon," "all insects have eight legs." An informed or reasonable respondent would intuitively understand "true" to mean "well-established," but the discrepancy in the operative definitions of science embedded in the two sections of this survey points to a troubling ambiguity in the way Durant and others would have the public understand the scientific process. In fact, the real processes of science are entirely obscured by a teleological view of science that derives the process from the outcome. While we are encouraged to equate science with the continual production of new knowledge and the correction of older knowledge, the process itself is hermetic, pure in its scientific rigor and impermeable to outside influence. Durant et al. expect scientifically literate respondents to recognize that "new technology does . . . depend on basic scientific research" but do not expect them to recognize also that basic research is often driven by new technology as well as the interests of those who stand to benefit from the growth of that technology.

It is perhaps all the more surprising that the concept of science literacy espoused by Durant et al. would exclude the cultural matrix out of which science operates given that their first argument for an increased public understanding of science is that "science is arguably the greatest achievement of our culture" (11). To illustrate the problem of the public's failure to appreciate "science as a cultural achievement," the authors note that "most of the public appears not to have caught up with Nicholas Copernicus and Galileo Galilei" (13). But is a familiarity with great names and their associated paradigms equivalent in any way to an understanding of science as practiced today? To focus on the name and the discovery is to reproduce what Roland Barthes describes as "the myth of Einstein," the myth of

the unity of nature, the ideal possibility of a fundamental reduction of the world, the unfastening power of the world, the age-old struggle between a secret and an utterance, the idea that total knowledge can only be discovered all at once, like a lock which suddenly opens after a thousand attempts. The historic equation $E = mc^2$, by its unexpected simplicity, almost embodies the pure key, bare, linear, made of one metal, opening with a wholly magical ease a door which had resisted the desperate efforts of centuries.[16]

"Cartoons of Einstein," Barthes points out, "show him chalk still in hand, and having just written on an empty blackboard, as if without preparation, the magic formula of the world."[17] Alternatively, the board is cluttered with arcane notations pointing teleologically to that "magic formula." Popular representations of science frequently duplicate this image of science, though without the humorous intent of the cartoon, in an effort to impress their audiences with the grandeur of science: science, understood not as the vast, wasteful, precarious, and fascinating world of "experiment," but as a series of brilliant "discoveries."

To offer a faithful rendering of the scientific process as something more complex than the hypothetico-deductive model and less mysterious than Barthes's magical "key" might require opening what Bruno Latour calls "Pandora's black box," in which "context and content fuse together, . . . mixing hydrogen bonds with deadlines, the probing of one another's authority with money, debugging and bureaucratic style."[18] Henry Bauer, who is both a critic of conventional constructions of scientific literacy and an advocate of a more heavily contextualized version, argues that "no bits of specific information about one or more of the sciences could be nearly as meaningful as a sense of what position science and technology play, and have played, within human culture."[19] Although Bauer does not go as far as Latour in treating science as a cultural enterprise, his contextualized scientific literacy would help to diffuse the aura of the scientist and to situate the scientific process among other related social processes. Only in this way will individuals and communities ever be able to make an informed (and often critical) use of science for the real betterment of their lives.

Science Writing in a Maze of Metaphor

The success of a radio program about science or anything else is never measurable in science literacy scores. Nor can we expect an easy accommodation of complex social analyses to the two-minute module. First and foremost, radio has to be entertaining, memorable, and enjoyable. The disproportionate number of science radio programs on public, as compared to commercial, radio suggests that public radio's listeners take greater pleasure in intellectual self-improvement, but if the lessons fail to maintain the listener's interest, the station will discontinue its subscription to the program. The problem is particularly acute in the case of radio, which rarely commands the full attention of its audience. Unlike television, radio attracts its largest number of listeners during the 6 A.M. to 10 A.M. "drive time" slot, listeners who are usually busy driving a car, washing dishes, or performing some other activity.[20] Even if we choose to tune in to a specific radio program, the freedom that a strictly aural medium offers us to look around, put away a few dishes, or pick up a magazine means we are more likely to be distracted than we would be in front of a television with its more tyrannical claim on our sight as well as hearing.

For this reason, memorable narratives, visual images, concrete metaphors, and familiar analogies, all proven strategies for explaining technical or abstract information, are especially important in radio. As one hand-book for presenting scientific information notes, "comparing a computer to a brain (or vice versa, depending on the audience), a chemical procedure to a culinary technique, or a space probe's sensors and appendages to the parts of an organism can help your audience to grasp and appreciate your point."[21] Radio is different only in the degree to which it depends on rhetorical, rather than visual, modes for making abstract ideas concrete.

As long as the science writer aims at nothing more than an intelligible explanation of whatever scientific principle or discovery currently requires explanation, nothing more is needed than lucid prose buoyed by a judicious placement of images, metaphors, and analogies, all embedded in a memorable narrative. In fact, that is precisely what modular science radio programs are best at: like the sound bite, the two-minute format is just long enough to instill some nugget of truth without overwhelming a busy or distracted listener. For example, one episode of *Everyday Science* takes us on an imaginary journey into an octopus, where we learn how that creature propels itself through the water; in one "Moment of Science" we learn that the movement of lightning is like "a frog jumping from lily pad to lily pad across a pond";[22] another "Moment of Science" explains the organization of the genome into chromosomes, genes, codons, and nucleotides by invoking the familiar analogy of the book, with its chapters, sentences, words, and letters.[23] This is good writing because it allows an audience of nonspecialists to grasp difficult and technical concepts. Collectively, these programs suggest a view of science as something accessible, straightforward, even easy. "There's nothing mysterious or underhanded about science," they seem to say, "just close observation and common sense."

Also contributing to this simplification of science are the simple experiments popular science programs often give listeners to perform at home. One "Moment of Science" I wrote on emulsions encouraged listeners to make mayonnaise and to experiment "with different varieties and amounts of oils. You'll not only learn about emulsions, but make better sandwiches, too" (22). Listeners often told me these were some of their favorite programs: "Even if I never do the experiment," one listener commented, "I enjoy imagining it." This approach to science has pleased listeners, program directors, and sponsors of *A Moment of Science* for nearly fifteen years now. What often troubled me, however, were the tendencies to distort the real practice of mainstream science and simultaneously to promote an uncritical respect for scientific authority. As I will explain, I believe that radio offers unique means for overcoming these tendencies, but first let me explain the source of my concern.

First, there is what I call the colonizing impulse of "everyday science," the idea that science is everywhere and that therefore any discussion of the natural world properly belongs to science. For example, Durant et al. assume that identifying as false the proposition "All insects have eight legs" indicates an understanding of science. Anyone with even a rudimentary knowledge of entomology knows that insects have only six legs, but so would anyone else with an interest in the natural world. Similarly, when *Everyday Science* answers the question "Why do potatoes have eyes?" the answer is interesting and perhaps useful (they are the beginnings of new roots), but it was common knowledge thousands of years ago in South America long before, and far away from, the rise of anything resembling modern science. Indeed, it is simply not true as populizers of science like to claim that "all children are born scientists" or that "the toddler who pours the juice onto the floor is making fundamental discoveries about gravity [and] fluid dynamics."[24]

Before the existence of the modern disciplines and institutions of science, the term "science" did indeed designate general knowledge or else described "a particular body of knowledge or skill, as in, 'his science Of metre, of rime and of cadence' (Gower 1390); "thre Sciences . . . Divinite, Fisyk, and Lawe' (1421)."[25] In 1840 William Whewell's use of the neologism "scientist" signaled a powerful new idea that science might designate a distinctive field of human endeavor. It was not until this time that "a particular and highly successful model of neutral methodical observer and external object of study became generalized, not only as science, but as *fact* and *truth* and *reason*."[26] With the institution of that idea in today's laboratories, universities, journals, and professional organizations, the equation of science with general knowledge becomes more exclusionary than inclusive. The effect is to marginalize certain types of knowledge based on their distance from dominant scientific practice. Insofar as the paths of science are deeply influenced, if not determined, by specific institutional, political, economic, and cultural interests, using the category of science as the highest arbiter of legitimate knowledge grants excessive authority to those interests.

This is hardly the place to explore the social and economic influences on science, but the displacement of natural history and field biology by molecular biology should demonstrate the power these influences have to

direct the course of science. Given the increasingly tight connections between industry and the sources of knowledge (including the sources of
funding), it is hardly surprising that cancer research, for example, would be
directed primarily at developing new drugs and technologies for treatment
rather than at identifying the environmental contaminants to which a good
deal of cancer must be attributable. As mainstream biology turns increasingly toward the holy grail of a perfectly legible genome as the ultimate
explanatory tool, ecologists and field biologists find funding more and
more difficult and their work increasingly marginalized. (For example,
nonmolecular developments in biology rarely make the cover of *Science* or
Nature.)

One might argue that the broadly inclusive definition of science often
assumed by its popularizers represents an openness to alternative perspectives, an effort to ground science in the material realities of everyday life
(unlike the questions on the Harris poll), or even an invitation to challenge
the authority of the scientific establishment. Yet there is rarely any acknowledgment that legitimate knowledge might exist outside of, or prior
to, the advent of modern science. One common exception is the announcement that a scientific basis has been found for some item of folklore such as
the medicinal properties of chicken soup. However, the occasion for the
story is not so much the belief, which some people had always held to be
true, but the power of science to legitimate or, in other words, colonize that
knowledge.

In recent years, the colonization by science and its corporate owners of
alternative forms of knowledge has led to intense confrontations between
Third World countries (often represented by nongovernmental organizations) and multinational corporations seeking patents on indigenous
knowledge. The World Trade Organization's rules on trade-related intellectual property rights (TRIPS), established at the Uruguay Round of the
Global Agreement on Trade and Tariffs, give corporations broad license to
patent indigenous knowledge with little or no alteration from its original
form. One patent granted to two researchers at the Mississippi Medical
Center for the medicinal use of turmeric was rescinded only after the
Indian Council for Scientific and Industrial Research produced an article
from 1953 in the *Journal of the Indian Medical Association* describing the
medicinal efficacy of turmeric. Because U.S. patent laws "allow patents for
inventions in use in other countries unless they have been described in a
publication,"[27] the medical knowledge and use of turmeric by indigenous

people—going back thousands of years—would have been irrelevant. Another patent, held by W. R. Grace and Co., for the fungicidal properties of neem tree oil (long recognized by Indian farmers) was successfully challenged in the European Patent Office but remains in force in the United States.[28] Meanwhile the Texas-based Rice Tec is threatening Southeast Asian farmers with its patents on basmati rice. At the heart of these efforts is a systematic denial of the rights of communities outside the circuit of international law, science, and industry to the fruits of their own knowledge. While collaborations like International Cooperative Biodiversity Group Maya (ICBG-Maya) between ECOSUR, Mexico's College of the Southern Frontier, and the Institute of Ecology at the University of Georgia promise greater returns to indigenous communities and respect for indigenous rights, the response among representatives of those communities has ranged from deep skepticism to a guarded optimism.[29]

Sharing the royalties of technological innovation with the cultures whose knowledge provided the original impulse for that innovation would be an important step toward some kind of global equity. Even so, the dissociation of indigenous knowledge from the cultures that produced it (perhaps because they could not identify the gene responsible for the medicinal value of some plant, for example) would tend to legitimate the colonization of that knowledge by science. The situation is comparable to the long history of colonialism, also made possible by the advances of modern science, which required a systematic denial of the claims of indigenous people to the land they occupied, or even of the people's existence altogether. The "discovery" by modern science of the healthful properties of chicken soup or the correct number of legs on an insect or the healing powers of neem tree oil are discoveries only in the same limited sense that Europeans may be credited with having "discovered" the "New World." Tragically, the consequences for those who were there first may be comparable as well. To treat all observations of nature as material for a science radio program may seem a comparatively benign activity, but if the program fails to recognize the existence of legitimate knowledge independent of modern science, it runs the risk of abetting this latest incarnation of Western imperialism.

My second concern is with the presentation of science as something easy, simple, and straightforward. Too often, popular science reduces science to its results in the form of discrete facts: "When antibiotics don't work in this Moment of Science" is a typical lead for that program, while

Everyday Science introduces its programs with questions like "How do animals hear?" and "Why do we sweat?" Programs like these might improve scientific literacy in the narrow sense defined by the Harris poll, but they also reaffirm the passivity of the listener, gratefully receiving the fruits of scientists' unquestionable, even magical, knowledge. When a modular radio program does introduce listeners to the process by which scientific knowledge is produced, the medium itself encourages a misleading simplification of that process. The very first "Moment of Science" described an experiment by Benjamin Franklin demonstrating the relationship between color and the absorption of the sun's energy:

On a bright winter day, when the ground was blanketed with freshly fallen snow, Franklin laid [samples of different colored cloth] on the snow, in the sun, and left them for a few hours. When he came back, he saw that the black square had sunk deeper into the snow than any of the others. . . .

Even two hundred years ago, people knew that dark-colored things get warmer in the sun than light-colored things. But Franklin's little experiment demonstrated it scientifically by comparing cloth samples that were all the same except for one thing: color.

The dyes in the samples absorbed different amounts of sunlight.[30]

Having listened to this program, those of us in northern climates can head out into the snow with half a dozen scraps of cloth to participate in the grand enterprise of science.

However useful such a program might be in explaining the experimental method and in capturing an archetypal moment in the history of science, there is a danger in treating such a simple gesture (laying the cloth in the sun, waiting a few hours, and recording its depth in the snow) as an accurate miniaturization of modern scientific enterprises such as the Human Genome Project (HGP). Yet that is precisely the idea that popular science tends to promote. By treating the genome as a book, as in my earlier example (or a map or computer code), we suggest that to the molecular biologist, the genome is as easily and unequivocally legible as Franklin's bits of cloth are to the untrained observer. In fact, as Thomas Fogle points out, "metaphors comparing hereditary information to books, programs, and blueprints . . . can be extremely misleading about the significance of the HGP toward understanding the human phenotype."[31] Such metaphors suggest the possibility of linking complex characteristics in a one-to-one relationship with individual genes and implicitly raise the specter of a narrow biological determinism. Even more pernicious is the suggestion implicit in the book metaphor of a second tier of literacy: as nonscientists, we are barred from the genetic book, but we must also take for granted the book's legibility in the hands of the molecular biologist. When we dutifully or curiously lay our squares of cloth in the snow, we are not so much participating in real science as we are affirming the legibility of a text to which we ourselves will never have access. Perhaps most frightening about this delegation of the task of genetic explication to a field of experts is the assumption by many that what is really being explained is our very identity as human beings, and as men, women, blacks, whites, alcoholics, aggressors, gays, and straights.

Ironically, in attempting to make science familiar and relevant to a nonscientific audience, such metaphors actually obscure or mystify what makes science so relevant to all of us, namely, its embeddedness in ideology. Alice Dreger notes that the metaphor of the genome as a "genetic frontier" provided strong support for the Human Genome Project in part because "it implied a definite, realizable goal whose progress could be measured and which would presumably not require endless funding."[32] More important, however, the metaphor "made the Project appear ethically unproblematic and value-neutral, since maps in themselves do not seem dangerous or imbued with particular values," even as it "situated the Project rhetorically as part of the great American tradition of manifest destiny; it made the project 'American' in style and gave Congress an imperative to beat other nations, especially Japan, to the promised and yet-unclaimed land." Thus metaphors may operate as more than heuristic devices for elevating scientific literacy: they become the tools by which the HGP is sold to Congress and to the public. Without any such agenda, writers of science radio programs make frequent use of metaphor as a tool for conveying information to their audience, but by consistently failing to consider the history or political entailment of our metaphors, we frequently assume positions of advocacy incompatible with the objectivity one looks for in journalism.[33]

The two dangers I have identified as endemic to popular science—first, the tendency to exclude important bodies of knowledge from the canon of scientific literacy and, second, the construction of the listener as passive recipient—are in fact closely connected. As the study by Durant et al. illustrates, "science literacy" often becomes a measure of the public's acceptance of the authority of science as the arbiter of meaningful knowledge rather than of its ability to use knowledge for personal or communal betterment. Does a rejection of the proposition "Natural vitamins are better for you than laboratory-made ones" really indicate, as Durant et al. suggest, a degree of science literacy? More likely it indicates an atomistic view of food according to which chemicals can be meaningfully isolated and evaluated independently of any context. What it disregards and therefore devalues are the holistic bodies of knowledge that would understand nutrition only in relation to a whole diet, an individual, or even a community. A "correct" response would indicate not so much a general understanding of scientific principles and findings as an uncritical acceptance of a reductively scientific view of nutrition and a willingness to accept what science has "found" to be true. Paolo Freire's argument for the inherently political nature of teaching general literacy is clearly adaptable to an analysis of scientific literacy. Both types of literacy posit implicit or explicit definitions of the Subject in relation to the world, and both are actively engaged in the production of political categories. In the case of scientific literacy in the United States, these are not categories of (literally) enfranchised and disenfranchised people but the categories of orthodox and heterodox scientific knowledge that structure public discourse on issues of science and technology. To accept the model of scientific literacy as suggested by the Harris poll or the study from *Nature* is to accept the assumption Freire identifies with conventional literacy programs that "man is a passive being, the object of the process of learning to read and write, and not its subject."[34]

Some Ways Out of the Maze

In a society as heavily reliant as ours on science and technology, the media and those familiar with the practices and findings of science have an obligation to make information about science available. To that extent, science writers and the pundits of science literacy share at least one fundamental goal. The real task for the science writer, however, is to overcome the limitations and exploit the possibilities of the medium so as to encourage less adulation and more skepticism, a respect for what science has contributed to our lives, but also a more honest recognition of science's implications in the realms of the social, the political, and the economic. We do not need to treat science as merely a fabrication to understand the constructed element of scientific reality. In seeking a middle ground between constructivism, with its view of science as only a projection of human desire, and realism, with its view of scientific knowledge as utterly unconditional, Bruno Latour suggests that we treat both the objects and the results of scientific inquiry as "quasi-objects, quasi-subjects," things "much more social, much more fabricated, much more collective than the 'hard' parts of nature, but . . . much more real, nonhuman and objective than those shapeless screens on which society—for unknown reasons—needed to be 'projected.' "[35] Such an approach demystifies science and changes the questions we ask: instead of asking, "Who discovered the shape of the DNA molecule?" we might ask, "What were the conditions that led, not to the 'discovery,' but to the 'determination' of that shape?" At the same time, we might begin to challenge both the boundaries of and the assumptions behind the current canon of scientific literacy.

Although it is perhaps more difficult, a critical approach to science is not impossible in the medium of the modular radio program, a medium that may in fact fill an important niche in this regard. One strategy, available to any medium, is simply to do more than is usually done with conflicts and inconsistencies in scientific knowledge. This not only encourages a less adulatory attitude toward science but presents a more realistic picture of intellectual inquiry kept alive by reasonable disagreement. One "Moment of Science," for example, explores the scientific concept of "biodiversity" at the same time that it explains the role of genetic engineering in promoting monoculture (155). In this way, the program explores science as a field of conflict: whereas biodiversity is most meaningful to the ecologist (whose focus is ecosystems and interactions), the object of analysis and manipulation for the geneticist (who may, as a concerned human being, also value biodiversity) is the DNA of individual organisms. The conflict is both epistemological and social, for it represents not only two different ways of looking at the world but also the source of significant differences in public policy in matters of agriculture, the environment, and business.

Getting the Signal

Setting aside questions of content analysis, a great deal of research remains to be done on the reception of science radio programs. What is the impact of a program's context on how it is received and understood by listeners? And in what distinctive ways might individuals or distinct groups assimilate the material they hear? Such questions will require the kind of research that is only just now being done on television audiences, but there are good grounds already to begin speculating. On commercial radio, science might take its place alongside popular call-in talk shows, "shock jocks" like Howard Stern, and self-help gurus like Dr. Laura. Would such placement help diffuse the aura of authority that surrounds science, encouraging listeners to challenge the assumptions of science as they challenge whatever other ideology had been the target of the preceding talk show? Or would a listener who had been listening attentively to Dr. Laura's firm directives fall into the same attitude of timid obedience in relation to the science program immediately following? One might reasonably worry that situating science modules among radio talk shows would encourage listeners to "challenge" science with only the superficial analysis and identity politics typical of those other shows. None of these attitudes toward science is consistent with what either scientists or serious promoters of science literacy would espouse, but until we understand better how the context of the module influences its reception in the listener's mind, it will be difficult to say just what these modules do for the public understanding of science.

Orson Welles's famous broadcast of *The War of the Worlds* is evidence enough for the capacity of radio to induce an entirely uncritical suspension of disbelief. Yet, as Susan Douglas has argued, the aurality of radio exercises a less tyrannical hold on the individual consciousness: "Hearing something rather than seeing it allowed you to hold something in reserve that was just yours. . . . Your image . . . was simultaneously yours and part of a collective vision."[36] In a study of one woman's radio diary, Pamela Riney-Kehrberg shows how Mary Dyck, isolated on a remote farm in Kansas, incorporated radio broadcasts into her life in ways their producers might never have expected.[37] The relatively flexible demand radio makes on a listener's attention, while making unique demands of the writer, also gives the listener more control over his or her consumption of the information. In his analysis of the experience of television viewers, John Fiske argues that viewers appropriate the meanings of the programs they watch in ways that may support, reinterpret, or even reject the ideological position of the actual program.[38] If we accept even Fiske's most basic premise that the meaning of television grows out of a negotiation between the viewer and the program, we might argue that the radio listener, free from the visual demands of television, negotiates from a stronger position by virtue of a greater physical and intellectual independence from the source of the message.[39] Again, there is an element of speculation here that would require careful studies of radio reception, but what I want to suggest is that what makes radio writing difficult, namely, the mobile and evanescent quality of the audience, may make it a natural medium for encouraging a critical distance from the familiar metaphors and narratives of popular science.

Getting around the News Values

One of the difficulties in presenting a realistic view of science in the news is the need to accommodate science to the basic news values of timeliness, relevance, prominence (of the news maker), and human interest. As a result, we tend to get a disproportional number of stories about recent successes and "breakthroughs" involving popular topics. Ninety percent of the respondents in the Durant study reported that they "might read" or would "definitely read" an article beneath the headline "New Clue in Hunt for AIDS Cure." The figure goes down to 71 percent of the headline "Astronomers Discover New Galaxy," and one might reasonably suspect a much bigger drop for a letdown headline like "Scientists Unable to Locate Gene for Drosophila Growth Hormone" or even "New Findings Cast Doubt on Recent Hope for AIDS Cure." We cannot easily get around the fact that listeners quite reasonably want to know what *has* happened, the bigger the better. Articles about science with no apparent relevance or human interest, or articles retracting the news of last week's apparent breakthrough, simply do not have the news appeal of stories that promise a more immediate impact.

However, because most science modules take a nonnews focus, they may enjoy more flexibility than news reporting and thus offer a corrective to the biases associated with news reporting on science. Two minutes is long enough to describe a scientist's simple and largely inconclusive research into tickling,[40] point out the environmental risks posed by genetically engineered crops, or show how the unexpected results of another researcher's work sent her back to the drawing board for a new approach.[41] Often these possess neither the news values to make them suitable for a news program nor the obvious appeal required of features in a print medium. Inserted as brief modules into an already interesting and diverse day of programming, however, they will be heard by whatever radio listeners are already tuned to that station. Reviewing changes in science writing over the centuries, Bob Coleman notes that "a frank, humane discussion of errors, troubles and limitations was once considered essential to objective scientific writing. The revival of such discussion might make us all more comfortable with the course and uses of science in the late 20th century."[42] Coleman acknowledges that changes in the way science is practiced, as well as its entrance into the marketplace, make it unlikely that scientists will again include that kind of discussion in scholarly articles. However, we might well look to science modules as one medium for restoring science in the popular mind to its human and social context.

The Local Scene

The problem of the scientific bias toward general rather than local knowledge, a problem exacerbated by the globalization of media, might be addressed effectively in the radio module. Widely syndicated programs will always have difficulty addressing local situations as anything other than instances of more general knowledge, but by promoting an understanding of sciences such as ecology and natural history, which must take into account the local environment, even these programs may help validate local knowledge. One "Moment of Science," for example, explored the relationship between acorn production and mouse populations in the Appalachian Mountains. Even listeners from regions without oak trees may be encouraged to consider similar relationships among species indigenous to their own areas. Some programs like *NatureWatch* and the *90-Second Naturalist* focus almost exclusively on natural history, avoiding all reference to "science." In giving up the legitimating affiliation with science, these programs may risk devaluation in the eyes of those accustomed to the traditional standards of "science literacy," but at the same time they remind us that the realms of science and of knowledge are not necessarily identical. One potential pitfall in this approach, however, is the tendency to capitalize on the exotic, thereby devaluing whatever is local and accessible. *A Moment of Science* has always avoided programs on exotic species in the belief that treating nature as exotic would contribute to the alienation of the listener from the natural world. The *90-Second Naturalist* combines programs on exotic animals with programs that deepen the listener's appreciation for animals with which they are already familiar (on owls' adaptations for night hunting, for example).

Radio deregulation in the 1980s boosted the radio industry to a prominence it had not known in decades but also brought tremendous changes in the relationship of radio stations to their communities. With the removal or near removal of restrictions on the number of stations one company could own and of the holding period required before a station could be resold, station licenses became readily marketable assets.[43] One result of this change was a consolidation of radio stations in the hands of a relatively small number of media conglomerates, and consequently a trend toward more national programming.[44] Under this changed system, radio stations lost their ability or willingness to address local and regional issues.

Excellent locally oriented radio modules do exist, as evidenced by *California Field Notes,* a series of five-minute programs on local natural history produced in Santa Cruz, California, by a collective of volunteer writers and producers. As producers of *California Field Notes* found out, however, the same emphasis that made their material immediately relevant to its local audience created problems for national funding agencies. According to Rachel Goodman, one of the show's producers, media foundations prefer to fund larger projects, whereas environmental foundations are more interested in promoting research and advocacy. Fortunately radio is relatively inexpensive to produce and distribute compared to television, and so for five years, the group researched, wrote, and produced the program using their own equipment and that of KUSP. The programs on CFN tended to be of general interest but with a local focus, for example, on local species (the acorn woodpecker or the Allen's hummingbird) or on local stream systems and watersheds. Rather than treating these as instances of some general principle, local programs like this one are free to focus on the local phenomena, with their distinctive characteristics and histories. One CFN program on soil mites, for example, followed the familiar pattern of taking the listener into the world of its subject matter. Unlike the world of *Everyday Science,* however, which takes a similar approach in all its programs, the world of CFN was geographically specific and engaged the listener as more than a passive observer. The soils in some forests apparently contain as many as one million mites per square foot, but Rusten Hogness (the producer of this show) moves quickly to the more local situation:

The soils in California forests aren't quite so mite-rich. But imagine yourself sitting down cross-legged, leaning back on your hands to gaze up at the trees overhead. Your hands and knees are at the corners of a square. And in just the top four inches of soil in that square, right underneath you, maybe half a million mites are chewing on fungus or maybe on each other, slurping up nutrients leached from the litter above.[45]

The program concludes with the provocative suggestion that "we live on the rooftops of a hidden world," but whereas programs on the hidden genetic world typically impress listeners with the explanatory and manip-ulative power of science, this program encourages a sensitivity to the world immediately underfoot.

One innovative response to this situation is the creation of regional consortia of stations to share information of regional importance. The High Plains News Service of the Western Organization of Resource Coun-cils began ten years ago in response to what executive producer Bob Reha saw as the national news agencies' neglect of issues affecting the High Plains from Idaho to the Dakotas and south into Colorado. Today Reha solicits ideas and material from throughout the region to produce a weekly series of three four-minute modules. The modules, about one-third of which deal with scientific or environmental topics, are distributed to some seventy-five public and community-based stations, mostly within the re-gion. A similar series with a somewhat greater emphasis on science and the environment is produced by the Great Lakes Radio Consortium, based at the University of Michigan. In contrast to "the media's tendency to cover environmental issues as a narrowly defined 'beat' " (from an earlier mission statement), the consortium produces and distributes modular features on "the relationship between the natural world and the everyday lives of peo-ple in the Great Lakes region."[46] These features, which are now distributed to 140 stations in ten states, not only foreground the issues of local impor-tance but also contextualize science. "When science becomes part of the political process," not only should "science writing . . . become part of political reporting," as Rae Goodell contends, but politics should become part of scientific reporting.[47]

These organizations return radio to its roots, but with a much stronger grassroots element. In the early 1920s, radio became the medium through which farmers kept track of prices, weather, and other variables. In rural far more than in urban life, radio became the principal source of informa-tion and entertainment, the connection to the rest of the world. From the beginning, however, agricultural broadcasting was organized for the dis-semination of nationally produced material. "Market reports, compiled by the Department of Agriculture, were relayed by wireless from Washington, D.C., to . . . St. Louis and Omaha. Each of these cities served a territory within a radius of about 3,000 miles, and some 2,500 radio operators located in these regions took down the reports and helped transmit them to farmers by posting them in railroad stations, post offices and country stores."[48] Radio was celebrated as a means of civilizing the rural regions but also of subordinating regional difference to national identity:

The farmer heard through his battery set that electricity could make his life not only more enjoyable, but more profitable as well. He learned, too, that the old two-seater could be traded in for inside plumbing, and Mrs. Farmwife could do the family washing in a machine. Almost unconsciously the distinguishing characteristics of speech began to disappear, and the farmer shaved off his goatee. Radio's voice was bringing the farthermost segments of a nation's people closer together to a common ground for living.[49]

Through the Great Lakes Radio Consortium and the High Plains News Service, radio is again serving as a medium for the distribution of information of relevance to those overlooked by the national media, a means by which individuals might hope to improve the quality of their lives. The great difference, however, is the two-way flow of information: stations that broadcast the modules are often in the business of producing their own, and the clearinghouse for the programs is located in the heart of the region rather than in the nation's capitol.

Given the ubiquity of science in our lives and the power of science for good and ill, it goes almost without saying that a better public understanding of science would constitute a public good. Certainly high-tech companies like Bayer Corporation that underwrite popular science programs see in them the potential for the advancement of their own goals. If journalists and science writers are to act as more than public relations agents for mainstream science and the high-tech companies that benefit from its findings, they must be more alert even than other writers to the ideological implications of both genre and medium as well as to opportunities within the medium for promoting a more critical stance in relation to the subject material. "The purpose of science journalism, after all," Nelkin points out, "is not to promote science but to help create an informed citizenry aware of the social, political and economic implications of scientific activities, the nature of evidence underlying decisions, and the limits as well as the power of science as applied to human affairs."[50] The radio science module ex-emplifies the contemporary, perhaps postmodern, mode of communication—the decontextualized sound bite, available for insertion anytime in any program, at home everywhere and nowhere. As such, these programs may be embedded deeply in contemporary ideological structures but still flexible enough to provide a greater degree of manipulation than some more established formats. In this essay, I hope to have laid some of the groundwork for further study of both the ideological embeddedness and the flexibility of the science module, a format we are likely to see with increasing frequency in coming years.

Notes

1 For a good overview of this movement, see Jane Gregory and Steve Miller, *Science in Public: Communication, Culture, and Credibility* (New York: Plenum Press, 1998), esp. chaps. 1 and 2.

2 E. D. Hirsch, *Cultural Literacy: What Every American Needs to Know* (New York: Vintage Books, 1988), 21.

3 See, for example, David Sarnoff, "The American System of Broadcasting and Its Function in the Preservation of Democracy," in *Democracy and American Ideals* (New York: Town Hall, 1938). See also Steve Wurtzler's discussion in this volume of AT&T's 1923 proposal for a "decentralized array of noncompetitive local broadcast stations" with content controlled by community leaders and the general public.

4 *Everyday Science* is an exception to this rule, with its more elaborate use of sound effects.

5 Salvatore Tocci, *Chemistry around You: Experiments and Projects with Everyday Products* (New York: Prentice Hall, 1985), iv.

6 Ibid.

7 Richard Brennan, *Dictionary of Scientific Literacy* (New York: Wiley, 1992), ix.

8 Bayer Corporation Web site, http://www.bayerus.com/about/community/main.html. This Web page has since been changed to eliminate any reference to "our company's values and beliefs," but continues to stress "our commitment to helping improve the quality of life in the communities where we live and work." More information on *Everyday Science* can be found at http://www.bayerus.com/msms/fun/pages/everyday/index.html.

9 Leon Trachtman, "The Public Understanding of Science: A Critique," *Science, Technology, and Human Values* 6 (summer 1981): 10–15.

10 Boyce Rensberger, "Scientific Literacy," *Washington Post*, 23 May 1994, A3.

11 Carolyn Merchant, *Radical Ecology: The Search for a Livable World* (New York: Routledge, 1992), 219.

12 Material cited here comes from *90-Second Naturalist*'s old Web site at http://www.cincyzoo.org/90.htm. Current information and sample programs can be found at http://www.nsnaturalist.org.

13 *A Moment of Science* aims to "remove some of the mystery from science, but not

the wonder. A Moment of Science makes you think 'Wow, that's neat!' " See http://www.wfiu.indiana.edu/amos/about. An earlier Web site and brochure described the series as "educational in an entertaining way, an enjoyable diversion."

14 Inferring a radio program's critical orientation from its source of funding would be a risky speculation at best, but clearly a corporate sponsor is less likely to support a program with aims antithetical to its own. During the time that *A Moment of Science* was funded by the Indiana Institute for Molecular and Cellular Biology, whose mission is to "promote research and research training in the sciences basic to biotechnology, and to provide resources for biotechnology research," we aired several programs on problems associated with biotechnology. Thane Maynard, however, who has produced the *90-Second Naturalist* for fifteen years without external funding, chose not to accept an offer of funding from Chem-Lawn on the grounds that it would compromise the integrity of the program.

15 John R. Durant, Geoffrey A. Evans, and Geoffrey P. Thomas, "The Public Understanding of Science," *Nature* 340 (1989): 12.

16 Roland Barthes, *Mythologies* (New York: Hill and Wang, 1972), 69.

17 Ibid.

18 Bruno Latour, *Science in Action: How to Follow Scientists and Engineers through Society* (Cambridge: Harvard University Press, 1987), 6.

19 Henry Bauer, *Scientific Literacy and the Myth of the Scientific Method* (Urbana: University of Illinois Press, 1992), 16–17.

20 Vincent M. Ditingo, *The Remaking of Radio* (Boston: Focal Press, 1995), 16.

21 Barbara Gastell, *Presenting Science to the Public* (Philadelphia: ISI Press, 1983), 4.

22 Don Glass, ed., *How Can You Tell If a Spider Is Dead? And More Moments of Science* (Bloomington: Indiana University Press, 1996), 170. Except as noted, all page references in connection with *A Moment of Science* are to this book.

23 Don Ulin, "How Bacteria Teach Scientists to Read," wfiu, Bloomington, Ind., 6 February 1991.

24 Boyce Rensberger, *How the World Works: A Guide to Science's Greatest Discoveries* (New York: Morrow, 1986), 9.

25 Raymond Williams, *Keywords: A Vocabulary of Culture and Society,* rev. ed. (New York: Oxford University Press, 1985), 232.

26 Ibid., 235.

27 Anil Agarwal and Sunita Narain, "Pirates in the Garden of India," *New Scientist* 152 (26 October 1996): 14–15. Vandanna Shiva, "The Threat to Third World Farmers," *The Ecologist Report: Globalising Poverty,* September 2000, 40–43.

28 Ulrike Hellener and K. S. Jarayaman, "Greens Persuade Europe to Revoke Patent on Neem Tree," *Nature* 405 (18 May 2000): 266–67.

29 See " 'Stop Biopiracy in Mexico!' Indigenous Peoples' Organizations from Chiapas Demand Immediate Moratorium," 23 October 2000, a publication of the Action Group on Erosion, Technology, and Concentration (formerly Rural Advancement Foundation International). For more information on corporate

takeovers of indigenous knowledge, see the ETC group's other publications, available on their Web site at http://www.etcgroup.org. In October 2001, after two years of local opposition, ICBG-Maya was canceled, ending the project with unanswered questions about information already collected. For more information, see the ETC Group's updated news release, "U.S. Government's $2.5 Million Biopiracy Project in Mexico Cancelled," http://www.etcgroup.org/documents/news_ICBGterm_Nov2001.pdf.

30 Stephen Fentress, *Why You Can Never Get to the End of the Rainbow and Other Moments of Science,* ed. Don Glass (Bloomington: Indiana University Press, 1993), 1.

31 Thomas Fogle, "Information Metaphors and the Human Genome Project," *Perspectives in Biology and Medicine* 38, no. 4 (1995): 536.

32 Alice Domurat Dreger, "Metaphors of Morality in the Human Genome Project," in *Controlling Our Destinies: The Human Genome Project from Historical, Philosophical, and Ethical Perspectives,* ed. Philip R. Sloan (South Bend, Ind.: University of Notre Dame Press, 2000), 160. Equally compelling is Lily Kay's exposé of the genome-as-code metaphor and its contribution to the efforts of molecular biology to reconfigure "itself as a pseudo-information science and [represent] its objects in terms of electronic communication systems (including linguistics)" ("A Book of Life? How a Genetic Code Became a Language," in Sloan, *Controlling Our Destinies,* 124).

33 Dorothy Nelkin offers compelling documentation and analysis of the lack of objectivity regarding science that pervades the print media as thoroughly as it does radio and television. "While political reporters go beyond press briefings to probe the stories behind the news, science writers rely on scientific authorities, press conferences and professional journals. And they are reluctant to challenge their sources—in part for fear of losing access to them" ("Selling Science," *Physics Today* 43, no. 11 [1990]: 46). For a more extended discussion of the problem, see Nelkin, *Selling Science: How the Press Covers Science and Technology* (New York: W. H. Freeman, 1995). Jeanne Fahnestock makes some related and equally important claims in a close rhetorical analysis of science writing. Journalistic "accommodations" of science, she writes, "emphasize uniqueness, rarity, originality of observations, removing hedges and qualifications and thus conferring greater certainty on the reported facts" ("Accommodating Science: The Rhetorical Life of Scientific Facts," *Written Communication* 3, no. 3 [1986]: 275).

34 Paolo Freire, "The Adult Literacy Process as Cultural Action for Freedom *and* Education and Conscientização," in *Perspectives on Literacy,* ed. Eugene R. Kintgen, Barry Kroll, and Mike Rose (Carbondale: Southern Illinois University Press, 1988), 400.

35 Bruno Latour, *We Have Never Been Modern* (Cambridge: Harvard University Press, 1993), 55.

36 A number of other contributors to this volume have made important related

points. In her analysis of Gracie Allen's radio and television appearances, Leah Lowe, for example, notes that to a greater degree than more visual media, "radio representations unfold through time and require an imaginative completion by the listener," and that "the lack of visual context in radio . . . creates possibilities of multiple points of identification across gender lines." Although less amenable to the agency of the individual listener, Susan Squier's argument alerts us to the complexity of the process of reception: "Radio functioned as a powerful new site of cognitive activity in the twentieth century, . . . activating basic brain structures that are then inflected differently by different cultural contexts, permitting a pleasurable shared simultaneity while reserving a deep sense of individualized interior experience."

37 Pamela Riney-Kehrberg, "The Radio Diary of Mary Dyck, 1936–1955: The Listening Habits of a Kansas Farm Woman," *Journal of Radio Studies* 5, no. 2 (1998): 66–79.

38 In *Reading Television* (London: Methuen, 1978), John Fiske develops the argument that television programs operate according to an ideological framework of codes, and that the audience is "spontaneously and continuously confronted with this framework and must negotiate a stance towards it in order to decode and thus enjoy the entertainment in which it is embodied" (19). In later work, he elaborates on the importance of social categories of race, class, ethnicity, and so on, in explaining the nature of a viewer's response to the program, which may take many forms, including the "dominant reading," the "oppositional" reading, and, what is most common, the "negotiated reading" ("British Cultural Studies and Television," in *Channels of Discourse, Reassembled: Television and Contemporary Criticism*, 2d ed., ed. Robert Clyde Allen [Chapel Hill: University of North Carolina Press, 1992], 296–97). See also Robert C. Allen, "Audience-Oriented Criticism and Television," in the same volume (101–37).

39 In practice, watching television is not always as slavish an activity as I have suggested. One study by Peter Collett found that "most of the time the set was on, his subjects were doing something else in addition to or instead of watching television" (cited in Allen, "Audience-Oriented Criticism and Television," 128). If this is the case with television, it must be more so with the purely auditory medium of radio.

40 Glass, *How Can You Tell*, 44–45.

41 Ulin, "From Chicago to the Mountains," *A Moment of Science*, WFIU, Bloomington, Ind., 1 October 1996.

42 Bob Coleman, "Science Writing: Too Good to Be True?" *New York Times Book Review*, 27 September 1987, 47.

43 Vincent M. Ditingo, *The Remaking of Radio* (Boston: Focal Press, 1995), 3.

44 Ibid., 17.

45 Hogness, "Soil Mites," *California Field Notes*, KUSP, Santa Cruz, Calif., February 1998.

46 http://www.glrc.org/about.

47 Rae Goodell, "How to Kill a Controversy: The Case of Recombinant DNA," in *Scientists and Journalists: Reporting Science as News,* ed. Sharon M. Friedman, Sharon Dunwoody, and Carol L. Rogers (New York: Macmillan, 1986), 170–81.

48 E. P. J. Shurick, *The First Quarter-Century of American Broadcasting* (Kansas City: Midland Publishing, 1946), 271.

49 Ibid.

50 Nelkin, *Selling Science,* 110.

Works Cited

Adler, Richard, and Douglass Cater. *Television as a Cultural Force.* Praeger Special Studies in U.S. Economic, Social, and Political Issues. New York: Praeger, 1976.

Agarwal, Anil, and Sunita Narain. "Pirates in the Garden of India." *New Scientist* 152 (1996): 14–15.

Allen, Robert Clyde. *Channels of Discourse, Reassembled: Television and Contemporary Criticism.* 2d ed. Chapel Hill: University of North Carolina Press, 1992.

Barthes, Roland. *Mythologies.* New York: Hill and Wang, 1972.

Bauer, Henry H. *Scientific Literacy and the Myth of the Scientific Method.* Urbana: University of Illinois Press, 1992.

Brennan, Richard P. *Dictionary of Scientific Literacy.* Wiley Science Editions. New York: Wiley, 1992.

Coleman, Bob. "Science Writing: Too Good to Be True?" *New York Times Book Review,* 27 September 1987, 47.

Ditingo, Vincent M. *The Remaking of Radio.* Broadcasting and Cable Series. Boston: Focal Press, 1995.

Douglas, Susan J. *Listening In: Radio and the American Imagination, from Amos 'n' Andy and Edward R. Murrow to Wolfman Jack and Howard Stern,* New York Times Books, 1999.

Dreger, Alice Domurat. "Metaphors of Morality in the Human Genome Project." In *Controlling Our Destinies: Historical, Philosophical, Ethical, and Theological Perspectives on the Human Genome Project,* ed. Phillip R. Sloan. Notre Dame, Ind.: University of Notre Dame Press, 2000.

Durant, John R., Geoffrey A. Evans, and Geoffrey P. Thomas. "The Public Understanding of Science." *Nature* 340 (1989): 11–14.

Fahnestock, Jean. "Accommodating Science: The Rhetorical Life of Scientific Facts." *Written Communication* 3, no. 3 (1986): 275–69.

Fentress, Stephen. *Why You Can Never Get to the End of the Rainbow and Other Moments of Science.* Ed. Don Glass. Bloomington: Indiana University Press, 1993.

Fiske, John, and John Hartley. *Reading Television.* New Accents. London: Methuen, 1978.

Fogle, Thomas. "Information Metaphors and the Human Genome Project." *Perspectives in Biology and Medicine* 38, no. 4 (1995): 535–47.

Freire, Paolo. "The Adult Literacy Process as Cultural Action for Freedom *and* Education and Conscientização." In *Perspectives on Literacy,* ed. Eugene R. Kintgen, Barry M. Kroll, and Mike Rose. Carbondale: Southern Illinois University Press, 1988.

Gastel, Barbara. *Presenting Science to the Public.* The Professional Writing Series. Philadelphia: ISI Press, 1983.

Glass, Don. *How Can You Tell If a Spider Is Dead? And More Moments of Science.* Bloomington: Indiana University Press, 1996.

Goodell, Rae. "How to Kill a Controversy: The Case of Recombinant DNA." In *Scientists and Journalists: Reporting Science as News,* ed. Sharon M. Friedman, Sharon Dunwoody, and Carol L. Rogers. New York: Free Press, 1986.

Gregory, Jane, and Steve Miller. *Science in Public Communication, Culture, and Credibility.* New York: Plenum Trade, 1998.

Hellener, Ulrike, and K. S. Jarayaman. "Greens Persuade Europe to Revoke Patent on Neem Tree." *Nature* 405 (2000): 266–67.

Hirsch, E. D. *Cultural Literacy: What Every American Needs to Know.* New York: Vintage Books, 1988.

Kay, Lily. "A Book of Life? How a Genetic Code Became a Language." In *Controlling Our Destinies: Historical, Philosophical, Ethical, and Theological Perspectives on the Human Genome Project,* ed. Phillip R. Sloan. Notre Dame, Ind.: University of Notre Dame Press, 2000.

Latour, Bruno. *Science in Action: How to Follow Scientists and Engineers through Society.* Cambridge: Harvard University Press, 1987.

——. *We Have Never Been Modern.* Cambridge: Harvard University Press, 1993.

Merchant, Carolyn. *Radical Ecology: The Search for a Livable World.* Revolutionary Thought/Radical Movements. New York: Routledge, 1992.

Nelkin, Dorothy. "Selling Science." *Science* 43, no. 11 (1990): 41–46.

——. *Selling Science: How the Press Covers Science and Technology.* Rev. ed. New York: W. H. Freeman, 1995.

Rensberger, Boyce. *How the World Works: A Guide to Science's Greatest Discoveries.* 1st ed. New York: Morrow, 1986.

——. "Scientific Literacy." *Washington Post,* 23 May 1994, A3.

Riney-Kehrberg, Pamela. "The Radio Diary of Mary Dyck, 1936–1955: The Listening Habits of a Kansas Farm Woman." *Journal of Radio Studies* 5, no. 2 (1988): 66–79.

Sarnoff, David. "The American System of Broadcasting and Its Function in the Preservation of Democracy: A Series of Addresses Given at the Annual Town Hall Celebrities Luncheon at the Hotel Astor, Thursday, April 28, 1938." In *Democracy and American Ideals.* New York: Town Hall, 1938.

Shiva, Vandanna. "The Threat to Third World Farmers." *The Ecologist—Special Report: Globalising Poverty* 30, no. 6 (2000): 40–43.

Shurick, Edward P. J. *The First Quarter-Century of American Broadcasting, by E. P. J. Shurick.* Kansas City, Mo.: Midland Publishing, 1946.

" 'Stop Biopiracy in Mexico!' " Indigenous Peoples' Organizations from Chiapas Demand Immediate Moratorium. Rural Advancement Foundation International, 23 October 2000. Available on-line at http://www.etcgroup.org/documents/geno_stopbiopiracy.pdf.

Tocci, Salvatore. *Chemistry around You: Experiments and Projects with Everyday Products.* New York: Prentice Hall, 1985.

Trachtman, Leon. "The Public Understanding of Science: A Critique." *Science, Technology, and Human Values* 6 (1981): 10–15.

Williams, Raymond. *Keywords: A Vocabulary of Culture and Society.* Rev. ed. New York: Oxford University Press, 1985.

NOT HEARING POETRY ON PUBLIC RADIO

Martin Spinelli

Words evaporate on public radio.[1] They evaporate especially and most ironically at the very moment when they should be the most present: the presentation of poetry on literary programs. Listening closely to this peculiar treatment of words allows one to hear how public radio imagines its audience and how it conceives of the dynamics of the relationship between its producers and its consumers. The first step in this analysis is a study of the poetry itself: public radio's poetry is chosen for a lack of formal characteristics (or deliberately shorn of them), characteristics that might dislodge listeners from absorption in a narrative or a sentiment and encourage a meditation on the nature of communicative systems or a participation in the linguistic play of so much contemporary writing. Second is a study of the presentation of poetry that has implications for radio semantics and community far beyond literature. In short, the presentation of poetry is the commodification of poetry:[2] by ensuring that the poetry meshes into what Raymond Williams described as the "seamless flow" of media through narratization and biographical grounding,[3] these preferred presentational modes render the "poetry packages" acoustically and semantically exchangeable with public radio's news features and stock quotes. An argument based on the poetry of the National Public Radio program *Fresh Air*, NPR's only daily program with foregrounded literary intention and the de facto standard for literary programming, uses empirical and textual evidence to describe a method of audience conceptualization that neither anticipates complex individual listener interaction with the poetry nor facilitates literary exchange or literary community. This essay then explores how the methods and materials used by stations and networks to make programming decisions reinforce the effects of public radio language use. It argues that work done under the sign of "audience" preselects programs to fit anticipated listener desires in such a way as to effectually limit potential fulfillment of those desires through an actual limiting of listener choice.

Ultimately, a tiny but critically significant practice is suggested for unsettling public radio assumptions about audience and for facilitating less determinant listening options.

According to its Web site, *Fresh Air* provides its audience with "probing questions, revelatory interviews, and unusual insights" as a result of host Terry Gross's "trademark meticulous research."[4] But although *Fresh Air* makes the author interview its bread and butter, to describe it as public radio's "literary" series can seem like something of a mis-attribution. Guests are typically chosen not for their writing but for a perceived personal appeal to an imagined audience. They are usually best-sellers or are merely famous or interesting people who happen to have written something. *Fresh Air* shies away from poetry and often feels the need to justify its inclusion or to bracket it off in a special context, the most comfortable bracket being April, National Poetry Month. The legitimating effect of National Poetry Month to *Fresh Air* cannot be overstated and gives the program license to more than double its typical monthly poetry presentation.[5] *Fresh Air*'s choice of poetry is usually highly narrative or a species of identity-based writing in which the author's identity is fixed before the poem begins. In both cases, formal innovation is either minimal to start with or suppressed in favor of other aspects.

What *Fresh Air* does to and with poetry can be documented to a great extent by listening closely to interviews from 1997's National Poetry Month programs. An examination of the posthumous rebroadcast of an interview with Allen Ginsberg will precede analyses of interviews with Sekou Sundiata and Jane Shore. Particular attention will be paid to how Gross conducts the interviews and to the selection and presentation of the poetry.

The Ginsberg interview demonstrates five facets of public radio's approach to poetry: (1) the deferral to an interest in a "cultural figure," which leads to (2) an almost complete exclusion of discussion of the writing itself and (3) a staggeringly short amount of airtime allowed for the actual presentation or performance of the writing (only two minutes and forty seconds in Ginsberg's twenty-five-minute interview, (4) a fixation on poetry as an emotion or sentiment machine to the exclusion of its textual and aural qualities,[6] and (5) extensive amounts of biographical contextualization before and after the poetry.

In her introductory remarks, Gross describes Ginsberg as someone "on the forefront of cultural change," who "inspired hippies," "spoke out against the war in Vietnam," and "explored Eastern religions."[7] The introduction also features a recorded snippet from the first, most linear, and—in most respects—least-challenging section of "Howl." The section begins with "I saw the best minds of my generation destroyed by madness, starving hysterical naked, / dragging themselves through the negro streets at dawn looking for an angry fix," and ends with them "contemplating jazz." This recording is contextualized by Gross as being important as a historical artifact: it was the original recording of the now famous poem. But more significantly here, the selected lines lack the range in language use evident throughout the rest of the poem. One finds in the following line, for example, transcribed vocalizations and non sequiturs resistant, or at least not readily suited, to a project of mustering clear associations that lead to narratization or even to recognizable abstract ideas: "yacketayakking screaming vomiting whispering facts and memories and anecdotes and eyeball kicks and shocks of hospitals and jails and wars."[8]

After telling Ginsberg, "Everything about your life kind of sets you apart," Gross takes the already quite self-contained poem fragment from "Howl" and firmly grounds it in Ginsberg's biography, attributing its inspiration to the life of Ginsberg's mother, who had spent time in a mental hospital. (Here "meticulous research" seems to have overlooked the poem's dedication to Carl Solomon, whom Ginsberg had met during his own institutionalization.) The method of reducing lines of poetry to a simple reference to neurosis informs (on several levels) Gross's approach to literature: despite a wealth of more complex and interesting questions, observations, and connections suggested by the extract (poetry's position within the charged racial climate of the 1950s, for example), she has turned the poetry away from itself and focused it onto events in the life of the author. At the end of her initial analysis, the poetry is little more than a slightly stylish self-portrait, while Ginsberg's life is simply a straightforward and directly referential key to understanding the poetry.

It should also be stated that this life being called into service as the guide to reading the poetry is, obviously, something of a narrative fiction created for radio. Gross culls only the largest and most famous moments from Ginsberg's past, moments that indicate a progression. Gross suggests that Ginsberg's family life made him into a "provocateur," citing a connected sequence of communist mother, gay lifestyle, and "being an intellectual."

She then asks for anecdotes of encounters with other literary superstars such as Burroughs and Kerouac. As she proceeds through this account of Ginsberg's life, some of her assumptions about her audience begin to reveal themselves: that it is interested in only the most direct connections and simplest causal relationships, and that it wants some gossip concerning names it recognizes, if only to confirm hackneyed stereotypes about the marginality of poets. (Which, it should be noted, Ginsberg provides by relating a story of his sleeping with Kerouac.) At this point, the interview could be summed up in a simple sentence without much disservice: A marginal cultural star, who happens to be a poet, destined for distinction from childhood, does expectedly marginal things with other marginal cultural stars. The consequences of this mode of reading through the veneration of a cultural figure are many, the most important being a presentation of an exclusionary and static relationship between producers and consumers. Because a possible discussion of process has been displaced by a kind of idolatry—because writing (n.) has been allowed to eclipse writing (v.)—listeners are not invited to think of themselves as potential writers or producers but are conceived of as satisfied with the relatively limited and prescribed range of engagement being offered.

At one point Ginsberg does attempt to steer the interview in the direction of intonation and the possibilities open to performances with different inflections. But Gross prevents any discussion of performative possibilities before it develops by fixing Ginsberg's performance style in his Jewish background and hurrying along to his poem "Kaddish." Her effect is to direct any nascent discussion of any of the formal qualities of poetry back to biographical material in order to render causal connections as the only valid reading. Biographical readings are, obviously, not bad in and of themselves, but the absolutist manner in which they are deployed on *Fresh Air* produces most often merely sentimental vignettes. The "Kaddish" redirection, for example, moves the conversation back to Ginsberg's mother and to how he received a letter from her after she had died, a letter that upset him and inspired him to learn how to perform the Kaddish and subsequently to write the poem. We ultimately learn that "Kaddish" is a difficult poem for Ginsberg to read because he cries at certain passages in which the image of his mother is particularly present.

Ginsberg ends the interview with a statement of his own poetic and philosophical project that could also serve as a cursory sketch of public radio's approach to language forms:

Terry Gross: Tell us a little bit about your life now.

Allen Ginsberg: Candor ends paranoia. If I can make my own mind transparent, so that people know what I'm really thinking, they don't have anything to be scared of and they can use it as a mirror to their own minds.

Poetic language is to give direct, literally "transparent" access to the mind of the great poet; and further, this transparency is a lesson to be learned and applied by all through observation. Transparency and its dissemination are beginning to reveal themselves as the main components in *Fresh Air*'s literary editorial policy, and here Ginsberg's advocation of these principles makes him perhaps the perfect *Fresh Air* poet. Yet even before he utters this aphorism, his interview vivifies its content: His life is sufficiently big and glamorous as to encompass, if not blot out, his poetry; he facilitates an iconographic, celebrity, or "great author" reading of his work, and this image is both easily represented and within the imagination of *Fresh Air*'s imagined audience.

The National Poetry Month *Fresh Air* interview with "performance poet" Sekou Sundiata further clarifies the program's approach to poetry and assumptions about language. Its study expands an understanding of how the method of biographical contextualization displaces discussions of form and performance practice and establishes poetry as a product of a generalized racial experience before the poetry is even presented.

In the setup for the interview, Sundiata reads "Harlem, a Letter Home," which Gross describes as "a poem about how his old neighborhood has changed."[9] In light of Gross's opening comment, "It's easy to listen to Sekou Sundiata's poems over and over again like songs, because you like the music," and her subsequent comparison of his poetry to rap, it seems important to make two observations about the broadcast version of "Harlem, a Letter Home": First, *Fresh Air* has Sundiata read the poem in the studio, rather than play the version on his CD (promoted on the program), *The Blue Oneness of Dreams*—the read version being slower, less precise and decided in terms of inflection, and also containing several key alterations.[10] Second, and more instantly apparent, the read version stands out from the rest of Sundiata's work as almost completely uninfluenced by rap. Sundiata's work, on the whole, *is* songlike—borrowing arrangements from jazz and pop music—and can share the frenetic pace, quick turns, and verbal collisions of rap. His "Ear Training," on *The Blue Oneness of Dreams* collection, is an excellent example of Sundiata's use of a rap-influenced verbal play and density, and songlike vocal variation. It is also thematically similar to "Harlem, a Letter Home," choosing inner-city life as its subject. In "Ear Training," "the city returns to humming just below middle C," while the elements of that hum periodically emerge as snatches of urban dialogue with onomatopoeic renderings of street sounds keeping the rhythm of various urban moments. In a selection such as "Ear Training," Sundiata comes closest to today's most intricate and powerful examples of African Diaspora poetry in the likes of Amiri Baraka and Nathaniel Mackey, poets whose work has at its heart the forms of African American culture—from blues musician to preacher to griot.

The *Fresh Air* reading is singularly noteworthy for how unthreatening it would be to the expectations for poetry of *Fresh Air*'s imagined audience. It is vocally staid, often resorting to the clichéd "poetical" method of a rising and trailing-off last syllable on each line. The text is scenic, with Sundiata functioning as a tour guide, ticking off landmarks and personages of a Harlem of decades past:

Over by Harlem River Drive
Where years ago you went underground
Leaving two dead policemen in your trail
Then backstage at the old Apollo Theatre
Where we used to be waiting
Pulling on the stars

. . .

You don't belong to Bird or Billy anymore
You don't belong to Malcolm or Langston anymore

Already existing in popular culture and popular history, these experiences and icons (these memories) are generic enough, familiar enough, for an imagined audience to assimilate easily. One does not ever have to have been in Harlem to understand, or indeed to have written, this poem. These are simple remembrances of something once seen, and like photos of Harlem in an old *Life* magazine, they are clearly focused and designed to be easily accessible.

I walk around with this photograph of you
At the African American Day parade
Looking like a thirty-third-degree Mason

A Parliament Funkadelic
An old African
An eastern star

The effort at poignancy fueled by nostalgic renderings of the familiar is exacerbated by alterations made in the *Fresh Air* reading. Most significantly, an extra line is added to the end of the poem: where the slow, ever-quieter repetition of "O Harlem" five times ends the version published on the CD, the line "It hurts me to my heart to see you like this" is added on *Fresh Air*. This line functions to enact the appropriate response for the audience; it signals that if it was not already obvious, the poem is over and one should now feel suitably softened by it, moved by it, feeling its hurt even if one could not describe that hurt precisely; it is enough to *feel* it, and here is how. As one should expect of all commodities, the poem's realization is located in its generalized effect on an abstract consumer, not in the poem itself, and not in the possibilities of responses to it or meanings derived from it. Within this terrain, the very project of considering the medium, form, and location of poetry—which might be in sum described as its "artifice"—is deemed unsuitable for radio.[11] But even in light of what is emerging as a radio ethic that justifies itself in terms of ease of consumption, the premise of the reaction against form in favor of transparency is misguided: it is felt that the foregrounding of artifice implies a reciprocal suppression of all-important meaning. But a formal consciousness potentially opens up more avenues to meaning and participation than it closes.

The second alteration in the *Fresh Air* version of "Harlem, a Letter Home" is the removal of the only repeated line in the poem. The CD version proceeds:

To Malcolm and Langston's words
The songs the speeches the poems
The songs the speeches the poems
More alive now than them

This repetition is arguably (along with the repeated "O Harlem") the only formally noteworthy or conscious moment in the poem. In removing it, any hindrance to an immersion in the poem as visceral experience, where words are used as tools for composing images that are in turn meant to evoke feelings, is removed as well.

In terms of identity politics, in the *Fresh Air* version of "Harlem, a Letter

Home" especially, issues of race and ethnicity are not advanced, discussed, worked out, or worked with so much as they are merely (re)presented in the shape in which they already exist. A known identity is the presupposition (or pretext) for the poem, so much so that it again seems a magazine photograph of the African American Day parade that the narrator carries with him, not a personal snapshot. Here identity is merely another object about which, or a genre within which, someone has chosen to write a poem.

On issues of form, in terms of performance style and texture, Gross seems to raise the question only to take it away in the same breath. She asks: "You're a poet who uses your voice in, I think, a particularly musical way, and I wonder if you were always reading that way, or if you had to find your voice." There is no discussion of that voice beyond the nebulous "musical way," no attempt to detail its qualities and effects, only an immediate rush to fix that voice within the confines of the biographical detail of Sundiata's development. Similarly biographical questions avoid a broad range of other possible, and even "acceptable" (in the terms of what is emerging as *Fresh Air*'s interests and format), questions. The interview manages to evade, for example, the potentially difficult areas of the ostensible subject of Sundiata's writing: the real experiences of ethnic minorities and social tensions in urban areas. When Gross asks, "What were you writing about when you first started to write?" Sundiata responds not by describing Hughes-inspired verse but by saying he wrote adventure and explorer stories. This, when coupled with his ultimate response to questions about his literary origins, that "poetry and literature saved my life," locates him as the ideal correspondent to reveal Harlem to an imagined *Fresh Air* audience. He writes about Harlem nostalgically, as a memory, but also as something he has escaped: "Your protruding ribs where once I entered and lived." Poetry has allowed him to leave the life about which he writes; poetry has succeeded in removing him from his subject. His presentation of the specific subject matter in this poem, a vision of Harlem, validates the stereotype of its being violent and depressing, and something from which one should try to escape in order to nostalgize from a safe suburban distance, much more than it documents or contributes to a particular understanding of Harlem life. Any positive aspects, such as the cultural icons of Harlem, only exist as specters in the melancholy haze of memory and a recognizably poetic delivery that have very little relation to the life of

Harlem today. An imagined audience can thus feel the thrill of being given the tour of an old Harlem that was simultaneously "tough" and full of culture, while admiring the poet both for his authenticity and for his self-salvation via his own hard work at writing.

The relative safeness of *Fresh Air*'s presentation of Sundiata, along with its voyeuristic appeal to neoliberalism, is summed up in Gross's last question about content: "Did you ever write any revolutionary poems?" Sundiata responds that, yes, his poems have been about social issues; but ultimately he says, "I think of poetry as ritual," a move that first accepts Gross's naive connection and then relegates both poetry and political action to an anachronistic, "ritual" realm without a place in everyday life. There also exists the implication that any formal innovation or "revolutionary" gesture, any linguistic accoutrement outside of narrative conveyance or transparency, should be bracketed off in "ritual" so that it can be treated safely as something mystical rather than anything threatening, effectual, or even difficult. Through this thinking, even potentially disruptive poetry is consistently transformed into an easily consumable commodity for *Fresh Air*'s imagined audience. Gross's final question of the interview speaks directly to this issue and foregrounds the most common apprehension within public radio about poetry: that the audience might switch it off as demanding or merely bad entertainment. She asks, "People that like rap are really into rhyme; do you think that's made it safe for people to like poetry?" Poetry, defined by rhyme (a formal element), is *unsafe* in Gross's mind until it is raised to the status of commodity, exchangeable with other (established) commodities like rap songs.

Unlike Ginsberg and Sundiata, Jane Shore, author of the book *Music Minus One*, requires almost no processing by *Fresh Air*. Her poetry and interview are exceptionally helpful in illustrating public radio's use and propagation of abstraction as a central communicative principle and its attachment to the idea of nostalgia as an ideal vehicle for poetry (a mode already evident in Sundiata's interview). The selections of Shore's poetry used on *Fresh Air* function as an abstract, almost collective, memory intent on evolving a similar emotion across a wide swath of an imagined audience. This poetry, because of its quantity of simple, generic details seen through the blur of years, has the feel of those proliferating middle-market chain restaurants that seek to cultivate comfortable, nostalgic feelings in their patrons by covering the walls with bits of cultural detritus that could have come from any suburbanite's grandparents' attic. Gross introduces Shore as "a poet I've really been enjoying," whose work is informed by growing up in a Jewish family in the 1950s and 1960s in New Jersey, and whose poetry is about bargains at the five-and-dime, vacations in the Catskills, shaving your legs, and "the small details that form you."[12] Serializing those small but generic details constitutes her poetic practice.

I cut out their split-level house in the country,
their collie, their crew-cut lawn.
I cut out their flagstone patio, shady backyard.
The kit even had a fallout shelter
with walls of painted shelves
filled with canned goods and bottled water.

Too hot to talk, too hot to eat,
we lowered the blinds
and sat in the dark all day and evening—
turning on lamps only made more heat.
We camped out on the living room sofa.
Ozzie and Harriet. Canned laughter. The News.
The station signed off, jets flew in formation
to the strains of the national anthem.[13]

Like the bad postmodernity of that nostalgia restaurant, these lines from Shore's "Heat Wave, Cold War," which open her interview, are a clutter of benign and mundane images that neither muster themselves into coherence nor seek to question coherence as an idea. They function like the gentle jump cuts in middle-of-the-road music videos that might be interesting if it were not for their lack of juxtaposition and lackluster yet earnest intention to describe a scene, tell a story, convey a feeling, or engender a sentiment. In fact, her first reading is little more than a series of narratively arranged images about two days in the family home and store. After the reading, Gross says, "I think one of the things that I like so much in your poems is your sense of detail, and the triggers that some of those details set off in me. I think some of your poems just set off this—like these sense memory reactions—and I'm wondering if you always gravitated towards the details of your memories of day-to-day life?" Gross's question fails to interrogate the most interesting effect of Shore's poetry: how and why both Shore *and*

Gross should come to share the same memories of everyday life. In fact, their life memories are so much in accord that after Gross reads the next selection of Shore's poetry of childhood, the following exchange occurs:

Terry Gross: I remember the bathing cap, I had the ponytail, I sometimes remember getting into pools in the summer . . .
Jane Shore: I return to those specific objects of childhood; I just can't let them go. Something calls you to that.
Terry Gross: I think you've just described exactly the feeling I get when I read your poems.

This huge but unrecognized irony in Shore's work is compounded by her final comment: "Each person has a unique life, and that's the thing they can write about."

The method of abstraction through genericness marks more than just a contradiction in Shore's stated poetic project; here it helps to further elaborate Gross's function in relation to her audience. In the Shore interview, Gross reads almost as much of Shore's poetry as Shore does, which Gross usually follows with this shared-experience reading. In offering this kind of visceral reading that suggests an abstract and generalized feeling, Gross receives the poems as she expects her audience to receive them, a comfortable but passive consumption that resolves in a nostalgic and vaguely personal feeling. And where relevant, she facilitates this kind of reception by reining in anything too difficult, further abstracting any complexity or particularity, asking for clarification, and repeating and rephrasing issues into simpler English. She thus both facilitates an easy consumption of the poetry *and* demonstrates it.

It could be argued (as the program's Web site does) that *Fresh Air* undertakes to engage with its audience and to facilitate a kind of participation around each program. But this claim must be approached critically. Given all the cues for reading that surround *Fresh Air*'s representation of poetry, and the consistent examples of readings offered by the host, it must be viewed as a kind of participation best illustrated through Shore's paper-doll-kit family: kit form allows members of an imagined audience to feel as if they are actually creating something on their own, yet that end product (memories) must be generic enough to fit (or at least not to conflict) with the memories of a majority of consumers. Through the magic of commodification, a performance of something recognizably poetic and constructed out of remembered cultural commonplaces will allow audience members to feel something *personally,* to access individual memories that are also generic memories, as they most surely originate from the same culture industry. Yet under a consumption-centered programming ethic, these memories appear no less fulfilling.

Fresh Air's effects on poetry and on the potential for radio poetry discourse extend far beyond its own daily hour. Its prominence means that its selection criteria and presentational mode are the touchstones by which all literary projects are measured. Pitching a literary series produced by myself and the poet Charles Bernstein (featuring interviews and performances with authors from the best-selling to the avant-garde) generated a wave of suspicious responses characterized by the following e-mail from a public radio station program director: "These programs by academics are about the artifice of the book, the writing, the process of that kind of creativity— NOT about the final product! The final product could suck! but these people like talking about how they did the book. When Terry G[ross] talks to a writer she talks about the final output—the human everyday response to the topic—so even if I'm not a writer, have not read the book—I enjoy the subject."[14] In the course of relating his objections to airing our series in particular, and other independently produced literary series in general, this program director officially articulates both the public radio fear of artifice evident in the Sundiata program and the static nature of the writer/ producer–listener/consumer relationship apparent in the Ginsberg interview. Perhaps most important, the phrase "even if I'm not a writer" and the sentiment that surrounds it are the distillation of public radio's thinking about its literary audience. Coupled with Gross's paradigmatic approach to poetry, the notion that readers are not expected to be writers ultimately evolves into the idea that listeners are not expected to be producers either of any unforeseen interpretation or of actual radio cultural material. Ideally, listeners unproblematically consume, while producers merely facilitate that consumption. Such a conception of audience, which is at best incapable of nuance and at worst purely condescending, is the driving force behind a clearly articulated programming ethic designed to meet (but never exceed) the perceived minimal desires of the abstracted listener.

The sign of that abstracted listener, the sign of "audience" evident in our analysis of poetry, casts a long shadow over public radio programming. Ironically, work done under that sign almost always reduces actual listener choices and opportunities for participation through format streamlining.

Several public radio institutional devices exist to propagate streamlining among member stations. In addition to regular visits from marketing analysts and program representatives from national offices (who have personal pecuniary interests in seeing that the lessons of ratings-driven programming are learned), annual conferences reinforce this logic: "Focus Focus Focus Your Format/Appeal! One of the biggest hurdles still facing public radio is greater focusing of the appeals we offer to listeners. Too many stations are still trying to serve too many separate audiences, resulting in less service for everyone."[15] This flyer description of a panel at the 1996 Public Radio Conference fails to recognize that the same listener might want variety in her or his listening, or that a more diverse (and even larger) set of possible listeners might be served by a diversified format.

While "audience" is the clearly defined and generalized entry to which all programming questions are addressed, public radio's initial conceptualization of it is much more complex and nuanced than it might first appear; indeed, as stations tell us during every fund drive, listening alone does not constitute membership. The primary source used by public radio stations to build conceptions of audience is the annually published survey *Public Radio Listeners—Demographics, Consumption Patterns, Media Usage*.[16] Within the first pages of its bar graphs, an uncharitable reader might be tempted to rephrase its title to read: *Audience Equals Consumers*. One is not registered in these vital and formational statistics that influence almost every hour of public radio if one listens but does not consume (houses, cars, magazines, membership subscriptions, etc.). From a deconstructive perspective, though, the most interesting category of this survey is "media usage." Statistics on how and when an audience listens to radio are presented as the natural and immutable way people use radio. A consistent listening experience is offered as the target mode for successful radio, and in aspiring to it, a radio programming of consistency reinstates, reproduces, and expands its hegemony. Put more precisely, the application of media usage statistics in program scheduling and development creates an unexamined feedback loop between programming and listening: programming engenders a mode of listening that is in turn used to justify the expansion of that very programming. If, for example, a station chose to offer mostly popular classical music, an analysis might show that people primarily use that station in a secondary manner as little more than acoustic wallpaper. These findings might then be used to justify the thorough reduction of other kinds of programming offered on that station because the data clearly show that the audience wants wallpaper. This method fails to recognize on a macrological level what it embraces on the small scale: that the shape, form, and content of radio affect how it is used by listeners.

At this point, I should distinguish between the programming I have described as utterly deferential to a particular construction of a consuming audience and the laudable efforts of the past thirty-five years of cultural studies to celebrate the scene of consumption as the site of autonomous pleasure, cultural value, and critically engaged decoding. The reigning public radio programming ethic builds its conception of audience around simplistic and repetitive notions of consumption that fly in the face of many cultural studies caveats. Deployed in its rhetoric are a generalized consumption and a stereotyped consumer the likes of which Raymond Williams—a tireless champion of the cultural consumption of everyday life—would have found thoroughly repugnant: "There are in fact no masses; there are only ways of seeing people as masses."[17] While my criticism of the consumption-based programming ethic is certainly not directed against efforts to describe and valorize activities that occur through consumption, it is very much concerned to address the problems that arise when notions of consumption are used in overwhelmingly restrictive ways *to dictate production,* when the audience survey becomes the most important component of program design. Even as we may look for fulfillment in decoding around the scene of consumption, radio programs are being produced and production decisions are being made *that affect opportunities for kinds of consumption.* Under the consumption-centered programming ethic, a unique and proprietary knowledge of "what people want" is used to legitimate not a clique of esthetes paternalistically disseminating high culture (which has always only been a bogeyman on American radio) but a clique of culture industry producers even more privileged and intractable.

Positing a production-centered programming ethic in opposition to a consumption-centered one is, again, not to disparage the cultural opportunities of consumption but merely to underscore the *different* opportunities that occur around material cultural production. In fact, in that this alternative ethic is not at all motivated to protect selected producer privilege by whitewashing questions that occur around the means of production, it is free to engage with consumption in novel ways. In that such an ethic would not necessarily aspire to a radio and a language of maximum ease in consumability (or what our *Fresh Air* study has revealed as maximum "transparency"), it might even, as the 1938 broadcast of *War of the*

Worlds did, anticipate certain expectations for consumption and draw attention to their assumptions or even chide their existence and naturalization. Conversely the consumption-based ethic enacted on *Fresh Air* not only configured how consumption was to happen but provided a guide for the appropriate mode of that consumption. While the consumption-centered ethic might seem sensible for commercial radio, it presents more than just serious philosophical problems when adopted by public radio. The schizophrenic nature of public broadcasting in the United States (part state-financed, part commercially financed, and part listener-financed) both contributes to this tendency toward commercialism and exacerbates its danger. Program directors and station managers typically suppress the obvious but potentially devastating threefold conclusion of emulating a streamlined format with a more commercial sound: (1) it will cause the loss of listeners who have gone to public radio seeking an alternative to that commercial sound (reducing donors); (2) listeners will begin to ask why they should support public funding of public radio if they can hear a similar programming approach on commercial radio (further reducing support for state funding); and (3) since public radio stations, by definition and by virtue of the legalities of their licenses, simply cannot run commercials in the manner that the commercial stations they emulate can, the use of underwrites can never hope to compensate for losses in the other two sources.

Never given the chance to develop under the weight of an imagined audience and the simplistic contextualization it engenders, the experience of poetry and the possibility for poetic exchange within and across communities on public radio's premier literary forum are replaced with a generic radio experience, something thoroughly at home at the end of the afternoon news. This species of contextualization, the goal of which is to associate the poetry with a narrative of the author's life, and which takes the form of questions such as "How did taking care of your mother influence you?" "What was it like meeting Jack Kerouac?" and "Do you see your sister in yourself?" constitutes nothing but a giant evasion—a way of not talking about, and not performing, poetry. Poetry is evaded because even in its most banal instances, it differentiates itself from more earnestly transparent language. It is poetry not only by virtue of its line breaks or its unconversational cadences in performance but also because it does not hope to hide (not that anything ever could) its existence within the medium of language; it is audible as opposed to the attempted inaudibility of discursive prose (the prose of the radio interview and newscast proper). The preference for commodified and transparent speech is but a symptom of a much larger fear of form in general, a fear of anything that exposes the materiality or structure of means of communication. Such modes threaten to reveal the concentration of social power and cultural authority accrued in access to the means of media production, in this case, by program directors, network producers, and underwriters/advertisers. Any broadcast that does not present itself as a natural and uncomplicated conveyance of content potentially raises questions in the minds of listeners about how, by whom, under what conditions, and to what ends radio is being produced, the answers to which would argue for a diversification in production. Modes of self-referentiality, then, must not be encouraged because they might describe public radio gatekeeper practices as "antipublic" in the very public space that they manage. On public radio the unavoidable recognition that poetry is opaque is the source of anxiety because by analogy it threatens to force radio to locate *itself* in its medium, to call it to examine the means and effects hidden behind its own hopes for transparency.

When one listens carefully to an installment of *Fresh Air,* one is immediately struck by its production values; in fact, one could say that production values, not poetry, poetic exchange, or exposing listeners to new ideas, are the focus and central work of the program's literary segments (in fact, the entire program).[18] Because it is recorded near flawlessly in a studio with exceptional acoustics, on the best microphones, and with painstakingly seamless editing, imperfections on the level of sound quality are usually discernible only to the professional ear. No expense is spared to make the content perfectly smooth and to render the material production of the radio program inaudible; it is to sound like disembodied voices having a conversation in a vacuum.[19] In addition to ignoring the diverse spheres of interest and the possibilities for radiophonic experimentation that could be investigated, this smoothness of radio and its ironic emphasis on production values sets a de facto sound quality standard that presents a serious initial obstacle for would-be or low-budget radio producers. It is the first and easiest thing program directors listen for when presented with new material. Dismissing something by virtue of poor sound quality is much easier than dismissing something because it is deemed inaccessible, unconventional, or too difficult to find room for within an established format. The effect of this standard, regardless of its professionalistic justifications, is to limit access to production and to support the existing and exclusion-ary relationship between cultural producers and listeners/consumers.

It is indeed possible to be disheartened by these observations, to feel as if the only option is to throw up one's hands, sell one's microphone, and switch off one's radio. But I contend that the prevalent public radio anxiety around form should be approached as an opportunity, not an endgame. The hostile reaction to formal innovation, and to poetry and radio con-scious of their location in or as media, reveals a weakness, a volatile terrain, that might be exploited by those interested in unsettling conceptions of poetic exchange on radio, diversifying opportunities to be material cultural producers, and interrogating the claim for radio itself to be a public or community space.

An emphasis on the form of a medium (language included) potentially opens up a discussion about the terms and conditions of, and access to, its production. The conundrum is then how to insinuate formal innovation into a public radio that is more wary of it than anything else. In my own experience, I have found it possible to use promos to make such an inter-vention. Promos, the short promotional announcements for upcoming programs, are not usually subjected to the scrutiny of transparency that the programs themselves undergo; once a program has passed muster with a public radio gatekeeper, the style of its promos is usually taken for granted. Further, by virtue of their being played at all hours, in the midst of "popu-lar" programs, after newscasts, before weather reports, and so on, promos will always be heard by significantly more people than hear the actual program broadcast itself. With this ubiquity in mind, an innovative ap-proach to promo production would proceed not in the traditional man-ner—the rendering of ultracommodities (commodifications of already commodified program content)—but in the production of independent entities that might unsettle the smooth surface of the other public radio programs in and around which they would be aired. Instead of attempting to encapsulate an author's work and significance in a tightly scripted thirty seconds, as *Fresh Air* often does with *two and three* writers per program promo, innovative promos for an innovative literary program would give a maximum amount of time to excerpts of authors performing their work. (I have been unable to uncover a single *Fresh Air* promo that has had *any* performance in it.) Further, these excerpted readings would not seek to be definitive or representational, or even to end in rhythmically conclusive places (a practice that would be anathema to the standard public radio aesthetic). Hence they would be brief moments of formally innovative poetry dropped into the otherwise perfectly smooth surface of public radio programs engaged in abstraction and rendering themselves and language transparent. Puncturing this smoothness, if only for a few seconds, consciously draws listeners' attention to the very artifice of language typically abjured. Promos might then serve as tiny countercommodification missives within very large and finely wrought public radio commodities. This is a minor example to be sure, but it does begin to show the critical possibilities open to the generation of radio (and radio poetry) meaning beyond those currently explored in programs designed with the uncomplicated consumption of a generalized audience in mind.

Notes

1 By "public radio" I refer to professionally managed, public-radio-network member stations, usually connected to major universities. While noncommercial independent, community, and college radio stations in the United States typically make available more extensive and innovative literary programming than their professional counterparts, their effect and presence is severely limited by weak transmissions, deteriorating equipment, licenses that limit broadcast hours, and, primarily in metropolitan areas where the former limits are often less applicable, bandwidth competition from commercial stations, as well as other factors.

2 "Commodification" here refers to exchangeability, that is, programs or elements having similar enough sounds, textures, and presentational modes as to be interchangeable. Drawing on the Marxist tradition of the word, a commodity is anything (in this case language or thought) produced for its capacity to be exchanged or distributed en masse rather than something produced for a value it might have on its own terms (a use value).

3 Raymond Williams, *Television: Technology and Cultural Form* (Hanover, N.H.: Wesleyan University Press, 1992), 80–112.

4 WHYY, Philadelphia, "About Terry Gross" (cited 7 October 1997), available on-line at http://whyy.org/freshair/aboutterry.html.

5 In 1997 *Fresh Air* averaged fewer than two people describing themselves as "poets" per month, peaking with four poets in April. (*Fresh Air* is broadcast five times a week with between two and three interviews per program.) These figures are based on the program descriptions available at the *Fresh Air* Web site (WHYY, "*Fresh Air*" [cited 7 January 1998], available on-line at http://whyy.org/freshair/).

6 It must be noted here that although Ginsberg's work might not be as formally self-conscious as that of some of his contemporaries (Barbara Guest and Hannah Weiner being but two examples), it does show a significant awareness of

form, of itself as located within language. This quality and understanding are given short shrift on *Fresh Air.*

7 Allen Ginsberg, interview by Terry Gross, *Fresh Air,* National Public Radio and WHYY, Philadelphia, 7 April 1997.

8 Allen Ginsberg, *Howl and Other Poems* (San Francisco: City Lights Books, 1980), 10.

9 Sekou Sundiata, interview by Terry Gross, *Fresh Air,* National Public Radio and WHYY, Philadelphia, 16 April 1997.

10 See Sekou Sundiata, *The Blue Oneness of Dreams,* Mercury Records, 1997, compact disc 31453 43972.

11 In her book *Radical Artifice: Writing Poetry in the Age of Media* (Chicago: University of Chicago Press, 1991), Marjorie Perloff also suggests that the hegemony of mass-media institutions demands a poetic response that challenges transparent formats (x–xiii). She argues for an emphasis on precisely the "artifice," on the awareness of syntax and language forms (54–55), that public radio finds so troubling in order to prevent cultural products from being simply "absorbed into the discourse of the media" (78).

12 Jane Shore, interview by Terry Gross, *Fresh Air,* National Public Radio and WHYY, Philadelphia, 16 April 1997.

13 This quotation is taken from Jane Shore's *Music Minus One* (New York: Picador, 1996), 19; copyright ©1996 by Jane Shore; reprinted by permission of St. Martin's Press, LLC.

14 Much of the information used in this section comes from a fourteen-year career in public radio, which includes work as a reporter and producer for two National Public Radio member stations (WBFO, Buffalo, and WVTF, Roanoke), and work as an independent producer on several nationally distributed long-form radio projects. Through this tenure, I participated in a number of nationally organized public radio conferences, was exposed to numerous radio marketing consultants, and witnessed firsthand their impact on programming.

15 For accounts of marketing's effects on innovative radio, see Dan Lander, "Radio Art: The Pubescent Stage," *Musicworks* 53 (1992): 21; and Judith Strasser, "The Uses of Radio," *To the Best of Our Knowledge,* Public Radio International, 14 July 1996.

16 The title changes slightly from publication to publication and is typically headed by the year (*Audience 98,* for example). The book is an audience/consumer profile compiled by Simons Research (a marketing analysis company that measures "more than 800 products, over 4,800 brands, and all types of media") and National Public Radio's office of Strategic Planning and Audience Research in Washington, D.C. Copies are sent to all member stations and to producers distributing programs over the public radio satellite system.

17 Raymond Williams, *Culture and Society: 1780–1950* (New York: Columbia University Press, 1983), 300.

18 "Production values" here refers to the level of technology required to produce a particular aural effect or, more precisely, a fidelity to established radio sound and aesthetics. High production values are thought to enhance listeners' absorption in radio content and paradoxically to divert attention away from the means and circumstances of material radio production.

19 Each hour of programming in a series such as *Fresh Air* has an estimated cost of $25,000 (Tatiana Schreiber, "Double or Nothing: A Recommendation for Improving Freelance Rates," *Airspace,* September–October 1997, 1).

Works Cited

Ginsberg, Allen. *Howl and Other Poems.* San Francisco: City Lights Books, 1980.

——. Interview by Terry Gross. *Fresh Air.* National Public Radio and WHYY, Philadelphia, 7 April 1997.

Lander, Dan. "Radio Art: The Pubescent Stage." *Musicworks* 53 (1992): 21.

Perloff, Marjorie. *Radical Artifice: Writing Poetry in the Age of Media.* Chicago: University of Chicago Press, 1991.

Schreiber, Tatiana. "Double or Nothing: A Recommendation for Improving Freelance Rates." *Airspace,* September–October 1997, 1.

Shore, Jane. *Music Minus One.* New York: Picador, 1996.

——. Interview by Terry Gross. *Fresh Air.* National Public Radio and WHYY, Philadelphia, 16 April 1997.

Simons Research and National Public Radio. *Audience 98: Public Radio Listeners— Demographics, Consumption Patterns, Media Usage.* Washington, D.C.: National Public Radio, 1998.

Strasser, Judith, prod. *To the Best of Our Knowledge.* Public Radio International, 14 July 1996.

Sundiata, Sekou. *The Blue Oneness of Dreams.* Mercury Records, 1997, compact disc 31453 43972.

——. Interview by Terry Gross. *Fresh Air.* National Public Radio and WHYY, Philadelphia, 16 April 1997.

WHYY, Philadelphia. "About Terry Gross." Cited 7 October 1997. Available on-line at http://whyy.org/freshair/aboutterry.html.

——. "*Fresh Air.*" Cited 7 January 1998. Available on-line at http://whyy.org/freshair/.

Williams, Raymond. *Culture and Society: 1780–1950.* New York: Columbia University Press, 1983.

——. *Television: Technology and Cultural Form.* Hanover: Wesleyan University Press, 1992.

RADIO IDEOLOGIES

IN THE RADIO WAY:

ELIZABETH II, THE FEMALE VOICE-OVER,

AND RADIO'S IMPERIAL EFFECTS

Adrienne Munich

Windsor, October 13, 1940. Vibrations from bombs dropped in London by what Prime Minister Winston Churchill called "the Hun" shake the chalk hill on which Windsor Castle had stood guard over the Berkshire plain since William the Conqueror erected a wooden castle there. In September, six bombs hit Buckingham Palace, where King George VI and Queen Elizabeth determined to sit out the war. A bomb might drop at any time, but particularly just after sunset. Dusk is beginning to lower, and "the children's hour" poeticized by Henry Wadsworth Longfellow descends.[1] On a radio program of the same name, a girl's clear, well-modulated, and carefully rehearsed voice issues from wireless receivers all over the globe. She pauses at the right moments, with her voice slightly rising when she gestures to the young listeners and to the world of their common future: "And when peace comes, remember, it will be (voice rising) for us (voice lowering), the children of today." Yet this inclusive gesture gains its power from the unique position of the speaker. This is no ordinary girl. She was photographed at a microphone sitting in a sumptuous study, at a leather-topped desk, where her father, George VI, and her grandfather, Edward VII, broadcast to their empire.[2] Her words are simple, but her rank, the moment, and the place lend them particular gravity. Beaming her voice to a global audience, the fourteen-year-old future sovereign conveyed her love and good wishes from the children "at home" yet in the place of danger to the "children of the Empire," particularly children in the countryside, separated from their families.[3] "I can truthfully say to you," she pledged, "that we children at home are full of cheerfulness and courage. We are trying to do all we can to help our gallant sailors, soldiers, and airmen, and we are trying, too, to bear our own share of the danger and sadness of war. We know, everyone of us, that in the end all will be well."[4]

Spunky words (especially the "rather sweet human touches" admired by the royal governess, Marion Crawford), particularly inspiring from the mouth of a genuine princess.[5] Because her voice projected from a box located in whatever meant "home" to the listener (no matter that the speaker's actual "home" for the five war years was usually that huge medieval fortress, recently further secured with a bomb shelter), the moment was made all the more intimate at the broadcast's finale when the princess turned to her silent sister, saying, "My sister is by my side, and we are both going to say good night to you. Come on, Margaret," and the ten-year-old Margaret Rose added, "Good night, children," to her sister's farewell.[6] Perfect.

Perfect because this first broadcast set the tone for the family-oriented position of the future queen's radio voice. Listening in at this first instance of it, Jock Colville, Churchill's secretary, was disappointed at the "sloppy sentiment she was made to express," but he considered "her voice most impressive and, if the monarchy survives, Queen Elizabeth II should be a most successful radio Queen."[7] Colville did not appreciate that the sentiment was of a piece with the voice in establishing feminine sovereignty. Moreover, it was not the voice alone that conveyed the regal patent; the voice along with what the radio program itself came to represent heralded England's Queen Radio the First.

The program initiated other radio firsts. *The Children's Hour,* one of the first BBC programs, forty-five minutes long, transmitted every day after the evening news and thus programmed an extended time of family togetherness. Because it was the first regular program of its length to be broadcast by the BBC, its effects on defining radio's cultural position and on those who listened would be difficult to overestimate and impossible to specify.[8] *The Children's Hour* played a "disproportionately large part in the early life of the broadcasting stations. The BBC had succeeded remarkably well in mobilizing its child audience. It had made them feel that the world of *The Children's Hour* was one in which they could participate."[9] The idea of children within a family context thus played a key role in constituting and defining British radio's kind of power. The notion of family it established was a child-centered one within a benevolent patriarchy. Young people constituted an effective listeners' pressure group with responses to the broadcasts published in the corporation's magazine, *Radio Times.* Children of the empire wrote back, and Uncle Mac (Mr. McCulloch) or others of the uncles and aunts, the corporation staff metamorphosed into family, would respond. In reporting the story, the *Times* specifically mentioned that "'Uncle Mac' introduced the Princess and at the end of the broadcast, thanked both her and Princess Margaret for their presence at Children's Hour."[10] It was precisely the sense of royal presence that emanated through radio receivers; as the press noted, her "sweet" voice resembled that of her mother, and the actual presence of both parents in the broadcasting room, also widely reported in the press, brought the royal family into the family circle.[11] In acknowledging its community of listeners as part of its program, *The Children's Hour* performed family beyond ordinary family borders. Encouraging a belief in reciprocity, equality, and respect, the program started its consumers young and formed them in the radio way.

From its outset, the program created by fiat an extended "family" of its staff, who were initially reluctant performers of a radio family unity. Asa Briggs points out that the BBC staff "had to reconcile themselves to becoming 'uncles and aunts', with all that this meant, not only to children but to some extent at least to the public as a whole."[12] Briggs only gestures to radio's power in harnessing cultural ideas of an extended family to its appeal. Perhaps because the evocation of family implicitly carries its idealized image that assumes understanding of what "all that this meant," he cannot specify what the staff was taking on when the program anointed them uncles and aunts. But to appreciate Elizabeth's impact, one might speculate a bit more. What *did* all this mean? More precisely, what did it mean for the October 13 broadcast that the future sovereign should speak as a child to the empire, and to *what* "extent" could this family thing have meaning, not only to children but "to the public as a whole"?

For that moment, in that context, it meant that Elizabeth joined the radio family, and the radio family took her in, or, in radio terms, "heard" her. Placing the radio in the family way meant or implied a genetic stake in caring, in nurturing. But this was a family of millions, an invisible family— a family in the radio way. In families, the uncle or aunt occupies a liminal position, augmenting the nuclear circle, either by enlarging it or, for the image of the radio wave, by forming concentric circles around it, radiating family outward in waves of concern. This wholesome view of the radio family ignores—or perhaps better, *because* it is a radio family, it can more easily ignore—potentially dangerous functions of uncles and aunts, at an extreme, in seducing little children, a pornographic stock-in-trade. Less ominously, aunts and uncles can provide a different but often subversive view of the world for nephews and nieces, attested to by diverse literary characters such as Uncle Toby, Aunt Betsy Trotwood, Auntie Mame, and Uncle Remus. BBC uncles and aunts gave a wider world to their nephews and nieces, a world that, generously, was available to parents as well.

The Children's Hour family is a nostalgic, disembodied family. Princess Elizabeth, as the privileged child of this family, elicits a longing, not simply on the part of the parents for the perfect child but from the subjective position, for the inner child that no one could ever be. This listener could be an adult in chronological years, but she or he listened in as a child. Thus by inaugurating the future queen as a radio niece, the listener is positioned to join the queen's family as a compatriot but also as a niece or nephew. Because she could be imagined as an equal (yet a special equal), the radio family provided the ideal venue for Elizabeth's initial performance of imperial authority in a new, more democratic key.

The new key depended on the kind of power exerted by sound alone. Tim Wilson finds that radio can reproduce a deeply satisfying auditory experience, similar to that found in the acoustic experience of premicrophone cathedral masses, where the echoing, familiar sounds create an experience independent of semantic meaning. He argues that the cathedral hearing experience reproduces an ontological auditory experience of prebirth. Wilson quotes an audiologist, Dr. Alfred Tomatis, who "maintains that it is via the ear, the first of our sense organs to develop in utero, that we form our primary connection: first with the inner, and then the outer world."[13] Psychologically primitive, disembodied sound can evoke in the listener an early auditory memory. Like the transcendent experience of sound one experiences in a cathedral, where the sound swirls upward, absorbed in the air, familiar but vaguely incomprehensible and therefore reassuring, the ear in utero picks up the higher frequencies. Literally drawn to a "higher" power, the echoing voice that the fetus hears prepares one for such transcendent and regressive moments so effectively deployed in the religious chant of Christian liturgy. Disembodied sound in its higher registers strikes a note of nostalgia, takes us out of our body to that moment when, suspended in amniotic fluid, we discerned an echoing maternal voice accompanied by rhythmic pulsations and organic sounds. Earthly institutions such as religion can exploit such aural power to create the deeply private yet communal experience that draws one out of one's physical body while plumbing its psychological depths.

Radio, so Wilson proposes, possesses a power similar to the cathedral service to elicit transcendence through sound. When radio finds its distinctive sound or "acoustic profile," it sells the program. More than any semantic content, the sound *is* its content.[14] *The Children's Hour* sold through its acoustic profile, and it sold Princess Elizabeth. Because the program's acoustic profile evoked the experience of listening as a child, Wilson's connections between religion, prebirth, and radio are even more compelling for a program such as *The Children's Hour* than they would be for adult programs. The listener's association to a safe place reinforced the comfort of Elizabeth's message, giving its reassurances sonorous authority. That many thousands heard her speech in their actual places of worship only reinforced a conjunction between religious and royal sanctity.[15] Its profile enabled the sound of her voice itself to seem as if it were Princess Elizabeth's inevitable call to sovereignty.

The program's acoustic profile delivered a message in the princess's semantic content as well as in the sound of her voice. Wilson's insight about the religious effects of the medium applies to her message as well as to the auditory experience of it. Her voice gains in authority because it belongs to a real princess, carrying with it the collective mythology of royalty, a position where it is fantasized that one gets what one wants. Princess Elizabeth, the embodied fulfillment of fairy-tale desire, solidifies her female authority by becoming Everygirl, but "alone of all her sex." In that paradox, she, like a quasi-religious figure, speaks for all children, but unlike them, she can perform miracles through royal command. Her speech seems to perform a transformative miracle whereby a medieval pile could repel the Hun's slings and arrows rather than the Nazi's bombs. "All will be well," articulated by a princess, establishes a link between an anointed royalty's connection to the Almighty and registers as word from God, promising eschatological justice.

So much the better that all will be well "in the end." Depending on what one thinks "all" and "well" might mean, the wishful platitude spoke to the British will to defend itself against Hitler. But it also spoke to an empire beyond political borders, an empire that desired fairy-tale royalty. The once and future queen had become the familial sybil to that audience. It spoke out-of-bounds. Brigg's "public as a whole," I believe, is that larger public, drawn by primordial desire into the family circle. This is fulfillment on a secular register of the prophecy "And a child shall lead you." It testifies to the power inhering in that basically Christian wish, transformed to nineteenth-century romanticism by William Wordsworth, that the child be father to the man.[16]

If the particular wisdom that the child is father to the man signifies a belief in the oracular powers of the man-child, what if the child is a girl? In this particular case, the child's gender (and her unique position as heiress to an imperial monarchy) is crucial to the remainder of my argument, for if the voice is the voice not of a child/man but of a child/woman, the very nature of that voice is differently constituted and differently heard. Her child's voice "mothers" the woman and produces in its listeners a fantasy of authority different from that produced had the child's voice fathered the man.

The mothering voice, carrying a particular resonance of prebirth to the listener, theoretically produces a satisfying acoustic experience, reminiscent of prenatal life and linked to auditory feelings of religious transcendence. In listening to Elizabeth's relatively high pitched, though carefully schooled, girlish voice, which spoke reassuring and animating words, one's auditory experience in listening to *The Children's Hour* might be considered a pleasurable (but fraught) regressive moment, one that puts the listener in touch with the potentially ominous desire for an enveloping and echoing chamber where time stops and life is simple. This is a life before gendering, but distinctions between higher (female) and gruffer (male) voices prepare for gendered distinctions in voice.

The listener experiences the radio voice as both far away (in that it issues from some invisible location, a place not here) and very close (in that one can see the place from which the voice emanates). In addition to its register and the acoustic profile of the program, its bodiless distance from the listener recalls a primal loss, the loss of the maternal connection. Because of its resemblance to what has been lost, the girl's radio voice can be fetishized. It promises a presence in its intimacy of audibility surrounding the listener. According to Lacan, the remnants of various objects the child previously experienced as part of itself (such as the breast and the mother's voice) retain a particular resonance of meaning. They are Other, but also the part of oneself that forces recognition of loss. Lacan terms these objects *objets petits autres*, or objects with only a little "otherness."[17] Because the female voice retains its primal familiarity, it can thus function powerfully in a liminal space of me and not-me, no matter what the gender of the listener.

Elizabeth's voice in 1940 is liminal in another way. It is not quite the voice of the mother but the voice of a child on the brink of maturity. As such, it is a border voice, pointing the listener both to childhood and to the mother that the child hears before it can see her. That "female" sound inaugurates or mothers the person into the world. That many listeners identified the young girl's voice with that of her mother reinforces the dual sense of what one hears when the princess speaks.

While the concept of objets petits autres usefully places the loss in relation to the mother, it can also be understood as a loss of one's earlier self, a self that could not know one's own voice as one's own. The child's voice speaks of that loss in language, itself the recompense for loss. As a child's voice, it carries traces of a not-yet-gendered sound. At the same time, a fourteen-year-old voice speaks of what is about to come, for the woman and for the queen-to-be. Elizabeth's quasi-maternal turn to her little sister and Margaret's somewhat thinner, younger voice remind the listener of that liminal position. In wartime, when homes stand at the bat-tlefront as they did in London, psychological liminality maps onto the terrain. The children's place, at home in the place of danger or away in the place of relative safety, highlighted the complexities of loss and the fetishiz-ation of objects reminding one of loss.

The fetishized voice that Elizabeth's became by means of her radio speech only promises fulfillment in its creation of nostalgic desire, a prom-ise for homeland it cannot fulfill. Radio generates its promise by taking away some primary senses, most obviously the visual. Its success is mea-sured not by how it can restore in the imagination what is beyond its power to provide but by how it can convey a sense of plenitude without sight. Rudolph Arnheim praises radio's "blindness" not as a loss but as a purging, a purification of the world, "the reception of pure sound . . . which comes to [the listener] through the loudspeaker, purged of the materiality of its source."[18] In such purity, the voice creates its own intimacy, a sense of innerness, the potential for psychological space. If subjectivity is "from the very outset dependent upon the recognition of a distance separating self from other,"[19] the radio listener can experience a partial closing of that distance. Listening can cause pleasurable regression where boundaries be-come more blurry but where the listener is firmly rooted in a (usually familiar) place. The configuration of an authoritative girl's voice counter-ing patriarchal authority constitutes a regressive pull to a primary object of desire. Along with its Christian (and romantic) radio overtones, a psycho-analytic perspective adds gender to the acoustic message: the voice of a female child shall lead thee both backward (to prebirth) and forward (to an afterlife), both figured as timeless pleasure.

Concepts of the female voice-over from psychoanalytic film theory provide some conceptual tools for theorizing different effects produced by Elizabeth's more mature voice from that, say, of her father's in his radio speeches. Kaja Silverman sternly points out that recent psychoanalytic theory shares with classic cinema a *fantasy,* "the trope of the maternal voice as a sonorous envelope." This fantasy plays itself out against the equally powerful myth of the mother as a trap, a power that imprisons or, worse, consumes its helpless victim. Against this threat, the maternal authority is appropriated by the male, whose voice speaks with the authority gained by divesting the female voice of its earlier role as a "language teacher, commentator, and narrator."[20] Silverman claims that because of the desire to contain her, the female cinematic voice must be cloistered or sequestered within the diegesis. Silverman is correct in her estimation of the cultural fantasy that keeps the cultural mother in a sentimental and idealized position within a carefully specified plot. The engine of the fantasy, its hold on thinkers such as Julia Kristeva, depends in part, however (and this Silverman denies, I think), on the power of fantasy to construct one's lived reality. Silverman warns about waxing nostalgic for this voice without also recognizing its fantasy aspect and the fears of, as well as desires for, envelopment that the experience of a female voice can elicit. The voice can reinforce the wish for the simplicity of a child about complex subjects.

Even if one considers the historical stage as analogous to a film's diegesis, Elizabeth's radio voice functions beyond a conventional family configuration. Some historians have accused it of existing independent of historical fact. This ability, however, to seem timeless, in this case by explicitly using the family as metaphor, characterizes the female voice-over's power. Elizabeth refers to history, speaks in real time, to an actual occasion, but references history to a family context that creates an aura of family benevolence, working toward common, even universal, ends. Hers is the voice of the collective nation, the female voice, speaking for the male authority in the same way that mothers tend to do, yet her maternal voice creates a fiction, a fantasy world of the imagination that points to a world of absolute safety beyond any situation to which she speaks. The voice of a queen, Elizabeth's voice and its effects engendered a family fantasy with a little less of the fantasmic. Her voice-over drew on powerful cultural desires, fundamental ones that can shape history.

Seven years after Elizabeth's radio debut, the queen delivered another momentous radio speech that added an element to the radio family she had engendered during the war. The youthful voice had modulated into a young woman's. The war was over, but was that the most one could extract from the princess's platitude that "all will be well"? It was true that George VI had gained in stature as a symbol of stalwart Britishness. But the monarchical image was not that of a solitary man but that of a father within a devoted family unit. The king's notion of the monarchy depended for its representation on the nuclear family. It was an image initiated by George III, naturalized and perfected by the king's great-grandmother Victoria, and consciously emulated by George VI. Although he restored some Victorian customs and Victorian uniforms, he also modernized the Victorian monarchical concept by merging the idea of family with an idea of corporate commercialism. Capitalizing on an idea of a family business, the king referred to himself, his wife, and their children as "The Firm." It represented itself as deeply connected to each other for mutual profit. This firm depended in part on the concept of family that had made the bbc's *The Children's Hour* such a success. Like the program, it acted as if the audience could talk back.

In 1947, parallels between the family and the realm were uncannily linked because both were besieged. The Firm was being invaded by a suitor for the princess's hand, and the British Empire (now also known as the Commonwealth) was asserting some independence. King George felt that Prince Philip, no matter how unobjectionable, even appropriate, as a suitor, threatened the shield against political dissolution afforded by the myth of "The Firm."[21] The conflict centered on the timing: Elizabeth wanted to announce her engagement to Philip at the moment that The Firm was about to embark on a tour of South Africa. If the engagement were made public, Philip would join the expedition. The king believed in the tactical importance of the trip as solidifying the bonds of commonwealth, and in the words of Elizabeth Longford, "the Royal Firm of four . . . were poised to capture South Africa as a single compact unit, and by this operation the King set much store."[22] Metaphors of conquest, though possibly unconscious on the part of the biographer, are apposite in describing the trip. Representation of a nuclear family seemed crucial to the king in establishing a patriarchal authority, loving and devoted, yet under the protection of the paterfamilias, who is also king.

The king's mission was not only to thank South Africa for its part in the war but also to endeavor to keep it within the family circle. The situation was tense because the Boer-supported Nationalist Party was standoffish, not feeling in the family way.[23] Hence, operating on the powerful fantasy of family power, the king depended on the fealty of his daughters to set the paradigm for his visit. To the king, a suitor would highlight the complexities of the family romance as a figure of empire.

Extending the metaphor into the political realm, suitors were carrying off their various brides. Gandhi was about to carry off the Jewel in the Crown, with Earl Mountbatten, viceroy of India, giving away the bride. Whether the coincidence that Prince Philip was to English himself by taking the name of this same British relative who had changed his name from Battenberg to Mountbatten figured in the king's conscious mind is unlikely. Yet the Victorian precedents for turning the German Hanovers and relations to English Windsors and Mountbattens determined the context for diplomacy as a family act. The family monarchy was also symbolized by the vessel HMS *Vanguard,* on which the family embarked. Queen Mary noted in her diary "how many fittings from the old *Victoria & Albert* had been adapted to *Vanguard.*"[24] Of course, Queen Victoria, a prototypical family monarch, was the first to reign as empress of India, and her "I" for "imperatrice" was about to disappear from the royal crest. In the face of such an actual and symbolic loss—to nation and to family monarchy—the king determined to present a family face. George VI, supported by his queen, won the argument, and the about-to-be-reconfigured Firm embarked for the Union of South Africa without the suitor.

The journey evoked royal progresses to far-flung lands. Such journeys, reported back at home in periodicals such as the *Illustrated London News,* typically portrayed them as entertainment: a circus, or great exhibition, with the natives in colorful costumes performing indigenous rituals involving dance, song, or some other indication of their difference from their sovereign. By implication, these portrayals solidified a concept "at home" of colorful colonies, somewhat backward, perhaps, but entertaining in their confirmation of the vast spaces under imperial domination. Against the complexities of imperialism, the Firm attempted to affect the course of history by evoking an empire in a family model.

The trip was eventually commemorated in a radio speech delivered by the Radio Princess. The notion of a radio speech to forge ties among far-flung units of an imperial entity began in 1933, when the monarchy appreciated radio's power to draw people together. James Lawrence notes the inauguration of the radio monarchy:

[The wireless was] the ideal device to enkindle a sense of community among the separate races of the empire; to strengthen the ties of kinship between Britain and the dominions; and, most important of all, to focus the loyalty of all the empire's subjects on the figure who symbolised imperial unity, the monarch. It was therefore appropriate that on Christmas Day 1933 members of the extended imperial family heard the gruff, fatherly voice of George V speaking from Sandringham. In the first royal Christmas message, the King thanked his subjects for their loyalty, pledged them his continued service, and sent them the season's good wishes. This brief, simple and warm address had been preceded by an hour-long programme made up of short pieces contrived to convey a sense of familial closeness among the peoples of the empire. There were short live broadcasts from Canadian, Australian and New Zealand towns and cities, Gibraltar, and a ship lying off Port Said.[25]

Each subsequent year, the Christmas broadcasts appealed to "family values" with the homey, unscripted voices of ordinary people juxtaposed to that rehearsed sovereign paternal voice. From the perspective of these celebrated performances of family, one appreciates that Elizabeth was raised to assume the radio mantle, along with the orb and scepter. Before Secretary Colville approved of her sovereign fourteen-year-old voice, Elizabeth was born into a radio monarchy, one that depended on the family metaphor. The Commonwealth had already been prescripted as family before her actually ever confronting actual lands belonging to it. The trip to Africa was Elizabeth's first trip outside the British Isles, and therefore her first physical experience of the idea of commonwealth. Coincidentally the Commonwealth, originally formed at the Imperial Conference of 1926, the year of Elizabeth's birth, was undergoing a change—in the metaphors of this essay, was, along with Elizabeth, coming of age. Both were twenty-one.

As The Firm approached the Cape of Good Hope, Elizabeth proposed to her father that she broadcast a coming-of-age speech. Debates ensued. The representation of the stakes of this debate is almost as interesting as the actual fact of the broadcast, for it reflects the importance of family dynamics at the intersection of the personal, figured as family, and the political, also figured as driven by family dynamics. For instance, Brigadier Stanley Clarke, O.B.E. described the royal decision to allow the princess's political coming-of-age speech by evoking the wholesome sexuality of a young maiden in flower, with the father controlling the daughter's sexual initiation:

It [the desire to broadcast] was something that the King had always hoped to hear, but he was anxious not to ask his daughter to take over her vast responsibilities before that was essential. . . . His Majesty realized that Princess Elizabeth had arrived, almost without his having noticed it, at full womanhood. . . . The laughing girl with the lovely golden hair, wonderful pink-and-white complexion, and beautiful blue eyes had been a child to him throughout the War years. Now she was suggesting a full entry into the world. So, though he was cautiously responsive to her plan, it was with mixed feelings . . . that he accepted the fact that his elder daughter was now ready to bear some of the burden of one of the world's most difficult jobs.[26]

Stanley's description of the father's attraction to his daughter details those body parts fetishized as the pinnacle of Anglo-Saxon feminine beauty: golden hair, pink-and-white complexion, and blue eyes. The passage glides from the sexualized white princess to "her full entry into the world," at the point where its rhetoric prepares for a statement referring to her sexual, rather than political, maturity. The bearing of the burden of empire echoes both Kipling's "white man's burden," since the speech is going to be made in Africa, and the seamier stories about white slavery, since the description of Elizabeth is so highly sexualized. Mixing the sexual with the political suggests the "innocent" sexuality of a debutante and its more subversive image of a white virgin sold into political slavery by her father, in the very home of the imperial Other, no less. Little wonder that the king is represented as having mixed feelings about his daughter's giving the radio speech. Furthermore, Stanley characterizes Elizabeth's bearing adult imperial responsibilities and the entry of her voice to the empire through the radio waves in terms of a family way.

The princess oversaw the carefully crafted speech, composed of touching memories and appropriate quotations, such as Rupert Brooke's line "Now, God be thanked Who has matched us with His hour," the saying of William Pitt about England saving herself by her exertions and saving Europe by her example. The spirit of self-sacrifice characteristic of patriotism in the body of her speech conveys a sense of maternal sacrifice in the context of the family metaphor: "To all the peoples of the British Commonwealth and Empire . . . I declare before you all that my whole life, whether it be long or short, shall be devoted to your service and the service of our great imperial family to which we all belong."[27] The voice itself had lost the charm of childhood and gained an aristocratic authority, with its plummy accents of "futshah" for future and "powah" for power. But it had not lost an innocent pleasure in finding "home" everywhere in the Commonwealth. "I am 6,000 miles from the country where I was born," she declared, "but I am certainly not 6,000 miles from home."[28] A "family of nations" could make the world a home for the princess. She acknowledges that radio power built this family home. Invoking an "ancient Commonwealth" and her ancestors' knightly coming-of-age vow of fealty, Elizabeth dubs herself as a knight of the radio realm: "I cannot do quite as they did [women cannot really be knights], but through the inventions of science I can do what was not possible for any of them. I can make my solemn act of dedication with a whole Empire listening."[29]

It is true that voice could, by its very accents, remind those unsympathetic to what it represented of oppression. On one level, everyone knows that the Commonwealth would not welcome its lesser nieces and sisters into all its homes. This regal voice, masquerading as the sister, niece, or aunt of the Other, must have been heard with some ambivalence by many indigenous auditors. In addition, given the cultural arena of its broadcast range, the imperial voice-over could be heard as anachronistic. In interpreting the connection between radio words and the context from which they draw, Longford comments on the speech's historical ironies: "There was no such thing as an 'imperial Commonwealth,' even in 1947, and South Africa, the very country in which she was speaking, was to 'support' her and 'share' her 'resolution' only for a limited number of years."[30] But if the words are ironic, they are so in context of royal representation and radio's imperial effects, for historical reality is not connected in a seamless relation to representation. The powerful realm of shared fantasy that the imperial radio voice supported effectively maintained the family metaphor against other realities to produce the reassuring tones of the empire as family in the radio way.[31]

Despite the realities surrounding the Cape Town coming-of-age speech, such as the separation of South Africa as a Commonwealth country, the dominance of the apartheid Nationalist Party, and the queen's support of the black cause, which essentially meant that she was not to return to South Africa for another forty-eight years, the family notion of the Commonwealth persisted in radio speeches.

Most strikingly, the family metaphor emerges fully developed in Elizabeth II's first Christmas broadcast when she performs the ritual of her forefathers. In this unrehearsed speech, the queen merges notions of the Commonwealth with thoughts of family. Alluding to a universal conception of the Christian holiday as a family event (of course, Christmas creates a collective divinity in the Holy Family), she observes that at Christmas our thoughts "are always full of homes and families."[32] Then Elizabeth moves into a meditation on the Commonwealth family, a family powerfully constituted by the radio:[33]

But we belong, you and I, to a far larger family. We belong, all of us, to the British Commonwealth and Empire, that immense union of nations, with their homes set in all four corners of the earth. Like our own families, it can be a great power for good—a force which I believe can be of immeasurable benefit to all humanity. My father and grandfather before him worked all their lives to unite our peoples ever more closely, and to maintain its ideals which were so near to their hearts. I shall strive to carry on their work.[34]

Monarchy is governed by family inheritance, and in her 1952 Christmas speech, broadcast at Sandringham from the very seat and desk of her blood relatives, Elizabeth invokes family loyalty, asserting it as her heritage and also the heritage of the "you" of her radio audience, an audience estimated at over one hundred million.[35] She enlists them in the family mission, when she is a new queen, just before her coronation. According to the press, she was successful. The *Daily Mail,* a paper published at Carmelite House, found her invocation to family particularly true: "The voice of the Sovereign brings to every home a feeling of reassurance. In those few minutes when each and every one of us is being addressed in person we feel that we 'belong,' and that we are, indeed, member of the same great family. . . . [the speech is] from the head of the family."[36] The voice has assumed the maturity of womanhood, and it is the voice of an actual mother. Different from her predecessors, then, her maternal voice, which speaks in its tonality and pitch of what has been lost, also promises to restore the loss through membership in a larger family, the family of Commonwealth and empire, a fairy-tale entity that gained in credibility from the fantasy-affirming radio.

That radio helped to maintain overlapping fictions: that families are good models for international relations, and that the Commonwealth operated as a family. Elizabeth could affirm this value as late as 1961, when, in recognizing Ghana as part of the Commonwealth, she defined the Commonwealth as "a group of equals, a family of like-minded peoples whatever their differences of religion, political systems, circumstances and races."[37] The political reality of Nkrumah's jailing his opposition enjoys no acknowledgment; the family fantasy prevails.

Radio, more effective for the family way than television, could reify the family image, for its blindness, in Arnheim's terms, could encourage individual fantasies of family independent of any concrete reality. The difference between the sovereign voice-over as a woman adds maternity to the radio queen's imperial effects. Such effects are initiated by radio's ability to create a "shadow world," defined by Dwight Frizzell and Jay Mandeville, as a world that "differs from the correct view assumed by society in direct proportion to the desire of an individual to accommodate fantasy to consensus."[38] Although the concept of "correct" is problematic in the context of the intersection between "the world" and "fantasy," the authors usefully signal the highly individual reception of the radio voice as it accommodates itself to cultural paradigms. When an Indian in New Delhi remarked, "We heard every word as distinctly as if she were in the room," he experienced the voice as embodied among his family.[39] Desire could conceivably transform Elizabeth into a queen of many colors, while to others the queen's very voice could create a barrier constituted of racial and status difference. My illustrations of Elizabeth II's appeal to family emphasize her stimulating desire and thereby facilitating the participants' entry into a fantasy world combining their own desires with an already constituted family feeling. That radio extends its waves outside Commonwealth boundaries creates imaginary subjects from those receiving radio beams. The 1940 broadcast achieved just such an effect—in North America, New Zealand, Malta, and wherever the broadcasts were initially heard and finally recorded and commercially distributed.[40] The imperial effects of this essay's title, then, extend the Commonwealth boundaries to anywhere the radio waves can be accessed and to the desire of listeners to create their shadow world in relation to the imperial family. Furthermore, the concept of "Commonwealth" depends in part on the will of people to believe in it and follows few coherent paradigms as a whole; the queen's voice-over creates a disjunctive fantasy that is no less effective for its illogicality in answering a culturally constructed desire.

Marshall McLuhan gestures to radio's tribal effect, independent of any particular content, an effect I call "imperial" rather than his "fascist."[41]

Nonetheless imperial effects possess a similar force. They draw on what McLuhan terms the "tribal drum" to entice people into its rhythms. Particularly when the tribal drum's register is female and evokes a never-never land of unity, of fusion, of the annihilation of difference, is that tribal pull the more psychologically primitive. Those who heard the tribal drum, according to the fantasy invoked by the radio and responded to by their own individual desires, could synchronize their heart to its beat.

Like the desire of which the imperial family stands in for, however, the fulfillment cannot be measured. Its appeal to a higher sense can function in ways difficult to specify, for perhaps it averts conflict by merely denying, rather than erasing, it. As Sara Ruddick asserts in *Maternal Thinking*, a mother keeps fighting children from actually killing each other and provides a model for peace. It was to these higher ideals of family unity that Elizabeth II appealed, and it was her maternal voice-over that repeated the message in the radio medium. In their radio way, the voice's failures and dissonances can be documented, but its effects, like Ruddick's analysis of the powers of maternal thinking, are more difficult to assess. We are in the realm of incalculable influence, of trying to assess powers to prevent as well as to make things happen. It is impossible to know how much Elizabeth's appeal to a family as a group of mutually caring individuals whose mothers can prevent disasters by means of what Ruddick calls "preservative love" had an actual effect. We are in the realm of belief, faith, negative capability.

To return to Wilson's analogy between radio and religion, the Queen's speeches conjured a higher power. Appropriate to her diverse family, her Christmas speech evoked similar confident sentiments to her first radio speech, with a similar rhetorical gesture: "Many grave problems and difficulties confront us all, but with a new faith in the old and splendid beliefs given us by our forefathers . . . I know we shall be worthy of our duty."[42] Elizabeth's female voice thus places itself within a diverse but nonetheless patriarchal cathedral as a servant of it, while at the same time evoking through the aural medium a realm where patriarchy has no place. The Radio Queen, virtually anointed in 1940, seizes her crown.

Notes

1 The relevant lines of Longfellow's poem: "Between the dark and the daylight / When the night is beginning to lower, / Comes a pause in the day's occupation / Which is known as 'the Children's Hour.' "

2 The *Times* reported that she broadcast "from a room near to her own apartments. The King and the Queen stood in the room near her." "Princess's First Broadcast," BBC Archive, *Times* (London), 14 October 1940.

3 The eventual audience would be infinitely larger, since tapes of the broadcast were sold, and the History Channel makes available portions of the speech on the World Wide Web.

4 Dermot Morrah, *Princess Elizabeth: The Illustrated Story of Twenty-One Years in the Life of the Heir Presumptive* (London: Odham's Press, 1947), 82.

5 Sarah Bradford, *Elizabeth: A Biography of Britain's Queen* (New York: Riverhead, 1996), 93.

6 "Come On Margaret" reported with admiration that "many children in various parts of the country have seized upon 'Come on, Margaret' as a catch phrase." The reporter evidently missed the parodic possibility of the locution. "Come On Margaret," BBC Archive, *Times* (London), 14 October 1940.

7 Quoted in Bradford, *Elizabeth*, 93.

8 Two generations of English men and women grew up with the program, according to Derek Parker, who believes that "its influence was quite incalculable." Parker, *Radio: The Great Years* (Newton Abbot: David and Charles, 1997), 25.

9 Asa Briggs, *The History of Broadcasting in the United Kingdom*, vol. 1 (Oxford: Oxford University Press, 1961), 261.

10 "Princess's First Broadcast."

11 "Several times listeners noticed a striking similarity between the voices of the Princess and the Queen" ("Princess's First Broadcast"). "All who have listened to the voice of the Queen will have noted the inherited sweetness of tone in her daughter's" ("A Royal Greeting," BBC Archive, *Daily Telegraph* [London], 14 October 1940).

12 Asa Briggs, *The BBC: The First Fifty Years* (Oxford: Oxford University Press, 1985), 73–74.

13 Tim Wilson, "Acoustic Architecture," in *Radiotext(e),* ed. Neil Strauss and David Mandl (New York: Semiotext[e], 1993), 283.

14 Ibid., 284.

15 "Churches in some places had wireless receiving sets installed so as to ensure the attendance of their members who were determined to hear her." "Clear Reception in Canada," BBC Archive, *Times* (London), 14 October 1940.

16 From a philosophical point of view, it is useful to consider nineteenth-century British romanticism as English Protestantism without Christianity. Wordsworth's transformation of the Christian prophecy instantiates the movement from religious faith to romantic wish in regard to special children.

17 Kaja Silverman, *The Acoustic Mirror: The Female Voice in Psychoanalysis and Cinema* (Bloomington: Indiana University Press, 1988), 7. Silverman's application of Lacanian psychoanalysis to the female voice in her early lectures and in *The Acoustic Mirror* has been crucial to my thinking about the monarchical voice.

18 Rudolph Arnheim, "In Praise of Blindness," in *Radiotext(e)*, ed. Neil Strauss and David Mandl (New York: Semiotext[e], 1993), 24.

19 Silverman, *The Acoustic Mirror*, 7.

20 Ibid., 77.

21 That all biographers take seriously this imaginary corporate body testifies to its mythic power. See Elizabeth Longford, *The Queen: The Life of Elizabeth II* (New York: Alfred A. Knopf, 1983), 114; and Bradford, *Elizabeth*, 119.

22 Longford, *The Queen*, 115.

23 In fact, the British visit could not prevent a victory for the Nationalist Party the following year and the foundation of the apartheid regime.

24 Longford, *The Queen*, 116.

25 Lawrence James, *The Rise and Fall of the British Empire* (London: Little, Brown, 1994), 448.

26 Stanley Clark, *Palace Diary* (New York: E. P. Dutton, 1958), 10–11.

27 Quoted in descriptions of the African trip. See, for example, Bradford, *Elizabeth*, 120; and Trevor McDonald, *The Queen and the Commonwealth* (London: Thames Methuen, 1986), 20.

28 "Princess Elizabeth's Coming-of-Age," BBC Archive, *Times* (London), 22 April 1947.

29 Ibid.

30 Longford quotes the speech as referencing the Imperial Commonwealth, but others such as Bradford have her as saying "imperial family," a phrase more in keeping with Elizabeth's metaphors for her realm. In addition, the queen is known for her accuracy. It is possible that the script and the broadcast differ on the phrase (Longford, *The Queen*, 120).

31 It was just this family metaphor that received praise from the press. For example, the *Recorder* affirmed the appropriateness of this "wonderful idea, so convincingly given, that everywhere in the British Empire is equally home." "Who Wrote the Princess's Speech?" BBC Archive, *Recorder* (London), 26 April 1947.

32 McDonald, *The Queen and the Commonwealth*, 21.

33 Queen Victoria was represented as imperial mother by means of paper images in periodicals, and by extravagant celebrations of her birthdays and her Golden and Diamond Jubilee, where millions were fed, public buildings were erected, and monuments were dedicated in the extent of her realm.

34 Clark, *Palace Diary*, 95; McDonald, *The Queen and the Commonwealth*, 21.

35 Emery Pearce, "No Rehearsal for the Queen's Broadcast," BBC Archive, *Daily Herald* (London), 24 December 1952.

36 "The Voice of the Queen," BBC Archive, *Daily Mail* (London), 23 December 1952. The speech was anticipated by the press and reflects an already constituted desire to be part of the family, and it is this desire to which the queen speaks.

37 James, *The Rise and Fall of the British Empire*, 557.

38 Dwight Frizzell and Jay Mandeville, "Early Radio Bigwigs," in *Radiotext(e)*, ed. Neil Strauss and David Mandl (New York: Semiotext[e], 1993), 45.

39 "Americans Hear Message Repeated," BBC Archive, *Daily Telegraph* (London), 27 December 1952.

40 The *Times* reported that "a large and appreciative audience" in Canada received excellent reception. "Thousands of children were delighted by her voice." Children in Malta likewise heard the broadcast clearly and were supposedly thereby "full of courage" ("Clear Reception in Canada," BBC Archive, *Times* [London], 14 October 1940). Agency messages from the United States and New Zealand reported that "the broadcast was one of the most effective ever received from London" ("Children Cheered the Princess on Radio," BBC Archive, *Star* [London], 14 October 1940). The *Daily Telegraph* that same day concluded that it was the "happiest of thoughts that the voice of Princess Elizabeth should have been first to be heard in the new weekly programme of the BBC North American service" ("A Royal Greeting," BBC Archive, *Daily Telegraph* [London], 14 October 1940).

41 The relevant passage: "That Hitler came into political existence at all is directly owing to radio and public-address systems. This is not to say that these media relayed his thoughts effectively to the German people. His thoughts were of very little consequence. Radio provided the first massive experience of electronic implosion, that reversal of the entire direction and meaning of literate Western civilization." Marshall McLuhan, *Understanding Media: The Extensions of Man* (New York: McGraw-Hill, 1963), 300.

42 "The Queen's Call to Her People . . . New Faith in Old Beliefs," BBC Archive, *Times* (London), 27 December 1952.

Works Cited

"Americans Hear Message Repeated." BBC Archive, *Daily Telegraph* (London), 27 December 1952.

Arnheim, Rudolf. "In Praise of Blindness." In *Radiotext(e)*, ed. Neil Strauss and Dave Mandl. New York: Semiotext(e), 1993.

Bradford, Sarah. *Elizabeth: A Biography of Britain's Queen.* New York: Riverhead, 1996.

Briggs, Asa. *The BBC: The First Fifty Years.* Oxford: Oxford University Press, 1985.

——. *The History of Broadcasting in the United Kingdom.* Vol. 1. Oxford: Oxford University Press, 1961.

"Children Cheered the Princess on Radio." BBC Archive. *Star* (London), 14 October 1940.

Clark, Stanley. *Palace Diary.* New York: E. P. Dutton, 1958.

"Clear Reception in Canada." BBC Archive. *Times* (London), 14 October 1940.

"Come On Margaret." BBC Archive. *Star* (London), 14 October 1940.

Frizzell, Dwight, Rev., and Jay Mandeville. "Early Radio Bigwigs." In *Radiotext(e)*, ed. Neil Strauss and Dave Mandl. New York: Semiotext(e), 1993.

James, Lawrence. *The Rise and Fall of the British Empire*. London: Little, Brown, 1994.

Longford, Elizabeth. *The Queen: The Life of Elizabeth II*. New York: Alfred A. Knopf, 1983.

McDonald, Trevor. *The Queen and the Commonwealth*. London: Thames Methuen, 1986.

McLuhan, Marshall. *Understanding Media: The Extensions of Man*. New York: McGraw-Hill, 1963.

Morrah, Dermot. *Princess Elizabeth: The Illustrated Story of Twenty-One Years in the Life of the Heir Presumptive*. London: Odhams Press, 1947.

Parker, Derek. *Radio: The Great Years*. Newton Abbot: David and Charles, 1997.

Pearce, Emery. "No Rehearsal for the Queen's Broadcast." BBC Archive. *Daily Herald* (London), 24 December 1952.

"Princess Elizabeth's Coming-of-Age." BBC Archive. *Times* (London), 22 April 1947.

"Princess's First Broadcast." BBC Archive. *Times* (London), 14 October 1940.

"The Queen's Call to Her People . . . New Faith in Old Beliefs." BBC Archive. *Times* (London), 27 December 1952.

"A Royal Greeting." BBC Archive. *Daily Telegraph* (London), 14 October 1940.

Ruddick, Sara. *Maternal Thinking: Toward a Politics of Peace*. Boston: Beacon, 1989.

Silverman, Kaja. *The Acoustic Mirror: The Female Voice in Psychoanalysis and Cinema*. Bloomington: Indiana University Press, 1988.

"The Voice of the Queen," BBC Archive. *Daily Mail* (London), 23 December 1952.

"Who Wrote the Princess's Speech?" BBC Archive. *Recorder* (London), 26 April 1947.

Wilson, Tim. "Acoustic Architecture." In *Radiotext(e)*, ed. Neil Strauss and David Mandl. New York: Semiotext(e), 1993.

"IF THE COUNTRY'S GOING GRACIE,

SO CAN YOU": GENDER REPRESENTATION

IN GRACIE ALLEN'S RADIO COMEDY

Leah Lowe

In 1940, radio comedy star Gracie Allen staged a mock campaign for president of the United States.[1] According to her husband and partner, George Burns, Gracie's campaign was conceived one evening in their Beverly Hills home: "Gracie suddenly remarked, 'I'm tired of knitting this sweater, I think I'll run for president this year.' "[2] Running on the Surprise Party ticket, the candidate displayed the offbeat, "dizzy" comic persona familiar to her radio listeners. She promised voters, "If I can't do anything about the high cost of living, we'll just have to do without." Asked if she would recognize Russia, she mused, "Oh, I don't know. I meet so many people . . . "[3] Gracie announced her candidacy on Burns and Allen's weekly CBS radio broadcast, *The Hinds' Honey and Almond Cream Program*, in February. Most of the campaign was conducted on the air, both on *The Hinds' Honey and Almond Cream Program* and on other popular radio comedy shows, including *The Jack Benny Jell-O Program, Fibber McGee and Molly*, and *Dr. IQ*, when Gracie would burst in unexpectedly to court potential voters and explain her political positions.[4] Begun as a running gag, Gracie's campaign captured the attention of her audience and gained momentum, culminating in the Surprise Party Convention in Omaha in May.

Audio recordings of twelve episodes of *The Hinds' Honey and Almond Cream Program* featuring the "Gracie for President" campaign provide ample material for an exploration of gender construction in radio comedy. Although Gracie's anarchic performances are based on a derogatory stereotype—that of the eccentric, silly, scatterbrained woman—and devoid of explicit feminist content, I will argue that they retain a transgressive power throughout the campaign broadcasts and result in an exuberant femininity oblivious to many of the limitations imposed on women by patriarchal authority. I will also suggest that radio, the medium of transmission, is an integral element of Gracie's performance, as it constructs femininity differently and elicits different sorts of responses and identifications from its audience than do the visual media of television and film. Finally, the structure of the Burns and Allen radio comedy routine, more closely related to its vaudeville predecessor than to the later Burns and Allen television sitcom, works against a causal narrative drive and its demand for resolution and closure. In this sense, it too contributes to a representation of femininity that is not ultimately contained in, and reconciled to, the patriarchal order, but remains open-ended and multivalent. With regard to gender inequality and conflict, the "Gracie for President" campaign material demonstrates what popular culture theorist Richard Dyer calls the "utopian sensibility" of mass entertainment.[5]

The "Vote for Gracie" campaign did not directly satirize political events, nor did it offer a feminist or an alternative political agenda. In 1940 the United States had just begun to recover from the economic devastation of the Great Depression. The Nazi invasion of Poland in 1939 had drawn Britain and France into an overseas war that was increasingly difficult to ignore. With regard to foreign affairs, the country was anxious, and within the United States, the approaching presidential election was deeply contested. The field of presidential hopefuls was an unusually large one until the nominating conventions of June and July. Republican contenders included Robert Taft, Thomas Dewey, and Wendell Wilkie, the eventual nominee. The Democratic nomination, complicated by Roosevelt's silence on the much-discussed issue of a possible third term, was sought by John Nance Garner, Jim Farley, Burton Wheeler, and others. The number of possible candidates and the lack of clear front-runners lent an air of absurdity to the contest. On one broadcast, Gracie writes a letter to the other candidates thinking that if she can get all of them (at least fifty thousand, by her estimation) to vote for her, she will surely win.[6] References to actual political figures and events on *The Hinds' Honey and Almond Cream Program* are infrequent and innocuous. The real comic force and focus of Gracie's presidential bid lies in the absurdity of a woman, and scatterbrained Gracie at that, running for the presidency.

The classic Burns and Allen radio comedy routine, employed throughout their campaign broadcasts, drew on a vaudeville comic tradition based on fundamental differences between men and women. Burns and Allen perform themselves as essentially unlike, with vastly different perceptions and understandings of the world around them. Gracie plays an innocent eccentric, a screwball heroine, a "Dumb Dora," in vaudeville slang, while George serves as her normalizing foil. The scripted campaign broadcasts, written by professional (male) writers hired and supervised by Burns,[7] pit Gracie and the rest of the show's cast (announcer Truman Bradley, tenor Frank Parker, orchestra leader Ray Noble, and Gracie's secretary, Bubbles) against George, who grumpily resists Gracie's political aspirations. Throughout the various skits enacted in the campaign recordings, Gracie and the gang upset and subvert the social order while George struggles to undo the damage and reestablish the sense and stability of the reality that he assumes his audience shares with him. The campaign broadcasts do not represent an equally matched battle between men and women in the persons of George and Gracie, for against the comic exhilaration and sheer fun of Gracie's campaign performances, George's reality seems inordinately dull, rule bound, and predictable.

While Gracie's comic persona is reminiscent of the heroines of the Hollywood screwball comedies of the late 1930s and early 1940s, most notably the unruly Susan Vance played by Katharine Hepburn in Howard Hawks's *Bringing Up Baby* (1938), the differences between radio representation and cinematic representation are significant and deserve further exploration. In "The Technology of Gender," feminist critic Teresa de Lauretis argues that the representation of gender *is* its construction, and that gender is represented and constructed through a variety of "social technologies"—her examples include narrative, cinema, and theory. The "cinematic apparatus," she observes, constructs "woman as image, as the object of the spectator's voyeuristic gaze" through the use of film techniques such as lighting, editing, and camera positioning.[8] These techniques are employed in specific "cinematic codes (e.g., the system of the look)" that construct specific representations of femininity that are dependent on, but do not explicitly acknowledge, their formal and technological constructions.[9] Whereas the cinema represents woman as a visual sign, radio performance depends on sound and language as the means of representation and is devoid of a visual context or frame in which its signs are anchored. On the radio, Gracie is a voice in monologue, dialogue, or song, rather than a physical body.

Much of feminist film criticism is structured around analyses of visual aspects of the medium. Both images of women on the screen and theories of spectatorship predicated on the concept of the male gaze are central concerns. In theorizing radio performance, it is necessary to explore how the listener is constructed and addressed differently than is the spectator of visual media forms. Critic Don Druker describes radio representation as "a code defined not only by what radio lacks—visual homologies—but also by what is central to it: nonmelodic auditory structures."[10] Druker observes that radio performance requires the listener to piece together auditory information as it is given to him or her: "Where the painting constructs images homologous to reality, radio structures linguistic and auditory fragments from which images may be constructed by the listener, and these images may then be *construed* as homologies" (330). For Druker, "the listener is confronted with a text that must be constructed. . . . this is a difference in kind rather than degree from film or television" (334). While both radio and cinematic representations unfold in time and require active construction on the part of the audience, the lack of a fixed spatial objectivity in radio leaves the audience with more imaginative freedom to perform its receptive construction. The lack of visual context in radio creates a degree of "indeterminacy" that can be read as possibility (331). I would argue that the Burns and Allen campaign broadcasts take advantage of the indeterminacy of radio as a medium and create possibilities of multiple points of identification across gender lines.

Because radio is an auditory medium, character must be conveyed through language and sound. Much of Gracie's dialogue is designed to reveal her thought processes and demonstrate differences between the way she thinks and the way George thinks. For instance, in one campaign broadcast, George, Gracie, and the gang are preparing to leave for the Surprise Party convention in Omaha. George asks Gracie where the tickets are. She tells him that she gave them to a man standing outside the radio station. Alarmed, George asks, "What did he look like?" Gracie responds nonchalantly, "He looked like he wanted them." Through a long series of Gracie's non sequiturs, George's frustration and disbelief builds until she rather casually mentions that the tickets that she gave to the man were tickets to the broadcast and that the railway tickets are safe in her possession.[11] To get the joke, the listener must follow Gracie's thought processes, which results in a transparent characterization that highlights her internal reasoning. Off the air, George described Gracie's thought processes as "illogical logic"[12] and explained: "If you listen to Gracie's prattle on the radio, you may notice that her logic is faultless, though usually completely mistaken. . . . Gracie gets her laughs—we hope—because we often *think* the way Gracie *talks,* but we pride ourselves that *we* never talk the way Gracie thinks."[13] In broadcast recordings, Gracie explains herself; George does not need to, because our understanding of him is assumed—he is a citizen of the everyday world we all inhabit, but Gracie is not.

Because her representation of femininity is characterized by the revelation of internal thought processes and an idiosyncratic use of language, rather than a visually apparent, objectified body, Gracie's character is open and available to both male and female listening positions. In a 1940 magazine article, George described Gracie as "radio's Alice-in-Wonderland" and observed, "Gracie's remarks on the radio are very similar to those of a charming, good-natured child who is quite sure everything's in fun and everything is quite possible—there was a time we all felt like that."[14] Both men and women are encouraged to follow and identify with Gracie's reasoning and illogical logic; both men and women recognize the limitations of the reality George represents. The two characters each elicit some sort of understanding from the listening audience, and each retains a degree of ambivalence. George is the straight man, the "real" character, but he is regularly and passively subjected to Gracie's actions and wild escapades. While Gracie is constructed as the childlike woman who must have an adult man mediate between her and the world, she is also the privileged character who has all the fun and breaks all the rules. Although the campaign broadcasts exploit gender differences, they also encourage character identification across gender lines.

Gracie's peculiar use of language is the most obvious way that her character and femininity are constructed within the Burns and Allen radio routines. Malapropisms, puns, shaggy-dog stories, and non sequiturs are all featured in Gracie's dialogue, which regularly challenges the ordinary ways in which meaning is produced in the real world. Gracie tells George that her Aunt Clara lisps. He asks, "Oh, you mean she has an impediment?" "Yeah, but she traded it in for a Buick," she replies, and nonchalantly moves on to the next bit of dialogue.[15] On one of her campaign broadcasts, Gracie rehearses a speech she plans to give:

My opponents say they're going to fight me 'til the cows come home. So, they admit the cows aren't home. Why aren't the cows home? Because they don't like the conditions on the farm. The cows are smart. They're not coming home 'til there's a woman in the White House. . . . So my friends, what the American farm needs is the touch of a woman's hand. So I say that the hand that rocks the cradle should pull the plow.[16]

Performed, Gracie's speech sounds like a political speech. She uses declarative speech patterns and intonations, rhetorical questions, and strategic pauses. The humor arises from the discrepancy between the nonsense that Gracie utters and the earnestness and sincerity with which she utters it.

Gracie's use of language places her outside the bounds of everyday rules and the strictures of common interpretation; it destabilizes ordinary meanings and unravels causal sequence. As critic Susan Douglas points out, the "linguistic slapstick" that characterized much of the era's radio comedy provided opportunities for resisting social authority.[17] Ostensibly, Gracie's dialogue could be read as that of a woman who cannot use language appropriately and hence is an ineffective participant in the social realm, but this interpretation is at odds with the exuberance and appeal of her performances. Gracie's performances do not suggest someone who is being punished, humiliated, or made fun of for her lack of conformity. They reveal no sense of isolation or failure; if anything, they suggest there is something limiting and boring about the linguistic laws and humdrum reality that we routinely accept. As Gracie's use of language places her outside the bounds of normal discourse, it highlights the restrictiveness of this discourse and offers, if only for the duration of the broadcast, alternative ways of seeing and participating in the world.

In "Situation Comedy, Feminism, and Freud: Discourses of Gracie and Lucy," a 1986 essay, television critic Patricia Mellencamp examines Gracie's character on *The George Burns and Gracie Allen Show*, the couple's television show of the 1950s. Mellencamp describes Gracie's language as "derailing the laws of syntax and logic"[18] and notes Gracie's subversive potential: "Gracie equivocally escaped order. Despite being burdened by all the clichés applied to women—illogical, crazy, nonsensical, possessing their own, peculiar bio-logic and patronized accordingly—in certain ways, she seemed to be out of (or beyond) men's control" (321). However powerful her potential, Mellencamp argues, the sitcom Gracie is inevitably contained at the end of each episode by the sitcom George. Significantly, Mellencamp locates sites of containment primarily within the visual field:

George is center-framed in the mise-en-scene and by the moving camera; he is taller than all the other characters; and he has access to the camera via his direct looks at the camera. . . . In the end Gracie is frame left. She wins the narrative and the mink coat, but loses central screen space; perhaps more importantly, she never was in possession of "the look." (322)

The Gracie of the screen and the Gracie of the air are of different historical eras and production contexts. Their presentation includes significant differences in narrative structure in addition to other differences conditioned by their respective media. Still, it is interesting to note how a visual context can work against the power Gracie establishes through language. On the radio, the gaze absent, Gracie's voice suggests a woman free of real-world substance and unbound by real-world limitation.

Gracie's performance is not only composed of her use of language. In "Entertainment and Utopia," Richard Dyer argues that mass "show biz" entertainments operate through "an effective code that is characteristic of, and largely specific to, a given mode of cultural production."[19] This code, or social technology, employs both representational and nonrepresentational signs. Nonrepresentational signs, such as "color, texture, movement, rhythm, melody," convey meaning just as representational codes such as language do, though Dyer notes, "we are much less used to talking about them."[20] The emotional effectiveness of radio comedy depends on nonrepresentational codes, such as sound, inflection, and the rhythm of language, to a great degree. Much of what is funny arises from the vocal delivery of scripted dialogue rather than scripted dialogue in and of itself. In Gracie's campaign broadcasts, vocal performance, music, and the rhythm and structure of the Burns and Allen comedy routine contribute to the sense of transgressive power associated with Gracie's character.

The sound of Gracie's voice sets her apart from George, further emphasizing their differences. Gracie's is feminine and high-pitched. George's voice is gruff and deep; when he becomes exasperated by Gracie and the others, which happens frequently, his speech is punctuated with snorts, sighs, and other nonverbal sounds of anger, dismay, and frustration. Gracie and George frequently perform in rapid-fire, back-and-forth sequences of dialogue, such as the following discussion of campaign finances:

Gracie: Yeah, but does Jim Farley have to spend seventeen dollars on a permanent?
George: Well, I wouldn't know.
Gracie: And does Mr. Garner have to pay ten dollars for a snood?

George: You got me, you got me.

Gracie: And does Mr. John L. Lewis have to pay three dollars to get his eyebrows plucked?

George: You got me.

Gracie: You know what's wrong with this program?

George: You got me.

Gracie: You guessed it.[21]

Gracie's laughter is a crucial element of her vocal performance. Gracie laughs throughout her campaign broadcasts; sometimes she laughs at things that are funny, sometimes she laughs at George's bad jokes, and sometimes she laughs for no reason at all. On one broadcast, Gracie bursts into laughter, and when George asks her what's funny, she replies, "I don't get it."[22] She often laughs right over George's lines, completely disrupting the smooth flow of dialogue and forcing him to repeat himself, sometimes more than once. Her laughter is infectious and conveys an utter lack of concern about George's frustration and judgment. Gracie's laughter is a stark contrast to George's perpetual irritation. Throughout the campaign broadcasts, Gracie and the rest of the cast (who regularly side with her) are happy with the current state of affairs, whatever it may be. It is George who is dissatisfied and tries to pull the others back to "reality."

The use of music in the campaign broadcasts further emphasizes a sense of community and solidarity between Gracie and the other characters of the cast and excludes George from that community. The half-hour radio programs follow a standard format: opening comic dialogue; commercial;[23] song by tenor Frank Parker; comic dialogue (Bubbles, Gracie's secretary, joins the rest of the cast in this part of the show); instrumental piece, group song, or song sung by Gracie; more talk; second commercial; closing. Frank Parker, Ray Noble, and Gracie regularly sing on the show; Truman Bradley and Bubbles join in on group numbers. Although George wants to perform musically, he is a singer of limited abilities, and the rest of the cast discourage him. On one of the campaign episodes, Gracie apologetically announces, "George wants me to do my campaign song again, on account of he does a chorus in it." The entire cast participates in an elaborate brass arrangement of "Vote for Gracie," and in the middle, Gracie says, "Alright George, here's what you've been waiting for." The band suddenly stops, and to a single piano playing "Ain't Misbehavin'," George sing-speaks:

Oh, vote for Gracie
So I can be by myself,
Please vote for Gracie
So I'll be happy on the shelf.
If she's elected,
I'll be neglected,
And I can stay home and play solitaire,
And keep that silly dame outta my hair.[24]

Gracie and the rest of the cast easily participate in the song that George cannot master. Dyer describes music as a form of expression that works through emotional appeal and exists outside the realm of logic.[25] Gracie's musical ability is consistent with her playful emotional appeal, just as George's inability to communicate musically reinforces his identification with the prosaic real world and sets him apart from the other characters of *The Hinds' Honey and Almond Cream Program.*

The structure or form of George's and Gracie's comic patter, another "social technology" through which gender is constructed, is derived from their earlier vaudeville routines. Vaudeville comedy developed as a single component of larger variety shows that could include performances ranging from song and dance to animal acts. Individual acts were designed to fit into standardized slots within the larger shows, and comedians often performed comic versions of themselves, rather than identifying their performance personae as explicitly fictional. Film historian Henry Jenkins notes that the vaudeville performance aesthetic was often diametrically opposed to that of the legitimate theater. In vaudeville, virtuosity and self-conscious performance were valued above the realistic theater's unified artistic product and psychologically coherent characters.[26] In the vaudeville-based Burns and Allen radio comedy routines, character and comic virtuosity are prominently featured, and a disregard for causal narrative can be observed. The relative unimportance of the narrative drive frees these routines from the expectation of closure and resolution. George does not contain Gracie's socially disruptive performances, in part, because he does not have to. The two are working in a form that is open-ended and driven by multiple perspectives, a collage approach, rather than a plot-driven sequence that carries with it an implicit demand for reconciliation and the tying-up of loose ends. Gracie's campaign, rather than suggesting a coherent story line for a series of broadcasts, provided the couple with a series of weekly opportunities; within these weekly situations, several "miniroutines" were enacted.

Richard Dyer asserts that popular entertainment is the product of utopian impulses: "Entertainment offers the image of 'something better' to escape into, or something that we want deeply that our day-to-day lives don't provide."[27] He observes that the utopia of popular entertainment is not a reasoned alternative to the world we inhabit, as is found in classical literary utopias, but an emotional and empathetic one. Dyer asserts that entertainment's utopianism "is contained in the feelings it embodies. It presents, head-on, as it were, what utopia would feel like, rather than how it would be organized."[28] Although feminist positions and agendas are not acknowledged or developed in the "Vote for Gracie" routines, the representations of gender differences and gender relations reflect Dyer's emotional utopianism. Politically, men and women, in the persons of George and Gracie, are represented as unlike but not unequal. Domestically, both George and Gracie are represented as powerful partners in a relationship in which professional ties are clear, but personal bonds are somewhat ambiguous. Within this partnership, Gracie retains her power and a sense of personal and sexual autonomy.

The radio spoof attacked real political anxieties by banishing all serious political issues, destroying the gravity associated with the presidency, and relocating the campaign in an essentially domestic context. For instance, in a cab on the way to Union Station, where they plan to catch a train to her Omaha convention, Gracie asks George if he has her campaign speeches. He says that they are in his pocket, and she responds, "Oh, don't move them, I have sandwiches wrapped up in them." "Sandwiches?" George questions. "Yeah, swiss cheese sandwiches." When George sputters in exasperation, she calmly announces that she brought an apple for him.[29] Although the initial subject of the conversation, Gracie's campaign speeches, might suggest a discussion of the public aspects of her campaign, the talk quickly moves to food and the domestic sphere. Repeatedly throughout the campaign broadcasts, public and private spheres are playfully interchanged, blurring the distinctions between stereotypical male and female concerns.

Gender utopianism can be seen in the support Gracie's bid for the White House garners from the others on the program. The cast members, primarily other men, embrace Gracie's candidacy and are actively involved in her campaign, much to George's dismay. Gracie initially engages the other characters by promising them prestigious jobs: Frank Parker is going to be a Supreme Court justice; Ray Noble, the secretary of the Navy; and Truman Bradley, the postmaster general.[30] The absurdity of a woman running for the office, the implicit comic assumption of the entire campaign, is rarely acknowledged by the other male characters. The campaign broadcasts downplay gender inequality by giving Gracie's political aspirations the approval of the program's men. Conflicts are refigured by their participation: George's disapproval of Gracie's campaign is not just a dispute between George and Gracie—it is a rift between George and everyone else.

The Burns and Allen routine is predicated on the notion of conflicting gender differences. Throughout the broadcasts, differences and conflicts exist but do not destroy the relationship because one character cannot overpower the other. Conflicts exist, but George does not achieve dominance by forcing a resolution or reconciliation between Gracie and the real world. The characters are constructed in opposition to each other, and through the demonstration of difference. In some senses, their continuity from episode to episode depends on their continued conflict. The on-air relationship between George and Gracie is complicated by their well-known real-life marriage. At the time of Gracie's presidential campaign, the two had been married for fourteen years and had two children. Various self-conscious references to performance within the context of their performances, such as George's improvised comment about "a very old script" following a bad joke, blur the distinction between the performed character and the real George.[31] Along with the lack of narrative drive, the off-the-air marriage between George and Gracie implied that the on-air differences and conflicts did not need to be resolved. A utopian vision of gender differences can be seen in the representation of conflicts that can be left open and are suspended rather than resolved.

Gracie, married to George off the air, is represented on the air as ambiguously attached to George, but not necessarily married to him. Truman Bradley refers to the two as a couple on one episode: "She goes out with George Burns, if you could call that living."[32] However, Gracie-the-candidate, Gracie's fictive radio persona, is not married and interacts freely with the show's male characters. She has a running flirtation with Ray Noble, the British orchestra leader, who functions as a sort of male version of Gracie:

Ray: I say, Gracie, will you forget me when you are in the White House?
Gracie: Well, I will if you'll forget about me.
Ray: Let's just forget about each other, then.

Gracie: Well, let's write it down so we'll remember.
Ray: Or else we'll forget.[33]

Although Gracie's flirtations, particularly with Ray, are childlike and not overtly sexual, they are important. Gracie not only resists George's efforts to make her see the world his way but also, through her autonomous relationships with others, demonstrates an ability to take care of herself.

Gracie's performance and representation of femininity is complex and lends itself to several possible readings from different subject positions. An initial analysis of Gracie's run for president might highlight the silliness and absurdity of a woman running for office and interpret George's normality as evidence of Gracie's lack of consequence. It is my contention that a closer analysis complicates the matter and reveals that Gracie, although certainly silly, challenges the sense and order of the real world and is not reconciled to it by George. I have suggested that the radio medium itself contributes to Gracie's unruly femininity by structuring both characterization and the audience's perception of it in specific ways. Throughout her campaign broadcasts, Gracie retains her transgressive power and is not forced to repent or recant or change anything about her behavior as a concession to reality's demands. It is in this sense that Gracie is a feminist candidate—a utopian feminist candidate—who suggests what it might *feel* like to abandon gender hierarchies along with other social restrictions, rather than promoting a specific feminist political agenda.

Notes

An earlier version of this essay was presented at the 1998 Performance Studies International Conference. I thank the conference's participants, Catherine Cole, Ben Gunter, Carrie Sandahl, and Jim McFarland, for their helpful criticisms.

1 A series of twelve episodes of *The Hinds' Honey and Almond Cream Program* revolving around Gracie's campaign, originally recorded between February and May 1940, form the basis for my essay's analysis. Audiocassettes of these broadcasts were released as a boxed set titled *Gracie Allen for President* by Metacom, Inc., of Plymouth, Minnesota, in 1995. All quotations are from my own transcriptions. For clarity's sake, I will cite quotations from the broadcasts by the title of broadcast episode.

2 George Burns, "Gracie Allen As I Know Her," *Independent Woman*, July 1940, 214.

3 "Government Jobs."

4 "Candidette," *Time*, 18 March 1940, 36.

5 Richard Dyer, "Entertainment and Utopia," in *The Cultural Studies Reader*, ed. Simon During (London: Routledge, 1994), 276.

6 "Government Jobs."

7 Kate Davy, "An Interview with George Burns," *Educational Theatre Journal* 27, no. 3 (1975): 353; Arthur Wertheim, *Radio Comedy* (New York: Oxford University Press, 1979), 202.

8 Teresa de Lauretis, "The Technology of Gender," in *Technologies of Gender: Essays on Theory, Film, and Fiction* (Bloomington: Indiana University Press, 1987), 13.

9 Ibid.

10 Don Druker, "Listening to the Radio," *Theatre Journal* 43, no. 3 (1991): 334.

11 "Aunt Clara Kangaroo."

12 Larry Wilde, *The Great Comedians Talk about Comedy* (New York: Citadel Press, 1968), 134.

13 Burns, 214.

14 Ibid., 198.

15 "Aunt Clara Kangaroo."

16 " 'Til the Cows Come Home."

17 Susan Douglas, "Radio Comedy and Linguistic Slapstick," in *Listening In: Radio and the American Imagination* (New York: Times Books, 1999), 100–123.

18 Patricia Mellencamp, "Situation Comedy, Feminism, and Freud: Discourses of Gracie and Lucy," in *Star Texts: Image and Performance in Film and Television*, ed. Jeremy G. Butler (Detroit, Mich.: Wayne State University Press, 1991), 320.

19 Dyer, "Entertainment and Utopia," 273.

20 Ibid.

21 "The Biggest in the World."

22 Ibid.

23 Commercials for *The Hinds' Honey and Almond Cream Program* are performed by the announcer, Truman Bradley, and are integrated into the show. Hinds' Honey and Almond Cream, a hand cream, is a woman's product, and the commercials are targeted toward female listeners. This aspect of the show suggests that the audience included a large female segment—an intriguing point when considering the program's representation of femininity.

24 "Gracie's Triumphant Return."

25 Dyer, "Entertainment and Utopia," 273.

26 Henry Jenkins, *What Made Pistachio Nuts? Early Sound Comedy and the Vaudeville Aesthetic* (New York: Columbia University Press, 1992), 67.

27 Dyer, "Entertainment and Utopia," 273.

28 Ibid.

29 "Aunt Clara Kangaroo."

30 "Government Jobs."

31 "Rah, Rah in Omaha."

32 "Gracie Wins Wisconsin."
33 Ibid.

Works Cited

Allen, Gracie, and George Burns. "Aunt Clara Kangaroo." Audiocassette of radio broadcast presented 5 May 1940. In *Gracie Allen for President*. Plymouth, Minn.: Metacom, 1995.

———. "The Biggest in the World." Audiocassette of radio broadcast presented 24 April 1940. In *Gracie Allen for President*. Plymouth, Minn.: Metacom, 1995.

———. "Government Jobs." Audiocassette of radio broadcast presented 28 February 1940. In *Gracie Allen for President*. Plymouth, Minn.: Metacom, 1995.

———. "Gracie's Triumphant Return." Audiocassette of radio broadcast presented 13 March 1940. In *Gracie Allen for President*. Plymouth, Minn.: Metacom, 1995.

———. "Gracie Wins Wisconsin." Audiocassette of radio broadcast presented 10 April 1940. In *Gracie Allen for President*. Plymouth, Minn.: Metacom, 1995.

———. "Rah, Rah in Omaha." Audiocassette of radio broadcast presented 15 May 1940. In *Gracie Allen for President*. Plymouth, Minn.: Metacom, 1995.

———. " 'Til the Cows Come Home." Audiocassette of radio broadcast presented 3 April 1940. In *Gracie Allen for President*. Plymouth, Minn.: Metacom, 1995.

Burns, George. "Gracie Allen As I Know Her." *Independent Woman*, July 1940, 198, 214.

"Candidette." *Time*, 18 March 1940, 36.

Davy, Kate. "An Interview with George Burns." *Educational Theatre Journal* 27, no. 3 (1975): 345–55.

de Lauretis, Teresa. "The Technology of Gender." In *Technologies of Gender: Essays on Theory, Film, and Fiction*. Bloomington: Indiana University Press, 1987.

Douglas, Susan J. "Radio Comedy and Linguistic Slapstick." In *Listening In: Radio Comedy and the American Imagination, from Amos 'n' Andy and Edward R. Murrow to Wolfman Jack and Howard Stern*. New York: Times Books, 1999.

Druker, Don. "Listening to the Radio." *Theatre Journal* 43, no. 3 (1991): 325–35.

Dyer, Richard. "Entertainment and Utopia." In *The Cultural Studies Reader*, ed. Simon During. London: Routledge, 1994. First published in *Movie* 24 (spring 1977).

Jenkins, Henry. *What Made Pistachio Nuts? Early Sound Comedy and the Vaudeville Aesthetic*. New York: Columbia University Press, 1992.

Mellencamp, Patricia. "Situation Comedy, Feminism, and Freud: Discourses of Gracie and Lucy." In *Star Texts: Image and Performance in Film and Television*, ed. Jeremy G. Butler. Detroit, Mich.: Wayne State University Press, 1991. First published in *Studies in Entertainment: Critical Approaches to Mass Culture*, ed. Tania Modleski (Bloomington: Indiana University Press, 1986).

Wertheim, Arthur. *Radio Comedy*. New York: Oxford University Press, 1979.

Wilde, Larry. *The Great Comedians Talk about Comedy*. New York: Citadel Press, 1968.

"ARE YOU LONESOME TONIGHT?":

GENDERED ADDRESS IN *THE LONESOME GAL*

AND *THE CONTINENTAL*

Mary Desjardins and Mark Williams

This essay examines representations of two broadcast media performers of the post–World War II era whose openly gendered direct address was considered blatantly suggestive but also complementary to each other. *The Lonesome Gal* was a radio show begun in Dayton, Ohio, in 1947 and transported to Los Angeles in 1949. It featured a female disc jockey of unknown identity who adopted the persona of a woman-in-waiting, patiently longing for her desired (male) listener. Interweaving complimentary patter, sponsor-supported asides, and personalized introductions to romantic and popular musical selections, she opened and closed each program with her admonition "I love you more than anybody else in the whole world." Listeners were routinely addressed as "muffin," "baby," and "dreamboat." At what appears to be the peak in her popularity, Renzo Cesana premiered on local Los Angeles television as *The Continental*, a suave European date for his (female) viewer, whom he flattered and embarrassed (via direct visual address) into a position as a sexual fetish.

Examined together, these shows are representative of certain tensions and contradictions in postwar American culture, especially when related to the social and gendered status of the private sphere, the rapidly changing postwar broadcast industries, and the relationship of these media to the construction of that private sphere. A close look at the competing radio and television institutions at this time, and the discursive strategies and positionings in examples of program texts of these shows, reveals that the textual meanings and ideological effects of *The Continental* and *The Lonesome Gal* are not based on neat reversals or "separate-but-equal" policy for seducing heterosexual male and female viewers and listeners. We will argue that although the conditions of reception of these programs include the possibility of affirming the "difference" of female desire, this possibility only arises through a struggle with conditions that worked to secure male mastery over the physical space of the home, where women had become ensconced.

Our analysis will suggest how media institutions, program texts, audiences, and other cultural discourses worked to construct conditions of reception that operate from what Christine Gledhill argues are "competing frames of reference and experience."[1] Meaning, according to Gledhill, arises "out of a struggle or negotiation" between these registers, which renders the hegemony or dominance of meaning unstable and subject to continual renegotiation. One central negotiation at stake in the historical reception of *The Continental* and *The Lonesome Gal* is the postwar rejection of an effacement of difference allegedly characteristic of wartime "unity." This rejection was generally achieved through a defensive retrenchment within socially defined roles that served patriarchal consumer capitalism. Such retrenchments included the attempts to usher women back into the home, the massive movement to the suburbs (which were often stringently discriminating, characterized by several barriers of entry according to race, class, and religion), and the surveillance and persecution of people who blurred social, gender, and political boundaries.

Jean King as the "Lonesome Gal": Industrial Contexts

The Lonesome Gal went on the air in October 1947 as a local radio show in Dayton, featuring talk and recorded music. Within a year, "Lonesome Gal" host Jean King had won *Billboard*'s award for Top Disc Jockey of the Year, and the press was claiming that the show had saved its sponsor (a local restaurant) from bankruptcy.[2] In 1949 King moved to Los Angeles, where she was at first unable to convince any local stations to give her show a try. With the help of a salesman and veteran radio producer Bill Rousseau (who became her husband), she was soon recording her program for syndication.

By June 1950, *The Lonesome Gal* was carried by fifty-seven stations throughout the country, with King recording 285 programs a week. (The show was heard five nights a week on each of the fifty-seven stations; King recorded programs with separate, personalized commercials for local sponsors in each city.)[3] She corresponded with local chambers of commerce in order to include hometown atmosphere, mentioning local streets and people in her chats. This marathon recording schedule necessitated a studio in her own home, where she lived with her husband/producer (who was also for a time the producer of the *Dragnet* radio program) and his two children from a previous marriage. To maintain her air of mystery and the illusion of her availability—not to mention her "loneliness"—King never mentioned her name, her husband, her two children, or her remarkably labor-intensive production process within the Lonesome Gal's pleasant patter.[4] However, she did recount anecdotes about personal concerns such as her garden and cats (i.e., preoccupations that fill the time between visits to or from her "desired" listener) as interstitial remarks between jockeying records chosen from her own collection.

The success of *The Lonesome Gal* can be situated within its negotiation of a number of major shifts experienced by the radio industry in the late 1940s and early 1950s. As a national advertising medium, radio had nearly reached a point of audience saturation, with limited potential for future growth. Rising production costs and a threatened loss of audience to television meant decreasing network revenues and profits. As a result, the industry as a whole began to reconfigure its policies and practices regarding national and local advertising, and the use of transcribed programming. The shows of many major stars were canceled because they were too expensive, and much performing and technical talent drifted to television.

Although radio talent had always performed tasks associated with disc jockeying, it was only in the late 1940s that such a role became central to the industry. Since the beginning of its existence as a mass entertainment medium, the radio industry had been discouraged from playing "canned music" by the FRC, FCC, ASCAP, and the AFM. There had been court battles over the copyright legality of playing records bought through retailers, and the FCC had mandated that stations identify to listeners the recorded nature of such music at regular intervals, helping to produce an ideologically informed "distaste" for seemingly less-genuine or less-"live" radio performances.[5] Consequently, it had been mostly small local stations that risked playing records as regular programming fare. King's first radio venue, for example, WING in Dayton, had recently disengaged itself from network affiliation and therefore had to produce more of its own original programming. By the late 1940s, larger stations and network affiliates also started to produce more shows with disc jockeys playing records. The FCC had let up on its restrictions for record playing after the Supreme Court ruled that once bought, a record could be played by a station at any time. These "record" shows were cheaper to produce and could also be tailored to reflect local tastes, an important advantage in selling advertising time to the local sponsors, who were now increasingly more important as supporters of radio programming.[6]

The production and distribution of *The Lonesome Gal* were compatible with these sorts of shifts in the industry. Because of the emerging gap between network and local station interests, and the changing valuation of transcribed recordings (from condemned, to condoned, to commended), King was able to independently produce and syndicate a popular, successful non-network program. Radio stations and advertisers were not paying for an expensive network personality. At the same time, King's practice of remaining a mystery behind *The Lonesome Gal* format, enhanced by her insistence on wearing a mask in public appearances or in photos, gave her persona the fetishistic and charismatic qualities of a star. Her commitment to weaving local information into her intimate chats complemented stations' attempts to create unique local identities in what was becoming a more decentralized industry, and also complemented local advertisers' desires to personalize their products.

The success of *The Lonesome Gal* must also be seen within the context of the changing role of women in the radio industry. Since the rise of radio in the 1920s, debates surrounding the aesthetics of radio broadcasts had often centered around the supposedly displeasing qualities of the female voice—it was alternately deemed too monotonous, too shrill, or displaying too much personality.[7] Yet even though no women became important announcers on a national level at this time, the popularity of radio homemakers, especially notable in the Midwest, suggests that many listeners had no problem with the voices of helpful women who eased listener isolation and shared some of the labor and scheduling burdens of the domestic sphere.[8]

Even though listeners—as opposed to scientists, critics, and broadcasters—did not seem to have a problem with the female voice, Michelle Hilmes has noted that the network-controlled radio industry confined programs that featured the female voice and expressed women's concerns to a schedule and a set of promotional discourses that associated them with the "disparaged commercialized form of the daytime serial" (a disparagement echoed by cultural critics in reviews and editorials).[9] By the 1940s, especially in cooperation with the propaganda efforts of the OWI to get women into the World War II home-front workforce, network radio did use women's voices in programs like *Listen Women* to expand notions of the female sphere beyond the domestic. Although such shows conveniently alternated stereotypes of the home-front superwoman with the housewife as "weaker sex," Hilmes argues that "wartime media succeeded in recasting the identity of the audience to whom they appealed."[10] Radio's wartime "success" in reaching women, then, involved its mass circulation of tensions between private domesticity and public achievement, making visible (or more precisely, audible) aspects of women's lives that had earlier been obscured by debates about the unsuitability of their voices or the relegation of their programming to less-esteemed daytime hours.

By the early post–World War II period, concerns about female pitch and voice quality had become selectively ignored. In an era when the recently "freed" FM band caused a proliferation of new channels, and some AM affiliates were cut loose as networks turned money and attention to television, local or syndicated programming was even more important.[11] The lady, or "glamour" disc jockey, was seen as an exploitable novelty in this competitive climate—a "novelty" status determined in part by an implicit mandate that women's voices be experienced as innocuous on U.S. radio, especially in contrast to the possibly dangerous qualities of the female voice exemplified in anti-American propaganda broadcasts by Tokyo Rose in Japan and Axis Sally in Germany. These women were tried for treason during the very period in which the glamour disc jockey was a successful experiment on American radio.

A perceived threat of, and desire to control, the encroachment of women in the domestic radio industry occurred within a broader context of anxiety about self-determined women in the postwar United States. This was not conceived as a problematic involving women's voices alone, however, and extended across institutional as well as industrial and textual matters. A 1948 issue of *Broadcasting* magazine rather bluntly evidences a nexus of anxieties regarding the movement of women into male-dominated (and typically male-exclusive) preserves of the communications field. In an article announcing the swearing in of Frieda Hennock, the first female member of the FCC,[12] commission chair Wayne Coy is described congratulating Hennock with the following welcome: the commission as always had "rectitude, fortitude, and solemnitude—but never before pulchritude."[13] A cartoon from a July 1948 issue of *Broadcasting* depicts members of the FCC in a nighttime meeting (figure 1). As the newest member primps before her pocket mirror, her male colleagues are having what seems to be a collective misogynist dream of their "castrating" wives. Images of sour-looking old

Drawn for BROADCASTING by Sid Hix

"By order of higher authority, there will be no night sessions henceforth."

FIGURE 1. Cartoon from *Broadcasting,* 12 July 1948.

women appear over the heads of all the male members, prompting one to suggest, "By order of higher authority, there will be no night sessions henceforth."[14] The professional working woman, as seen by the radio industry (or at least by this prominent industry organ), is thus depicted as narcissistic, a threat to what are assumed to be the concerns of domestic women, and a problematic object of desire for her male coworkers.

A few years later, a complimentary article about Hennock displays a different ambivalence about the power of professional women in the media. Seemingly oblivious to any threat she might pose to wives of FCC members, "The Lady from the FCC" suggests that men nevertheless fear her because Hennock's law career had focused on helping widows and orphans, and "the women and children still love her."[15] After an initial "quiet period" during her FCC tenure, Hennock's profile on the commission became that of an open advocate for more educational television programming to "develop the minds, the hearts . . . of our youth" (39). Such altruistic and socially minded goals are more indicative of an institutionalized sense of the maternal than a stereotypical feminine narcissism implied by the cartoon, though the article does assure readers that Hennock "is no less feminine now that she is a Commissioner. She wears gay, frothy gowns and the most frivolous hats." It goes on to claim, "she is a very attractive woman and as feminine as only a really good-looking woman can be, but she can be as dogged as the toughest Senator, and tougher than some of the male law-makers with whom she has to tangle" (39). Ultimately, then, the article works to portray/defend Hennock's "difference" in terms of a potential "threat," due not only to what it positions as her "essential" femininity but also to a strategic combination of femininity with more typically "masculine" tenacity and competitive spirit.

In depictions such as these articles and cartoon, industry publications display an anxiety over summoning a visual fantasy of Hennock to both demonstrate and contain her power. In the cartoon, the fantasy visualizes Hennock and the male members' wives to suggest that Hennock's public power threatens the private realm where traditional wives are supposed—but apparently fail—to satisfy male desires. In the articles, Hennock's "pulchritude" and concern for fashion are the visible manifestations of a femininity that is presumedly at odds with, or not readily discernible from, her "dogged" toughness as a professional woman.

Radio listening itself at this time had a similar fantasy status, one in which visible versus invisible, public versus private, invocatory ethereality versus imaged concreteness, dominated as tensions in its listeners' pleasures and psychic investments.[16] In its April 1949 issue, *Radio Best* presented "Mental Television," a feature by comic strip artist Mel Graf, in which his drawings of disc jockeys are placed alongside their photographs. Graf describes how his drawings reflect the fantasies inspired by the disc jockey's voices, and how those frequently clashed with the reality of their actual appearances. The feature was so popular that the magazine had Graf repeat the exercise—this time including a cartoon rendering and photo of the Lonesome Gal—in the next issue.[17]

As the portrayals of Hennock suggest, the tensions of visibility/invisibility and public/private had a particular valence when associated with women and radio. Jean King's use of a low, sexy voice in creating *The Lonesome Gal* had the potential to suggest the femme fatale, the stereotype used to link powerful women to personal downfalls and political subversiveness in both the immediate post–World War II and the HUAC periods. And although both industry and mass-market publications marveled at King's success, with her husky voice cooing sweet nothings to her special

FIGURE 2. "Who's Your Favorite Glamour Disc Jockey?" Contest, *Radio Best* magazine, May 1948. Library of American Broadcasting, Hornbake Library, University of Maryland, College Park.

FIGURE 3. Second page (ballot page) for "Who's Your Favorite Glamour Disc Jockey?" Contest, *Radio Best* magazine, June 1948. Library of American Broadcasting, Hornbake Library, University of Maryland, College Park.

"guy," there is indication that the disembodied female voice was not entirely unthreatening and was best "enjoyed" if contained within a sexually defined female body.

Such a strategy of containment is exemplified in *Radio Best* magazine's 1948 contest to elect the "most glamorous" female disc jockey, with readers sending in votes.[18] The candidates are pictured in the contest announcement, ostensibly because the disc jockeys at this time were all on local stations (including King in this, her presyndication period), and so not familiar to all readers of the magazine. But it is significant that most of these "glamour" pictures are cheesecake images, modeled on the poses and attitudes used in stills produced to accentuate the sexual allure of female film stars (figures 2 and 3). Posing for the objectifying gaze of the presumed male reader, some of the disc jockeys are dressed in bathing suits, strapless gowns, tight sweaters, and, in King's case, wearing a facial mask that hides—and consequently fetishizes—the area around her eyes. Some have their chests pushed forward to appear "busty"; legs are posed to show off both calves and thighs; some have lips slightly open, or eyes looking off-camera. Of the sixteen candidates pictured, only one—one of two "cowgirl" disc jockeys—is posed in a relaxed, nonsexualized manner.

King won second place in *Radio Best*'s glamour contest, but she would ultimately prove to be the most successful in terms of airtime longevity and national fame (once her show was syndicated). In 1951 MGM bought the film rights to the Lonesome Gal personality and announced that either Ava Gardner or Lana Turner would star in her story.[19] Although MGM was promising the allure of one of two of their most glamorous stars, the studio never made the picture. Universal bought the rights from MGM in 1956, this time with King herself to write the story treatment, but once again the project was shelved.[20]

Despite King's frequent visual depiction in glamorous poses (especially when masked), and MGM's plan to approximate her appeal through casting sexy Ava Gardner or Lana Turner, over the ten years she was on the air, King was increasingly understood as a savvy businesswoman, and the Lonesome Gal as a devoted friend in her shows and publicity. The erotic qualities of King's performance as the Lonesome Gal seem to have been increasingly propped onto what can be recognized as a maternal address concerned with the every need of *The Lonesome Gal*'s man. This propping, while it diffuses the gendered nature of the addressee (i.e., allows her address to cast its net over the imaginary of female listeners as well), aligns

The Lonesome Gal with more traditional female roles—ultimately closer to the "neighboring," interpersonal address of the radio homemakers than the aggressive, "treasonous," seductive address of Rose and Sally and the femme fatale.

Textual and Audience Analysis

On a textual and discursive level, the success of both *The Lonesome Gal* and *The Continental* is due in large part to each program's use of direct address—a strategy that compels the listener or viewer to enter into and identify with the program's gendered but porous fictive space. Such an invitation is immediately apparent from *The Lonesome Gal*'s opening line: "Sweetie, no matter what anybody says, I love you better than anybody in the whole world." The following is an excerpt of her continued opening address for one program (circa 1951):

(Singing, with accompaniment)
Lonesome, I'm a real lonesome gal.
I can't stop feeling lonesome. Heaven knows when I shall.

(over theme music)
Hi, baby. This is your Lonesome Gal. Are you as lazy as I am right this minute? Then keep on being lazy, and forget everything for awhile, except us. I have no profound knowledge to impart, but I sure do love ya and I want to tell you so. So light up a pipe full of Bond Street, lover, and relax.

(Singing)
Who knows what tomorrow may bring?
I wonder whether I'll know when my heart starts to sing?

(over theme music)
Cutie, this is a very special event for me, to be back with you again. Gee, I've missed you. And a lot of things have happened since I was with you last. But I won't try and tell you everything at once. I'll spread my news over a long period of time. Cause you know me—the more visits I get with you, the better I like it. (music out)

There's one thing I bet you didn't notice: my new winter window-box. Know what those plants are? Martha Washington geraniums. Just a little something for me to tend to when you're not here. But with you back, I'll have lots to do. And this time, baby, I hope it's for keeps. Nobody can break this up. Course anyone who'd think of trying that would be a cockeyed optimist.

(Recorded song follows immediately: "Cockeyed Optimist")

The seductive hailing of the listener as "sweetie," coupled with the declaration of an exclusive intimacy between them, is a strong draw into the fictive space of *The Lonesome Gal*'s world. But her musical lament (that she can't help feeling lonesome) contradicts the permanence of their intimacy and opens to question the power of female desire initially asserted with so much confidence: the show suggests that the seductive, unattached woman is fated to be lonely. In this way, it negotiates a maintenance of women's assumed desire for marriage, even as it acknowledges an uncontrollable melancholic desire that marriage won't necessarily appease. As a means of sustaining interest in the show's textual developments and encouraging regular listening, it intimates the necessity of an ongoing resolicitation of male desire, in order to help the Lonesome Gal overcome her loneliness. Within each show, the textual economy between her concluding phrases and the songs that follow them afford a forward momentum, a flow based on a kind of iterative wit—a pleasantly predictable rhyme between textual units. On an institutional level, the repetition and serialization of sexual desire is compatible with advertisers' needs to continually reopen the desire of the listeners to consume their products.

The facilitation of consumption also operates within the Lonesome Gal's positioning of her time with the male listener as a time to be "lazy," the leisure time so often fantasized by contemporary advertising discourses to create their products' appeal, to place them in the life schedule of postwar consumers. One of the most consistent characteristics of the textual operations of *The Lonesome Gal*'s chats is the smooth transition or slippage between the seductive descriptions of being lazy together with the listener and their constitution as a couple that enjoys his use of the sponsor's product:

Dreamboat, every girl likes to be with a man of good taste. And sweetie, I'm no exception. That's why I like being with you. I like the ties you pick, I like the clothes you wear, and the music you choose. And most of all I like the Bond Street tobacco you smoke. Good taste is just another name for Bond Street. Sweetie, I don't have to tell you about Bond Street tobacco. You smoke it, you taste it, you enjoy the full, rich, mellow pleasure that comes out of that wonderful Bond Street blend.

But what I do want to tell you is what it means to me, what it means to the girl you're with, when you're smoking Bond Street. It means the joy of seeing you happy. It means the pleasure of enjoying with you the gentle, delicate aroma that only Bond Street has. It means the good taste of a kiss between boy and girl. Maybe this isn't news to you, but it's good to know these things about Bond Street tobacco. The mild, clean, good-tasting tobacco that pleases not only you, baby, but the girl you're with. It's a man's tobacco that keeps a girl feeling good about the man who smokes it. You'll remember that, won't you baby? I know you will—you've got good taste. You're my everything.

(Recorded song follows immediately: "You're My Everything")

The Lonesome Gal's attraction to her male listeners is linked here to their possession of "taste." She takes pride and self-satisfaction in being associated with such good taste. Bolstering the male ego is thereby accomplished by persuading the listener that using Bond Street tobacco conforms to a dynamic in which both the product and women/a woman accessorize men/a man appropriately. This address is also open to women, ostensibly "overhearing" this conversation, who might share the Lonesome Gal's melancholic unattached status—or, even if married, share her loneliness—and who may be inclined to purchase such products for their own boyfriends, husbands, and so on. The threat of the single or lonely female subject is repositioned in a more commercially sanctioned space as "male accessory," sexual object, and/or retail conduit.

Although we do not have access to demographic figures for the program, there are some textual and extratextual discourses (such as publicity, etc.) that suggest there were indeed numerous female "eavesdroppers" on these intimate conversations. In a 1985 interview, King said that many women wrote in to say she "made their ironing easier and to thank her for showing them how men liked to be talked to."[21] Over time, products advertised become less male centered (from tobacco and beer to restaurants, antique stores, and car dealerships), and the persona of Jean King in popular magazines shifted from a woman of mystery to a basically happy homemaker, whose overwork in radio production had caused her to occasionally collapse from exhaustion.[22]

The patter in the show also became less determinedly male directed, with comments more oriented to social observation, including the addition of a "food for thought" segment during which the Lonesome Gal read words of advice sent in from listeners, many of whom were women. The show continued to create a slippage between advertised products and suggested listening positions, but delivered by a persona now less constructed as an ideal sexual mate and more as an ideal oral/aural mother, a comforting fantasy figure promising pleasurable fusion for listening subjects of both genders. From this perspective, the Lonesome Gal as a radio mother exists as a voice that cannot be subordinated in visual spectacle, taken in by a listening ear. Even though promotion and publicity of King (and other women disc jockeys) attempted to "contain" the female radio personality visually, the actual vocal performance broadcast over the airwaves cannot be readily incorporated through the gaze, as the maternal body is by cinematic or televisual textual regimes. However, this fantasy projection of the maternal, whether constituted through visual or aural corporeality, generally supports a conservative subject positioning.[23]

The Lonesome Gal and its seductively maternal aural space can be seen to function as a trope for radio's shifting institutional, textual, and cultural identities circulating at this moment. In a post-atomic-bomb Cold War American culture, the annihilation of subjectivity not only was a genuine possibility but was often represented in popular discourses as virtually coterminous with aspects of female desire and subjectivity.[24] The fictive aural space offered by The Lonesome Gal manages anxiety through a sonorous envelopment of the listening subject, involving a pleasurable play with the desire of fusion/annihilation (with the maternal). One way for radio to survive in the age of television was by not competing with television's stars and narratives, which offered viewers a series of discrete identifications, but instead seeking new functions aligned with a fragmented and mobilized audience increasingly listening to the popular car radio, or the newly developed clock or transistor radios. By the mid-1950s, radios were imagined to be—and could increasingly be found—most everywhere in the urban and suburban topography. The Lonesome Gal offers one voice and format that suggests a pleasurable and soothing omnipresence. In this way, it harkens back to the "neighboring" of radio homemakers but also anticipates talk radio hosts and therapists, programming formats that have also responded to a specialized and dispersed audience through a slow development of ongoing intimacy between listener and host.

The Continental: *Textual and Industrial Analyses*

Conversely, an aggressive address is central to the discursive strategies of *The Continental,* a persona and format that Renzo Cesana appears to have

FIGURE 4. The Continental offers his "date" a glass of champagne.

borrowed and transposed from *The Lonesome Gal.* Premiering on local Los Angeles radio in February 1951, and directly following *The Lonesome Gal* in station KHJ's late-night schedule, *The Continental* found little success and was soon canceled. Cesana convinced local television station KNBH (channel 4) to air a visualized, direct-address fifteen-minute version of the show in June, which quickly gained considerable notoriety and national magazine attention,[25] propelling Cesana into a contract with Capitol Records and then a twice-weekly CBS network version of the show (Tuesday and Thursday at 11:15 P.M., running from January 22 to April 17, 1952; see figure 4).[26]

Institutionally, Cesana's career rise can be positioned within industry economics and practices almost wholly reversed from those that King was taking advantage of in radio. Unlike the economically stalled radio industry, the television industry (in pursuing the established broadcast industrial paradigms) had an imperative to grow: to sell more sets, and to increase both local audiences and television's national saturation. To achieve this meant attracting more and different viewers, filling in and expanding broadcast schedules, and in general maintaining television as a topical and attractively "new" consumer purchase, while at the same time indicating that it could be both flexible and substantial enough to maintain viewer interest. As a result, there was a much greater tendency to take risks on formats and performers. For the networks in the East, this included seeking out talent from local markets. *The Continental*'s brief rise to national attention played a part in this dynamic.

Los Angeles had become a primary source market for such transplanted programs as networks assimilated locally successful shows and performers such as Mike Stokey's *Pantomine Quiz*. Even Hopalong Cassidy, whose career as a heroic cowboy was revived by television at this time, was first aired and rose to popularity on local Los Angeles television. In addition, enterprising local stations had syndicated some of their programs nationally, including *Time for Beany, Wrestling from Hollywood, Life with Elizabeth* (which starred Betty White), and the most successful of these shows, *Liberace*.

Cesana's success with *The Continental* was a notable if fleeting example of this trend. Premiering on the CBS network in January 1952, twice weekly in late-night spots, he received photo spreads in *Life* magazine the following month, and then *Look* magazine, which documented the various spoofs of his format that other network shows had performed: Jimmy Durante, Red Skelton, Robert Q. Lewis, Jackie Gleason, Alan Young, and Donald O'Connor had each parodied him.[27] The instant recognizability of his format, derived from a certain creative ingenuity in resolving budgetary limitations (e.g., the use of direct address), was combined with the show's inherent camp value in making opaque the sexual content latent in common stereotypes of swarthy Europeans. All of this was readily acknowledged and lampooned—an early example of television's self-referential humor, which has always served in part to elevate TV as a significant source of intertextual reference. In this way, the show was perfectly compatible with, and valuable to, the industry's agendas of growth.

But the degree to which such parodies critiqued or otherwise defused the implicit gender politics of the show (or of television at large) seems to have been slight. *The Continental* was parodied, but it was also considered to be in some way threatening to the security of heterosexual couplings, a response that we will discuss in more detail later. Institutionally, the show took part in a quite polarized depiction of televisual sexuality and desire, indicated by one industry response to the show's almost immediate popularity and notoriety. Counterprogramming in some local markets featured a five-minute seduction by a female "counterpart" dressed in a provocative negligee, wishing the (male) audience good night.

Such representations of women on early TV, though rarely so baldly suggestive, were actually not uncommon, as featured personalities such as Faye Emerson, Dagmar, Zsa Zsa Gabor, and countless dancers and chorus girls "entertained" in part via provocative attire and décolletage. Such renderings were often excused or even applauded for their function in providing (male) diversions from what were perceived to be incessant and increasing social pressures and threats. In other words, sexually suggestive programs were positioned as sites of leisure, in answer to what seemed to be growing "external" threats and personal pressures that the postwar consumer culture was suggested to be able to allay or resolve. *The Continental*, while seeming to, and in many cases undoubtedly succeeding to, genuinely address female desire, is a notable if partial exception to the general trend of such shows. We will suggest that although his attention to female desire is not wholly recuperable, the program's allegedly dystopian potential (as sexual rival) is not-so-subtly compromised, so that Cesana's gendered address was actually complementary to TV's general regime of sexual representation at this historical moment.

The suggestiveness of the direct address employed by Cesana as "the Continental" is virtually unchecked.[28] Cesana speaks for himself (and for his "guest") and tempers his aggressiveness only as it approaches a limit point of taste and propriety (he embarrasses "her"). *The Continental* directly attempts to induce a fetishization of women in their social existence via an evocation of some idealized, imaginary construct of the woman-as-fetish.

Especially in the network version of the show (which are, to our knowledge, the only kinescope copies available), the program has a distinctive and important "frame": it is sponsored by Burr-Mill Cameo stockings, which offer "the fashion advantage of face powder finish." Although we never see Cesana's "date" during the show, we do see, before and after his monologue, fetishized models raising a skirt, blowing on a powder puff, and exhibiting clothes, suggesting how a viewer might approximate the ideal fetish that the show evokes. Within one show, Cesana details his modes and practices of fetishization (saving lost gloves, charting the length of skirts, etc.), offering to the implied female viewer an identification with them. He offers an imaginary construct of his "guest" in a strapless, sleeveless, backless, "slightly frontless" gown, in a progressively shorter skirt, with exquisitely sized and formed hands, and so on.

Within his address, the Continental creates a space for women's sexuality but assigns it to the purpose of male desire: he opens the process of fetishization but presents it as a double bind of women's intentionality. Cesana's opening remarks in this undated CBS episode indicate that a woman's acceptance of a position of fetishization should be seen as a "gift" to men, which men have misunderstood as narcissism:

You know, I've always wanted to thank you for making me so happy—with the pains you take to always look your best: so well-dressed, well-groomed, well-coiffed. And all for me. Oh yes, [there are] others that say that women are supposed to dress to please themselves. But you and I know better. That probably must have been started by a man, who wanted to blame you instead of himself for those little charge accounts you open with such gay abandon.

A woman's sexuality is flattered into a position of object status and also related to her activity to spend and consume—to actively pursue making herself into a fetish by investing monetarily into the suggested libidinal economy (for example, to buy Cameo stockings). Any contradiction or difficulty in assuming or maintaining this object status—especially in the form of traditional male complaints of feminine "irrationality"—is similarly flattered away. After Cesana breeches the assumed limit point of tact in his address, by virtually implying his "guest" is naked, he apologizes:

Oh darling, now you're unhappy? Oh, I've embarrassed you; I'm sorry. Well then, you know, you might be unhappy for no reason at all. That's what makes you women so fascinating. You see, to have a reason for being happy or unhappy, well, that is a superfluity to which I, a mere man, still cling. But you—you're a woman, darling, you are above all sorts of reasons or causes or anything.

We do not have figures that describe the viewership of *The Continental,* either locally or nationally, but it seems significant to consider the program in relation to the postwar generation of married couples who were progenitors of the baby boom, especially in addressing housewives tied to, and largely defined by, their (asexual) domestic responsibilities. The few newspaper and magazine articles about the show that we have located indicate a half-joking dystopian threat perceived via its attention to female desire.

Hal Humphrey, television columnist for the *Los Angeles Mirror,* titled his review of *The Continental*'s local L.A. premiere "Comes Now 'The Other Man,'" offering a corrective to his previous day's column, in which he had warned housewives in TV homes of the danger they run by getting careless about their appearance while their husbands ogle the beauty parade on the video screen. *The Continental,* Humphrey suggested, is "a program which is designed to put another strain on family ties," and he concluded that "if you catch the little woman turning to channel 4 tonight at 11, break her arm. At 11:15 it will be too late."[29]

An article in *TV-Radio Life,* a local Los Angeles publication, suggested a decidedly gendered split of affection for Cesana. In the article, Cesana is described as evidencing during an interview an awareness of, and appreciation for, the domestic chores previously mentioned:

Renzo, with great waving of hands and in his inimitable and fascinating accent, carried the typical American housewife through a whole day's activities. And very accurately done it was. He finished with a beam of pride for all American femininity . . . "and at the end of this day's work they are as gracious and lovely as no other woman in the world can hope to be!"

Certainly the husbands of America can't disagree with him on this. But while they are out working calculators, riveting with machines, or swinging golf clubs, Renzo is working in TV toward entertaining their wives. And they loathe him for it![30]

The husbands reportedly offended and enraged were doubtless disturbed that the show offered to women the opportunity to identify with the position of a mistress in an extramarital, if not adulterous, affair. (At the conclusion of one episode, when Cesana requests that his "guest" bring a friend along next time to accompany a friend of his—"He's not particular, as long as it's a woman"—he does stipulate that she should be "unattached.") This reaction to a program so thoroughly engrained in patriarchal positionings of women is a sign of just how repressive this system can be regarding female sexuality.

In conclusion, we would suggest that the relative failure of *The Continental* to achieve lasting popularity (none of Cesana's various local and national shows appear to have stayed on the air at one station for more than a year), as opposed to the approximately decade-long run of *The Lonesome Gal,* is less due to media specificity than to differences in the way the two shows sustained and serialized the gendered desires they evoked.[31] Whereas *The Continental* offered only an unrelated series of seduction ploys and scenarios, which ultimately repeated with little variation from week to week, *The Lonesome Gal* not only shifted from a more sexually seductive address to one that facilitated a sense of emotional well-being but also forged an intimacy with listeners that developed gradually over time, on the basis of shared experiences and a past history together. Such an intimacy over time did not threaten the appeal of the show for men and also agreed with reading competencies more likely to be cultivated by, and socially induced in, women. By examining these shows and formats across industrial, institutional, and programming contexts, we hope to have suggested a more complete understanding of the goals and stakes implicit in what may appear to be merely complementary texts—and complementary media—especially as they illustrate historically specific valences of gendered media practices.

Notes

Thanks to Ron Wolf of the Pacific Pioneer Broadcasters and John and Larry Gassman of SPERDVAC for making available several episodes of *The Lonesome Gal* found in their respective collections of transcribed radio programs. Thanks also to Ned Comstock at the USC Cinema-Television Library for research assistance.

1 Christine Gledhill, "Pleasurable Negotiations," in *The Female Spectator*, ed. E. Deidre Pribram (New York: Verso), 68.

2 "Lonesome . . . by Choice," *TV-Radio Life*, 14 July 1950.

3 "How Are You Baby," *Time*, 26 June 1950, 47–48.

4 The Lonesome Gal was revealed to be Jean King as early as 1948 in a variety of magazines, both specialized radio-TV publications and mass-market general-readership magazines (such as *Time*). However, she never mentioned her name or marital status on the air, nor did she show her face unmasked in either photos or personal appearances.

5 In December 1946 the FCC had allowed transcription recordings of less than one minute to go unidentified as such, which led to a boom in transcribed ads. Bing Crosby, whose 3M Company pioneered various recording technologies, had begun to transcribe his ABC network show that same year. While NBC and CBS initially refused transcribed shows, ABC and Mutual relished them, and independent syndicators such as the Keystone Broadcasting System (a transcription quasi "network") and Frederick W. Ziv, who would go on to great success in television, flourished. See "Transcription Boom," *Newsweek*, 19 January 1948, 58. Regarding another transcription company, see Linda L. Painter, "The Rise and Decline of Standard Radio Transcription Company," *JEMF Quarterly* 17, no. 64 (winter 1981): 194–200. On a related topic, Robert Vianello has detailed how major U.S. radio networks used an enhanced, expensively produced rendering of (national) "live" programming, which demarcated their address from that of the qualitatively less spectacular (local) "live." See Robert Vianello, "The Power Politics of 'Live' Television," *Journal of Film and Video* 37, no. 3 (summer 1985).

6 Arnold Passman, *The Dee Jays* (New York: Macmillan, 1971). Typical of most historians of radio, Passman does not discuss the female "glamour" disc jockeys, even though radio and general readership magazines of the time frequently mention them. Passman does discuss the economic, industrial, and cultural

factors that led to the predominance of DJ-oriented and Top 40 radio programming in the postwar era.

7 The debates about radio and the female voice are discussed by Anne McKay in "Speaking Up: Voice Amplification and Women's Struggle for Public Expression," in *Technology and Women's Voices: Keeping in Touch,* ed. Cheris Kramarae (New York: Kegan Paul, 1988), 187–206; and Michelle Hilmes, *Radio Voices: American Broadcasting, 1922–1952* (Minneapolis: University of Minnesota Press, 1997), 141–45. See also Amy Lawrence, *Echo and Narcissus: Women's Voices in Classical Hollywood Cinema* (Berkeley: University of California Press, 1991), 29–32.

8 See Jane Stern and Michael Stern, "Neighboring," *New Yorker,* 15 April 1991, 78–92; Robert Birkby, *KMA Radio: The First Sixty Years* (Shenandoah, Iowa: May Broadcasting, 1985); and Evelyn Birkby, *Neighboring on the Air: Cooking with KMA Radio Homemakers* (Iowa City: University of Iowa Press, 1991).

9 Hilmes, *Radio Voices,* 141.

10 Ibid., 264.

11 See Hilmes, *Radio Voices,* 272–73, for an excellent discussion on the impact of these changes on the development of African American programming.

12 Erik Barnouw suggests that President Truman had put Hennock forward as a nominee to the commission in order to invite an uncooperative Congress "to go on record as anti-feminist or anti-Semitic. They risked neither and confirmed her quickly." *The Golden Web: A History of Broadcasting in the United States, Volume II, 1933–1953* (New York: Oxford University Press, 1968), 293.

13 "Madame Commissioner," *Broadcasting,* 12 July 1948.

14 *Broadcasting,* 12 July 1948.

15 Saul Carson, "The Lady from the FCC," *TV Screen,* August 1951, 38.

16 For a discussion of radio's invocatory ethereality, see Susan J. Douglas, *Listening In: Radio and the American Imagination* (New York: Times Books, 1999), 40–54. Douglas argues that radio has historically had a special relationship to the male listener.

17 Mel Graf, "Mental Television," *Radio Best,* April 1949, 36–37; and Mel Graf, "Mental Television," *Radio Best,* May 1949, 40–41.

18 Coverage of the contest is found in the May through August 1948 issues of *Radio Best.* Pictures of the various candidates accompany the contest announcements (May issue, p. 21, and June issue, pp. 32–33); King's masked image as the Lonesome Gal is present in all four issues.

19 "Radio's 'Lonesome Gal' Acquired for MGM Film," *Hollywood Reporter,* 27 September 1951.

20 "'Lonesome Gal' Will Be Biopictured by UI; MGM Project Off," *Variety,* 6 July 1956. It is not clear from any of the blurbs about the "Lonesome Gal" film in the industry trade press whether the narrative would detail the life of Jean King or her alter radio ego, the Lonesome Gal persona. An unpublished interoffice

memo at Universal-International Pictures dated 23 February 1954 indicates that the MGM project had been based on the Lonesome Gal character (USC Cinema-Television Library, Universal Collection, Box 719, Folder 22972). Apparently Jean King was hired by MGM to do voice-overs for some of their film trailers. Her voice is recognizable in the trailer for the 1956 MGM film *Diane.*

21 See Richard Lamparski, *Whatever Became Of . . . ?* 9th series (New York: Crown Publishers, 1985), 100–101.

22 See especially "Put Legs to Your Prayers," *TV-Radio Life,* 28 October 1955, 6.

23 Of course, recent critical theory about audience/spectators/listeners reminds us that responses are unpredictable and open to multiple positionings. That *The Lonesome Gal* offered a conservative subject positioning—or, for that matter, primarily a maternal projection—was not necessarily the position or fantasy of every listener. In Lamparski's 1985 interview, King recounts how one woman had a distinctly sexual, lesbian fantasy regarding *The Lonesome Gal.* She would write King passionate letters, send yellow roses, and was persuaded by police to desist from such practices after she wrote a detailed letter describing the lovemaking she expected to share with King/Lonesome Gal (Lamparski, *Whatever Became Of . . . ?*).

24 This relationship between the atomic threat and female desire/subjectivity literally climaxes in *Kiss Me Deadly* (Robert Aldrich, 1955), one of the most pointed critiques of masculine narcissism and the Cold War context to appear during the period. At the end of the film, Gabrielle, one of the transgressive female characters in the film, sets off an apparent atomic explosion via her curiosity about "the Great Whatsit." Significantly, a radio show with an address very similar to that of King is playing on protagonist Mike Hammer's car radio during the opening scene of the film. For an example of nonfiction televisual disclosure that relates atomic blasts and an image of women, see Mark Williams, "History in a Flash: Notes on the Myth of TV 'Liveness,'" in *Collecting Visible Evidence,* Visible Evidence Series, ed. Jane M. Gaines and Michael Renov (Minneapolis: University of Minnesota Press, 1999).

25 See "Latin Lover," *Time,* 5 November 1951, 104–5; and "Lonesome Guy," *Newsweek,* 5 November 1951, 58. Cesana had begun his career in his native city of Rome, Italy, where his father was publisher of a newspaper, *Il Messaggero.* As a youth Cesana wrote and produced experimental plays and was a schoolmate of Roberto Rossellini. MGM brought Cesana to the United States in the mid-1930s to help adapt their films for Italian audiences. After a failed promotion as a budding star ("The Shark of the Tiber"), he appeared on radio in San Francisco, and later became U.S. advertising director for a prominent Italian wine company, and also started his own advertising agency. After Rossellini invited him back to Italy to appear as the priest in the film *Stromboli* (Rossellini, 1950), Cesana appeared as a priest in several more films before returning to radio as "the Continental." See "Give Him Paradise," *Fortnight,* 24 December 1951.

26 Jack Gould's *New York Times* review of Cesana's network premiere wryly suggests that CBS was attempting a strategy toward network parity with station-rich NBC, by hiring "the first electronic gigolo." It is intriguing to note that both Gould and Philip Hamburger (is this a pseudonym?) in *The New Yorker* figure their gendered resistance to *The Continental* in class terms, by reporting their desire for a bottle of beer. See Jack Gould, "Radio and Television," *New York Times,* 1 February 1952; and Philip Hamburger, "Television," *New Yorker,* 16 February 1952.

27 See "Woo-Pitcher Gets Network," *Life,* 11 February 1952; and "Kidding the Continental," *Look,* 22 April 1952.

28 Cesana would sometimes phone female viewers in response to their letters to him, a practice that apparently could disturb the fetishization process for at least some viewers. See Jack Gould, "Radio and Television," *New York Times,* 1 February 1952.

29 Hal Humphrey, "Comes Now 'The Other Man,'" *Los Angeles Mirror,* 14 June 1951, 27.

30 Jane Pelgram, "Husbands Loathe Him!" *TV-Radio Life,* 14 September 1951, 39.

31 Cesana was subsequently featured in two short-lived series: *First Date,* on which he spoke to couples taking part in the show's titular activity, ABC (and possibly syndication), 1952–1953; and a program called *Love Story* (several programs have shared this title; it is unclear which one Cesana appeared on). He also briefly reprised his most famous role in a new format, in which he interviewed women, *Ladies! The Continental* on local Los Angeles station KTLA in 1961. Over his career, he appeared in dozens of films in the United States and Italy, and a great many more television shows, including hits such as *Mission Impossible* and *That Girl.* See "The Continental: 15 Years Later," *TV Guide,* 21 November 1970, 49.

Works Cited

Barnouw, Erik. *The Golden Web: A History of Broadcasting in the United States, Volume II, 1933–1953.* New York: Oxford University Press, 1968.

Birkby, Evelyn. *Neighboring on the Air: Cooking with KMA Radio Homemakers.* Iowa City: University of Iowa Press, 1991.

Birkby, Robert. *KMA Radio: The First Sixty Years.* Shenandoah, Iowa: May Broadcasting, 1985.

Carson, Saul. "The Lady from the FCC." *TV Screen,* August 1951, 38.

"The Continental: 15 Years Later." *TV Guide,* 21 November 1970, 49.

Douglas, Susan J. *Listening In: Radio and the American Imagination.* New York: Times Books, 1999.

"Give Him Paradise." *Fortnight,* 24 December 1951.

Gledhill, Christine. "Pleasurable Negotiations." In *The Female Spectator,* ed. E. Deidre Pribram. New York: Verso.

Gould, Jack. "Radio and Television." *New York Times,* 1 February 1952.

Graf, Mel. "Mental Television." *Radio Best,* April 1949, 36–37.

——. "Mental Television." *Radio Best,* May 1949, 40–41.

Hamburger, Philip. "Television." *The New Yorker,* 16 February 1952.

Hilmes, Michelle. *Radio Voices: American Broadcasting, 1922–1952.* Minneapolis: University of Minnesota Press, 1997.

"How Are You Baby." *Time,* 26 June 1950, 47–48.

Humphrey, Hal. "Comes Now 'The Other Man.' " *Los Angeles Mirror,* 14 June 1951, 27.

"Kidding the Continental." *Look,* 22 April 1952.

Lamparski, Richard. *Whatever Became Of . . . ?* 9th Series. New York: Crown Publishers, 1985.

"Latin Lover." *Time,* 5 November 1951, 104–5.

Lawrence, Amy. *Echo and Narcissus: Women's Voices in Classical Hollywood Cinema.* Berkeley: University of California Press, 1991.

"Lonesome . . . by Choice." *TV-Radio Life,* 14 July 1950.

" 'Lonesome Gal' Will Be Biopictured by UI; MGM Project Off." *Variety,* 6 July 1956.

"Lonesome Guy." *Newsweek,* 5 November 1951, 58.

"Madame Commissioner." *Broadcasting,* 12 July 1948.

McKay, Anne. "Speaking Up: Voice Amplification and Women's Struggle for Public Expression." In *Technology and Women's Voices: Keeping in Touch,* ed. Cheris Kramarae. New York: Kegan Paul, 1988.

Painter, Linda L. "The Rise and Decline of Standard Radio Transcription Company." *JEMF Quarterly* 17, no. 64 (winter 1981): 194–200.

Passman, Arnold. *The Dee Jays.* New York: Macmillan, 1971.

Pelgram, Jane. "Husbands Loathe Him!" *TV-Radio Life,* 14 September 1951, 39.

"Put Legs to Your Prayers." *TV-Radio Life,* 28 October 1955, 6.

"Radio's 'Lonesome Gal' Acquired for MGM Film." *Hollywood Reporter,* 27 September 1951.

Stern, Jane, and Michael Stern. "Neighboring." *The New Yorker,* 15 April 1991, 78–92.

"Transcription Boom." *Newsweek,* 19 January 1948, 58.

Universal-International Pictures memo, dated 23 February 1954. Universal Collection, Box 719, Folder 22972. University of Southern California Cinema-Television Library.

Vianello, Robert. "The Power Politics of 'Live' Television." *Journal of Film and Video* 37, no. 3 (summer 1985).

Williams, Mark. "History in a Flash: Notes on the Myth of TV 'Liveness.' " In *Collecting Visible Evidence,* Visible Evidence Series, ed. Jane M. Gaines and Michael Renov. Minneapolis: University of Minnesota Press, 1999.

"Woo-Pitcher Gets Network." *Life,* 11 February 1952.

WIRELESS POSSIBILITIES,

POSTHUMAN POSSIBILITIES: BRAIN RADIO,

COMMUNITY RADIO, RADIO LAZARUS

Susan M. Squier

The possibility of the posthuman is not to do with the transcendence of the human, its replacement, but rather with the recognition and exposure of the networks of production which constitute human techno-genesis.—Catherine Waldby, *The Visible Human Project*

Radio, by cultivating different modes of listening, also fostered people's tendency to feel fragmented into many selves, which were called forth in rapid succession, or sometimes all at the same time.—Susan Douglas, *Listening In*

We've been able to transplant the brain, as a separate organ, into an intact animal and maintain it in a viable or living situation for many days. . . . we've been able to retain the brain . . . in the skull and in the head, and some people designate this as a head transplant, but it is also a brain transplant, and under those circumstances of course the organ can see, hear, taste and smell because the nerves are left intact in the head. This has also been accomplished in the monkey and under those circumstances it becomes conscious and functionable [*sic*].—Robert White, BBC interview

Even your body has a biological radio set, which can be triggered by a seizure of the temporal lobe. Radio knows no boundaries: its signal is as unavoidable as it is unstoppable.—Neil Strauss, Introduction, *Radiotext(e)*

In 1924 a British physicist named A. M. Low published *Wireless Possibilities,* a slim volume arguing that radio had the potential to reshape human identity. "Oscillation—that is all we mean by Radio," Professor Low observed, "and oscillation is at the base of life itself."[1] From his vantage point early in the era of modern radio, Low predicted a change in the whole trajectory of human life. "Once we understand the theories of electrical sonics," he predicted, a vast array of knowledge would be open to us: "Theories of preventing local thunderstorms, of growing babies and wheat effectively, by electrical or other similar oscillating means, of helping our- selves to see by wireless, and of effecting our health at the end of many generations for the better, may all be developed in the time to come."[2]

Low's bold prophecy foretold that radio would not only increase the effectiveness of human activities, from weather forecasting to agriculture, but improve the human being itself. His vision of "growing babies . . . [and] helping ourselves to see" by wireless seems a remarkable anticipation of the posthuman subject, that "material-informational entity" whose ap- pearance N. Katherine Hayles traces back to the Macy Conferences on cybernetics held in the United States between 1946 and 1953. Hayles argues that those conferences marked a shift in our conception of the human being, from sovereign possessor of a discrete and malleable technology, to enmeshed participant in an amorphous and unstable informational circuit.[3]

But radio is a technology dating back to the nineteenth century, its crude first demonstrations by Marconi in 1896 and 1899 evoking "nothing so much," according to radio historian Susan Douglas, "as the apparatus in the labs of Frankenstein movies."[4] To consider *radio* as part of this shift toward the posthuman plunges us into a debate over the relations between human beings and technology. If we see the wireless as implicated in the production of a posthuman subject, we must rethink radio, seeing it no longer as a quaint, nearly obsolete technology but instead as the leading edge of later developments in cybernetics. Alternatively, if we hold on to our awareness of the nineteenth-century roots of wireless technology, we will find ourselves rethinking our understanding of the term "posthuman." We may understand the posthuman not as *a new type of being,* part human and part informational circuit, but as a *new perspective* on the complex and enmeshed relations that human beings have always had to the technologies we develop.[5] In short, our assessment of wireless possibilities will both depend on and inform our understanding of the relations between tech- nology and human beings, in the modern and postmodern periods.

With the larger question of the relations between human beings and our technologies in mind, in what follows I will trace three moments in radio's oscillatory embodiment of human life. The first moment, a well-known part of the modern radio scene, embodies what might be called "brain radio"; the second, a classic fictional expression of midcentury malaise, I call (with some irony) "community radio"; and the third, a science fiction narrative of the biomedical life-extension possibilities of radio in the new millennium, we can call "radio Lazarus." Beginning with the modernist preoccupation with a mechanist extension of the brain, these three embodiments of radio gradually work outward to a digitized reformulation of the boundaries of the human being. In the process, they reframe the subjective nature of the individual, the nature of the human social collective, and finally the species itself.[6] While these by no means represent all of the "wireless possibilities" explored in the course of the twentieth century, they do embody the general direction that radio representations have taken in the course of the last hundred years. In their sequence, they will enable us to assess the role that radio technology played in the production of the posthuman, whether we understand it as a new point of view or as a wholly new subject, in the twentieth century. And they will have something to say about the complex relations between science, technology, and the human body.

Brain Radio

Modern writers loved to speculate about the ways the human body could be improved on as an information-processing machine, and one of their favorite fantasies was what we might call the "brain in a beaker": a perfused brain in a cylinder, connected to the world around it by artificially enhanced sense organs.

The brain thus guaranteed continuous awareness, is connected in the anterior of the case with its immediate sense organs, the eye and the ear—which will probably retain this connection for a long time. The eyes will look into a kind of optical box which will enable them alternatively to look into periscopes projecting from the case, telescopes, microscopes, and a whole range of televisual apparatus. The ear would have the corresponding microphone attachments and would still be the chief organ for wireless reception.

This image comes from crystallographer J. D. Bernal's 1929 fantasy of mechanical human evolution, *The World, the Flesh, and the Devil: An Enquiry into the Future of the Three Enemies of the Rational Soul*. Although the radio is only one of the technological instruments by which Bernal's superhuman of the future would extend his powers, it is central to another modern tale of the scientific attempt to perfect the human, the radio play

"Donovan's Brain." Based on Curt Siodmak's 1943 novel by the same name, this radio drama aired on May 18 and 25, 1944, on *Suspense, Radio's Outstanding Theatre of Thrills*.[7] "Donovan's Brain" takes Bernal's notion of the brain in the beaker one step farther, by imagining it hooked up to an electrical amplifying system. The brain thus *becomes* a radio set, capable of transmitting and receiving signals.[8]

This radio play was followed in the same year by a film version, *The Lady and the Monster,* starring Erich von Stroheim, and later by the United Artists production of *Donovan's Brain,* which starred Nancy Davis (later Reagan).[9] Despite the same theme, there are some significant differences between the film and the radio play. Film versions of the brain in a beaker celebrated the notion of an autonomous individual who exercised free choice as a citizen of the liberal civil state. As one critic has observed, "brainfilms unleashed the awesome power of the mind only to contain it. They rehearsed the anxiety of a subjectivity besieged by mental science only to restate emphatically the strength of human identity. In the end, the conquering brain always falls in defeat, and in doing so, signals a victory for the individual subject both as a political citizen and as a metaphysical category."[10] In contrast, in the radio play, human identity is both less easily defined and more conflicted. The dialogue and plot spring from the point of view of a God-fearing, law-abiding citizen of a state in which scientific power is limited. However, sound effects and other nonverbal aspects of the radio play offer a more ambiguous construction of selfhood, science, and the state.

"Donovan's Brain" concerns a celebrated and idiosyncratic brain researcher, Dr. Patrick Cory, who has been experimenting with the in vitro culture of capuchin monkey brains when an airplane crash gives him the opportunity to extend his experimentation to a human brain. Neurosurgeon turned thief and murderer, Cory removes the brain of William H. Donovan, a brilliant industrialist who was gravely injured in the accident. Cory sends the body off to be buried, its cranial cavity stuffed with cotton wool, but secretly keeps the brain alive in a beaker in his laboratory. Yet something goes awry when Cory extends his experiment with brain culture from the monkey to the human. The brain begins to function as a powerful radio, transmitting signals that—in the end—overwhelm the mind of the researcher until he is a mere automaton, controlled by Donovan's brain.

In this tale of biomedically produced intersubjectivity, Orson Welles reads the parts of both the murderous Dr. Cory and his innocent victim, Donovan. Thus the radio play forces its listeners to use specifically auditory cues to distinguish between individuals. We know when Welles is playing Donovan's *brain* rather than the fully embodied Dr. Patrick Cory because the accent, word choice, and timbre of his voice change. Cory is a man of clipped, crisp, and impatient diction, while Donovan, the industrialist—or more precisely, his brain—has a gruffer, thicker tone of voice and a crude set of word choices. Moreover, Donovan's brain has a characteristic speech tag: a repetitive "Sure sure sure." Familiar from our first auditory encounter with him, by the end of the radio play this muttered phrase functions to cue the moments when the transmitting brain overwhelms its receiving host body and Donovan submerges Cory.

As it traces the fluctuating identities of Donovan and Cory, as their two selves interpenetrate and overwhelm each other, the radio play moves from a visual to an auditory register, and from a modernist articulation of the scientific construction of the self to one that is more nearly postmodern in its refusal of binary oppositions and its challenge to the explanatory regimes of science *and* religion. The play opens with the discovery that Dr. Cory has succeeded in keeping a capuchin monkey brain alive in "a variation on Carrel's mechanical heart." He has confirmed the brain's continuing viability by monitoring its emission of "infinitesimal electrical impulses" through an "encephalograph [hooked] to a small amplifying system." As Cory explains to his assistant, Schrott, "The brain impulses can actually be heard. Here, I'll turn it on. [Humming noise] Quite effective, isn't it?"[11] In Siodmak's novel, the visual cue that the brain is transmitting is a glowing light. In the radio play, however, that light has been replaced by a humming noise, creating a constant, ominous background for the listening audience. This shift to an auditory mode has philosophical and ontological implications, as Steven Connor has observed:

The most important distinguishing feature of auditory experience [is] . . . its capacity to disintegrate and reconfigure space. With the development of radio in the early twentieth century, this effect was intensified. The rationalized "Cartesian grid" of the visualist imagination, which positioned the perceiving self as a single point of view, from which the exterior world radiated in regular lines, gave way to a more fluid, mobile and voluminous conception of space, in which the observer-observed duality and distinctions between separated points and planes dissolve.[12]

As the perspectives of the perceiving self proliferate, the moral and epistemological picture becomes more complex as well. Thus the animal experimentation in "Donovan's Brain" provokes debates about the morality of vivisection that recall the rationalist rhetoric of H. G. Wells's Dr. Moreau. To research assistant Schrott's appalled exclamation on first hearing the humming noise, "Why, it feels! It thinks!" Dr. Cory replies, "I wouldn't go so far as to say that, but it certainly shows marked reactions to an external stimulus." The reductive nature of Cory's "mechanistic philosophy [that] reduces life to a mere matter of chemicals and test-tubes" horrifies Schrott, as does Cory's familiar litany "You can't stop the progress of science!" Yet Schrott, speaking for the humanist reader, gets the last word in the first scene: "When you can manufacture love and sympathy and kindness in a test tube, I'll be back."

Given Cory's single-minded pursuit of scientific knowledge, it doesn't surprise us that he, like Moreau, transgresses the bounds of medical ethics, removing Donovan's brain from his critically injured but still living body. Cory's hopes are clear: "For a while, at least, Donovan's brain will *live!*" The faithful assistant echoes him: "William Donovan had one of the greatest minds . . . *has* one of the greatest brains . . . in the world today." Yet with the move from monkey to man, mind to brain, the experiment goes awry. The human brain shows a marked difference in behavior to the monkey brain, or at least its behavior is *interpreted* differently: the brain is not only alive; it is empowered. So when Cory urges Schrott to turn on the encephalograph and tap on the glass, he says: "Delta waves! It was asleep! You woke it up! There are three of us conducting this experiment now, Schrott. You, me, and William Horace Donovan." The brain increasingly takes control of both Dr. Cory and Schrott.

The brain's shift from the merely alive to the empowered receives a more detailed explanation in Siodmak's novel. There Cory's living-room radio gives him the inspiration for his experiment with Donovan's brain: "Last night I had an impulse to turn on the radio in the living-room. I do not know what impelled me: I never listen to it. Actually, I dislike this instrument, which only distracts me. . . . I found a short-wave Spanish broadcast, turned the dial, and a French one came in, less clear, the fadings sometimes blotting out the music. I dialed again and an American coast-to-coast hook-up came through strongly. Suddenly I knew what I was looking for and the inspiration made me flush hotly."[13] Cory has made the very connection that Low articulated in *Wireless Possibilities:* "Oscillation— that is all we mean by Radio; and oscillation is at the base of life itself." An oscillating electric current is present in brain waves as well as radio waves, and the principle of amplification can be applied to each. As Cory explains, "If you broadcast from a station with a weak transmitter, a receiver cannot amplify the sound waves beyond a certain distance, and increasing the power of the receiver does not help. The power of the transmitter has to be increased . . . we must increase the electric thought discharge of Donovan's brain until it can contact a sensitive brain."[14]

Whereas the novel can rely on a leisurely exposition to show the brain's progress in assuming command of Dr. Cory's actions, the radio play must move quickly, for it is limited to two hours of direct dramatization. Orson Welles uses to good effect Mary Shelley's convention of the laboratory notebook, which, when juxtaposed to his letters home, gave us a chilling, double-faceted view of Victor Frankenstein's character and activities. The laboratory notebook of Dr. Patrick Cory works to establish the many-layered auditory event that is the radio play, staged in the multiple spaces of American consumer culture, Hollywood stardom, and gothic science. After a surge of strings and the tolling of an ominous bell, the announcer's authoritative voice intones, "Roma Wines presents SUSPENSE! This is the man in black, here to introduce this weekly half hour of *Suspense*. Tonight from Hollywood we bring you a star, Mr. Orson Welles, as the protagonist of Curt Siodmak's novel, *Donovan's Brain*." Music swells, followed by the sound of scribbling, and then we hear the rich voice of Orson Welles speaking as if directly to us: "As I sit now outside my laboratory door, writing, under the heading Experiment 87, this final entry in my casebook, I know that these are the last words I shall ever write upon this earth. I neither ask nor expect forgiveness, now or hereafter, but for those who seek some explanation I refer them simply to this casebook. Let them read it carefully, from its first entry on that ill-starred day of July the 13th." Speaking in the persona of Dr. Patrick Cory, Welles draws us into the sequence of events recorded in Cory's laboratory notebooks, so that to "read" them soon becomes to participate imaginatively in the conditions of their unfolding. Yet in doing that, we are necessarily inserted into three different subject positions—consumer, experimenter, and suspense-gripped radio listener—for the sound of Cory's scientific scribbling is sandwiched between the sponsor's jingle and the reenactment of the story for the radio audience. Moving between the commercial, the scientific, and the gothic, the radio play both presents and undercuts the unified perspective that its title promises. Donovan's brain takes possession of Dr. Cory, compelling him to place his wife in a mental institution, and then forcing him—in the play's climax—to sever his own son's spinal cord, leaving the still-breathing body as a new home for the now dominant brain. Only in the conclusion is the intersubjective link severed between Donovan's brain and Dr. Cory. The radio play ends with a final laboratory notebook entry written by Cory alone. As he confronts his guilt for killing his son, he asks himself how he has come to commit such a hideous crime.

I only know that at the instant my son died under my own hand, I was set free; at that instant, I saw and understood for the first time that monstrous plan born in the brain of William Donovan, of which I was to be the instrument. . . . Donovan *did* aspire to the domination of the world, and with those tremendous mental capacities that I myself had given him, it was literally within his power to become the absolute ruler of all mankind. Only one thing was lacking: a body, a body, a young strong body into which those ever growing brain cells could graft and affix themselves to live on, and on, perhaps for centuries.

Planning to seize the body of Cory's son, Donovan's brain aimed at unstoppable dominion. Yet in the end, the malevolent brain is stopped by Cory himself, a victory also registered in radio waves. When the doctor's final speech ends, and the finale music swells, we hear through the shrilling of brain waves and the crash of wreckage the pulsating noise of the brain dying, a muttered "Sure . . . sure," and a thump as Cory and the brain fall together to the floor.

   The radio play "Donovan's Brain" gives its listeners the opportunity to experience a new, absolutely powerful, superhuman intersubjectivity, but only briefly. The denouement returns us to reason and order: a celebration of "good science" and critique of bad or false science, and an affirmation of good Christian paternity over Dr. Cory's bad scientific fatherhood. Investigators who arrive at Cory's laboratory discover "the brain itself . . . in such a state of decomposition as to indicate that it had been dead, and slowly decaying, for at least three months." Although we find in the end that the brain radio was only Cory's mad delusion, as Welles's voice oscillates between Donovan and Cory, it has given us the chance to experience the precise reconfiguration of human life and health predicted in Low's *Wireless Possibilities.*

Community Radio

Low's suggestion in 1924 that radio could breach the boundaries of the individual, giving rise to long-distance forms of communication—telecommuting, faxing, even telepathy—anticipates the second cultural representation I want to address. This is what I will call—in a deliberate inversion of the normal meaning of the term—"community radio." "Who knows," Low asked, "but that the electrical operations of thought may be reduced to a science so that our very ideas are not secret without protection? How many of us to-day could risk all our thoughts being known? It would probably improve moral standards if they were published: science tends to effect an average improvement."[15] John Cheever's "The Enormous Radio" tests precisely that premise. In ways I will return to, this story offers a prophetic glimpse of radio's future as well as our own, for the enormous radio purveys a particularly significant, and particularly noxious, brand of community radio.

Published in 1957, Cheever's story is on one level an exposé of 1950s-era hypocrisy. Yet this short story takes a further step toward the posthuman "material, informational entity" in its tale of a radio that exposes the collective psyche of an entire vertical community: a New York apartment building.[16] The protagonists, Jim and Irene Wescott, are "the kind of people who seem to strike that satisfactory average of income, endeavor, and respectability that is reached by the statistical reports in college alumni bulletins" (253). The story portrays a challenge to the enforcement of normalcy that moves from the social to the biological, suggesting that technology is altering our very sense of our own boundaries, calling into question both the limits of the self and the meaning of moral agency.

Wholesome young marrieds, Jim and Irene are docile citizens of the new consumer state. When their radio breaks ("an old instrument, sensitive, unpredictable, and beyond repair"), they quickly replace it with a new one. But the new instrument is shocking in its ugliness, violence, and power, marked by all the stigmata of the science fiction brain radio: "like an aggressive intruder," the radio's "dials [flood] with a malevolent green light" (253, 254). A privileged postwar stay-at-home mother, Irene customarily listens to the radio for recreation while the maid feeds and bathes the children. However, the new radio disrupts this domestic peace. When Irene settles down to enjoy a Mozart quintet, she finds herself venturing beyond the culturally and socially normal. A "crackling sound like the noise of a burning powder fuse" emerges from the radio, followed by a bewildering static mingling technological and human cacophony. Irene realizes "that the radio was sensitive to electrical currents of all sorts, [and] she began to discern through the Mozart the ringing of telephone bells, the dialing of phones, and the lamentation of a vacuum cleaner. . . . The powerful and ugly instrument, with its mistaken sensitivity to discord, was more than she could hope to master" (255).

The encounter with the radio not only shakes Irene's sense of control but threatens her husband's mastery as well. When Jim Westcott comes home, he goes "to the radio confidently and work[s] the controls. He ha[s] the same sort of experience Irene had had. A man was speaking on the station Jim had chosen, and his voice swung instantly from the distance into a force so powerful that it shook the apartment" (255). Repairs to the radio don't help: it begins to transmit songs from Irene's past as well as the garble of static, and then it broadcasts arguments from the other apartments. The couple's first response to this technological voyeurism is negative; Jim remarks, "This is strange," and Irene urges, "Turn that thing off. . . . Maybe they can hear *us*" (256–57).

However, by the time evening falls, with ironic Cheever significance, the radio's strange behavior has come to seem not alarming but exciting. "Isn't this too divine?" Irene exclaims. "Try something else. See if you can get those people in 18-C" (257). Eavesdropping soon becomes an addiction, and from breakfast onward Irene overhears "demonstrations of indigestion, carnal love, abysmal vanity, faith, and despair. Irene's life was nearly as simple and sheltered as it appeared to be, and the forthright and sometimes brutal language that came from the loudspeaker that morning astonished and troubled her" (258). Overwhelmed by the babel of financial, sexual, and medical anxieties and troubles that the radio broadcasts, Irene finally breaks down, pleading for reassurance from her husband: "We're not hypercritical or worried about money or dishonest, are we?" Yet that is precisely what they have become, as we learn when we overhear an argument that exposes Irene's calculating self-aggrandizement and Jim's despair. In the end, the revelations of the radio are too upsetting. Once again, Jim gets the radio "repaired," this time successfully. When he brings it home, Irene turns the radio on and is "happy to hear a California-wine commercial . . . [and] Schiller's 'Ode to Joy'" (261).

By the conclusion of Cheever's story, Irene's radio tour of the collective psyche has permanently altered not only her sense of what is *normal* but also Irene herself. She now exhibits precisely the hypocrisy, greed, and dishonesty that she earlier recoiled from in her eavesdropping. "Why are you so Christly all of a sudden?" Jim shouts at her in the story's climax. He recites a litany of her sins, ranging from stealing from her mother's estate before her will had been probated and cheating her sister out of her share to coolly having an abortion without "any good reasons" (262). "Disgraced and sickened," Irene turns to the "hideous cabinet," holding "her hand on the switch before she extinguished the music and the voices, hoping that the instrument might speak to her kindly" (262). Instead "the voice on the radio was suave and noncommittal," delivering the sort of network broadcast we have all become familiar with in the world of the "global village": "An early-morning railroad disaster in Tokyo . . . killed twenty-nine people. A fire in a Catholic hospital near Buffalo for the care of blind children was extinguished early this morning by nuns. The temperature is forty-seven. The humidity is eighty-nine" (263).

Cheever's story illuminates both radio's history and its role as a twentieth-century technology of the subject. First, consider the phrase "community radio." As will have become evident, I have chosen this term to highlight Cheever's ironic inversion of its customary usage: taking community radio as a tool for eavesdropping on a community rather than enabling communication between its members. "Community radio" is generally understood to be local programming that serves the cultural, civic, or informational needs of an audience that is either geographically or demographically limited. In short, as Richard Barbrook observes, "non-profit-maximizing, democratically-accountable, listener-access stations [are] usually called community radio."[17]

As opposed to corporate radio, which increasingly dominates the U.S. market and exists to make a profit, and to nonprofit public radio that is federally funded and centrally programmed, community radio is locally focused, locally programmed, and locally owned. Whereas corporate radio is increasingly geared to standardization and niche marketing, tailoring its playlist to the needs of specific consumer categories, community radio preserves a place for diversity, for it can afford to be interest driven rather than consumer driven. Although such service to the community was one of the earliest mandates of radio, developments at the end of the twentieth century made genuine community radio an increasingly scarce entity. In 1980s Britain, where the Conservative government launched an experiment

in community radio, the term itself was subject to controversy: did it mean
"small-scale commercial stations or [was it] a form of voluntary service on
the airways?" (84–85). Was community radio a commendable instance of
small business, or a dangerous new voice for radical political extremists?
The Conservative experiment in community radio foundered in 1986,
when a review of the pending low-power station licenses suggested that
they would provide a voice for opponents to the Conservative party, especially ethnic minorities (83). In the United States, a consolidation of the
radio industry at the end of the 1990s led to a drastic reduction in the
numbers of African American and Hispanic owned FM radio stations, and
thus a national homogenization of radio programming.[18] This drastic decrease in the number of radio station owners, coupled with the emergence
of increasingly sophisticated transmitting technologies, has catalyzed a new
interest in microradio. The recent intense debate about whether the Federal Communications Commission should issue licenses to hundreds of
low-power FM radio stations, operating at a range of between 100 and 1,000
watts, and serving areas of a radius between 3.5 and 8.8 miles, suggests some
of the complex issues in play in the realm of community radio. Critics of
low-power radio, or microradio, often with ties to the radio industry, have
framed the debate in terms of "spectrum integrity" (transmitter capacity,
clarity, and the possibility of interference), broadcast quality, and political
extremism. So Billy Tauzin, chairman of the House telecommunications
subcommittee, spoke of an "open-ended question about who will get these
stations, whether or not they would be platforms for hate groups in America."[19] Yet issues of programming quality and potential interference are
weak counterarguments. While community radio can be idiosyncratic and
uneven as community cable TV, parodied in the 1990 hit movie *Wayne's
World*, it is not inevitably so. And while there is the potential for interference, early tests of low-power radio suggest that it can avoid disrupting
existing stations.[20] The real danger of community radio to the corporate
radio industry is in the competition that it would produce for monopolistic big radio, through the extension of radio licenses to individuals, community groups, educational institutions, and others not part of the giant
radio corporations.[21] As Richard Barbrook has observed, "In radio broadcasting, as with the mass media in general, it is not so much what *is* said, as
what is *not* said that is important. The mass media do not simply 'brain-
wash' the population, nor do they create some form of 'false consciousness'

through popular culture. What they do is to prevent any mass participation in broadcasting."[22]

In its ironic reinterpretation of community radio, Cheever's short story offers a commentary on twentieth-century Anglo-American radio history. The way the enormous radio distorts the voice(s) of the apartment house dwellers points to the increasing distortions of local programming in the United States during the second half of the twentieth century, as "big radio" gets bigger. While ideally community radio might provide a voice to local arts, culture, politics, and educational institutions, as broadcast by the enormous radio, it is precisely the opposite: an imagined cacophony of disturbingly nonnormative voices. Hardly surprising, then, that the West-cotts retreat to the sanitized uniformity of network news and weather, preferring things *not said* rather than *said*. This short story, composed in the heyday of the corporate man, can be read as an allegory of the victory of corporate radio.

If we move from a focus on radio history to a broader inquiry into radio's role in twentieth-century technologies of subject production, we may find in the conclusion to "The Enormous Radio" a neat embodiment of radio's liminal position between the modern and the postmodern, the human and the posthuman. The story dramatizes radio's power to produce three kinds of tension: between rational detachment and passion, between normalcy and the abnormal, and between sanity and insanity. First, whereas modern-ist radio has as a central strategy the move to "dehumanize the announcer as much as possible," so that his voice is merely "distinct, clear, and pleasant," Cheever's enormous radio gives us an eruption of the posthuman, a clamor of disparate voices speaking with passion, love, hate, anger, fear (even irrationality, when the Sweeneys' nurse reads Edward Lear's nonsense poem "The Yonghy-Bonghy-Bo").[23] Those disruptive voices are silenced when the radio is "fixed," however; afterward that "suave and noncommittal" mod-ernist announcer once again commands the airwaves. Second, whereas American radio under modernity takes as its goal the surveillance and enforcement of the normal, as John Corbett has observed, Cheever's enor-mous radio has the opposite effect. It releases the chaotic and abnormal under the surface of normalcy. Take, for instance, Irene's musings about the women she encounters in her building's elevator after a stint of radio listening: "She stared at their handsome and impassive faces, their furs, and the cloth flowers in their hats. Which one of them had been to Sea Island, she wondered. Which one had overdrawn her bank account?"[24] Once the radio is "fixed" and reinserted into the regime of the normal, that normalcy is signaled by the return not only of high culture but also of consumer society. Irene hears a commercial for "California wine," just as radio listeners in 1944 heard a jingle promoting "Roma wine" when they tuned in to "*Suspense!*" to listen to "Donovan's Brain."[25] Finally, in both "Donovan's Brain" and "The Enormous Radio," a character's experience of radio-induced intersubjectivity calls attention to the thin line separating sanity from insanity, the ordinary from the uncanny.

There is a difference between these two representations of radio, however. Both tales exist in the realm of the gothic, but the twenty years between them have seen a displacement of the uncanny from the mental to the mechanical. Cheever's gothic genre casts doubt less on Irene's sanity than on the ordinary-ness of the "enormous radio." The unusually large machine, with its hideous gumwood cabinet, its instrument panel studded with dials and switches, and its "malevolent green light," fills the apartment with an uncanny agency, seizing control of Irene and changing her, just as Donovan's brain *initially* seems to have changed Dr. Cory. In "Donovan's Brain," the coda to the story reveals that when Patrick Cory dies, Donovan's brain is found in an advanced state of decomposition, and we find ourselves wondering just how sane and objective this scientist really was. However, no such coda occurs in "The Enormous Radio." Instead, the very return of the ordinary, with the "suave and noncommittal" announcer's concluding newscast, emphasizes just how uncanny the radio remains.

Radio Lazarus

An understanding of the continuous oscillation central to radio might lead to "a better understanding of the nature of life . . . affecting our health at the end of many generations for the better," Low argued in 1924.[26] Whereas "Donovan's Brain" and "The Enormous Radio" reveal that oscillation occurring at the macrosocial level—between human and machine, self and other, sanity and insanity, the ordinary and the uncanny—another more recent work of fiction moves to the microsocial, using the actual oscillation of electrical transmissions to explore the ways that radio might be used to improve the health of the human body. Linking the notion of brain radio with the intersubjectivity of "community radio," Robert Mawson's *The Lazarus Child* (1998) tells the story of a dedicated neurologist, Dr. Elizabeth

Chase, whose quest is to bring children back to life, rescuing them from a particularly extensive and deep coma known as a "persistent vegetative state."[27] Chase's strategy, first conceptualized during sessions of hypnotherapy with patients suffering from post-traumatic stress disorder, is to create a network of brains, mediated and stimulated through computer hookups, to goad and lead her comatose patients back to consciousness.

In its play with the boundaries of life and death, waking and dreaming, *The Lazarus Child* evokes not the technology, nor even the sound of radio, so much as its potential to mingle the spiritual and the material, first revealed when Sir Oliver Lodge added his notion of sympathetic resonance to Marconi's wireless telegraphy. Just as Lodge believed that "if he could match certain aspects of the circuits in wireless transmitters and receivers and make them electrically resonant, they would respond 'sympathetically,' as he put it, to each other but not to [an] apparatus not similarly adjusted," so Elizabeth Chase has bet her career as a physician on her conviction that patients in persistent vegetative states can, if properly connected, communicate with each other, drawing each other out of their comas and back to life.[28] The novel recalls J. D. Bernal's vision of a human being whose senses are prosthetically enhanced. But this time, it is not the very old whose lives are extended but the very young. Moreover, the computer-mediated prosthesis serves not to replace flesh-and-blood functions but to reactivate them, boosting their neurological capacities by stimulating them through interlinking neural networks. Dr. Chase's theory behind this practice is remarkably reminiscent of the early spiritualist take on radio. As she explains it: "The subconscious, the spirit, the soul, call it what you will, it goes on, it continues, it exists, unconstrained, unfettered but on a totally different plane from anything we have experienced or can relate to. It may even coexist with others."[29]

Her theory has striking resonances to the way P. T. McGrath, a contemporary observer, described the world revealed by Marconi's work in "wireless telegraphy": "It would be almost like dreamland and ghostland, not the ghostland cultivated by a heated imagination, but a real communication from a distance based on true physical laws."[30] Gregory Whitehead's description of the essence of radio could equally well describe the essence of the technique that saves the Lazarus child: "Radio *happens* in sound, but sound is not really what matters about radio. What does matter is the bisected heart of the infinite dreamland/ghostland, a heart that beats through a series of highly pulsed and frictive oppositions: the radio signal as intimate but untouchable, sensually charged but technically remote, reading deep inside but from way out there, seductive in its invitation but possibly lethal in its effects."[31]

Mawson's novel recapitulates for the computer era those experiments mingling science and spiritualism, in which the powerful oscillating frequencies of the wireless were deployed, by Sir Oliver Lodge and Sir Arthur Conan Doyle, to commune with the dead. Only this time, the dead are merely comatose, and the communications occur via electrodes. As one of the researchers explains, "Two of the kids appeared to set up some sort of brief common awareness field with each other via the control room array. . . . They bypassed us, just hijacked the gear for their own use."[32] Or, as one of the perennially available skeptics puts it, " 'Common, subliminal, goddamn awareness fields,' he stammered. 'It's a crock! I mean, what exactly are we talking about here? Transferring thoughts down a wire?' " (163–64).

Technology has an accumulative cultural effect, with earlier forms persisting along with later ones. *The Lazarus Child* also invokes the 1950s view of radio as entertainment with an ominous edge: "The patients, young girl and an older, dark-skinned boy, were both naked, their heads shaven. Their bodies were sheathed in their electrode nets, the tangled wiring converging into thick bundles plugged into the control room wall. On the other side of the wall Nathan sat at the master control console. . . . A mesmerizing display of flowing oscilloscope traces, TV monitors, blinking status lights, liquid-crystal arrays and switch panels. The home entertainment center from hell, Nathan called it" (108). Nathan's phrase flippantly recalls the predominantly masculine popular audience from the earliest days of radio, hepped on "hi-fi" delivered from the "home entertainment center." But in its techno-gothic complexity, this passage provides a gauge of the distance we have traveled from the early image of "brain radio" and Welles's "Donovan's Brain," and the later notion of an unholy "community radio" in Cheever's story, to the science fiction notion of "radio Lazarus," an application of radio that can wake the (nearly) dead. In Welles's radio play, Dr. Cory's obsession with the malevolent power of Donovan's brain finally testifies to his insanity, but in *The Lazarus Child* neither the transmitting nor the receiving human beings (both children) are perceived as insane. Instead the doctor's sanity is questioned when she persists in her experimental interventions on patients in persistent vegetative states, despite a barrage of criticism. Having in her youth lost her ten-year-old brother to an irreversible coma, Dr. Chase uses her neurological skills and a range of dramatically powerful electronic and chemical strategies in the effort to bring her patients back from the verge of death.

Dr. Chase's first success brings her "a spiraling whirlwind of media attention" that finally catches up the head of her own neurology department, who takes part "in a radio call-in program about the trailblazing work being undertaken 'under my guidance' by his talented team" (48–49). But the media stir up opposition as well, and she must fight angry parents, obtuse state regulatory authorities, technical difficulties, and even her own skepticism, to continue her work. In the end she manages to revive the comatose young girl in her care. But she does so at a great, and ironic, price: the loss of her own consciousness, which she surrenders to free her patient from the coma. When the novel closes, the roles have been reversed. Dr. Chase's young patient is now able to power about freely in her little electric wheelchair, to wave and even to accomplish a semblance of speech, but the independent neurologist Elizabeth Chase is now comatose "Lizzie," dependent on her new husband, who summarizes her state of mind and body with chilling cheeriness: "Lizzie continues to be really well, fit and healthy. She has made wonderful progress over the past few months. It's hard to say for certain whether she is fully aware of herself, and us, but somehow I sense she is and that she is at peace, even when she seems to withdraw for a while. . . . Eliot [her father] . . . is indefatigable in his researches into her condition and confident that her motor and cognitive functions are improving all the time. One day she'll be restored to us, of that I'm certain . . . " (301).

Exploring the Matrix

As brain radio, community radio, and, finally, radio Lazarus, the radio has functioned in fiction and film to express tensions central to twentieth-century culture: in the 1930s, between human and machine; in the 1950s, between individual and community, high and consumer culture; and finally in the nineties, between the human and the informatic.[33] Implicit in each of these conflicts is a gender role negotiation as well, over the masculine and/or feminine properties invoked by intersubjectivity. To some extent, radio's ability to express core cultural conflicts like the gender binary reflects its binary structural principal, the reliance on oscillation that, as Low put it in 1924, "is all we mean by Radio; and . . . is at the base of life itself." But just what aspect of the oscillation is marked as "alive" is now being reevaluated, marking a substantive difference in the role radio plays and the concerns that it expresses.

Marshall McLuhan has identified one of radio's major effects—the externalization of the human body: "Today men's nerves surround us; they have gone outside as electrical environment. The human nervous system itself can be reprogrammed biologically as readily as any radio network can alter its fare."[34] Whether it is ethical to engage in such an act of reprogramming; whether the environment constructed from that externalized neural network is emancipatory or oppressive; whether, finally, life resides more fully in the internal human brain or the external, reprogrammed environment—these are the themes of a film providing our most recent exploration of wireless possibilities, Larry and Andy Wachowski's 1999 incarnation of the "entertainment center from hell," *The Matrix*. This film references the intersubjective potential of computer, radio, and telephone technologies to animate the horrifying future unleashed by the victory of the machines. A world "of seeming reality that is actually controlled by artificial intelligence," the landscape of the matrix recalls the vision of an alternative world transmitted by Donovan's brain.[35]

A sort of vast cosmic valley presided over by the colossal figure of a young man whom I seem to recognize yet I never see his face. It is as though the entire population of the earth were moving past him in review, at his command. . . . The dream of the young giant bestriding the earth, the figure without a face pursues me now even in my waking hours. Increasingly I seem to live in a world of evil fantasy peopled and controlled by the mind of William Donovan. It was the plan I had glimpsed, but never grasped, in the recurring dream. Donovan *did* aspire to the domination of the world, and with those tremendous mental capacities that I myself had given him, it was literally within his power to become the absolute ruler of all mankind. Only one thing was lacking: a body, a body, a young strong body into which those ever growing brain cells could graft and affix themselves to live on, and on, perhaps for centuries.[36]

The Matrix recalls the human/machine interface of "Donovan's Brain," but with the difference that the relation is reversed. Rather than Donovan's brain doing the controlling (fueled by the radio machinery that enhances its transmission abilities), now it is the radio machinery that controls, fueled by the electrical output of the human beings it rules. We have gone one step farther than the oscillatory neural network of *The Lazarus Child*.

As an early press release for the film explains, "*Matrix* is set in the 22nd Century, when a race of vast and powerful computers rule the earth, using human beings as their energy source. The earthlings' passivity is ensured by a virtual reality device which convinces them they are experiencing life in the 20th Century."[37] The metaphor of the man/machine resemblance that sustains this plot is a familiar one, extending from Samuel Butler's *Erewhon*, with its threateningly human machines, to *The Lazarus Child*, in which the people seem increasingly machinelike. In one episode, the father of a comatose girl struggles to start the diesel generator that will power the bank of transmitters for the neural net with which they hope to revive her. Hands deep in engine grease, he contemplates the life of his family, which he describes as a machine in need of repair:

"We used to be a team, a unit, a self-sustaining system, something strong and alive that existed independently of anything else, ran itself like a—like a little engine. . . . But then, at some point, somewhere, it all began to fall apart, to break down. . . . Bad maintenance, I suppose."
"Yes, but bad maintenance can be fixed."
"Or maybe a defective component . . ."[38]

The Matrix presents a world in which the threat avoided by the citizens of Erewhon has come to pass: the machine metaphor has become literal. Rather than electrically powered machines serving to call humans back to life as they did in *The Lazarus Child*, now human-powered computer networks enable the new life of machines. And "human powered" is meant literally: a "fetus farm," a bank of human batteries grown in slimy extra-uterine cases, fuels the interlinked computer networks that constitute the matrix. They are maintained in this perpetual machine gestation, their electrical energy drawn off to power the cybernetic systems needed to maintain the illusion of a normal twentieth-century world in what is really the twenty-second century.

Recapitulating the neural networking of Dr. Elizabeth Chase, and the gothic subtext of "The Enormous Radio," *The Matrix* rounds back to the vision with which we began: the notion of radio as a liminal technology capable of negotiating the boundary between human and animal, human and machine, life and death. The dilemma of Dr. Cory, trapped by the telepathic brain radio transmissions of Donovan in vitro, anticipates the dilemma of Keanu Reeves in *The Matrix:* "A man apparently dead can hear and see, still receive impressions in his mind, but is paralyzed in voice and motion. I was listening and looking on. To be declared dead while still alive must be the most horrible of all tortures, but there is peace to be found in knowing the worst."[39] For Reeves, freed by Laurence Fishburne from his illusion of life, all that remains is to fight to "liberate mankind from the scourge of living in 'the matrix,' a seeming reality that is actually controlled by artificial intelligence."[40] Yet his fight against the mental tyranny of the matrix, like Dr. Cory's battle against Donovan's brain, calls into question not only the difference between machine and human, dead and living, but also the boundaries between the sane and the insane. As film critic David Denby observes, "the free life, which takes place in a cramped space module, is so much less attractive than existence on earth, within the matrix, that no one not certifiably insane would fight to achieve freedom."[41]

Wireless Possibilities: Reconfiguring the Brain

In moving from "Donovan's Brain" and its image of brain radio, to Cheever's "Enormous Radio," and finally to the revivifying force of Radio Lazarus, we can be said to have moved from a modernist construction of life and identity to a postmodernist one. Yet to make that point is to falsely stabilize, unify, and thus distinguish between the modern and the postmodern moments. In fact, two uncanny transmutations of radio flank Cheever's familiar console with its glowing dial and its imposing polished wooden box: Siodmak's brain in a beaker that transmits humming electrical impulses, and Mawson's bank of computers that, by linking two comatose brains, yank them back to life. These transmutations of radio may share more than any differentiation of them into modern and postmodern representations acknowledges. How do we explain the relations between these three cultural representations of the radio?

We can begin by thinking about cognition itself. Susan Douglas has argued that "*cognitively,* [radio] revolutionized the perceptual habits of the nation."[42] Radio functioned as a powerful new site of cognitive activity in the twentieth century, linking different states of awareness, from passive reception to active listening; encouraging visual and spatial imaging in response to what we hear; activating basic brain structures that are then inflected differently by different cultural contexts; permitting a pleasurable shared simultaneity while reserving a deep sense of individualized interior experience. These three representations express radio's power to reconfigure modern cognition, embodied from the earliest years of the century in the image of "brain radio." Activating experiences aurally, addressing our individual interiority, radio taps a powerful and deep connection to the human brain, as cognitive scientists are discovering. Moreover, Douglas argues, radio schools us in different modes of listening: informational (a relatively flat conveying of facts), dimensional (a highly textured and detailed construction of three-dimensional space), and associational (linking different experiences and concepts due to the random juxtaposition of a particular moment in life) (33–34). Although they differ in format (whether aural or written), the three representations of radio we have considered reflect the special positioning and power of this new medium, as well as recapping some of the distinctive moments of its developmental history.

"Donovan's Brain" emphasizes dimensional listening: a linguistically cued transmission from one brain to another that enables the superimposition of one will on another, with the ultimate goal of creating a new world under the total domination of that new transhuman will. In its eerie play of reversals with the boundaries of Donovan's death and Cory's life (and vice versa), the radio play recaps one of the most interesting legacies of early radio: the link between radio and spiritualism promulgated by the radio pioneer Sir Oliver Lodge. As Douglas details, this famous physicist, who had patented a method of radio tuning known as "syntonized telegraphy," responded to the death of his youngest son in the battle of Ypres by undertaking a highly publicized series of public lectures in which he advocated wireless contact with the dead and affirmed that radio can provide proof of the existence of a spirit world (42–43). A remarkable example of the complex and contradictory uses to which radio was put in the twentieth century, the lectures of Sir Oliver Lodge used scientific principles to affirm the spiritual: "He moved back and forth between the language of physics—especially of wireless telegraphy—and the language of spiritualism, so that the ether was a medium of transmission but so was a person who 'allows his or her hand or arm or voice to be actuated by an intelligence not their own'" (45). When Dr. Patrick Cory comes under the control of Donovan's brain, arguably we have an explicit reference to this aspect of the history of radio. And like radio itself, the representation is remarkably double valenced: the kernel of the tale affirms spiritualism, as Cory takes on the position of medium for Donovan's dead/undead will, while the coda reassures the more skeptical audience that the brain was definitively "in an advanced state of decomposition" and that Dr. Cory is simply insane. Although this tale of the occult, like the craze for spiritualism that Sir Oliver Lodge triggered a decade earlier, may seem merely a frivolous coda to the solid technological history of radio, Douglas provides support for arguing otherwise. "Overlooking the spiritualism craze, and Lodge's role in it, would be a mistake," she argues, "for it gives us important clues about the imaginative terrain that radio would initially encounter, interact with, and reshape, a terrain that remains very much a part of the invention's legacy" (46).

Rather than embodying the quest for the spiritual, Cheever's "The Enormous Radio" moves beyond it to explore the material foundations and social effects of radio: its uncanny ability to access distant sites. Cheever's story does this by making an ironic return to one of the earliest modes of radio listening: "DX-ing—trying to bring in distant stations—and the farther, the better. (DX was early ham code for 'distance')" (73). Just as DXers were forced to tolerate static of all sorts in their quest for those distant stations, so too Jim and Irene Westcott are helpless when the transmission of their impressive new radio is disrupted by "electrical currents of all sorts," from electric lights and power circuits to vacuum cleaners, electric razors, telephones, and doorbells.[43] Yet after their initial dismay at the unpredictable nature of their radio's transmissions, the Westcotts experience the gratification of that earlier form of "listening in": "with DX-ing the anticipation rested on *not* knowing who or what you would hear, or from where: this was the delight of using your ears for discovery."[44] The Wescotts find a guilty pleasure in the kinds of transmissions they hear from the enormous radio, just as DXing brought a new freedom to an increasingly routinized world: "There was also the pleasure of eavesdropping, and the simultaneous sense of superiority and freedom from responsibility that accompanied listening in on others without their knowing who you were, or even that you were there. You could be taken out of your life, however briefly, and feel the liberation of anonymity. Like voyeurism, eavesdropping brought a sense of control over others, a power to judge them without them being able to judge you" (75).

The Wescotts' form of listening in differs in one significant way from the DXing so central to the early years of radio, however: it substitutes social for physical distance. Rather than pulling in transmissions that are geographically distant (and thus free from any demand for immediate response), the Wescotts receive transmissions from the apartment next door, upstairs, or downstairs. And unlike the DXers free to listen without response to the stations they pulled in, they—or at least Irene—feel impelled to intervene.

Thus one evening her husband returns from work to find "her face . . . shining with tears and her hair . . . disordered. 'Go up to 16-C, Jim!' she screamed. . . . 'Mr. Osborn's beating his wife. They've been quarreling since four o'clock and now he's hitting her. Go up there and stop him.'" Jim responds with impatience: "'You know you don't have to listen to this sort of thing,' he said. . . . 'It's indecent. . . . It's like looking in windows . . . you can turn it off.'"[45] When Jim gets the enormous radio fixed, and it transmits facts in the neutral tones of the radio announcer, the imperative of response has been eradicated. With that act, response has also been eradicated between Jim and Irene, and their relationship is not so easily repaired. In the tension between disasters and weather reports, empathy and disregard, intimacy and isolation, Cheever's enormous radio registers the gendered impact of the stresses of midcentury urbanization.

If Cheever's enormous radio demonstrates how the informational aspects of radio can increase social and emotional distance (at least in the men who are its technical masters), *The Lazarus Child* demonstrates how the associational aspects of listening can be harnessed to put human beings back in touch with each other, thus shoring up human community. Radio transmission, lights, computer signals: all form part of the wireless continuum, for radio is one aspect of a spectrum of energy that moves from the audible to the inaudible and finally to the visual.[46] It is this spectrum of energy that Dr. Chase harnesses to call the comatose patient back to consciousness. As a skeptical interviewer puts it to Dr. Chase, "It's alleged that you use strong lights, and high volume music, and other powerful aural and visual effects."[47] Indeed she does: using every aspect of the oscillating frequencies available to her, Dr. Chase calls the near dead back to life in a performance that, like "Donovan's Brain," recalls the spiritualist projects of early radio, enthusiastically put forward by Sir Oliver Lodge, Thomas Edison, and Arthur Conan Doyle.[48]

The Lazarus Child recalls radio's *materialist* as well as its spiritualist potential. Just as early radio drew commercial sponsors who saw in the new technology not "yearnings about immortality" but the potential for wealth, so too the new technology behind Dr. Chase's Perlman Institute has great investor appeal. As her partner explains: "Right from the beginning, I could see that what you were doing, what you had already achieved and might yet go on to achieve, was groundbreaking stuff. . . . the stuff of international recognition, Nobel Prizes and coffee at the White House. The stuff of massive government funding, overseas investment, unlimited sponsorship from industrial conglomerates. The stuff, therefore, of very serious money indeed."[49] The Perlman Institute draws the comatose Frankie, a young traffic accident victim, back to life by cueing the memories linked to certain melodies and phrases, so that the electronically transmitted, computer-generated sounds trigger the memory of the original accident that left her unconscious. In the case of her comatose younger brother, his grandmother's repeated rhyme, "Wasnae for your wellies where wud you be!" draws him toward life, just as a radio listener is drawn toward making a purchase by the repetitions of a commercial jingle. In each case, the associational properties of radio are key to the profit potential, whether it operates directly by triggering a sale or more indirectly by producing a life-saving technique that appeals to potential investors.

Published in 1998, *The Lazarus Child* represents the commercial and conceptual culmination of a trend that McLuhan dates back to 1844, with the development of the telegraph, that moment when "Western man began a process of putting his nerves outside his body." McLuhan explains that media have developed as "extensions of the central nervous system, an inclusive and simultaneous field. Since the telegraph we have extended the brains and nerves of man outside the globe. As a result, the electronic age endures a total uneasiness, as of a man wearing his skull inside and his brain outside."[50] The novel's vision of a computerized reanimating technology at the end of the century recalls radio's role as one of the inaugural electronic technologies enabling us to test the boundaries of human life, embodiment, subjectivity, and society.

What relation exists between the wireless possibilities envisioned by Professor Low and the networks of production that gave rise to these popular commodities, as articulated in these works of science fiction: a radio play, a short story, a film, and a popular novel? I would argue that the very capacities of the new technology of radio had a reflexive relation to (that is, they *both produced and were produced by*) the ensemble of social relations—scientific, social, artistic, and medical—embodied in these images of brain radio, community radio, and radio Lazarus.

Coda: Darwin's Radio

A. M. Low was right: "wireless possibilities" are the basis of life itself. Indeed, his prediction has been confirmed (at least in fiction): the wireless can be used to "grow babies," and to "[effect] our health at the end of many generations for the better." One year after the publication of *The Lazarus Child,* science fiction writer Greg Bear used radio as an extended metaphor for a form of "adaptive evolution . . . tied to something resembling a universal species consciousness."[51] Evoking and exceeding McLuhan's notion of an extended nervous system while incorporating the linkages between radio and computer technologies, in *Darwin's Radio* (1999) Bear traces the social and biological effects of a Scattered Human Endogenous Retrovirus Activation (SHEVA) that extends both spatially and temporally. Bear explains that the virus emerges in the human population because of the stress of contemporary life: "Endless nasty competition. Too much to learn. Too much bandwidth crowding the channels of communication. We can't listen fast enough. We're left standing on our tiptoes all the time."[52] When an excess of population collides with an excess of information to stress the species into reshaping itself, the viral signal is given to activate the genetic memory that has been "programmed" by its "adaptive genetic computer" (194). Just as computers have been succeeded by biocomputers that express the binary code in base pairs, so the mechanical radio has been succeeded by an organic one: "Darwin's radio." When SHEVA occurs, a signal is sent across time and space to produce (by infection) a new species of human being that will be more fit to survive in contemporary society. These new babies are characterized by enhanced ability to communicate and accelerated cognitive development: they have mottled skin that pulses to enhance their communication, and they can speak from the moment of birth.

In this image of the genome signaling to itself down the eons, Bear gives us the notion of an extended material and cognitive self. Yet this prosthetic self, forged from an uneasy symbiosis of human and informational circuit, is imaged as a fleshly, evolving radio. If, as Catherine Waldby has argued, "the possibility of the posthuman is not to do with the transcendence of the human, its replacement, but rather with the recognition and exposure of the networks of production which constitute human techno-genesis," this final radio fiction takes a reflexive turn. It draws our attention to the networks of cultural and material production that are embedded in, and predicted by, the radio: to the posthuman within the human, the silicon based within the organic, the computer within the radio, and the community within the individual.

Notes

1 A. M. Low, *Wireless Possibilities* (London: Kegan Paul, Trench, Trubner, 1924), 41.

2 Ibid., 41–42.

3 N. Katherine Hayles, *How We Became Posthuman: Virtual Bodies in Cybernetics, Literature, and Informatics* (Chicago: University of Chicago Press, 1999), 50–75.

4 Susan Douglas, *Listening In: Radio and the American Imagination, from Amos 'n' Andy and Edward R. Murrow to Wolfman Jack and Howard Stern.* (New York: Times Books, 1999), 49.

5 Catherine Waldby, *The Visible Human Project: Informatic Bodies and Posthuman Medicine* (London: Routledge, 2000), 48.

6 I use the term "modern" to refer to the period between 1900 and 1945 in Anglo-American culture, during which aesthetic distance, technoscientific progressivism, rationalism, unity, and objectivity were dominant values. In contrast, "postmodern" refers to the period after 1945, characterized by a decline of master narratives (including those of technoscientific progress, rationality, and objectivity) and an increase in fragmented subjectivity, pastiche, and hybridity.

7 Siodmak, who died on November 19, 2000, at age ninety-eight, was better known as a screenwriter and film director. Author of "The Wolf Man," Siodmak had a doctorate in mathematics and had worked as a train engineer and a reporter. One of his first journalistic assignments was an article on Fritz Lang's *Metropolis* (*New York Times*, 19 November 2000, 42).

8 This first appeared as a short story in the pulp detective magazine *Black Mask*, then as the novel *Donovan's Brain* (New York: Knopf, 1943).

9 Jeffrey Sconce, "Brains from Space: Mapping the Mind in 1950s Science and Cinema," *Science as Culture*, 5, no. 2 (1996): 278.

10 Ibid., 299.

11 All citations in the text to the radio play are from my transcription of "Donovan's Brain," in *Suspense* (Washington, D.C.: Radio Spirits, with Smithsonian Institution Press, 1995).

12 Steven Connor, "The Modern Auditory I," in *Rewriting the Self: Histories from the Renaissance to the Present* (London: Routledge, 1997), 207.

13 Siodmak, *Donovan's Brain*, 61.

14 Ibid., 62.

15 Low, *Wireless Possibilities*, 69–70.

16 John Cheever, "The Enormous Radio" [1957], in *American Gothic Tales*, ed. Joyce Carol Oates (New York: Plume/Penguin, 1996), 253–63.

17 Richard Barbrook, "A New Way of Talking: Community Radio in 1980s Britain," *Science as Culture* (London), pilot issue (1987): 82; also see Mark Raboy, "Radio as an Emancipatory Cultural Practice," *Radiotext(e), Semiotext(e)* 6, no. 1 (1993).

18 Paul Van Slambrouck, "A Push to Reconnect Radio to Local Roots," *Christian Science Monitor*, 28 January 1999, 3. "The Telecommunications Reform Act of

1996 led many broadcast companies to acquire additional radio stations," explains Frank James in "FCC Plans to License Low-Power FM Radio," *Chicago Tribune,* 28 January 1999, sec. 1, p. 13. See also Frank Ahrens, "What's the Frequency, Kennard?" *Washington Post,* 7 September 1999, C4; and Stephen Labaton, "FCC Offers Low-Power FM Stations," *New York Times,* 29 January 1999, C1.

19 Bruce Alpert, "Low-Power Radio Stations Proposed," New Orleans *Times-Picayune,* 20 April 1999, A6.

20 Ahrens, "What's the Frequency, Kennard?"

21 Nina Huntemann, "Media Monopoly and Space for Dissent—Take Radio, for Example, Whoops, Already Taken," paper presented at the "Rethinking Marxism" conference, Amherst, Mass., September 2000.

22 Barbrook, "A New Way of Talking," 92.

23 Rudolph Arnheim, "In Praise of Blindness" [1936], *Radiotext(e), Semiotext(e)* 6, no. 1 (1993): 24.

24 Cheever, "The Enormous Radio," 258.

25 "The underlying function of American radio is surveillance (the contemporary form of Enlightenment's disinfection of the dirty human being). Defense of normalcy is the goal of surveillance. Underlying the underlying function of American radio is the defense of normalcy. . . . Surveillance and normalization constitute the foundation of American radio (both commercial and public)." John Corbett, "Radio Dada Manifesto (An Excoriation with Six Histories)," *Radiotext(e), Semiotext(e)* 6, no. 1 (1993): 71.

26 Low, *Wireless Possibilities,* 41–42.

27 Robert Mawson, *The Lazarus Child* (New York: Bantam, 1998), 26.

28 Douglas, *Listening In,* 50.

29 Mawson, *The Lazarus Child,* 191.

30 P. T. McGrath, "Authoritative Account of Marconi's Work in Wireless Telegraphy," *Century Magazine* 63 (March 1902): 779–80, cited in Gregory Whitehead, "Out of the Dark: Notes on the Nobodies of Radio Art," in *Wireless Imagination: Sound, Radio, and the Avant-Garde,* ed. Douglas Kahn and Gregory Whitehead (Cambridge: MIT Press, 1992), 263 n.3.

31 Whitehead, "Out of the Dark," 254.

32 Mawson, *The Lazarus Child,* 163.

33 Of course, these tensions develop and fade away unevenly, overlapping each other, so that no era is characterized by a single source of tension.

34 Marshall McLuhan, "The Agenbite of Outwit," in *Media Research: Technology, Art, Communication,* ed. Michel A. Moos (The Netherlands: OPA, 1977), 86.

35 David Denby, "School Spirit: The Moral Perils of Flatness, and Airborne Special Effects," *New Yorker,* 26 April and 3 May 1999, 194.

36 "Donovan's Brain," my transcription.

37 Andrew Hindes and Paul Karon, "Fishburne Near Deal for 'Matrix,'" *Daily Vari-*

ety, 19 September 1997. Available on-line at www.reevesdrive.com/news/sep97/ htm.

38   Mawson, *The Lazarus Child,* 276.

39   Siodmak, *Donovan's Brain,* 190.

40   Denby, "School Spirit," 194.

41   Ibid.

42   Douglas, *Listening In,* 9.

43   Douglas, *Listening In,* 71; Cheever, "The Enormous Radio," 255.

44   Douglas, *Listening In,* 74.

45   Cheever, "The Enormous Radio," 260.

46   Douglas, *Listening In,* 37.

47   Mawson, *The Lazarus Child,* 116.

48   Douglas, *Listening In,* 42–43.

49   Mawson, *The Lazarus Child,* 87.

50   McLuhan, "The Agenbite of Outwit," 121–25.

51   Greg Bear, *Darwin's Radio* (New York, Del Rey, 1991). For an insightful reading of this novel, see Lisa Lynch, "Not a Virus but an Upgrade: The Ethics of Epidemic Evolution in Greg Bear's *Darwin's Radio,*" *Literature and Medicine* 20, no. 1 (spring 2001): 71–93.

52   Bear, *Darwin's Radio,* 196.

Works Cited

Ahrens, Frank. "Budget Bill Curbs Low-Power Radio: Stations Would Be Kept Out of Cities." *Washington Post,* 20 December 2000, E3.

Alpert, Bruce. "Low-Power Radio Stations Proposed." New Orleans *Times-Picayune,* 20 April 1999, A6.

Arnheim, Rudolf. "In Praise of Blindness" [1936]. *Radiotext(e), Semiotext(e)* 6, no. 1 (1993): 20–25.

Barbrook, Richard. "A New Way of Talking: Community Radio in 1980s Britain." *Science as Culture* (London), pilot issue (1987): 81–129.

Bear, Greg. *Darwin's Radio.* New York: Del Rey, 1991.

Cheever, John. "The Enormous Radio" [1957]. In *American Gothic Tales,* ed. Joyce Carol Oates. New York: Plume/Penguin, 1996.

Connor, Steven. "The Modern Auditory I." In *Rewriting the Self: Histories from the Renaissance to the Present,* ed. Roy Porter. London: Routledge, 1997.

Corbett, John. "Radio Dada Manifesto (An Excoriation with Six Histories)." *Radiotext(e), Semiotext(e)* 6, no. 1 (1993): 71–84.

Denby, David. "School Spirit: The Moral Perils of Flatness, and Airborne Special Effects." *New Yorker,* 26 April and 3 May 1999, 192–94.

Douglas, Susan. *Listening In: Radio and the American Imagination.* New York: Times Books, 1999.

Hayles, N. Katherine. *How We Became Posthuman: Virtual Bodies in Cybernetics, Literature, and Informatics.* Chicago: University of Chicago Press, 1999.

Hindes, Andrew, and Paul Karon. "Fishburne Near Deal for 'Matrix.' " *Daily Variety,* 19 September 1997. Available on-line at www.reevesdrive.com/news/sept97/htm.

Huntemann, Nina. "Media Monopoly and Space for Dissent—Take Radio, for Example, Whoops, Already Taken." Paper presented at the "Rethinking Marxism" conference, Amherst, Mass., September 2000.

James, Frank. "FCC Plans to License Low-Power FM Radio." *Chicago Tribune,* 28 January 1999, 1:13.

Labaton, Stephen. "FCC Offers Low-Power FM Stations." *New York Times,* 29 January 1999, C1.

Low, A. M. *Wireless Possibilities.* London: Kegan Paul, Trench, Trubner, 1924.

Lynch, Lisa. "Not a Virus but an Upgrade: The Ethics of Epidemic Evolution in Greg Bear's *Darwin's Radio.*" *Literature and Medicine* 20, no. 1 (spring 2001): 71–93.

Mawson, Robert. *The Lazarus Child.* New York: Bantam, 1998.

McGrath, P. T. "Authoritative Account of Marconi's Work in Wireless Telegraphy." *Century Magazine* 63 (March 1902): 779–80. Cited in Gregory Whitehead, "Out of the Dark: Notes on the Nobodies of Radio Art," in *Wireless Imagination: Sound, Radio, and the Avant-Garde,* ed. Douglas Kahn and Gregory Whitehead. Cambridge: MIT Press, 1992.

McLuhan, Marshall. "The Agenbite of Outwit." In *Media Research: Technology, Art, Communication,* ed. Michael A. Moos. The Netherlands: OPA, 1977.

Raboy, Mark. "Radio as an Emancipatory Cultural Practice." *Radiotext(e), Semiotext(e)* 6, no. 1 (1993): 129–34.

Sconce, Jeffrey. "Brains from Space: Mapping the Mind in 1950s Science and Cinema." *Science as Culture* 5, no. 2 (1996): 277–302.

Siodmak, Kurt. *Donovan's Brain.* New York: Knopf, 1943.

——. "Donovan's Brain." In *Suspense.* Washington, D.C.: Radio Spirits, with Smithsonian Institution Press, 1995. My transcription.

Strauss, Neil. Introduction to *Radiotext(e), Semiotext(e)* 6, no. 1 (1993): 9–17.

Van Slambrouck, Paul. "A Push to Reconnect Radio to Local Roots." *Christian Science Monitor,* 28 January 1999, 3.

Waldby, Catherine. *The Visible Human Project: Informatic Bodies and Posthuman Medicine.* London: Routledge, 2000.

CONTRIBUTORS

LAURENCE A. BREINER is Professor of English at Boston University. His book *An Introduction to West Indian Poetry* was published by Cambridge University Press in 1998.

BRUCE CAMPBELL is Assistant Professor of German Studies at the College of William and Mary, where he specializes in right-wing culture during the Weimar Republic, paramilitary organizations, the biographical study of Holocaust perpetrators, state violence, and German cultural studies. He is the author of *The SA Generals and the Rise of Nazism* (1998) and the editor, with Arthur Brenner, of *Death Squads: Murder with Deniability* (2000).

MARY DESJARDINS is an assistant professor at Dartmouth College, where she teaches film, television, and women's studies. She has published essays on stardom and feminist film and television theory in many journals and anthologies and is currently completing a book entitled *Recycled Stars: Film Stardom in the Age of Television and Video.*

LAUREN M. E. GOODLAD has recently joined the English Department at the University of Illinois, Urbana-Champaign, after spending several years at the University of Washington in Seattle. She is the author of *Victorian Literature and the Victorian State: Character and Governance in a Liberal Society* (forthcoming from Johns Hopkins University Press) and the coeditor of *Goth: Un-Dead Subculture* (forthcoming from Duke University Press).

NINA HUNTEMANN is an assistant professor of communication at Westfield State College. She is producer and director of an educational documentary, *Game Over: Gender, Race, and Violence in Video Games,* completed in 2000 and distributed by the Media Education Foundation.

LEAH LOWE is a visiting assistant professor in theatre at Connecticut College.

ADRIENNE MUNICH is Professor of English and Women's Studies, State University of New York at Stony Brook.

KATHY M. NEWMAN is Associate Professor of English at Carnegie Mellon University. Her book *Radio-Active: Advertising and Consumer Activism, 1935–1947* will be published by the University of California Press in 2003. She also writes a biweekly column, "What's Left on TV?" for the *Pittsburgh City Paper.*

MARTIN SPINELLI is Assistant Professor of Radio and Media Studies at Brooklyn College, the City University of New York. His essays on media and literature are widely published, and he is currently the producer of the syndicated public radio program *Radio Radio.*

SUSAN MERRILL SQUIER, Julia Brill Professor of Women's Studies and English at the Pennsylvania State University, is the author, most recently, of *Babies in Bottles: Twentieth-Century Visions of Reproductive Technology* (1994) and editor, with E. Ann Kaplan, of *Playing Dolly: Technocultural Formations, Fantasies, and Fictions of Assisted Reproduction* (1999). She is past president and member of the Executive Committee of the Society of Literature and Science.

DONALD ULIN is Assistant Professor of English at the University of Pittsburgh at Bradford.

MARK WILLIAMS is Associate Professor and Chair of the Department of Film and Television Studies at Dartmouth College. His book *Remote Possibilities: A History of Early Television in Los Angeles* is forthcoming from Duke University Press.

STEVE WURTZLER is an assistant professor in the English Department at Georgetown University.

INDEX

Library of Congress Cataloging-in-Publication Data
Communities of the air : radio century, radio culture /
edited by Susan Merrill Squier.
p. cm.
Includes bibliographical references and index.
ISBN 0-8223-3083-0 (cloth : alk. paper) —
ISBN 0-8223-3095-4 (pbk. : alk paper)
1. Radio broadcasting—Social aspects.
I. Squier, Susan Merrill.
PN1991.6 C66 2003
320.23'44—dc21   2002151217